URBANISATION IN DEVELOPING COUNTRIES

Institute of Social Sciences

Urban Studies Series

I. Urbanisation in Developing Countries: Basic Services and Community Participation
Edited by **Bidyut Mohanty**

II. Urbanisation in India: Basic Services and People's Participation
by **K. C. Sivaramakrishnan, Biplab Dasgupta, M. N. Buch**

III. Basic Services for Urban Poor: Case of Baroda, Bhilwara, Sambalpur, Siliguri
by **Archana Ghosh, S. Sami Ahmad, Shipra Maitra**

IV. Rapid Urbanisation and Access to Basic Services in India: A Status Report

Urban Studies Series-1

URBANISATION IN DEVELOPING COUNTRIES

BASIC SERVICES AND COMMUNITY PARTICIPATION

Edited by

BIDYUT MOHANTY

INSTITUTE OF SOCIAL SCIENCES, NEW DELHI

and

CONCEPT PUBLISHING COMPANY, NEW DELHI

ISBN 81-7022-475-6

First Published 1993

Published and Printed by
Ashok Kumar Mittal
Concept Publishing Company
A/15-16 Commercial Block, Mohan Garden
New Delhi 110 059

Layout by
Institute of Social Sciences
B-7/18 Safdarjung Enclave
New Delhi 110 029

Dedicated to
the memory of
Prof D T Lakdawala
our first Chairman (1985-92) and
an ardent advocate of the
public provision of minimum needs
and decentralised planning

Acknowledgement

I thank the authors who patiently endured my several queries and revised their articles in time. Ms.Priti Anand and Mr. G.S. Bhargava deserve special mention for their editorial help. I would also like to thank Mr. P.K.K. Namboodiri, Mr. P.N. Kuttappan and Ms. Sapna Sharma for patiently working on several drafts of the manuscripts and preparing the computer print-outs. Mr. Bachi Ram, the cartographer, helped in the preparation of maps and figures.

I thank my colleagues, Mrs. Archana Ghosh and Dr. S. Sami Ahmad for helping me in organising the seminar and making this publication possible.

Finally my thanks to M/s Concept Publishing Co., our publishers.

Editor

Preface

WHEN the Institute of Social Sciences was founded one of the areas of concern was the 'urban poor'. Under the guidance of Mr Inder Mohan, Senior Fellow of the Institute, work in this area was launched and it has achieved certain concrete results. Another area where the Institute concentrated its attention was local self-government especially in rural India (*panchayats*) and people's participation in development through grass-roots level democracy. These areas of study of the Institute attracted Dr Thomas Mayer, a distinguished social philosopher and political scientist and Resident Representative of Friedrich Ebert Stiftung (FES), to our work (FES is a German non-governmental organisation committed to the principles of social democracy). We held several long discussions on the problems of urbanisation, relative under-development of our villages and their relationship to the political system. A research project on "Basic Amenities in the Context of Rapid Urbanisation: Drinking Water and Sanitation Issues" evolved out of our meetings. Our common concern was the empowerment of the less privileged and the marginalised in our urban centres.

An international seminar focusing on the experiences of developing countries in the area of urban basic services was conceived as part of the research project. Dr. Thomas Mayer's successor Dr. Heinz Bongartz, a sociologist with vast experience in India and Indonesia, was equally committed to this programme. We held a successful international seminar, in co-operation with FES, in November 1992 and this book contains selected papers presented at that forum. Our research team led by Dr (Mrs) Bidyut Mohanty has done commendable work to make the international conference a watershed in our urban studies programme and her hard work has made it possible to bring out this edited volume, the first in a series of publications by the Institute on urban studies.

New Delhi
May 18, 1993

George Mathew
Director

[illegible] Institute of Social Sciences was founded [illegible] of the [illegible] the [illegible] Under the [illegible] [illegible] [illegible] [illegible] where the [illegible] concentrated [illegible] was [illegible] self-government [illegible] capacity [illegible] and people's participation in development through grassroots level democracy. The areas of study of the Institute attracted Dr Thomas Meyer, a distinguished social philosopher and political scientist and Resident Representative of Friedrich Ebert Stiftung (FES), to our work (FES is a German non-governmental organisation committed to the principles of social democracy). We [illegible] discussions on the problems of [illegible] relative [illegible] development of our villages and their relationship to the political system. A research project on "Basic Amenities in the [illegible] and [illegible] Issues" emerged out of our meetings. Our common concern was the empowerment of the less privileged and the marginalised in our urban centres.

An international seminar focusing on the experiences of developing countries in the area of urban basic services was conceived as part of the research project. Dr. Thomas Meyer's successor Dr. [illegible], a sociologist with vast experience in India and Bangladesh, was equally committed to this programme. We held a successful international seminar in co-operation with FES in November 1992 and this book contains selected papers presented at that forum. Our research team led by Dr (Mrs) [illegible] has done commendable work to make the international conference a watershed in our urban studies programme and her hard work has made it possible to bring out this edited volume, the first in a series of publications by the Institute on urban studies.

New Delhi, May [illegible] 1993

George Mathew
Director

Contents

PART II
INDIAN EXPERIENCE

Contributors

M Arunachalam – Union Minister of State for Urban Development, Government of India, New Delhi.

K C Sivaramakrishnan – Vice-President, National Institute of Urban Affairs, New Delhi.

Geoffrey K Payne – Professor, Development Planning Unit, University College, London.

Jibgar Joshi – General Manager, Nepal Housing Development and Finance Company.

B L Panditharatna – Professor, Department of Geography, University of Perideniya, Sri Lanka.

Jinggan Zhang – Professor, Consultant Beijing Municipal Institute of City Planning and Design, China.

Margaret Mwangola – Executive Director, Kenya Water for Health Organisation, Niarobi.

Renato Arnaldo Tagnin – Coordinator of the Inundation Control Team for the Town Council of Sau Paulo, Brazil.

Daniel Faudry – Head of Research, Institut national de Genie Urbain Lyon, France.

Ashish Bose – Nehru Fellow, Jawaharlal Nehru University, New Delhi.

B K Roy – Director, National Atlas and Thematic Mapping Organisation, Calcutta.

Amitabh Kundu – Professor, Centre for the Study of Regional Development, Jawaharlal Nehru University, New Delhi.

Archana Ghosh – Research Faculty, Institute of Social Sciences, New Delhi.

Arup Mitra – Research Associate, Delhi School of Economics, Delhi 110007.

Sabir Ali -- Senior Research Fellow, Council for Social Development, New Delhi.

Rajkishor Meher – Lecturer, Nabkrishna Choudhury Centre for Development Studies, Bhubaneswar.

Abhijit Datta – Professor, Indian Institute of Public Administration, New Delhi.

Tapan K Banerjee – Director, Urban Development Agency, West Bengal.

Meera Mehta – Senior Fellow, Urban Settlement Management Institute, New Delhi.

Dinesh Mehta – Director, National Institute of Urban Affairs, New Delhi.

K S R N Sarma – Professor, Indian Institute of Public Administration, New Delhi.

P S N Rao – Lecturer, School of Planning and Architecture, New Delhi.

D Ravindra Prasad – Director, Regional Centre for Urban and Environmental Studies, Osmania, Hyderabad.

Sara Ahmed – Fellow, Institute of Rural Management, Anand, Gujarat.

Asok Mukhopadhyay – Professor, Department of Political Science, University of Calcutta, Calcutta.

L N P Mohanty – Director, All India Institute of Local Self Government, Bhubaneswar.

Gangadhar Jha – Research Professor, National Institute of Urban Affairs, New Delhi.

H M Golandaz – Director, Regional Centre for Urban and Environmental Studies, Bombay.

Saraswati Haider – Research Scholar, Centre for the Study of Social Systems, Jawaharlal Nehru University, New Delhi.

Introduction

Bidyut Mohanty

> **Future historians may well decide that the crucial phenomenon of our time is the massive urbanization that is engulfing the Third World. Within the span of the last two decades towns and cities all over Asia, Africa and Latin America have been doubling and tripling in size.**
>
> —*Report of the National Commission on Urbanization, Government of India, August 1988*

ONE of the most remarkable features of the second half of the twentieth century has been the spectacular growth of the urban population in the world. Developing countries, in particular, have experienced rapid urbanisation and the mushrooming of huge metropolises. Of the fifteen cities in the world with more than ten million people, twelve are situated in the developing countries. Increasing urbanisation accompanied by an increasing concentration of the urban population in bigger cities has not only posed the problem of pollution, crime and congested housing but has also led to severe pressure on the basic civic amenities and, consequently, a decline in the living standards of the city dwellers. As a result, although the situation is no better in the rural areas, the urban areas suffer from inadequate provision of safe drinking water and sanitation facilities. It is estimated that over 2.3 billion inhabitants of the globe lack access to the minimum sanitation facilities, while 1.5 billion persons lack access to safe drinking water and health services. Nearly 40 countries facing these and related problems belong to the developing world. These problems are expected to become acute by the end of the century. Some fear that it may even lead to international warfare!

Many factors, such as a resource crunch, lack of proper management, too much dependence on central authorities as well as very little involvement on the part of the community have contributed to such a situation, particularly in the urban areas. To deliberate on these and other related questions, an International Conference was organized by the Institute of Social Sciences in New Delhi (27-29 November 1991). It was a gathering of seventy-five experts and included urban administrators, academicians, specialists on urban affairs and social-action groups from different parts of India as well as from Brazil, Mexico, Kenya, Sri Lanka, Pakistan, Afghanistan, Bangladesh, the U.K. and the USA. Altogether thirty-five papers were presented in different sessions. The contributions to this book comprise a selection of twenty-eight papers among those presented at the conference. The selected papers underwent a revision following the suggestions received in the working sessions of the conference, and on the basis of certain guidelines from the Institute's research group.

The objectives of the conference were (a) to deliberate on the magnitude of the specific problems faced by patterns of urban growth, particularly in the developing countries; and, (b) to learn from the experiences of other countries and to suggest concrete recommendations to improve the situation. In addition it aimed at stimulating further thinking and research on the subject.

The experience of some of the developing countries such as Pakistan, Turkey, Egypt, Nepal, Sri Lanka, China, Kenya and Latin America, form the first part of this book. The authors deal not only with the patterns of urbanisation but also with the status of basic services in terms of drinking water and sanitation facilities, problems of decentralized planning, community development and the role of social-action groups. The second part of the book is devoted to the Indian experience. The dimensions of the problems of urban growth, the status of basic services, problems of resource mobilization, policies and programmes, community participation and functioning of local self-governments, are just some of the aspects under which the experience in different cities in India is analyzed.

The underlying theme running through the various chapters included in the book is that there has been a concentration of urban population in certain regions in the developing countries. These may be the 'urban corridors' in India, or the mega-cities like Sao Paulo and Mexico City in Latin America. Even Beijing, whose expansion was considered to be exemplary (the growth rate of this city was lower than the national average), has of late outgrown its resources for supplying the basic amenities to its inhabitants. In contrast, the Colombo experience shows less concentration of population as compared to other South Asian cities. The uneven distribution of the urban population has led to the need for asking what constitutes the "optimum size" of a city, definable in relation to its resource base. The concentration of twenty million people in one small place is not desirable from any point of view and policies encouraging balanced urban growth should be implemented forcefully.

What is it that has contributed to the growth of cities in India, particularly in the eighties? Generally, natural growth, net-migration to urban areas and the impact of reclassification of areas have been the major factors leading to this growth. According to the census authorities, rural to urban migration has played a relatively less important role in India during 1981-91 (37% in contrast to 40% during I971-81). Some experts on urban studies tend to agree with this. Others, specially scholars in the field, refute this contention, maintaining that this decline in the contribution of migration to the growth of cities may only appear to be so due to gross under-enumeration in the big cities. Migration continues to be an important factor in other cities like Beijing, Kabul, Sao Paulo and Mexico City and Colombo being an exception.

There exists a large-scale inequality in the distribution of basic services in general and drinking water and sanitation in particular, not only at the inter-city but also at the intra-city level. For example, the per capita water supply of Delhi is officially reported to be 200 litres per person, per day. But thirty percent of the population of Delhi (8.5 million in 1991) gets only twenty-five litres or less per day. Even a planned city like Rourkela faces the problem of unequal distribution of basic services. In such situations, the low income groups suffer the most. The inhabitants of the *bustees* and *jhuggi jhompris* in India, the shanty towns of Sao Paulo or the *katchi abadis* in Pakistan do not have access either to adequate quantities of clean water or proper sanitation facilities. Colombo's experience of unequal distribution of basic services, instead, is attributed to historical and technical factors like the lay-out of pipelines and location of sanitation facilities, which had been designed in a particular way. As a result, adverse environment and health conditions prevail in all the low income areas of Colombo.

The policies towards urban sectors and especially those referring to basic services in urban areas have been the subject of discussions and debate. Several authors of this book, especially those from India, are critical of these policies. It is well known that India did not have a comprehensive urban policy till 1988 when the National Commission on Urbanization (NCU) submitted its report. Two important recommendations of the NCU were: (1) urban centres which are growing very rapidly should be given more importance in future development (Generation of Economic Momentum or GEM); and (ii) Spatial Priority Urbanization Regions (SPURS), and the small towns which serve as the rural hinterland, should be supported fully.

For the basic services, like drinking water and sanitation, the NCU suggested a "holistic rather than a compartmentalised view of water resource management." It is a sad comment on the working of the Indian Government that it has not yet taken effective steps to implement the recommendations made by the NCU. Half-hearted attempts do not lead anywhere except in aggravating the problem. Studies show that, conversely, there has been a reduction of government investment in real terms on urban basic amenities such as drinking water and sanitation and, therefore, some opine that urban-ward migration has declined. Is it feasible to hypothesize that deteriorating civic conditions are acting as a push-factor, leading to a decline in the pace of urbanisation? Of course, there are others who argue that the total investment in providing water and sanitation has not declined at all. Further, there are push-factors at the village level showing that rural to urban migration continues and is likely to continue in the future also, and this trend is generally not influenced by the deteriorating civic conditions of the urban centres.

What about structural adjustments, which have been attempted in India since 1985 and which got a further boost in 1991? The experience of structural adjustment the world over, by and large, has not been positive in fostering the welfare needs of the weaker sections of society. This is because, among other things, in order to curb deficit financing it is generally the state's expenditure on social sectors which receives drastic reduction.

It is in this context that the question of the privatization of basic services assumes significance. The question arises whether the private sector can be entrusted to deliver these basic services keeping the efficiency and equity issues in mind. Private initiative in this sector has been tried in several parts of the world, including Colombo. In some places, the acute problem of availability of water has been solved to some extent. The basic issues of efficiency and equity, however, have yet to be squarely faced. Again, if the private sector organizations insist on the full cost-recovery of the services provided, the poor may get priced out. At the same time it is to be noted that the public sector may not be able to deliver the goods because of constraints such as corruption – administrative and political – red-tapism and the like which have frustrated the people who cherish social control in the name of equity. At any rate, the state should make strategic intervention and should not leave basic services solely to the forces of *laissez faire*.

Issues of physical management, including the conservation of water at source, the distribution network at users level, and other crucial issues related to this subject attract our attention. It is a shocking revelation that at least forty per cent of available water gets lost at various levels of distribution in India. It is a well known fact that out of the 70 per cent of water resource used by agriculture (as against seven per cent of available water resource used for domestic purposes), only 30 per cent is utilized efficiently. In this context, it may be recalled that the tariff systems and distribution arrangements of water have no link whatsoever with the total expenses incurred either for the conservation of water or for recycling waste water. The Minister of State for Urban Development, Shri M. Arunachalam, had this in mind when, while inaugurating the conference, he made the observation that water should be used like money, and that this must become a dictum not only for the consumers but also for the technocrats who manage water in our cities.

When there is an 'acute deficiency' in basic services, the question of financial resource mobilization and other related issues becomes important. It is true that a city might not be able to generate enough resources on its own for providing basic services to its entire population, or may not even utilize the same in the desired manner because of structural as well as organizational constraints. At a macro level, therefore, issues like 'financial optimization', 'mobilization of additional fiscal resources through taxation and fees', become increasingly relevant.

Another area of concern is the prevailing non-coordination at the administrative level between the urban local bodies and other special purpose authorities. On many occasions, special agencies usurp the authority of the local bodies. They plan and construct facilities without consulting the local bodies, making it difficult for the latter to maintain them at a functional level. This is particularly true of India. Further, there is a trend towards transferring functional responsibilities and local tax bases to the state domain. Nevertheless, the case study on Sao Paulo presents a different picture, as here the municipality has satisfactorily utilized hydro-resources for the generation of electricity, for supplying water and for drainage, in coordination with the state government.

What about the notion of 'standard'? The adoption of standard in terms of access to a societally determined minimum level of infrastructure should be done taking into account factors such as local availability of resources and culture-sensitivity. Incidentally, this goes contrary to the idea of the NCU, which had suggested a 'minimum norm' for installation of infrastructure, irrespective of local conditions. The pricing policy of the services should also, to a certain extent, be guided by the principles of 'affordability' and 'self-financing' in terms of operation and maintenance.

Scholars from countries like Kenya and India agree that policies regarding the access to basic amenities have worked well wherever the government, the municipalities and the community in general, and women in particular, have interacted among themselves continuously. Experiments in Nairobi and Hyderabad have emphasized the need for involving women in the implementation of the urban basic services programmes. Issues of community participation in the effective delivery of goods is crucial when we talk about access to basic services in cities. If the community is taken into confidence, the programmes meant for them will work effectively. Examples may be cited of the Orangi Pilot Project in Pakistan, the Community Development Project in Hyderabad, the Sulabh low-cost toilets in various parts of India as well as the Ankara experiment in Turkey. Programmes like the Ganga Action Plan have not had much success as they could not generate sufficient community involvement.

The need to identify the social and economic characteristics of the community involved was also stressed. Otherwise people would continue to use structures meant to be toilets as storage facilities or would drink water from the shallow hand-pumps in spite of warnings, as they do in the 'resettlement colonies' of Delhi. In other words, people's perspective should be taken into consideration when planning and designing such programmes. This, naturally, takes us back to the crucial topic of the involvement of the community.

For some authors, all these vital issues (of providing basic amenities and of policy-making) hinge on the devolution of powers and resources to the local bodies and on community participation, so that ultimately the urban poor may attain decent living conditions. Even though decentralization has moved to the centre-stage of discussions on political systems, the question of empowerment of the disadvantaged through a philosophy of 'power-sharing' is crucial, in the opinion of some, in order to face the growing problems of the urban areas.

The experience of the Latin American countries has shown that there is a trend towards decentralization but the objective is more towards freeing national governments from the burden of administration than that of ensuring efficiency. Even in the case of Nepal, where grassroots political institutions are functioning fairly well, the bureaucracy and political interests resist the strengthening of local government. However, in some places in that country, institutions of local government function efficiently because the community has played a positive role in implementing the programmes. Test cases from Turkey, Egypt and Pakistan develop our understanding for the importance of effective leadership and community involvement. For example, Ankara's (Turkey) experience of appointing *muhtars,* who have assumed the same role they had fulfilled in the traditional village system, has helped in promoting efficiency even at the city level. But the *pradhans* (elected chiefs) of the slums of Delhi, according to some studies, are more interested in personal benefits rather than arranging for basic amenities for the slum dwellers. However, one distinction between the two types of communities should be kept in mind. The community in Ankara is perhaps more cohesive than the one in Delhi. The role of political organization at the community level is yet another factor in the efficient functioning of municipal corporations, as has been demonstrated in the case study on Calcutta. It should be noted that the interaction between the community and the local government is more in the case of Calcutta than in Hyderabad. Some attribute this to the higher political organization of the community in Calcutta.

At this point, it is worth noting that in India some states, like Orissa, are encouraging "the bottom upwards" approach whereby community members are encouraged to participate in all stages of preparation of a project, from planning to execution. This approach is bearing some fruit in the slum areas of Bhubaneswar. A declining trend in the capabilities of urban local bodies can also be observed. In many town municipalities and city corporations, elections are often postponed or not held at all. Suspension of elected bodies has become the order of the day. Instead of people's representatives, administrators conduct the affairs of these local bodies. In the past three decades or so India has been repeatedly witnessing this scenario. This state of affairs holds true not only for urban bodies but also the rural ones, known in this country as *panchayats*.

Factors leading to this decline in the institutional capabilities of local government, particularly in India, have been identified in the inadequate resource base, weak executive system, extensive state control and lack of work culture, etc. The question of endowing local bodies with an effective constitutional status cannot be overlooked any longer. India has been making concerted efforts to vest powers in the local bodies – urban as well as rural – so that they become units of self-government. Since the second half of the eighties the efforts of political parties, the intelligentsia and the legislators have resulted in Parliament passing two significant constitutional amendments – 73d and 74h – the former (Panchayats) pertaining to the villages, and the latter (Nagarpalika) relating to municipal areas. The Panchayat and Nagarpalika Amendments have become part of the Constitution since 24 April 1993 and 1 June 1993, respectively. It is a major step towards the devolution of power to the people. India is one of the very few countries in the world which has worked towards the devolution of power through constitutional provisions.

It is well known, though, that mere legislation will not ensure empowerment of the people. We must ensure people's participation to make these local bodies function effectively. It is, however, doubtful whether the local bodies will function efficiently in the face of competing claims by other development agencies, and the switching of priorities from drinking water and sanitation to education, roads, etc.

Certain policy implications must be underlined here. Problems of the urban poor have to be seen in the context of the overall development perspective. Facilities for water and sanitation should not be approached sectorally. Women should be made the initiators of the programmes. A continuous dialogue should take place among the developing countries to learn from each others' experiences, and norms on per capita availability should be fixed by taking into account cultural factors and availability of local resources. The role of the media in general and of education in particular is important in making the community self-reliant. Two-way communication between the government and the community is also most crucial.

These and related issues are discussed in this book by scholars, urban planners, administrators and researchers. Their lucid expositions are based on sound theoretical knowledge and many years of valuable experience in the field.

1

Tasks Ahead: A Government Perspective*

M. Arunachalam

I am extremely pleased that you have organised this seminar on basic amenities on the birth anniversary of Pandit Jawaharlal Nehru, the great visionary and builder of modern India. He laid emphasis on development of the society scientifically and especially on the provision of basic amenities to all strata of the society. Water and sanitation are basic needs for any human habitation and also essential from the point of view of a safe and healthy environment.

The problems faced by the urban population are many and of diverse nature. The growth in the infrastructural facilities in cities cannot keep pace with the growth in urban population. The large size of the floating population puts excess strain on the already over-stretched urban facilities.

The problems of water supply and sanitation facilities are more disturbing in urban areas. Although the deficiency in supply affects all classes of population, the poor suffer the most. In 1981 even though 72 per cent of the urban population was covered by safe drinking water, sanitation facilities could reach only 25 per cent of them. In view of this, India joined the International Drinking Water and Sanitation Decade Programme which was launched the world over in 1981.

Under the programme, hundred per cent of urban population was to be covered by safe drinking water and 50 per cent by sanitation facilities. But due to resource constraints and other difficulties the targets were reduced to 90 per cent and 50 per cent respectively and it is expected that full coverage will be achieved by the year 2001.

---

* Inaugural Speech.

It may be recalled that at the conclusion of the Global Consultation on Drinking Water and Sanitation, at the end of the decade which took place in New Delhi last year, it was decided that appropriate technologies should be adopted for providing "some for all rather than more for some". While we have repeatedly been emphasising the need for developing appropriate technologies, water supply and sewerage systems in the urban areas, however, still remain highly capital-intensive and most cities cannot finance them on their own. The need of the hour, therefore, is to go in for more conservation and better utilization of the resources.

Tasks Ahead

In the water supply sector, there is need for greater emphasis on improved management practices and reduction of the present levels of unaccounted for water. I understand that roughly 45 per cent of the water supply to a system remains unaccounted for and a large quantity of this is wasted due to leakages. The emphasis should, therefore, be on greater conservation and utilisation of the water already being supplied to the system before we go in for augmentation of supply levels into a leaky system. We have to realise that water, especially treated water, is not free. Unless we optimise our existing systems, we should not invest the scarce resources of this country in further augmentation of badly managed systems.

I would also urge that this sector gear itself to running on more commercial and viable lines by realising larger proportions of its costs from the consumers. There is no denying that there are sections of the population with limited paying capacity, but water should not be supplied free to any section of the population in order to bring home to the consumers that this is a precious resource which has to be conserved. This is even more necessary in the face of shrinking safe water sources.

As far as sanitation is concerned, while sewerage is the ultimate answer to taking care of the entire problem of waste water and sewage, we should not be undertaking these systems unless we have adequate provision for sewage treatment before discharging the same into rivers and other water bodies. In the interim, we have taken up the low cost sanitation scheme for the liberation of scavengers. It has also been decided by the Government that:

(i) At the end of this financial year there should be no government building with dry latrines; and

(ii) Dry latrines should be converted into low-cost sanitation units besides undertaking legislation for banning manual scavenging during Eighth Five-Year Plan.

The Government is also fully aware of the need to strengthen local bodies so that their resource position can be improved. This will enable them to take up water supply and sanitation schemes and provide better services to consumers. To achieve this, a Constitution Amendment Bill relating to urban local bodies was introduced in the Lok Sabha on 16 September, 1991. In the previous two bills introduced in the Parliament the municipalities were clubbed with the *panchayats*.[1] But considering the growing importance of the urban sector in economic and political terms, the Government has now introduced a separate bill for the municipalities. The bill has provisions to safeguard the democratic character of the local self-governments.

In conclusion, I would urge the present august body to address itself to this very acute problem being faced by the country and suggest pragmatic solutions which can be considered while finalising the Eighth Five-Year Plan. There is no point in making ambitious schemes when we are well aware of the present resource constraints and the weaknesses in our delivery systems. I would like to thank the organisers for inviting me to this seminar which is addressing a very critical sector of human habitation in the urban areas.

---

1. The Constitution (64th Amendment) Bill introduced in 1989 dealt only with the panchayats but the then Government indicated its intention to introduce similar legislation for urban local bodies as well. The present Constitution (72nd and 73rd Amendments) Bill deal separately with these bodies.

2

Provisions of Basic Services in Urban Areas: Some Issues*

K. C. Sivaramakrishnan

The Overview

THE pace and volume of urbanisation across the world and in developing countries has been documented extensively and no purpose will be served by repeating them here. Cities are no longer a western phenomenon. They are very much a part of the demographic and economic change which is swiftly and irreversibly altering the landscape of developing countries. Asia contained some of the most ancient cities of the world – Beijing, Patliputra, Babylon, Samarkand and Isfahan are some of the many names which conjure up memories of great civilisations and mercantile glory. But until this century the spread of urbanisation has not been a significant phenomenon. Today half of the East Asia's population is urban. South Asia's urban population has also increased from 17 per cent in 1960 to about 24 per cent in 1980. As of now out of 2.2 billion people in Asia, a quarter live in urban areas. By the end of the century it is estimated that the Asian population will surpass three billion and that the urban population will itself be close to a billion. In absolute numbers, countries like China and India will have urban populations far above the total population of several countries.

Yet the paradox is that China and India, as well as some other Asian countries will still be regarded as largely rural or agricultural. This is not a game of names or numbers. After all, when the size of the urban population is 217 million as in India and the number of cities and towns well over 5,000, there is little point in citing the rural

---

* Keynote Address.

population of 627 million and taking comfort in the statement that 'India lives in its villages'. Of course it does. But is it not time for us to accept that India lives also in its cities and towns?

Suggestions continue to be made of slower urbanisation, pointing out that the decennial growth of urban population in India during the period 1981-91 has been 36.19 per cent compared to 46.14 per cent in the 1971-81 decade. This is a rather misleading and somewhat mistaken conclusion. Since 1921 the rate of urban growth has been well above the overall growth percentage and in some decades nearly two or three times more. Even during the 1981-91 decade the urban growth percentage of 36.19 has been much higher than the overall growth rate of 23.56. Since independence urban population in the country has quadrupled. In 1951 it was 62 million. The urban growth rates are much higher in the agriculturally advanced States like Punjab and Haryana as well as in the States such as Karnataka and Maharashtra than rest of the country. The Indian experience only confirms the well known trend that agricultural development, better farm productivity, rising farm incomes as also the limitations in absorbing the growing labour force in agriculture, all contribute to an increase in urbanisation. I have elaborated on the Indian phenomenon because I feel the problem of urbanisation and the provision of services for the urban population are as much of perception, as of lack of resources.

Status of Water Supply and Sanitation

The global consultation on Safe Water and Sanitation which met here in Delhi in September 1990 started its proceedings on the modest note that globally the percentage of population covered by water supply increased from 44 to 69 per cent, which was largely due to progress made in the rural areas. On the other hand, the urban unserved increased by some 31 million, reflecting the position in Africa, Asia and the Pacific.

A part of the problem in measuring coverage is that the data are limited to simple arithmetics. Usually most national reports describe the total population of a whole town as 'covered' if there is some kind of water supply system functioning in the city. Per capita figures of supply are calculated even more simplistically by dividing the total installed capacity by population. We need not go very far to search for the truth. In Delhi itself the per capita water supply as officially reported is about 200 litres per day. This comfortable average, however, doesn't mean much to about 30 per cent of the city's nine million people who have access if at all to about 25 litres or less. Even in cities claiming 100 per cent reach, the per capita availability varies as much as 10 times between marginal settlements and the so-called better-off localities. The inequities in distribution are not just a statistical problem. They seriously distort tariffs and jeopardise cost recovery, apart from creating a sense of complacency in the minds of the decision-makers.

The coverage in regard to sanitation is even worse. The UNDP estimates that during the International Water Supply and Sanitation Decade, an estimated 748 million people received access to sanitation: 314 million in the urban areas and 434 million in the rural, due mainly to the large gains made in rural sanitation in Asia and the Pacific. Though in percentage terms coverage in urban areas rose from 69 to 72 per cent, in absolute terms, those left unserved rose from 292 to 377 million.

Perception of the Need

Most public policies or plan documents of most developing countries regard water supply and sanitation as "basic amenities". Yet this exalted position is not reflected in their budget allocations. What the Human Development Report of the UNDP terms as 'the human expenditure ratio' which is a percentage of national income devoted to human priority concerns, continues to be low in many developing countries and in some is probably going to be less. In the grim economic scenario which faces many countries burdened by external debt, adverse trade conditions, low economic growth and compulsions of security and defence, public expenditure on these human priority concerns such as primary education, health care and water and sanitation are first and easy casualties of budget exercises.

The comparison between rural and urban needs further exacerbates the problem. In India as well as some other developing countries, there is a needless but continuing preoccupation with comparisons of the severity of deprivation among the rural and urban poor. The Human Development Report has also presented an index of rural-urban disparity. Taking the urban average of access as 100, the HDR reports the disparity as 62 for water and 45 for sanitation. I respectfully submit these comparisons do not serve much purpose. I have already mentioned the all too simplistic and highly inadequate reporting on coverage of water supply. The figures are also not sensitive to the high density of urban settlements, in particular, the towns where congestion aggravates poor services. The mosquito that carries malaria or filaria or the waterborne germs spreading cholera, do not respect municipal boundaries nor urban-rural divisions. Morbidity characteristics tend to be rather similar and in fact in urban concentrations, the prevalence of gastroenteric diseases and jaundice is more pronounced. There is little point in comparing gross supply figures. The urban poor are as badly off as the rural poor in terms of quantity and quality of services as well as the time and effort spent in access to them.

A part of the problem in many countries is that water supply and sanitation are regarded as social sectors not directly connected to the production sectors of the country. The economic impact of poor water supply and sanitation is rarely understood and usually not quantified. In recent years as part of an increasing awareness of gender issues, studies have been undertaken in several countries to assess the time and effort that women and children have to spend to secure fuel and water for the household. In a recent study of Delhi, Hyderabad and Ghaziabad in India, Vinay Lal reports that on an average a woman has to spend 3.8 hours per day in fetching water for the household. Anyone who has seen the long queues of buckets and jerry-cans in the slums of Manila, Bangkok or elsewhere should have no problem in understanding what this time and effort means in terms of lost wages.

The Future Demand

The projections for 2000 and beyond indicate that out of the world urban population of 3.7 billion, 2.2 billion may be in the developing countries. In the African region the anticipated urban growth rate of 5.4 per cent will take the urban population to over 250 million, almost twice the number as was in 1988. Urban Asia will be about 880 million. As for urban poverty estimates, it is expected that the percentage of urban poor will decline slightly from 28 to 24 per cent. However, their absolute numbers are estimated to rise by nearly one-third from the current estimate of 330 million to 430 million. This assumes of course that per capita income growth will be similar to the levels as between 1965 and 1986. A more pessimistic assumption could give substantially higher numbers.

It is important to emphasize that it is not urbanisation which has caused or increased poverty. Cities have not invented poverty, they have only made it more visible.

But this visibility should not prompt leaders and decision-makers to close their eyes or flee the scene. Given the severe crunch on resources and the anticipated increase in numbers, we have to focus on critical issues of technology, finance and management.

The Issues

First, we have to recognize that at the present rates of consumption, over-use and wastage, many countries are literally running out of water. As it is, in Mexico, India, Pakistan and China, water-tables are dropping. In 1975, as many as 19 countries were classified as having less than 500 cubic metres of renewable water per person per year. After accounting for losses, this means an availability of 200 cubic metres per capita, which is not sufficient to meet domestic and irrigation water-supply demands. By 2000, ten more countries will be added to this problem list. If the present trend continues, nearly 40 countries will have a serious problem. The question is not how much water is needed but rather how best the water demand can be managed and how to optimise the use of available water.

Though only seven per cent of the world's water is used for domestic demands and 70 per cent for irrigation, the efficiency of water used in agriculture in most countries is around 30 per cent only. The inefficiency is no less in urban areas. Leakage and unaccounted for water in many cities in many countries is as high as 40 per cent. Distribution arrangements and existing tariff systems have hardly any relevance for water conservation, wastage reduction or recycling. This is as much an issue of technology application as of management.

In large cities, the cost of conveyance and distribution has become very high. The dependability of large-scale systems is also getting to be less. At the risk of offending public health engineers and those favouring large-scale water supply authorities, I would suggest a closer scrutiny of the limits of such large-scale systems. In cities like Manila, Calcutta, Shanghai or Cairo, are we sure that the economies of scale continue to be valid? Should we not explore the possibility of disaggregated supply arrangements which can be more sensitive to local needs and more easily managed at the local level?

Yet another issue of technology is the type of supply and sources within the urban settlement, particularly the periurban settlements and slums. The hand-pump has been heralded all over the world as having vastly improved access to water. Yet in urban areas, given the concentration of population and the very poor sanitation, hand-pump sources have also been easily exposed to contamination. The gastroenteritis epidemic in the slum settlements in Delhi in 1988 clearly established this.

Global warming, diminishing rain forests, protection of the ozone layer and preserving genetic diversity are all hot subjects of discussion today but closer to the ground is the problem of water pollution. The contamination of water resources is now wide spread in many developing countries, brought about by industrialisation as well as untreated sewage. In India 70 per cent of the total surface waters are considered to be polluted. The UNDP reports that in China out of 78 rivers monitored, 54 are reported to be seriously polluted by untreated sewage and industrial waste. Several rivers in Malaysia are devoid of fish and aquatic animals.

Surface water pollution is also a major problem affecting rural water supply sources. I am personally hopeful that strict adherence to the principle "pollutor pays" as well as the adoption of clean technologies will help us overcome the problem of water pollution from industrial sources. I am, however, much less hopeful about treatment of domestic sewage. Most of the Class I cities in India do not have a sewerage system at all. Even in the so-called metropolitan cities of more than a million population, only 50 per cent of the waste water is collected and treated partially or otherwise. Unfortunately, the costs of conventional sewerage system continue to be very high and the level of technology developed and application effort limited. While man has succeeded in putting one of his species on the Moon, he has not been able to deal with his own waste in an efficient, cost effective manner. Technologies like anaerobic treatment and those for recovery of resources from sewage continue to be applied on a limited scale only.

The Ganga Action Plan launched in this country in 1985 was the first comprehensive plan of action to address, in an integrated manner, conveyance and treatment of sewage, resource recovery through methane gas, fish-farming and irrigation, sustaining aquatic diversity, and river quality monitoring and management. But the plan is limited only to the Ganga.

Low-cost sanitation with pit latrines or pour-flush latrines has definitely helped to improve the sanitation coverage but there are serious limitations in adopting this approach everywhere. In India a major programme has been launched to provide low-cost sanitation wherever feasible in towns having a population of up to 500,000. The programme is an imaginative combination of loans, grants and beneficiary contributions, involving local bodies and aiming at the elimination of manual scavenging. Work is in progress in over 400 towns at a cost of Rs. 155 million. Under this programme, about 78,000 pour-flush toilets are being built. A complementary programme will help rehabilitate about 30,000 scavengers through retraining and placement in other occupations. Successive governments have continued to give top priority to this particular programme which demonstrates how much can be accomplished if different departments and levels of the government act in coordination.

Financing

It is estimated that during the International Water Supply and Sanitation Decade, various governments and external support agencies have spent about $ 120 billion which amounts to approximately $ 100 for each additional person served during the decade. These are according to 1985 prices. If the investment levels are not increased considerably in the 1990s to provide water supply and sanitation, the per capita expenditure may come down.

What then are the possible courses of action? Consider the following:

Should we strive to lower the cost further?
How much can we recover from the user?
Can we draw on private resources not used before? and
How can public expenditure allocations be increased?

I have already touched upon the need for cost reduction and cost effectiveness. Technology application, extension of trained man-power to build and maintain water supply and sanitation installations are all crucial. The plumber, whether in the United States or elsewhere, is an expensive and difficult person to get hold of. Our experience in low cost sanitation indicates how important it is to develop easily understood methods of latrine construction. Some of the public authorities, as in Tamil Nadu, have brought out handy little folders with pictures to describe the process. Still, for the average city dweller, the construction of a latrine is a complex and difficult business.

The position is much worse regarding water supply. Quality control in the sinking of hand pumps and their efficient operation and maintenance on a large enough scale are important aspects. As for piped systems, the net cost of production is increasing and currently averaging about 25 to 30 cents per kilolitre. While the Decade has provided a broad range of low cost technologies, scaling up is an important task which is pending.

The poor cost recovery should not give one the impression that there is no potential to pay at all. Even in slum settlements it is seen that about 40 per cent of the families do make some form of payment which is often more than what the higher income groups pay. The remaining households will also be prepared to pay for improved supply. Cost recovery mechanisms tend to rely heavily on individual metering and billing. The Kumpung Improvement Programme, Basti Improvement Schemes or Urban Basic Services are examples of converging basic amenities and services. This area based approach for provision of services has to be taken further towards operations and maintenance and cost recovery.

However, faced by the stark reality of declining budget allocations, local bodies and water authorities have of late begun to look for loan grant combinations. During the past one year, India's Housing and Urban Development Corporation, 'a parastatal', has sanctioned 54 projects for water supply and sewage in different cities at a total cost of about Rs. 800 crores. HUDCO itself is providing a loan of Rs. 330 crores on rates of interest varying 12 to 15.5 per cent. The bulk of the amount is for eight projects in some metropolitan cities. The significance of the HUDCO initiative is that it marks a departure from total dependence on public exchequer allocations.

Management

The role of urban local bodies in providing water supply and sanitation has varied from country to country. While in Latin America these are understood and accepted as patently municipal functions, there has been much ambivalence in Asia and Africa. Arguments about resource mobilization and the so-called efficiency considerations have led to the water supply function being taken away from municipal bodies in many countries. A study of 29 cities by the Operations Research Group in India indicates that as many as 22 provincial level bodies took up the capital works but only in five they were involved in operation and maintenance. The division between capital works and operational and management responsibilities has been a long-standing problem. If public accountability, better understanding of local needs and flexibility in delivery arrangements are required, there is, perhaps, no substitute for local bodies.

Unfortunately in many of our countries, decentralisation has been a tenuous and uncertain exercise. In spite of the vast and dramatic changes in the economy and political structure of many societies, the orthodox nation-state model, relying on external sovereignty against transnational influences and internal sovereignty against local and regional powers, continues to influence many minds. Recent events, however, show that even the largest country is too small to govern the world and at the same time too large to govern their cities. What holds for the USA and New York is as much true of Tokyo or Seoul, Shanghai and Jakarta, Bombay or Lagos.

There is, therefore, no escape or alternative to decentralisation. In a situation of rising aspirations, limited resources and the near impossible task of having rational, happy national budgets and self-expanding bureaucracies, decentralisation may indeed be the only approach to sustain large societies within some acceptable frame of government. Akin Mabogunje, the renowned African scholar, refers to the perception of central and provincial governments as fountainheads of patronage: the obvious fear is that decentralisation would cause hydraulic problems to the fountain. We have to get over these apprehensions and accept that local participation, through local governments as well as community participation, is as much a financial necessity.

The decade of the 1980s has been an extremely difficult one for domestic resource mobilisation and expenditure. It has not also been a bright period for external resource mobilisation. In fact, from 1986 to 1988 the net outflow from heavily indebted countries was over 100 billion dollars. The recent World Debt Tables confirm this sad trend and it is feared that many countries pay about five per cent of GDP in debt repayments. No one knows for certain how much governments in the developing countries are spending on water supply and sanitation. It is estimated that the current levels of investment in the sector are about $ 10 billion. The New Delhi Consultation last year concluded that a five-fold increase in that amount would be needed to provide water supply and sanitation to all by the year 2000. William Draper, the UNDP Administrator in his forthright opening address, suggested that a $ 50 billion a year might be called unrealistic but $ 15 to $ 20 billion a year would not. Perhaps he is right: perhaps not. But $ 50 billion is what it took to wage the 15-day war in the Gulf.

PART I

Experiences from Developing Countries

3

The Provision of Basic Services in Pakistan, Turkey and Egypt

Geoffrey K. Payne

Introduction

OF all the shelter and environmental issues facing cities in developing countries, the provision of adequate quantities of clean and affordable water is the most fundamental. The unprecedented scale of urban growth in developing countries makes this task difficult enough. To achieve this under conditions when both governments and residents lack adequate resources for conventional approaches is even more problematic. It is not even enough, however, to provide water, since increased consumption imposes a corresponding burden on systems of waste disposal to prevent contamination. By focusing on these key issues whilst the lessons of the International Drinking Water and Sanitation Decade are being absorbed, this Seminar is serving a vital need and it is an honour to have been invited to participate and contribute.

The focus of this chapter is on the experiences of three countries, Pakistan, Turkey and Egypt, each of which illustrates different forms of innovation in the provision of urban services. In reviewing and analysing these cases, special attention will be paid to issues of community participation, resource mobilisation and effective management systems.

Pakistan

In common with many other countries, Pakistan has experienced considerable problems in terms of urban services provision. Levels of access to public services are generally low, particularly in the larger and more rapidly growing urban areas. In 1980, only 25 per cent of the urban population had access to an indoor flush latrine; 48 per cent used pit latrines and 27 per cent had no access to latrines. At least 40 per cent of urban deaths are due to water and sanitation related diseases.

The rapid growth of unauthorised low-income settlements, known as *katchi abadis*, reflects the inability of public and formal private sector supply systems to keep pace with the demand for land, services and housing. The application of high standards, inflexible administrative procedures and limited institutional capacity, combine with limited resources to inhibit any prospects for early improvement.

Under these conditions, any examples of innovation deserve attention. In Karachi, the Orangi Pilot Project (OPP), is one such case. In 1980, Orangi accommodated about 800,000 of Karachi's 3.2 million *katchi abadi* population in an area of about 4,000 acres. People had acquired land illegally, but at acceptable prices and constructed houses of variable quality, which they proceeded to improve according to their means. The one problem they had not solved for themselves was sanitation. No public mains sewers served the area and people were dependent on either bucket latrines, soak-pits, or short sewer lines which discharged into the nearest *nullah*. As a result, the streets were filled with excreta and waste water, making movement difficult and creating enormous health hazards (Hasan, 1986).

In an attempt to address this problem, an NGO was formed in 1980 under the name of the Orangi Pilot Project (OPP). This sought to demonstrate that considerable improvements could be made if people worked together as a community and technologies were developed according to the requirements of local groups. The NGO encouraged people living on each lane to appoint lane managers, whose task was to resolve local problems, collect money and implement the works in collaboration with staff from OPP.

Initial works simply transferred wastes from lanes into the nearest *nullah*, which then became even more polluted. To overcome this problem, a single chamber septic tank, known locally as a *haudi* was placed between every connection and the sewer, to prevent solids from flowing into the drain. Even so, it was realised that the project lacked an overall plan for the area and that it required the design and construction of secondary sewer lines. Since these also had to be financed by the community in the absence of services from Karachi Municipal Council, a major education programme was conducted to explain the needs to lane managers and obtain local support to extend the project.

The OPP has now expanded to cover a large part of the entire settlement and adjacent communities have expressed interest in following the same approach. To achieve so much in such a short time would not have been possible without the availability of a committed NGO team and external financial support. However, the real question is to what extent can the approach be replicated in other parts of Karachi or Pakistan? Not all urban areas possess the gentle slopes which made it possible to install and extend the sewer system at costs which local people could afford. Local government officials also complain that the scheme merely concentrates the effluent at the edge of the settlement and makes the problem even worse for those living at lower levels. OPP staff answer that they can overcome the technical problems of working on flat sites, though this has yet to be established. It is hardly fair, however, to blame the NGO or local people for externalising the problem, when the local authority has been unable to undertake any improvements in any of the areas concerned.

Perhaps the real lesson of the Orangi project is that it demonstrates that even low-income people are willing and able to pay for services, providing they are designed according to their own needs and resources rather than those of government agencies, no matter how well intentioned. Furthermore, it suggests that hard pressed local authorities could benefit by collaborating more closely with local NGO's to develop local networks which can connect efficiently with off-site public mains services provided by government agencies and funded out of general revenue or property taxes.

The principle of involving residents in the services provision has recently been extended to a project for new development undertaken by the Hyderabad Development Authority in Sindh. All applicants to the *Khuda ki Basti* project who can demonstrate eligibility are allocated a plot without any on-plot services, with the intention that community services will be upgraded to individual connections as and when residents are able to afford them. This reduces initial costs and the need for subsidies, with the intention that the approach will be replicable. The approach has not yet, however, been adopted in other cities.

Turkey

The processes by which services have been provided in the Turkish capital Ankara are of particular interest for the ways in which they coped with rapid urban growth under conditions of scarce resources and weak local government (Payne, 1982).

Unlike most developing countries, the high levels of urban growth experienced in Turkey are largely the outcome of government policy, which stressed the need for modernization, industrialization and urbanization. To this end, urbanization was to be welcomed, though it was not until after 1945 that regional socio-economic imbalances and improved roads encouraged large scale rural-urban migration. From then on, many cities grew rapidly and Ankara's population doubled almost every decade, reaching three millions in the early 1980s from a base of 20,000 in 1924.

The demand for urban land, services and housing generated by this level of growth proved greater than the government or the formal private sector could supply. As a result, many migrants adopted the same approach which had been officially accepted under the Ottoman administrations, whereby villagers were entitled to claim and use any undeveloped state land, providing they farmed or lived on it. This approach had been developed to encourage the productive use of land in the under-populated Anatolian plateau, but was quickly adopted by the new urban population to solve the problem of finding a plot on which to build a house. Since Ankara was being developed according to a master plan, however, such settlements were regarded as illegal and became known as *gecekondus*, or buildings which 'landed by night'.

The ability to prevent *gecekondu* formation and manage urban growth was not made easier by the financial, administrative and technical weakness of local government and its enforced dependence upon central government. Municipalities did not even exist in Turkey until 1930 and most local government programmes depend upon grants and loans from the centre. Inevitably, this creates bottlenecks when the political party in power varies from one level to another.

For this reason, long term strategic planning has tended to be a somewhat unproductive exercise. However, this has been largely offset by adapting and expanding the traditional role of the *mahalle* (a district or ward). Under this arrangement, each *mahalle* is administered by a *muhtar*, or *headman* and a committee of elders. He serves as the representative of government in his *mahalle*, but is elected by the residents to represent their interests to government. He is therefore required to balance conflicting interests and needs to be able to deliver local benefits if he is to be re-elected.

In rural areas, the *muhtar* is expected to organise the provision of public works, such as the provision of water and sanitation, the construction of roads and the draining of swamps. The revenues for these works come from two sources: *imece*, a form of self-help in which it is compulsory for villagers to provide labour, and *salma*, which consists of a tax levied on each family in the village.

The inability of government to provide services to new settlements in Ankara led to the *muhtars* assuming the same role that they had traditionally fulfilled in the villages – of organising the provision of local services and public works, as well as keeping registers of births, marriages and deaths, etc. Since each *mahalle* was entitled to a share of the annual municipal budget, it was important for a new settlement to be registered as a *mahalle* as soon as possible. Since the criteria for approval were flexible, it was possible for most settlements with a population of about 10,000 to be allocated *mahalle* status and for larger ones to be sub-divided into two or more, irrespective of the legal status of the area. In this way, the administrative boundaries of the city expanded in line with physical development and population distribution.

The importance of this arrangement is that it enables the varied needs of different *mahalles* to be reflected in the claims they make on the municipal budget. For example, *mahalles* in inner city locations may request funds for open spaces, or more schools, whilst new settlements on the urban periphery may require access roads and a water supply. In addition to being familiar to everyone, another advantage of the *mahalle* system is that it provides a local scale to urban management. This combination encourages participation in community development and enables hard pressed local authorities to concentrate on providing technical back-up to *mahalle* initiatives and planning the distribution of public mains.

A good example of this approach in practice can be seen in the development of Sehit Mevlut Meric, in the south of Ankara. This area was initially developed in the early 1960s, and quickly became a *mahalle*. Since the settlement was off the main road, the first priority was to obtain a good access road, so that a bus service could be provided. To achieve this, the *muhtar* applied to the highways department to plan a road. The highway engineers duly prepared a plan which followed the most economic route over the hills and involved the minimum of house demolition. This plan was then sent to the *mahalle* for action and three options were open to the *muhtar* and local residents. They could accept the plan as it was, propose minor modifications, or reject it. If they followed the latter course, that was generally the end of the matter, since the highways department would already be dealing with applications from other *mahalles*. So the pressure was on to agree with the plan, or propose modest changes.

Since it was the local community which wanted the road, there was usually strong pressure on any residents who opposed the plan to agree. The most vocal opposition naturally came from residents whose houses or plots would be adversely affected. To obtain their agreement, neighbours would often agree to realign plot boundaries, or find another plot nearby and even help to demolish and rebuild an affected house. The important point is that such negotiations took place within the community and therefore avoided time consuming delays, or conflict between the community and the local authorities. The initial application *and* the final decision were taken at local level.

Once the proposal was approved by the *mahalle* residents, or their modifications accepted by the local authority, it was placed on the list of proposals for funding by the municipal council. Often, funds would not be forthcoming immediately to implement the scheme and in some cases *muhtars* were able to invoke the traditional levies of *imece* and *salma* to implement the works. Families would be expected to contribute cash and/or labour to dig trenches for water and sewer lines, or level the rights of way for access roads and in some areas, they even paid for the materials.

It would be incorrect to claim that this arrangement was the outcome of enlightened local government, or that it was faultless. However, given the circumstances, it enabled government agencies to provide a technically competent service to the expanding population of the city at a rate more or less equal to the high rate of growth and that must rank as a major achievement. Whilst the *mahalles* occupied a humble position in local government, they contributed substantially to the effective provision of roads, water supply and sanitation throughout the city. By assuming responsibility for their own housing, local communities also enabled scarce technical and financial resources in the public sector to be spread more widely and concentrate on major public works. For many years, infrastructure provision represented about two-thirds of the total municipal budget and enabled even low-income groups arriving in the city to obtain a plot and services within a short time. Over the years, the effectiveness of this arrangement has been reduced by the increasing commercialisation of the land and property markets. This has reduced the homogeneity of new settlements and the degree to which people are willing to collaborate on community developments, such as services provision. Nonetheless, it still operates in areas where there is strong demand for particular services.

Egypt

This case study is of interest because it shows how services provision can be designed as an integral part of projects based on incremental development strategies.

Ismailia is a relatively small city half-way along the Suez Canal and is the centre from which the Canal is administered. It was evacuated for eight years between 1967-75, during the two Middle East wars. In 1974, the Egyptian Government obtained funds from UNDP to appoint a firm of British consultants, Clifford Culpin and Partners (now Culpin Planning) to prepare a master plan for the city until the year 2000. This led to a proposal funded by the British Government to prepare 'demonstration projects' as a means of illustrating how the plan could be implemented and in 1977-78, three projects were prepared by the same consultants. These were designed to be self-financing urban developments which would provide housing plots and services for a wide section of the population, but also be affordable to low-income households.

At that time, many households were unable to afford legal, officially acceptable housing, or the cost of public services. About 60 per cent of the population lived in various types of unauthorised housing which they improved when and as they could afford it.

In attempting to upgrade and extend such areas to meet future needs, the consultants undertook extensive social surveys to identify the priorities of the target population. They then prepared 'community plans' for two low-income settlements which concentrated on putting the available land to the most efficient use in order to minimise unit land costs. The plan also accepted that the existing practice of incremental house building should be permitted to continue and that the same approach should be extended to the provision of services. In this way, it was found that even households earning (UK) pounds 18 (at 1978 rates) could afford the full cost of a plot and modest house, with minimal surfaced roads, community standpipes and an on-plot pit latrine (see below).

For those at the top end of demand, it was obviously possible to provide full services immediately. Care was therefore taken to prepare a package of services options which met the primary needs of households in a way which could be efficiently upgraded as incomes and demand increased. Seven distinct packages or thresholds were identified for the initial project at Hai el Salam. These were as follows:

Level 1:
- Administration, plot markers, compensation, registration
- pit latrines (including capitalised running costs)
- standpipes
- stage 1 access roads (graded district roads)

Level 2:
- Level 1 plus
- electricity
- landscaping

Level 3:
- Level 2 plus
- paved district roads
- stage 2 local roads (grading and transitable surface)

Level 4:
- Level 2 (less pit latrines) plus
- reticulated water network
- water connections
- reticulated sewer network
- sewerage connections

Level 5:
- Level 4 plus

- paved district streets
- stage 2 local roads

Level 6:
- Level 5 plus
- trunk sewers
- trunk water mains
- paved access roads

Level 7:
- Level 6 plus
- service core on plot

The cost of each of these levels varied according to plot sizes and density levels and for this reason a range of plot sizes was compared with each level of provision. The greatest single cost threshold occurred between levels 3 and 4, since the introduction of individual on-plot water connections raised consumption and disposal levels to the point where it became necessary to install public mains drainage. Whilst 79 per cent of all households in the new development area were estimated as being able to afford level 3, only 41 per cent could afford level 4.

To ensure that all households were able to afford a given level of services provision, the costs of each were related to estimated affordability levels and the appropriate ratio of each incorporated into the plan. The spatial distribution of each level of service was then related to the distribution and pricing of individual plots. For example, plots on main roads, which would be able to receive services first, were designed and priced for the upper end of demand and allocated at a higher unit price than other plots on secondary roads, which would be able to receive services at a later date.

The recovery of network installation costs from these relatively better off households reduced the cost of extending the networks to the lowest income households, though it is important to note that each group only paid for what they were receiving. The cross subsidy element was obtained by differential pricing of the plots and their allocation for commerce, industry or higher income housing.

By relating the design and phasing of services provision to levels of demand and local priorities, the Ismailia Demonstration Projects broke new ground in housing development in Egypt. In the event, however, the strategy was modified when USAID offered to fund the provision of full infrastructure for the entire Hai el Salam project on a grant basis.

This dramatically changed the way in which the area was perceived within Ismailia and was seen as making it one of the best serviced areas in the entire city. Before long, many higher income households than were anticipated began to buy plots in the area, forcing up prices and encouraging the low-income residents to sell out. In the event, it was many years before the services were provided at the level envisaged, so those who bought into the project had to endure the same modest level of services provision which had been envisaged for the poor. Since they were living at much higher densities in apartments, however, the demand on available services was often greater than they could cope with, so that environmental conditions have been lower than planned.

Ironically, modest initial services provision had been intended to discourage this tendency as well for reducing unit costs. Whilst this represented a dilution of the principles behind the project, this was more than offset by the Governor's decision to expand the project agency established to implement the project into the Ismailia Planning and Land Development Agency with responsibility for applying the incremental development approach on a city-wide basis. The central aim of the demonstration project was, therefore, fully vindicated.

General Observations

As these case studies have sought to demonstrate, the role of local communities is a key question in any programme of services provision. Of the three elements of shelter provision, e.g. land, services and buildings, services cannot easily be provided by people for themselves. In most countries, the private sector, (formal or informal) has been able to ensure the provision of land and most households have proved able to organise their own housing. In the initial stages of developing new settlements, when density levels are relatively low, residents may even be able in organising their own water supply from wells and sanitation through pit latrines or septic tanks. However, once densities increase, these are unlikely to be adequate and the intervention of local government agencies then becomes essential.

However, it is worth asking if professionals are always best placed to determine and maintain services and if the role of communities is merely to provide information and assist with construction? As Angel (1983) has observed, the successful implementation of services programmes requires collaboration between several groups of actors-professionals involved in housing; municipal engineers; community workers; politicians; international funding agencies and local residents. Services provision is not just a technical issue, though many professionals tend to consider it as such; it is increasingly a management issue, in which those arrangements which satisfy the prime needs of each set of actors will be the most successful. The experience of Ankara and the Hyderabad UCD programme are good examples of such a participatory and multi-disciplinary approach in action.

The only effective way to ensure that cultural factors are incorporated into services programmes would appear to be by involving communities in the design of the projects. Water consumption and wastes disposal impinge on extremely personal attitudes towards bodily hygiene, which are largely cultural in nature. Cultural concepts of purity, or cleanliness, do not necessarily correspond with the criteria assumed by engineers, yet if they are ignored, services systems which may function efficiently from a technical point of view, will not be accepted, used or maintained, by their intended beneficiaries. The international experience with communal toilets is, perhaps, a good case in point (though the Sulab toilets and wash places in India shows how a compromise can be achieved).

It is frequently considered that community participation increases the time and cost of services provision programmes and many professionals can probably provide direct evidence of this. However, this is often because the concerns of communities and the ways in which they arrive at decisions are invariably different from those of professionals. When professionals initiate or control the project, it is not surprising that community contributions are considered unhelpful. In cases where the initiative or control is vested in the community, as in Ankara, such limitations may not apply.

To what extent should affordability determine levels of services provision? It is now widely accepted that the poor should pay for what they receive, but is this justified unless the more affluent are treated in the same way? At present, high income groups commonly receive substantial direct and indirect subsidies on full services provision.

Another key issue is that the provision of services may stimulate house improvements, providing that residents feel sufficiently secure on their plots and have adequate resources. On the other hand, they may lead to increased rents which could displace low-income tenants. Of course, displacement may also result from the physical works themselves and the need to install services lines, so there is an advantage in combining upgrading with new development projects.

Assuming that a pragmatic approach is adopted, the level of services provision to be provided will be determined by the priorities of residents and their ability to pay, rather than arbitrary norms and standards. Priorities will usually relate to the minimum plot size considered suitable for permanent occupation, the level of services provided and the initial standard of superstructure.

As Kirke (1984) has noted, successful services provision can best be achieved when initial costs are minimised without prejudicing long-term potential standards. Incremental development can then take place as demand and resources require. The services which particularly affect costs and affordability are as follows:

- Access and circulation

  Reducing unit land and servicing costs can be substantially helped by reducing the rights of way of roads and footpaths to the minimum necessary for the amount and type of traffic likely to use them. In most cases, it should be possible to achieve appropriate layouts with a maximum of 20 per cent of the available area occupied by circulation and public open space. Not all plots need vehicular access, since few low income households will own cars, even in the medium future and it is more sensible to plan for an efficient public transport system for the majority of residents. The need for efficient land use has been accepted for many years in India and other countries would do well to familiarise themselves with the experience gained.
- Storm water drainage

  This needs to be adequate from the outset, but need not be capital intensive if carefully designed. Kirke recommends that providing storm drains are separate from sewers, open channels with earth banks are generally appropriate in that they are inexpensive to construct and easier to maintain.

Water supply and sanitation

These can usually be provided on an incremental basis according to costs and the ability to pay. It is also often socially acceptable for households to collect water from a communal standpipe, at least on a temporary basis and providing the distances involved are not too great. This is often part of rural life and would still represent an improvement over existing levels of provision for millions of people. Extensions can then be made as effective demand increases, which makes it important to design the mains network for eventual full supply. Kirke considers that standpipes do not encourage high levels of cost recovery and also impose high maintenance costs. The additional cost of providing on-plot taps may therefore be justified. Many technical options exist for on- and off-plot sewerage and wastes water disposal, all of which are well known. In situations where full sewerage is not affordable, waste stabilisation ponds are becoming widely accepted. These can reduce treatment costs of effluent to less than 10 per cent of a traditional sewage treatment works and produce an effluent that can be used for aquaculture or agriculture. Another option is the composting toilet, though this has only been introduced on an experimental basis so far.

Electricity and street lighting

According to Kirke, standards often provide for 1.5kV per plot, which may be three times what low-income groups need and can afford to pay for. An above-ground distribution system will also help to reduce installation and maintenance costs, while circuit breakers can be used to control levels of supply more cheaply than meters.

Solid wastes disposal

This should, of course, be incorporated into all schemes from the outset, though it is unrealistic to expect a higher level of services in new low-income developments than what hard pressed local authorities are able to provide elsewhere.

Conclusions and Policy Implications

The scale of urban growth in many developing countries during the past four decades has been without precedent in human history.

According to a recent World Bank Study (1984), India can expect an additional urban population of about 175 million between 1984-2000. This will apparently require about two million hectares of land, or about double the area of Bombay, each year. Against this background, it is hardly surprising that governments have often been unable to provide services at the rate required.

It is not only desirable to improve this situation in terms of public health and economic development, but also in terms of long term ecological survival. In many developing countries, the agricultural eco-system is already vulnerable to degradation because of deforestation, over-grazing and over-population. This trend is being intensified by the loss of essential soil nutrients in the form of crops which are consumed in the cities and transformed into wastes which are not returned to the soil. Urban water supply and sanitation policies need to be developed which reduce this linear process and replace it with a cyclical approach in terms of energy consumption and wastes management. As Giradet (1990) has observed, the soil fertility of much of North Africa was shoved through the stomachs of the Romans into the Mediterranean!

In practice, this means more use of treated sewage as fertiliser and a greater use of recycled materials in building and large scale tree planting. This inevitably brings us back to the cultural issue, since societies such as India's find it difficult to apply the same pragmatic approach that is taken for granted in others, such as China. One way of encouraging a change in attitudes would be through a pricing policy which provided adequate reward to those responsible for implementing such programmes. In India's case, this would also be consistent with social policy by improving the economic status of scheduled castes.

This returns us to possibly the most critical point in any discussion of urban development, whether it concerns land, buildings, or services provision; namely, that the main issues are not technical, but political and economic. The comprehensive series of studies published by the World Bank (1980), together with more recent publications (e.g. Cotton and Franceys, 1991), all demonstrate that the technologies required are already available. Resolving the political and economic issues cannot begin until they are accepted as central.

This will require professionals, such as engineers, architects, planners and surveyors, to develop an increased understanding of the implications of technical options and acquire skills in negotiating proposals according to needs and resources, rather than applying inherited standards. It also indicates the benefits of bringing municipal engineers into the planning process at the initial stages of development planning, rather than at the end. It would be desirable for municipal engineers to be included in the teams selecting project sites, so that they can advise on linkages to existing and proposed mains systems and likely drainage problems, etc. To play their part effectively, it would be necessary for such engineers to be sensitive to the social, cultural and economic aspects which will influence the nature of the services to be provided and how they are likely to be used.

It also suggests that there can be major benefits in reducing professional compartmentalism and encouraging all environmental professionals to collaborate more in multi-disciplinary teams, so that the implications of proposals for one sector on others can be anticipated and optimised.

Other aspects in need of urgent consideration are the standards and procedures for establishing services delivery systems. These are often over ambitious, compared to the immediate needs of the population and the resources available. Kirke (1984) cites the example of Cairo, where the master plan envisaged the supply of treated water for domestic consumption reaching a level of 500lcd within 20 years at a time when the majority of the population were not even connected to a piped water supply. (By comparison, per capita water consumption in London in 1980 was 346lcd). A standard of 100lcd was considered the most that could be achieved in high density, low-income areas.

The point being made by Kirke is that standards are of little relevance if they cannot be delivered in practice to all in need. A pragmatic approach on the part of all agencies and professionals involved in water supply and sanitation programmes is therefore necessary. Any increase in water consumption made possible through improved supply will generate a corresponding increase in wastes. It is therefore vital to adopt an holistic approach to services provision, especially where incremental provision is required. For this reason, it may well be necessary to install a public mains sewer system in inner city projects, since land prices may well be too high to permit plot sizes large enough to enable on-plot sewerage systems to operate efficiently. The consolation is that as density levels rise, the unit costs of installing full services are reduced, making the transition easier to achieve.

One way of approaching the problem is to prepare 'packages' of options. These should satisfy primary project objectives, the local community and the local authority, a process which will require skills in negotiation as well as design. For example, the provision of communal standpipes will reduce levels of water consumption to the point where on-plot sanitation systems will generally be adequate, while higher standards of supply will require higher standards of wastes disposal. Grouping such packages according to cost thresholds, as in the Ismailia Demonstration Projects, can enable project designers to minimise initial costs while meeting the primary needs of local residents.

In most countries, it is not possible to provide all communities with full services initially. Instead, approaches have to be developed which provide basic levels of provision initially, but in ways which can be upgraded and extended as resources become available. This incremental development process presents engineers with considerable problems in planning detailed services layouts, since it may not be possible to anticipate the rate at which an area may increase in density, or incomes may rise to pay for higher levels of provision in selected areas. However, the experience gained during the Ismailia Demonstration Projects described above, shows that it is technically possible to prepare services proposals which are efficient and affordable at all levels of demand and are capable of improvement and extension. Such examples need to be more widely disseminated.

The administrative structure is a key consideration in implementing an effective services provision policy. Ankara illustrates the advantage of a flexible arrangement which enables administrative boundaries to adapt to demographic changes within the existing built-up area population and expand to incorporate new peripheral development. By ensuring that each local ward or community is able to express its needs through the administrative and resource allocation systems, it is easier to identify what services are needed in each part of the city and prioritise them.

Of course, the existence of effective community leadership will not, in itself, guarantee that community needs will always be met. Community leaders may well have their own agendas and be able to exploit opportunities for personal aggrandisement at the expense of their constituents. There are many cases in Turkey where *muhtars* have used their community positions as a stepping stone for higher political ambitions at the expense of their *mahalle* residents. However, there are many more who have served their communities well and it is probably unrealistic to assume that community level politics should be any more altruistic than those at other levels.

This is not to claim that community participation can resolve all the issues involved in servicing expanding urban areas. As the Orangi Pilot Project demonstrates, communities can only operate at the local level. Local drains and sewers need to be connected to a public mains system which only urban development agencies can install and this requires co-ordination between agencies and groups working at local and urban levels. In Karachi, the lack of communication between the Orangi community and the agencies responsible for services provision led to sewage being discharged at the boundary of the adjoining neighbourhood. This problem was less apparent in Ankara because the agencies and community groups co-operated more effectively. The key consideration in this respect is accountability. The more transparent the decision-making process is, the more such corruption or exploitation can be contained and exposed. The more local communities are involved directly in the future development of their neighbourhoods, the more they are likely to play their full part in strengthening democratic institutions and contributing effectively to the local economy. The provision of services through such community initiatives can play a vital part in this developmental process.

REFERENCES

Angel, Schlomo, 1983, 'Upgrading Slum Infrastructure: Divergent Approaches in Search of a Consensus', *Third World Planning Review*, Vol 5, No 1.

Cotton, Andrew and Franceys, Richard, 1991, 'Services and Shelter', *Liverpool Planning Manual*, No 3, Liverpool University Press.

Giradet, Herbert, 1990, 'The Metabolism of Cities' in Cadman, David and Payne, Geoffrey (Eds.), *The Living City*, Routledge.

Hasan, Arif, 1986, 'OPP's Low Cost Sanitation Programme', Orangi Pilot Project, Karachi.

Kirke, John, 1984,'The provision of infrastructure and utility services' in Payne, G. K. (Ed.), *Low-Income Housing in the Developing World*, John Wiley, 1984.

Payne, Geoffrey, 1982, 'The Gecekondus of Ankara' in Ward, Peter (Ed.), *Self-Help Housing: A Critique*, Mansell.

World Bank, 1984, 'Efficiency in Land Use and Infrastructure Design'.

World Bank, 1980, 'Appropriate Technologies for Water Supply and Sanitation'.

4

Empowerment of Local Government and Community-based Programmes: The Case of Nepal

Jibgar Joshi

DURING the Panchayat Regime (1960-1990), the Government of Nepal has tried to devolve power to regional and local levels following basically a top-down approach. There has been adequate enabling legislation but bureaucratic resistance is also in operation to hinder its implementation. Without trying to implement laws with determination, more laws have been enacted, creating confusion and overlapping. However, the legal and institutional framework is sufficiently egalitarian to allow community based activities. At the same time, there have been considerable efforts at the grassroots level which in fact help bring new awareness and changes.

This paper is organised into five parts. The first part deals with enabling legislation and weaknesses in the laws. The second part deals with the advantages of community involvement. The third part describes projects where community involvement is substantial. The next part links the community based programmes with the process of creating legislative environment conducive to the provision of urban services. Finally a summing up follows.

Local Government and Enabling Laws

During the Panchayat Regime, the local panchayats (village, town and district) were established under the Village Panchayat Act, 1962 and the District Panchayat Act, 1982. The government had apparently been trying to integrate these political units into local development processes. The last five development plans incorporated the panchayat sector besides the public sector and the private sector. Under the panchayat sector, local development programmes, panchyat training programmes and other local activities were included. From the Sixth Plan (1980-1985) onwards the panchayat sector was made more comprehensive by incorporating the district plan. The government initiated several institutional arrangements to ensure coordination of various institutions at the local level. Regional directorates were established. Projects and development efforts spread far and wide and the need for distributing the development benefits among the people was felt strongly. The Decentralization Act, 1982 and the Rules, 1985 were enforced.

Before the implementation of the District Administration Plan 1975, there was no mechanism to co-ordinate the development works of district panchayats and the district level offices of the sectoral ministries and departments. The plan tried to strengthen the local development process and involve wider participation of the panchayats in planning and implementation. Integration of local planning with the national/regional planning objectives and priorities was its main objective. All the district level activities are co-ordinated, supervised and controlled by the Local Development Officer. With the enforcement of the Decentralisation Act, the district panchayat secretariat controlled the activities of line agencies. But the administration in the secretariat of the local panchayat was handled by an administrative staff seconded from the Ministry of Local Development which weakened the autonomy of local government (Joshi, 1991).

Similarly, the Town Development Committee Act, 1963 (TDCA) provided the legal base for the creation of such committees at local levels, chaired by respective zonal commissioners (recently dissolved) with the mayors nominated as member-secretaries. Heads of the line agencies and representatives from different class organisations were made members.

In 1972 Nepal was divided into different development regions and physical development plans of regional development centres were implemented under Town Planning Implementation Committee Act, 1973 (TPICA). The law entrusted the committee with the task of implementing development schemes prepared by the Department of Housing and Urban Development. These committees were also supposed to mobilize locally based sectoral agencies in implementing respective components of the plans. These committees although represented mostly by local panchayat organisations were also chaired by zonal commissioners (recently dissolved).

These committees (TPIC/TDC) and municipalities share a common jurisdiction and draw upon the resources of the same locally based agencies. There are considerable functional overlaps and conflicts between them. The original idea that such TPIC's or TDC's would be of crucial significance for all town development initiatives came into direct conflict with the role assigned to the district and town panchayats under the Decentralization Act.

The TPICA provides the authority to the national government to frame rules for the purpose of implementing the objectives of this law. At the same time these acts impose serious restrictions on raising funds. TDCA, for instance, requires the committee to call tenders to secure loans at the lowest rate of interest whereas the TPICA prohibits the municipalities from selling or alienating its title to any property including those purchased or acquired by it.

Institutional impediments to municipalities are numerous. These include interference by politicians in day to day administrative work; organizational set-ups which do not relate to functional requirements; lack of adequate and qualified manpower; lack of training support and unclear role differentiation of the municipalities *vis-a-vis* TPIC/TDC.

Various attempts made by the Panchayat Government towards decentralization had invariably failed. As viable political bodies could not be formed at different tiers of panchayats, most decentralization steps emerged from the top and reached down to district level where major local development works were to be implemented with the active participation of elected bodies ranging from the Ward Committees to the District Assembly. The major thrust of the decentralization policy has been to implement the district development plan under the coordinating role of the Local Development Officer. The Decentralization Act, 1982 (DCA), attempted to integrate panchayat bodies into the local development process by substituting the coordinating role of the Chief District Officer with those of the District Panchayat Chairman and Local Development Officer.

On the ground of technical incompetence, power is generally not delegated to local government. But as a matter of fact several enabling programmes including management support to municipalities have already been launched. However, the technical process is so specified as to make it very difficult for the local government to adopt those. When the performance standard of the national government is not satisfactory, it is paradoxical to ask the local government to adopt stringent rules and technicalities. The DCA and its rules are biased towards how plans should be formulated rather than the mechanism to implement them. A very elaborate procedure for approving plans is given under the DCA, from the ward to the district level.

The secretary of the district panchayat, an administrative officer, is appointed by the Ministry of Local Development. He is the executive head of the District Panchayat Secretariat. All the local offices of the concerned line agencies are brought under the secretariat and they have to work as the part of the secretariat for the implementation of the district plan. Almost all the government agencies are required to extend necessary cooperation in the formulation, execution and evaluation of the plan of the local panchayat.

The relationship between the District Panchayat and the Municipality had been one of friction and resistance because the power vested in the District Panchayat included the management of resources of the Town Panchayats. In terms of resource mobilization, town panchayats are in a favourable position.

The politico-administrative structure of the Panchayat government did not allow the local institutions to play a decisive role. The grassroots level demands were never politically processed upwards to the national system. Although the National Development Council resolves the local-national conflicts at the national level, there is no other institution between the national and district level, and local interests as such, could not be well reflected in the implementation stage.

Through the establishment of committees and project offices located at urban areas, the inter-level interactions have been formalized. The striking feature of these committees on projects is that these end up with the national government's control on local affairs either through liasion ministries or the zonal commissioner and the CDO.

After the political change of 1990, the government dissolved the panchayats and made interim provisions for conducting the local affairs. The executive secretary now heads of the municipality and representatives of line agencies are the members. The government is presently drafting legislation for the structure of local government which will soon be tabled in the winter session of the Parliament. Hopefully, the new legislation will help to empower the local government. Here two things are of critical importance. First, their ability to integrate the community based activities into the total city level infrastructure network and to work under a participatory development approach whereby they derive strength through local action and local politics. This can be termed as empowerment from below rather than through top down decentralization. This will avoid dependency of the local government on the national bureaucracy or national politics, irrespective of whether they are party-based or not. Second, their ability to adapt technological innovations to their specific needs. The two most dangerous elements hindering their full development have been technological and political subordination.

Advantages of Community-based Projects

Projects based on community involvement help enormously to create local institutions which are better placed in the provision of services including water and sanitation. Projects should not be judged by their physical targets only. While in the initial stages, the physical targets are likely to be in significant, there are several other advantages when viewed from a long term perspective. That has been the the experience of some of the activities undertaken in Nepal during the past few years. The advantages of such activities are:

- they help towards empowerment of the local government.
- they create communities.
- they exert pressure on government agencies.
- they create awareness in the field of sanitation and water supply.
- the possibility of improving their immediate environment gives new hope to most slum dwellers and squatters.
- through action, the methods of integrating their activities with the formal infrastructure network could be worked out.

There are other advantages specific to the Nepalese case:

a) The people did not know till recently how to obtain access to institutions responsible for infrastructure provision. As a result, institutional resources remained untapped and institutions continued to be liabilities rather than assets.

b) The cities of Nepal even now have rural features although they are fast disappearing. If timely intervention is not made, it will be more difficult to harness community-based resources as the city network becomes more complicated and sophisticated. There will be more problems in integrating such activities in the future.

c) Most of the local resources are administered by the national government. Most district level projects under the national plan, funded through the district offices, are generally tightly budgeted as the national budget is also severely limited. In fact, about 70 per cent of the national budget goes to carry-over projects. As widening the resource base is primarily a national concern linked with the broad issues of national economy, the major concern at the local level should be to activate the private sector including non-governmental organizations, private voluntary organizations, community organizations, and households. Once the private sector could be functionally linked with the public sector for local development processes, there will be no need to go on increasing the strength of the local bureaucracy under the national government. The activation of local institutions depends on its interaction with the people at large. Unless accessibility is increased, no amount of mushrooming of offices, top-down decentralization steps, stringent rules, or control mechanisms will strengthen the local government action. The only way to increase accessibility is through action at the grassroots level.

d) Nepal offers a unique opportunity to devise ways and means to use community based resources along with urbanization process where new approaches need not be thrust upon as in the case of cities of more urbanized developing countries.

Community Involvement

With the change in the government, there is already more awareness and political consciousness. More involvement of the municipalities in urban affairs, less central interference and unlimited access and participation of the people in development process will help urban development. Participation in local government offers a very good forum where local politics will be centred and people will see their political rights *vis-a-vis* their rights to the access to services and infrastructure.

Some of the projects and activities in the above direction are discussed below:

(a) **Dhalko Urban Community Development Project:** Dhalko is the name of a locality in Ward No 17 of Kathmandu Municipality where a sweeper community lives. The project is being financed by Redd Barna, Nepal. The project was approved in 1988. Durga Pariwar Club, a local organization is implementing the project.

The general objective of the project is to help support the socially deprived community within the Kathmandu Valley. The project will assist the community in improving their social and physical environment. Street sweeping and clearing garbage and solid waste have been their main job. The special feature of the project is to involve the community in fulfilling this objective. The problems were identified and implemented by the community whereas the project office including Redd Barna and Durga Parivar Club played the role of facilitators. Key activities were identified and prioritized with the help of the community. The line agencies such as the Water Supply Corporation, the Municipality, the Roads Department, TB and other hospitals, educational institutions, helped in the implementation of specialized works. The community contributed labour, played a significant role in supervision and users groups were formed to implement the programmes.

The project has already provided new sewerage and drinking water lines with connections to every household. A school building has been reconstructed after demolishing the old one. Programmes of health, family planning, nutrition and literacy have been launched. It has provided income generation opportunities (like mushroom cultivation, piggery training, etc.) to the people and first-aid training to community members.

The project has been a good experience in terms of community building, people's involvement and replicability. It does not involve huge financial commitment. However the project is too small to make a significant impact. Only Rs. 2.5 million has been spent for a population of 1800.

(b) **Training in Upgrading and Slum Improvement (TASK Project):** As an outcome of the continued involvement of the Norwegian Students and Teachers from University of Trondheim and Oslo School of Architecture, in the study of squatter settlements of the Kathmandu Valley, this project made a significant contribution in the training and planning for slum rehabilitation and urban upgrading.

The primary objective of the project is to develop skilled and trained manpower in government line agencies in the field of urban area upgrading. Another major objective is to prepare an area development plan of the study area in order to implement the plan and also to generate curricula and training manuals for similar types of trainings in other parts of Nepal. Other objectives include motivation of community groups, documentation and dissemination of the project experience, implementation of demonstration projects (upgrading) and the formation of users committees. The trainees provided technical assistance in drawing up the plan of action. Other achievements include installation of two hand-pumps with 53 per cent cost contribution by the community, rehabilitation of two court yards with 35 per cent of the cost shared by the community and total management by the community without outside help. The community was seriously involved and interested in the project. They have already come forward with additional proposals to be implemented in the project areas.

The project sites are located in the core area of Kathmandu and Lalitpur. The trainees are engineers, architects, sociologists, economists, geographers from sectoral agencies, municipalities, the Institute of Engineering and the Town Development Committee.

The positive aspects of this project are: (a) the programme produces valuable planning documents, (b) ensures considerable community involvement in the planning process, (c) provides a comprehensive action-oriented course in planning. The demonstration projects were highly appreciated by the community and stand a high chance of being replicated with community involvement.

(c) **Courtyard Rehabilitation Programme:** When Solid Waste Management Project began it was found that the waste from courtyards found its way to the streets which obstructed the normal function of solid waste collection. To solve the problem, the project cleared up the dumping in the courtyard with the help of the municipalities but after some time the people again began dumping the wastes in the courtyards. Hence the idea of courtyard rehabilitation cropped up and the residents themselves were encouraged to clear up the wastes and the labour cost was borne by them.

The government broadcasts the programme objectives and details over television and radio along with general information and rules and regulation for co-operation. On hearing the announcements, interested communities apply after which the Centre approves the programme. Technical support and advice are provided by the project for the rehabilitation of the courtyard and other works such as connection of their kitchen outlet to the drainage connection to the main sewer etc. The main objectives of the programme are:

- improved sanitary living conditions in and around courtyards through the removal of waste and their rehabilitation whenever deemed necessary.
- motivation of courtyard residents to regularly clean and maintain their courtyards after rehabilitation and to encourage maximum people's participation in the programme.

The drainage and sewerage system of the houses surrounding the courtyard were rehabilitated first as per necessity e.g. by providing drain pipes for individual kitchens, building manholes for sewerage for every house and also providing facilities for connection of toilets to the sewerage manhole or even to the main sewer. The project provided materials e.g. paving stone, pipes and other building materials while the community or the municipality contributed the labour or labour cost.

During the period 1986-88, 174 courtyards were rehabilitated at a total cost of Rs. 64,58,000. Of the total cost, about Rs.54,00,000 was contributed by the project. The courtyard rehabilitation programme became so popular that the demand for rehabilitation grew rapidly. The hygienic condition around courtyards improved. Seventy-four per cent of the courtyards were found to be kept clean after rehabilitation. A good response from the applicants demonstrated the popularity of the programme. This project is a good experience of community mobilization, motivation and participation. The cost involved is not much and such programmes can be replicated. These activities contribute enormously in the improvement of the urban environ- ment and use of potential open spaces (courtyards).

(d) **Urban Basic Services**: The Urban Basic Services (UBS) programme has been jointly launched by UNICEF and the government to address the need of the urban poor. The programme was initiated as it became increasingly difficult for the urban poor especially the women and the children to live in urban areas.

The overall objective of the programme is to provide basic services for children and women especially those in greatest need. The specific objectives are: (a) reduction in infant and child mortality, and (b) improvement in the situation and well-being of women through integrated delivery of basic social services.

The main objective of UBS programme is to identify needs of the poor and to work out a plan of action that will incorporate those needs together with other pertinent areas of UNICEF work, focusing on health and community development. The UBS is to be implemented in five towns of Nepal: Dhangadi, Nepalgunj, Lalitpur, Pokhara and Biratnagar from 1990-92.

Relatively disadvantaged wards of the town are selected by the municipality in collaboration with the Ward Chairman and UNICEF. The criteria for the inclusion of a particular ward in the programme include lack of access to adequate drinking water and low nutrition level among the children, participation of the poorest and disadvantaged groups of the locality. City level planning and implementation committees are headed by the Chairman of the Municipality comprising representatives of the departments involved in UNICEF assisted programmes. The committee is responsible for policy development and periodic reviews. All the activities are carried out by the municipality through sectoral services and organization of local community. The programme co-ordinator works in close collaboration with the Chairman of the Municipality and has operational responsibility for co-ordination, planning, programme implementation, monitoring and evaluation. The programme has made a good start. It has helped:

- increase awareness on health and hygiene.
- improve the sanitary condition in the area.
- provide basic services to the deprived community.
- motivate the community and revive their age old community organization.

Though the financial involvement is not much now, it will increase when other towns are covered. The contribution from the people should increase to make the projects replicable. This would require effective economic upliftment programmes which would enable people to pay.

(e) **Balaju Squatter Settlement Improvement Programme**: Women in Environment (W.E.), an NGO took interest in the Balaju squatter settlements and studied the area in detail. UNICEF approved the proposal in 1990 after making necessary amendments. The squatter settlements in Balaju is located along the western bank of Bishnumati river north east of Balaju bridge. There are altogether 68 dwellings with six persons per dwelling. The community lacks basic services like water, electricity and toilets. The quality of dwellings is very poor. Some of the achievements include:

- running a non-formal education programme for adult women.
- training for literacy facilitator.
- provision of water stand post.
- community motivation.
- management of kitchen gardens.
- river bank stabilization.
- greenery development along the river banks.
- primary health care.
- toilet construction etc.

An action committee comprising community members was formed for implementing the programme. Users committees were also formed for different components of the programme. Line agencies were mobilized to provide necessary materials and technical help in collaboration with W.E. and the community. For example, the Ministry of Education provided books, the project provided materials while the community contributed labour for all the programmes.

Lessons from Successful Community Programmes For Legislative Environment

When we assess the contribution of such projects as described above towards building local institutions, replicability of activities becomes a crucial criterion. As projects are generally judged by their physical performance, emphasis is generally laid upon the resources to be mobilized, systematic preparation of the planning documents, nature and extent of participation of the beneficiaries and so on. On the other hand, if the process is of any importance, it is that which has to be sustained, augmented and integrated within the urban community. Thus community cohesiveness becomes the most crucial element for strengthening local government action.

Implementation of an otherwise well intended legislative frameworks is a more critical aspect. Implementation process of urban planning is influenced by various interests. When the interest of the poor is not well represented, the existence of legal and institutional framework is meaningless. This is exactly what happened in Nepal. While the State professed to be an egalitarian one, it was not interested in the empowerment of local government. Then the question is where does the political forces emanate from? The success of the projects where community participation is substantial shows that power evolves through action at the grassroots level. Local empowerment is aided through awareness generation, through teaching people by their rights of access to services and basic amenities and by building of viable communities.

Conclusion

The objective of a good legislation is an increased access of the people especially the poor to institutions and resources ensuring at the same time greater autonomy local government. Nepal's experience in decentralization from the top shows that most legislations served to create confusions professing a decentralized egalitarian approach under a basically autocratic partyless panchayat system. The government enacted several enabling legislations but their implementation was deliberately resisted.

Yet this absence of effective enabling legislation could not deter grassroots action as it is still in an embryonic stage and apparently does not pose a threat to the government. At the same time, these efforts helped tremendously in generating awareness in the form of political demand making and helped in the interpretation of the existing legislation to achieve desired results in some areas.

REFERENCES

Development, Communication and Research Consultancy Group. Urban Basic Services: Baseline Survey Report, Biratnagar Nagar Palika, HMG of Nepal/UNICEF, Oct. 1990.

HMG - Nepal. Decentralization Act, 1982.

———. Decentralization Act: Rules and By-laws, 1985.

———. Land Acquisition Act, 1977.

———. Municipality Act, 1990.

———. Solid Waste (Management and Resource Conservation) Act, 1987.

———. Town Development Act 1988.

———. Town Development (First Amendment) Act, 1990.

———. Village Development Act, 1990.

Joshi, Jibgar. 1991. *Housing and Urban Development in Nepal*, Kathmandu: Lajmina Joshi.

———. 1986. *Regional Strategy for Development: A Case Study of Nepal*, Kathmandu: Lajmina Joshi.

Joshi, J. and Bjonness H.C. 1987. *Housing for the Urban Poor*, Report from a seminar March 1, 1987 in connection with the International Year of Shelter for the Homeless, jointly organized by Deptt. of Housing and Univ. of Trondheim and Oslo School of Architecture.

Kvamstad, V *et al.* Bas. 1985. *A Study of Squatter Settlements, Kathmandu '85.* published jointly by the Univ. of Trondheim and The Oslo School of Architecture, Trondheim/Oslo.

LCRC. *Urban Development through Nagar Panchayat*, Kathmandu: GTZ, 1984.

LCRC. "Various" Town Panchayats: An analysis of organizational structure, manpower distribution and job description. Sept. 1988.

LCRC/BDP. *Town Panchayat Finances*, Kathmandu: GTZ, 1985.

Mathema, M.B. and Jibgar Joshi. 1986. "Major National Urban Issues: Nepal." Country paper, regional seminar on "Major National Urban Issues," Asian Development Bank, December.

McCullough, James. 1984. *Institutional Development Program for Local Authorities*, Kathmandu.

———. Financial Assessment Reports on Eight Town panchayats, MSTP, various dates, 1985/86.

Redd Barna. *South Asia 1990.*

Solid Waste Management Board, *Report on Courtyard Rehabilitation*, 1985 and 1986.

Throndsen J. Kankeswori. 1990. *Kathmandu, Nepal: Urban Structure and Housing Upgrading for the Poor* M.Sc. thesis Univ. of Trondheim.

Urban Basic Services Programme for Lalitpur Nagar Panchayat, inter-office memorandum, 30/11/1990.

Women and Environment, A Progress Report on Slum Improvement Programme at Balaju Squatter Settlements, November 1990-February 1991.

5

Contemporary Urbanization of Sri Lanka: Impact on the Quality of Urban Environment

B. L. Panditharatna

CONTEMPORARY Third World urbanisation reflecting a strong western colonial legacy has been accelerated since the Third World nations gained independence. Metropolitan and urban economies experienced a rapid expansion of the secondary, and service sectors, resulting in population increase, high densities and an overload on the existing infrastructures. Residential segmentalization into areas of different levels of affluence and deprivation evolved, and were observed by Robert McNamara:

> "The urban poor are frequently denied access to basic public services not because these do not exist, but because these have been designed or located for middle and upper income city dwellers and are beyond the reach of the less privileged."

In urban morphology, a "formal sector" distinguished itself from an "informal sector" where over-crowding with substandard houses, high population densities with relatively poor access to public utilities, civic and community services were conspicuous features.

This paper is a presentation of Sri Lanka's experience of rapid and decentralised urbanization, and its implications for basic amenities, focusing on Colombo city. Sri Lanka is a small and compact country, 64,000 square kilometres (25,330 sq.miles) in area with an estimated total urban population of around 5.2 million out of a total of 18.4 million in 1991. The incidence of urbanisation is in inverse proportion to the proximity to the capital city of Colombo so that as one moves to the periphery from the centre one finds it more intense. Thus, Colombo's urban problems when compared to the multimillion cities of South Asia (India, Pakistan and Bangaladesh), appear in 'miniature form' as regards scale, intensity and variety. Even then, intra-city and inter-city access to basic services in Colombo is not much better than in other South Asian cities. However, several steps have been taken to improve the situation.

Sri Lanka's rate of urbanisation was just below 2 per cent per year for 1963-71 and was reduced to 1.4 per cent for 1971-81 period which may be regarded as modest compared to the high rates of 4-6 per cent for some of the African and Latin American countries. A major reason for this situation in Sri Lanka in recent decades was the government investment in the provision of better economic and social infrastructure such as power and irrigation, transport, health and education facilities which were distributed throughout the country. Improvement in the standard of living of the rural population, creation of job opportunities and the availability of satisfactory health and education facilities in the rural areas along with cheap public and private transport services between the urban and rural areas have been the other contributory factors for the decreasing rate of urbanization. The other reason was the official definition of urban areas which, following the British practice, was confined to municipalities, urban and town units. Thus certain towns with a population of more than 5000, urbanized areas in suburban situations and urbanized villages were excluded from the definition of urban area.

Several research studies provide a conceptual base and useful reference for comparative analysis for this study. These are: "Informal Sector in the Calcutta" (Bose, 1974), "Informal Sector" (Hart, 1973), "Informal Economy" (Geertz, 1963), "Proto Proletariat" (McGee, 1974), "Petty Commodity Production" (Moser, 1978), "Disguised Proletariat" (Jerry and Birbeck, 1981) "Upper and Lower Circuits" (Santhos, 1979), "Squatters" (Castells, 1988) and "Employment in the Informal Sector" (Hettige, 1986).

Process of Urbanisation

Sri Lanka's urban population in 1946 was 1.02 million representing 15.4 per cent of the total population. This doubled to 2.84 million in 1974, raising the urban proportion to 22.4 per cent. In 1981 the urban population increased to 3.2 million but in percentage terms it decreased from 22.4 to 21.4 per cent. Thus both the levels and rate of urbanization in recent decade (1971-1981) have been rather low, 21.4 per cent and 1.4 per cent respectively. But the picture has changed considerably in the 1980s.

A realistic assessment of the trend of urbanization should take into account the newly urbanized areas in the highly suburbanized south-west coastal region, the numerous road-railway junction centres, the fast developing new townships of the areas under Mahaweli Development Authority, the several urbanized villages of the Jaffna Peninsula and the on going decentralization process of devolution of administration to some 241 Assistant Government Agent's (AGA's) administrative centres spread throughout the island. The level of urbanization will then go up to about 30-32 per cent and the rate of urban increase to around two per cent (Fig.1).

Population increase from 3.2 million in 1981 to an estimated 5.2 million in 1991 was the most important factor contributing to urbanization. There were four reasons for this increase. Firstly natural increase which became the chief factor in the Colombo City despite its low rate of natural increase. Secondly Colombo's net migration rate was relatively very small (below 100,000 for the 1981-91 decade) as its pull by way of providing opportunities for better living both in the formal and informal sectors were limited. Thirdly, creation of several new towns in the newly developing areas of the Mahaweli Development Authority consequent on suburbanization and village expansion and fourthly extension of the boundaries of several municipal towns, urban and town units have contributed to the increase of urban population.

Colombo city registered growth rates exceeding two per cent per year up to 1963, decreased to one per cent during 1963-71 and to a very low 0.4 per cent in 1971-81 and is below 0.5 per cent in the 1981-91 decade. The towns having more than 100,000 population experienced high growth rates about four per cent per year during 1963-71 but decreased to 1.3 per cent in 1971-81 and increased to 1.6 per cent in 1981-91. The medium size towns (20,000) of Colombo district registered high growth rates around six per cent and is increasing continuously. The growth centres and new towns of the dry zone indicated very high rates above eight per cent. Colombo, the capital city had a population of 575,786 in 1981 and is estimated to be around 620,000 in 1991. All towns in the categories with a population between 5000 - 50,000 are experiencing rapid increase in population since 1971 (Table 1).

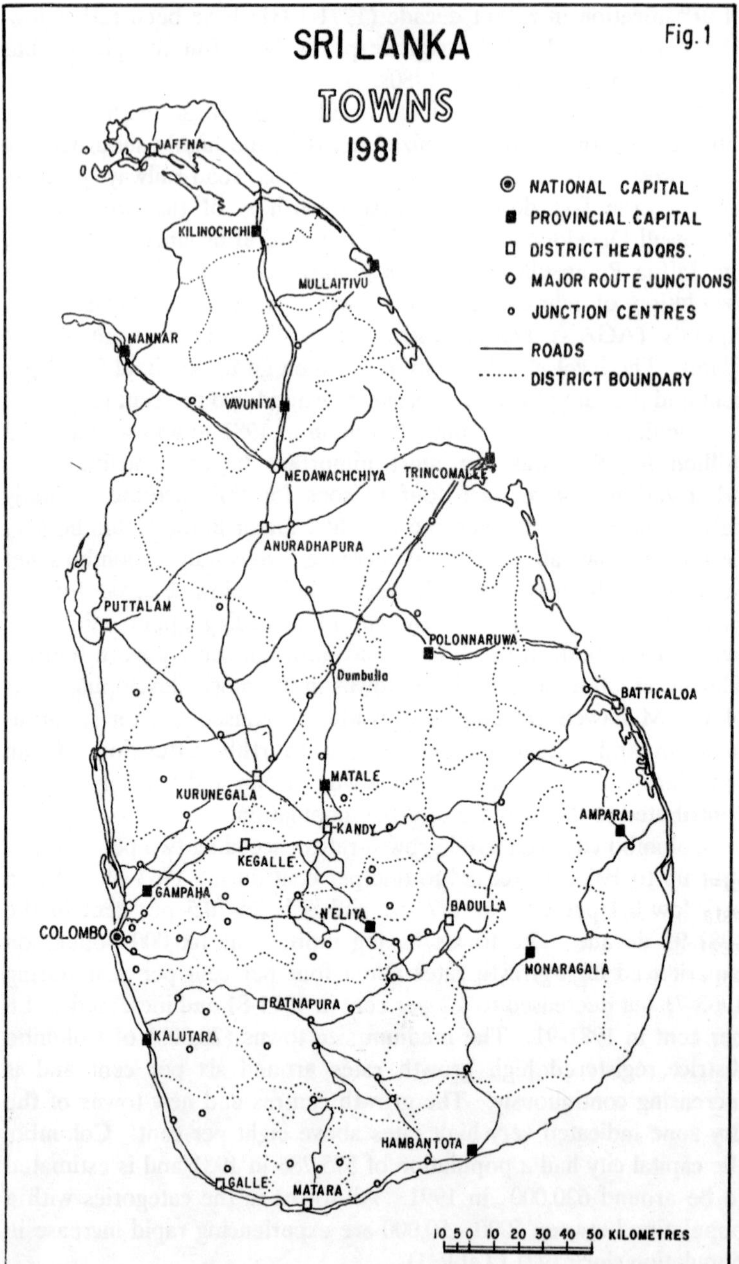

SRI LANKA
TOWNS
1981
Fig. 1
NATIONAL CAPITAL
PROVINCIAL CAPITAL
DISTRICT HEADQRS.
MAJOR ROUTE JUNCTIONS
JUNCTION CENTRES
ROADS
DISTRICT BOUNDARY
JAFFNA
KILINOCHCHI
MULLAITIVU
MANNAR
VAVUNIYA
MEDAWACHCHIYA
TRINCOMALEE
ANURADHAPURA
PUTTALAM
POLONNARUWA
Dumbulla
BATTICALOA
MATALE
KURUNEGALA
AMPARAI
KANDY
KEGALLE
GAMPAHA
N'ELIYA
BADULLA
COLOMBO
MONARAGALA
RATNAPURA
KALUTARA
HAMBANTOTA
GALLE
MATARA
10 5 0 10 20 30 40 50 KILOMETRES

Table 1
Sri Lanka Urban Population

	1971			1981		
Categories	No. of Towns	Population	% of total U. Pop.	No. of towns	Populat-ion	% of total U.Pop.
500,000	1	563,705	19.79	1	586,776	18.3
100,000	2	260,093	9.1	5	631,054	19.8
50,000	5	411,311	14.4	3	195,094	6.1
20,000	25	781,874	27.5	31	976,957	30.6
10,000	34	499,561	17.5	35	511,138	16.0
5,000	30	215,848	7.6	28	199,189	6.2
2,000 (and below)	38	114,914	4.1	31	95,671	3.0
All Towns	135	2,848,116	100.00	134	3,194,879	100.00

Source: *Census of Sri Lanka*, 1981.

After independence in 1948, Colombo, the colonial capital city and chief port, experienced population pressure which resulted in an overload on the existing infrastructure. Following depolarization measures from Colombo city around 1960, towns of the Colombo District came under a rapid process of residential infilling in relatively small residential lots. In these towns except for electricity supply, the other utilities namely water, sewerage, garbage collection, surface drainage had to be installed on an individual owner basis resulting in wide variations in the quality of the residential environment.

In the provincial and district towns, utilities were restricted to electricity and in a few towns water supply schemes as well which serviced the core areas only. Rapid residential growth and installation of water supply, sewerage and drainage facilities have created problems especially in small residential lots of 10-12 perch where both the source of drinking water (from wells) and sewerage (septic tanks) are contained within these lots.

Impact on Urban Environment

The housing conditions both in Sri Lanka and Colombo, its capital city, are an indicator of the quality of life of the people of the country.

The 1981 Census registered 2.8 million housing units for a total population of 14.8 million. This showed a substantial increase in housing coverage from 17 per cent during 1963-71 period to 26.8 per cent in 1971-81 period. Compared to the past, both quality and quantity of houses have also improved in the following directions:

a. site selection/soil, drainage and surface water considerations
b. structural features (floor, walls and roof and ventilation)
c. water supply, disposal of excreta and solid waste
d. limiting over-crowding by controlling housing and accommodation density and several measures to improve socio-economic environment, for example:
   i. to control insect, mosquito and rodent nuisance problems
   ii. pollution and precautions because of the presence of toxic and caustic substances for domestic uses, and planning to improve
   iii. nature of access to public utility services.

In Sri Lanka piped water supply was available for only 46.5 per cent of housing units and 48.7 per cent of the households obtained water from the wells. As regards sanitation 15.6 per cent households had flush toilets, 39 per cent water seal, 26 per cent pit or bucket type and nearly 20 per cent had no toilet facilities in 1981 (Table 2). Compared to 1971, the picture however, had improved in 1981.

The Status of Colombo City

In 1981 Colombo city had 84,500 housing units which accounted for only 3 per cent of the country's housing stock. 2999 units have not been approved and more than 30,000 units were unauthorized units categorized as slums and shanties. The distribution pattern of substandard housing (slums) is shown in Fig. 2 and these included:

a. Old dilapidated buildings in the inner zone converted into multiple residential units providing multiple family accommodation with shared water and toilet facilities
b. tenement garden house clusters of semi-permanent and improvised houses in very limited spaces exemplifying very high densities - 50 to 60 houses per acre and population densities exceeding 300/400 per acre

Table 2
Percentage Distribution of Occupied Housing Units by Source of Water Supply and by Types of Toilets by Sectors - 1971 and 1981

Source	All Sectors		Urban Sector		Rural Sector		Estate Sector	
	1971	1981	1971	1981	1971	1981	1971	1981
Water Supply								
Piped water on tap	20.1	17.3	45.3	46.5	4.8	5.1	74.7	65.6
Well	68.8	73.1	50.5	48.7	81.9	84.4	15.4	20.4
River, Tank or Other Source	8.9	7.0	2.0	1.1	11.0	8.5	7.3	5.8
Not Stated	2.3	2.7	2.1	3.7	2.3	1.9	2.1	8.1
Type of Toilet								
Flush toilet	6.7	4.8	22.8	15.6	2.2	2.1	8.2	4.9
Water Seal	14.3	21.9	19.2	38.9	9.9	17.5	33.9	24.2
Pit Type	38.8	37.9	18.3	17.0	44.4	43.5	38.2	32.3
Bucket Type	4.8	2.0	19.4	8.8	1.0	0.3	4.1	2.1
None	34.3	30.9	19.1	16.4	41.5	34.8	13.4	28.1
Unspecified	1.2	2.5	11.3	3.4	1.0	1.7	2.2	8.5
Total	100.0	100.0	100.0	100.0	100.0	100.0	100.0	100.0

c. temporary improvised huts along canals and water bodies
d. and improvised temporary structures along pavements and in open spaces.

Substandard houses and their residential population estimates in the city varied widely 30-42 per cent of the residential units (Fig. 2).

More than 50 per cent of the substandard houses have no electricity and use kerosene. It was observed that in a number of slum areas unauthorized electricity connections have been taken from public toilets or State buildings that posed a hazard in this crowded environment.

About 60 per cent of the houses had separate kitchens. The remaining had no kitchens at all and did their cooking in the verandah or outside the house using kerosene or fuel wood.

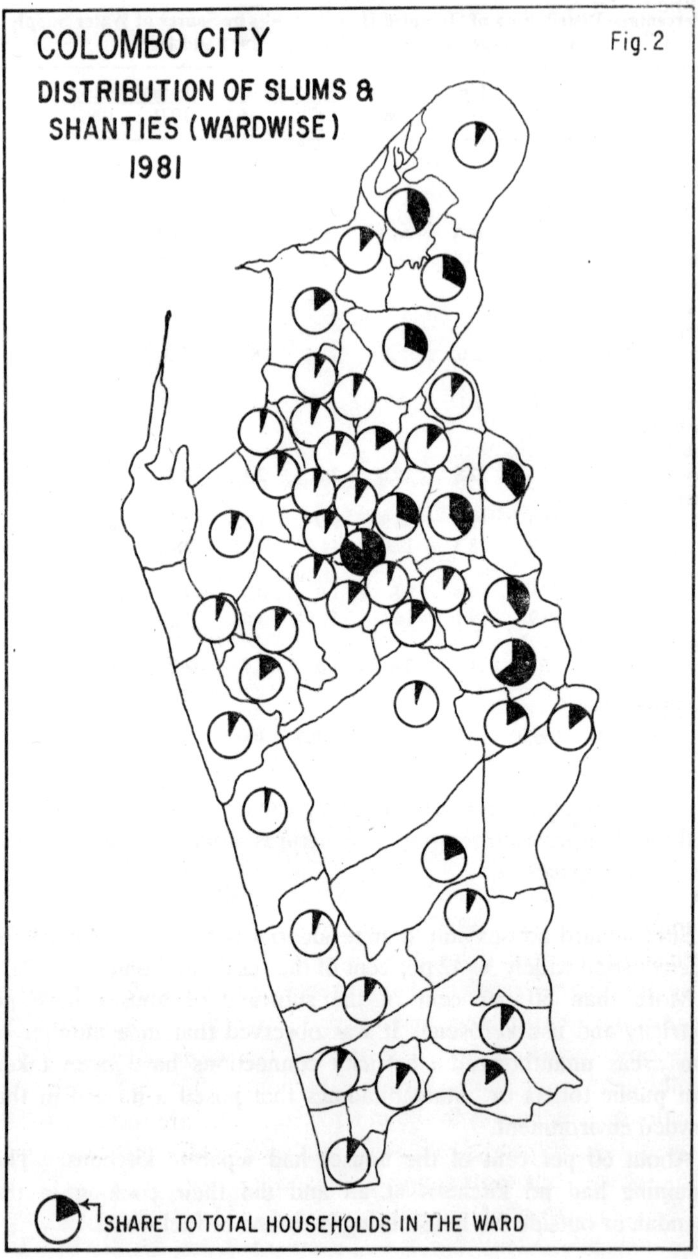
COLOMBO CITY
DISTRIBUTION OF SLUMS & SHANTIES (WARDWISE) 1981
Fig. 2
SHARE TO TOTAL HOUSEHOLDS IN THE WARD

Pipe-water was available everywhere except in the northern and eastern wards of the city. Only 38 per cent of the households had water taps installed inside the house. About 3 per cent used water drawn from wells which faced the possibility of contamination. Thirty-five per cent households had private bathing facilities. Public bathing either in public bathing enclosures or at the public taps (standposts) was very popular and thus the number of standposts had increased from 752 in 1971 to 855 in 1981. For each standpost there were more than 100 persons queuing up in the morning and late evening hours (Table 3).

Sixty-five per cent of the households had flush toilets. Water seal latrines have been partly replacing bucket latrines mostly in the northern and eastern wards, but at a low rate of 16.23 per cent. Approximately 6000 shanties and slums had no toilet facilities at all and the residents continued to pollute the open spaces, marshy areas, railway track corridors and canal embankments thus endangering community health (Table 3).

Access to Public Utilities

The sources of water for Colombo city are entirely surface supplies namely Kalatuwawa and Labugama reservoirs, Kelani River and wells. The reservoirs have a capacity of 145,000 cu m/d/20 mgd and Kelani River 190,000 cu m/d/20 mgd. After treatment water was pumped to three service reservoirs located at Maligawatta (East), Ellie House (North Central) and Dehiwela (South). The average per capita consumption of around 45 gallons per day was considered high. Considering other uses and wastage through toilet flushing, open taps, leaks and unauthorized uses, the actual per capita consumption is around 30-35 gallons per day. But the distribution pattern showed certain disparities.

The low income residential areas receive rather indifferent water supplies, because of the inability of the residents to pay the installation expenses of pipes and taps and the water rates and have to follow the long bureaucratic procedures for approvals of installations. The houses in the inner mixed zone are served better because of their proximity to State buildings. The affluent residential districts received adequate supplies of water.

The sewer system of the city consists of 152.5 miles of sewers, nine pumping stations and two treatment works. It is heavily

Table 3
Housing Characteristics: (A) On the basis of (i) type of lighting provided, (ii) cooking facilities available, (iii) type of water service, (iv) bathing facilities and (v) toilet facilities (B) (i) Walls, (ii) Roof and (iii) Floors in 1981

			No. of Units	Percentage
A.	i.	*Provision of Lighting*		
		Electricity	55,622	49.17
		Kerosene	35,683	49.26
		Unspecified	1,140	1.57
	ii.	*Cooking Facilities*		
		Separate Kitchen	43,020	59.38
		Shared Kitchen	2,363	3.26
		No Kitchens	24,806	34.24
		Unspecified	2,256	3.12
	iii.	*Provision of water*		
		Tap inside	27,318	37.71
		Tap outside	41,598	57.42
		Exclusive use of well	429	0.59
		Well shared	1,679	2.32
		Other	1,421	1.96
	iv.	*Bathing facilities*		
		Bathroom inside the house	25,427	35.10
		Outdoor bathroom	29,421	40.36
		Common bathing well	7,740	10.68
		Other	10,037	13.86
	v.	*Toilet facilities*		
		Flush toilets	47,233	65.20
		Water seal latrines	5,241	7.23
		Bucket latrines	11,611	16.03
		Pit latrines	1,283	1.77
		None	6,157	8.50
		Unspecified	920	1.27
B.	i.	*Walls*		
		Brick, stone & concrete	54,704	72.35
		Wattle and daub	4,709	6.23
		Wooden planks	14,800	19.57
		Cadjan/palmyrah	4,412	0.57
		Other	977	1.29
	ii.	*Roof*		
		Tiles	44,638	59.03
		Asbestos sheets	9,687	12.81
		Metal Sheets	13,467	17.81
		Cadjan/palmyrah	4,412	5.84
		Other	3,410	4.51
	iii.	*Floors*		
		Brick and cement	67,098	88.74
		Wood	907	1.20
		Mud	7,260	9.60
		Other	349	4.6

overloaded as it was designed to service the sewerage load of population around 250-300,000, and certainly not the present city population exceeding 600,000 and over one million commuters per day. Consequently raw sewerage has been emptied into the sea and the river, causing serious health hazards.

The Fort and Pettah wards, the core of the city and the administrative centre together with high class residential areas showed 'high connectivity'; 'low connectivity', was shown in the inner mixed zone wards and 'medium connectivity' in the wards south of the city. The answered areas were the wards of the North and North East mostly bordering the Kelani River.

Solid waste disposal is another public service which if neglected could have serious health consequences. The Municipality is solely responsible for refuse collection and disposal, and for keeping the city clean. Three factors are relevant:

a. the population distribution pattern and levels of income in the different areas
b. the transient commuter -- population of nearly 250,000-300,000 and
c. the location of State establishments

Northern Colombo has a larger population of around 353,000 and a concentration of 35-40 per cent substandard houses. The relatively small number of population, 232,000, and better housing and higher income in Southern Colombo generate small quantities of refuse. Sixty-seven per cent of the transient population passed through the Northern areas, another factor contributing to the sanitation problem in that area. In Central Colombo, State establishments are interspersed with substandard housing. The collection of refuse and disposal systems does not correspond with the load factor. As regards waste disposal as a municipal service, Southern Colombo with good housing, high income, concentrations of hotels, guest houses, embassies and clubs enjoys the "highest accessibility". Central Colombo has "medium accessibility" and Northern Colombo is characterized by "low accessibility" (Fig. 3).

The following problems have been highlighted:

a. area disparity between the better served and the poorly served

b. dumping of refuse in stagnant waterways and marshes
c. shortage of equipment for refuse collection
d. the relatively high organic content of the refuse and safeguards needed for personnel involved in the collection of certain types of refuse from hospitals, clinics and laboratories and
e. the need for self-help organisations, especially in the slum and shanty areas.

Electricity is the chief source of power in the city, distributed from five power stations connected to the hydro-generated power sources. The low energy consumption areas more or less correspond to the low income residential areas in the Northern, North-eastern and the Eastern wards of the city whereas the high energy consumption areas correspond with the high income residential wards.

Fuel wood is widely used for cooking purposes. A number of firewood selling points indicate the use pattern. These locations more or less coincide with the high density slum and shanty housing areas. Gas for cooking purposes has been increasingly popular with the affluent and State employed official class.

Road traffic both intra-city and inter-city point to the fact that passengers mostly by buses and railways, and goods are transported by lorries, container vehicles, vans, carts and bicycles. Bus commuting is popular and there were 175 bus routes which converge in the city from the suburban commuting areas at regular frequencies. Within the city, accessibility to public transport services has has made it possible for any person to reach the nearest bus stop in less than quarter of a mile and the frequency of operation of the buses is 15-20 minutes.

Urbanisation and Pollution

In the city and metropolitan region although pollution has not reached serious proportions, there are several dimensions to this problem.

a. Due to population pressure and sewer overload, raw sewage is discharged into the sea, polluting beaches and rivers.
b. In the wards of north and north-east, wells are the sources of

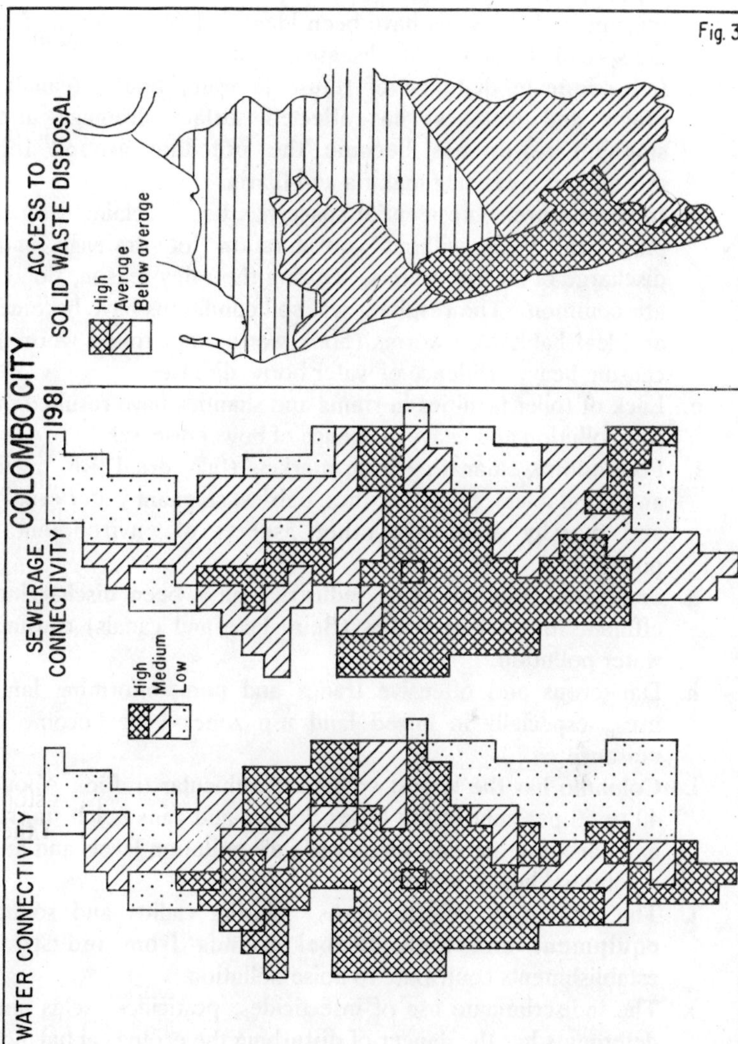
Fig. 3
COLOMBO CITY
1981
WATER CONNECTIVITY
SEWERAGE
CONNECTIVITY
High
Medium
Low
ACCESS TO
SOLID WASTE DISPOSAL
High
Average
Below average

water for drinking, washing and bathing. Contamination of water is possible as it is drawn on by several buckets tied to ropes. Washing of clothes also pollute the water through seepage and the wells have been identified as the source for the spread of water borne diseases.

c. Indiscriminate dumping of refuse in water bodies (canals, drains and marshes) has affected surface drainage and stagnant water has become the breeding ground for mosquitoes spreading malaria and filaria.

d. In certain areas, residential space has been reclaimed on a piecemeal basis without consideration for drainage and discharge of surface waters. During the rainy season, floods are common. The resultant wet soil conditions have become an ideal habitat or worms (hook worms and round worms) causing heavy incidence of water borne diseases.

e. Lack of toilet facilities in slums and shanties have resulted in soil pollution and heavy incidence of bowel diseases.

f. Foul odours emanating from markets (fish, dried fish, meat and vegetables), public latrines, dairies, stagnant water canals and marshy areas are other aspects of environmental pollution.

g. Small and medium scale industries have been discharging effluents into water bodies (Beira lake and canals) causing water pollution.

h. Dangerous and offensive trades and non-conforming land uses, especially in mixed land use zones have become a nuisance.

i. Colombo has the largest volume of vehicular traffic. About 40 to 50 per cent of the buses, lorries and vans belch smoke and carbon monoxide which raise air pollution levels and are a potential health hazard.

j. The tooting of vehicle horns, blaring radios and sound equipment and high decibel sounds from industrial establishments contribute to noise pollution.

k. The indiscriminate use of insecticides, pesticides, acids and detergents has the danger of disturbing the ecological balance and affecting human health. Further their easy availability has been a cause for high rate of suicides.

Institutions for Urban Development

Several State agencies namely Urban Development Authority (UDA), National Housing Development Authority (NHDA), National Water Supply and Drainage Board (NWSDB), Environment Authority (EA), Reclamation Board (RB), Municipality of Colombo and the Police Department have undertaken studies of several urban problems and have suggested remedial measures.

UDA in collaboration with NHDA and the Municipality have contributed to augmenting the housing stock and improving sanitary facilities. Slum remodelling, construction of low cost housing for low income groups, improvement of canal banks and environment have been some of the projects of UDA. Inducements have been offered to the private sector for the improvement of the living environment to achieve the following objectives:

a. redevelopment of inner city slum areas for housing and business
b. creation of health neighborhoods for families living in slums
c. mobilization of capital for rebuilding of slums

The State in this programme will provide the basic infrastructure (water, sewer facilities and access), while the private developers would bear development cost on a commercial basis.

NWSDB has recognized the urgency of improving environmental sanitation as a means of improving the standard of living of the urban poor. Rehabilitation of all water supply systems in order to expand services to the low income residential areas, as well as of canals and surface drainage schemes have been identified as projects for funding. Environmental Authority has begun monitoring the environmental situation as regards pollution of water by the release of industrial effluents and the use of toxic chemicals.

The Municipality of Colombo in collaboration with the Department of Health, United Nation Agencies, W.H.O, UNDP, UNICEF and NGOs has implemented several preventive health care programmes to control infectious diseases. These include immunization, a rodent control programme an educational programme focusing on the youth as regards drugs, social diseases, violence, suicide and family planning.

Who should Bear the Cost?

The sources of funding for capital development are two: local (from Central Government and local taxes) and foreign.

Allocation of Government funds reflects its priorities. Out of a total capital allocation of 149 billion rupees during 1989-93, Human settlement was allocated 13.3 billion rupees, approximately 11.5 per cent. Out of this, four billion was allocated for water supply of which, more than half of this was for rehabilitation of water supply. Water and sewerage schemes were planned to cover Greater Colombo towns, some of the provincial and district towns, rural towns and suburbs. For the improvement of urban housing particularly in slum and shanty towns 804 million rupees were allocated.

Generating local funds by broadening the tax base is not easy as nearly 40-45 per cent of urban residents are in the low income category who live in a tradition of State welfare and were enjoy free public utility services, although the access to these is limited and their quality relatively poor. Besides broadening the tax base has political and social consequences.

Expenditure on urban infrastructural development therefore has to depend to a large extent on foreign funding, but international opinion prefers the rural sector, for such assistance. "Urban investment which used scarce public funds would divert needed resources from the rural sector. Urban investment was frequently subsidized and benefited only a minority of the population. However, urban services with high unit costs, provided on a subsidized basis could not be extended to the urban masses. It was therefore essential that the urban sector could and should pay for itself and which provided services which were affordable to the urban poor and thus permitted replicability for the sector as a whole" (World Bank, 1983).

The efforts of resource mobilization and financing urban development should be based on city sizes. The large cities should carry the major proportion of financial responsibilities. But with a large proportion of the city population almost at subsistence level there is no way of sharing such responsibilities. Should we look on until the cities reach critical situations?

While rapidly growing cities are expected to bear a large portion of the fiscal burden of financing urban facilities and services, the question remains can they do so? Even if the task of planning and resource mobilization for financing urban development is devolved to large cities themselves and they are given them the authority and greater responsibility *vis-a-vis* their expenditures, perhaps they would not be able to grapple with the problems and solve them satisfactorily. The problems of South Asian cities require remedial policies and strategies of a different order.

Macro decisions of the State no doubt decide to a great extent urban processes and consequent urban morphology. However, a myriad of private decisions (individuals, households, firms and other entities) interact to bring about variations and differences. Thus planning and monitoring the implementation of rules and regulations in respect of urban land use, buildings, zonation, traffic and utilities become essential. And the problems of cities arising from rapid urbanization should be resolved by strengthening community action and with due regard for environmental health management.

Conclusion

Rapid urbanization in Sri Lanka has been accompanied by a policy of decentralized urbanization. Although Colombo the capital city showed signs of over-urbanization by way of increase of its substandard housing and a substantial proportion of its population living in these, creating an overload on the infrastructure, yet by implementing several remedial policies and strategies the situation was brought under control. As regards the accessibility and availability of basic amenities however, there were regional disparities which recent policies have reduced to some extent.

Rapid urbanization in suburban, medium and small towns have shown problems because of individualistic decisions particularly in the provisioning of water, sewerage and waste disposal services. And in the fast developing small towns of the areas under Mahaweli River Development Authority, basic amenities are restricted to the core areas of town only. With the filling up process in their outer zone, such facilities have to be installed as a measure of individual decision making.

REFERENCES

Bose, A.N. (1974). "The Informal Sector in the Calcutta Metropolitan Economy". ILO-WFP Working Paper, Geneva.

Castells, M. (1983). *The City and the Grass Roots*. London: Edward Arnold.

———. (1988). "Squatters and the State in Latin America" in Gugler, J. (ed.). *The Urbanization of the Third World*. Oxford: Oxford University Press.

Gerry. C. and Birbeck, C. (1981). "The Petty Commodity Producers in the Third World; Petite Bourgeois or Disguised Proletariat" in Elliot, B & Bachhofer. *Studies of the Uneasy Stratum*. London: Macmillan.

Geertz, C. (1963). *Peddlers and Princes: Social Change and Modernization in Two Indonesian Towns*. Chicago: Chicago University Press.

Hart, K. (1973). "Informal Income Opportunities and Urban Employment in Ghana" *Journal of Modern African Studies*, 11.

Hettige, S.T. (1986). "Employment in the Urban Informal Sector in Sri Lanka", Paper presented at the Policy Studies Conference. Institute of Policy Studies, Colombo

McGee, T.G. (1974). The Persistence of the Protoproletariat: Occupational structures and planning of the future world cities. Australian National University. Research School of Pacific studies, mimeo.

Moser, C.O.N. (1978). "Informal Sector or Petty Commodity Production: Dualism or dependence in urban development", *World Development*. Vol. 6.

Santos, M. (1979). "Circuits of Works: Interdependencies in the Urban Economy", in Wallman, S. (ed.) *Ethnicity at Work*. London: Macmillan.

World Bank Development Report. (1983)

6

The Development and Problems of Water Supply and Sanitation in the Past 42 Years in Beijing

Zhang Jinggan

URBANISATION has accelerated globally since the 1950s. It has led to a lag in the provision of urban basic services especially the water supply and sanitation in many developing countries. Beijing is an ancient capital with a long history; but it has had a short duration of urban modernisation. Many problems in the provision of urban water supply and sanitation have been solved since the founding of New China in 1949 but much needs to be done still.

Early in 1949, the water supply and sanitation systems of Beijing were very backward. There was only one water works (another was under construction) and 20 waterhead wells, with a total capacity of 50,000 m^3/d, in the city at that time. The total pipe length was 364 km and the filtered drinking water was available to less than 30 per cent of the total population of the city. Drinking water was available from wells or water carts which sold water drawn mainly from pumps. The old sewers, built during the times of the Yuan, Ming and Qing dynasties, had a history of 600 years but they constituted a combined water sewerage system. The total length of sewers was only 314 km in 1949. Even these had collapsed or silted up except for 22 km. Many streets and blocks were submerged during the rainy season.

People had to drain the storm water and discharged their domestic wastewater into rivers, ditches, hollows and cesspools. Especially in the outer city, where the labouring people lived in compact communities, there were reed ponds and puddles everywhere and several stinking ditches polluted the environment and caused epidemics.

The construction of urban water supply and sanitation systems since 1949 has made the following progress:

Construction of Water Sources

There are two main rivers outside the city, the Yongding to the west and the Chaobai to the east. To protect the city and its lower reaches from floods and to provide water for domestic, industrial and agricultural purposes, the Guanting and Miyun reservoirs, located in the upper reaches of the Yongding and Chaobai rivers respectively, were constructed in quick succession in the 1950s. The groundwater supply was comparatively plentiful because the city is situated at the diluvial and alluvial fan of the Yongding river.

Meanwhile the urban population increased from 1.61 million in 1949 to 5.29 million by 1990. Five groundwater works and two additional waterworks drawing water from the Miyun Reservoir were built to cater to the needs of the people. This raised the availability of urban water to 1.72 million m^3/d for the urban areas. By 1990, the total domestic water consumption of the city had reached 1.26 million m^3/d, which was 20 times more than that in 1949. This included water drawn from wells. The popularisation rate of tap water in the urban areas increased from 30 per cent in 1949 to 86.4 per cent; the average domestic water consumption standard, including private water, increased from 18 to 240 litre per capita per day during the same period.

Popularisation of Tap Water

After the founding of New China, the Beijing Municipal Government laid down a three-point guiding principle for water supply based on augmentation of production, improving distribution and monitoring and controlling the quality of the water.

Production

In 1950, the inhabitants used to draw water from public water stations. In the next 14 years till 1964, 1942 public water stations were installed to serve a population of 700,000, accounting for one-third of the total population provided with drinking water. Later, the average service radius of public water stations was reduced from 100 or 200 m to 50 m so that the water source was in closer proximity to the inhabitants. Subsequently, a project was launched to replace the public water stations by water pipes that reached every courtyard or household. All public water stations had been removed and tap water was available to every courtyard or household in the old city by 1977.

Prior to 1949, in Beijing, the inhabitants of the coal mining areas in the western part of the city, drank bitter groundwater or mine water, or otherwise had to carry water for long distances on their backs or by donkey. After Liberation, a water source was exploited to meet the needs of these people.

Distribution

Trunk water transmission and distribution pipes were constructed and an annular water pipe network was established in stages. By the end of 1990, the total length of the water supply system in the urban areas of Beijing had reached 4,915 km or 13.5 times that of in 1949.

At the same time close attention was paid to the monitoring and control of the quality of tap water. Chlorination is generally adopted to purify the groundwater. As regards surface water, the purification process consists of coagulation, sedimentation, silt filtration, ionisation and active carbon filtration. The test parameters for water quality have increased from 12 in 1949 to 76 presently, of which 50 are routine.

Sanitation

Between 1949 and 1952 the entire river and lake system in the city proper was dredged. At the same time, the old sewers from a bygone era were renovated and 160,000 m^3 of sludge removed, resulting in the reuse of 221 km of old sewers. Most praiseworthy was the removal of the Longxugou – a large foul-smelling sewerage ditch in the working peoples' settlement in the outer city, besides seven other smaller ditches. The residential conditions and environmental sanitation were thus vastly improved.

In March 1949, a movement for general cleaning of the whole city was launched and the Cleaning Movement Committee of all sections of the people was formed. Each district, state organ, school, industry and military unit in Beijing established corresponding organisations. At the time of general cleaning in 1949 and 1951,

373,000 people, 807 trucks, 3,290 handcarts and tram-cars and 32,100 animal-drawn vehicles were engaged in cleaning 600,000 tons of garbage that had accumulated since the end of the Qing Dynasty, changing the appearance of the ancient capital beyond recognition.

There were 20,000 subdistrict hygiene groups in the whole city by 1951 and a broad environmental sanitation control network came into existence. By 1980s, this had grown throughout the city, to carry out the responsibility system of Three Contracted Items in Front Gate, consisting of environmental sanitation, planting and public order within a designated section by state organs, social organisations, military units, schools, enterprises and private industry or commerce along the street. Since then, it has acquired a striking effect.

With a view to solving the problem of river pollution on account of wastewater from the combined sewer system, the sewers were separated from water supply channels. The laying of interceptor sewers along rivers and sanitary and storm sewers in the newly developing areas, kept pace with the development of urban construction. By the end of 1990, the total length of municipal sewers in the urban areas of Beijing was 2,178 km, 9.8 times the length of the old sewers in 1949, comprising of 665 km of storm sewers and 639 km of sanitary sewers. Two primary treatment plants with a daily treatment capacity of 304,000 m^3 were established in the urban areas.

Some rivers and lakes in the city proper were continuously dredged after 1952, especially during the period of patriotic public health campaign in 1958. Since the beginning of 1980s, the rivers in a bad condition have been renovated.

By 1990, the annual quantity of garbage cleared from the urban areas of Beijing was roughly 3.84 million tons. There were 165 hermetic container garbage stations greatly easing the workload of the sanitary workers. The problem of exposed garbage in the urban areas was tackled to improve the environmental sanitation in the residential districts.

There were more than 30,000 domestic dry latrines and 7,000 public dry latrines in single-storeyed houses and lanes in the old city. All of them were converted into flush toilets since the 1970s.

Enhancing Environmental Protection

The Beijing Municipal Environmental Protection Agency was established in 1971 to carry out the purification and treatment of wastewater and industrial effluents, as well as to promote environmental improvement. All the 6,000 or more smoky boilers in the old city were refitted, the amount of gas supply was increased and centralised heating was developed actively. Regulations regarding protection of groundwater sources and about 50 per cent of the industrial wastewater of the entire city was treated; over 4,000 pollution sources were brought under control; more than 200 highly polluting factories or workshops were renovated or removed; regulation of noise control was promulgated and over 1,000 fixed noise sources were eliminated.

Existing Problems and Solutions

Shortage of water supply has been a major restrictive factor in the urban development of Beijing. While the augmentation of water resources has been a great achievement since the founding of New China, still the water supply crunch continues to inhibit urban development.

Water supply remains inadequate on account of several factors. The growth of the city, especially the scale of industrial construction, has been excessive. Between 1949 and 1990 the built-up area expanded from 109 km^2 to 395.4 km^2, and the registered population increased from 1.61 million to 5.39 million. The scale of industrial construction especially grew by leaps and bounds after 1958. Within 33 years, from 1957 to 1990, the gross value of industrial output increased 5.6 times. Consequently, urban domestic and industrial water consumption has been rising constantly.

Meanwhile, the urban water sources have been decaying all round. Over the past 42 years, 270 reservoirs have been constructed in the upper reaches of the Guanting Reservoir, one of the major surface water sources of Beijing. The water-table has dropped over a wide area bringing down the capacities of six groundwater works. This has been due to the excessive exploitation of groundwater in the urban areas.

Wastage of water still continues although conservation efforts have been remarkable. There were 1,544 water saving projects completed from 1982 to 1987, and the total volume of water saved amounted to 210 million m^3. The average repeated-use-ratio of industrial water consumption has risen greatly, from 61.4 per cent in 1980 to 79.94 per cent in 1990. Water wastage, however, still exists due to use by large public buildings and due to insufficient use of water in agriculture.

Over the past 42 years, the problem of water source pollution has affected some sections of rivers, although the protection of water sources has been strengthened and a number of polluted rivers have been brought under control. Groundwater in some places has also been polluted.

The first reason is that the treated waste water which is seven per cent of the daily discharged industrial and sanitary sewage in the city proper, as well as most of the urban waste water directly flow into the rivers and ditches without further treatment. Secondly, the sewage from the combined sewers rushes into rivers, causing the pollution of water course during the rainy season. In addition, the non-treated waste water is used for irrigation by local farmers. This is one of the ways in which pollution of the ground water occurs.

Because the flow in the rivers is sluggish with a low capacity for diluting waste water, the rivers are easily polluted by the sewers in the combined system. These combined sewers have large cross-sections and low slopes, so sludge is easily deposited in them. This not only makes sewer maintenance difficult but also the accumulated sludge becomes corrosive and fermentable, emitting foul smell and creating insanitary conditions.

The majority of houses in the old city that have existed for long are old and shabby. In the past, on account of deficiency of funds the transformation of the combined sewer system had not been on the agenda. At the same time the reconstruction of old houses was restricted by the state of the sewer system.

Since the reform and the opening to the outside world, housing policies have been reformed. The housing of employees and workers is now undertaken by the government and the system of taking housing as a commodity is being carried out. It tackles the problem of funds for reconstruction of old houses. Last year, the Beijing Government decided to shift emphasis gradually from developing new areas to both reconstruction of old houses and development of new areas, and a Ten-Year Plan to reconstruct 8 to 10 million m^2 old houses was made.

The first group of 37 old housing districts consisting of 1.6 million m^2 dwelling area has been identified. Twenty-seven of these districts have already been renovated. Separate storm and sanitary sewers have to be laid to go along with the reconstruction of the old houses to create conditions for further enlarging the scope of reconstruction of the old houses.

The construction of infrastructure lags behind the development of the city because of inadequate funds. Urban water supply and sanitation are important components of urban infrastructure. In order to guarantee construction of infrastructure, investment in such infrastructure as a proportion of the total investment in urban fixed assets must also be inadequate.

Between 1949 and 1978 the average annual investment in urban infrastructure development amounted to 230 million yuan (1 Yuan = Rs. 5). This included inputs in electric power, telecommunication, postal services, the railways and civil aviation, which are beyond the purview of local government. After the reform and opening to the outside world, investment in infrastructure increased enormously from around 600 million yuan in 1979 to 3,160 million yuan in 1990. In contrast, the ratio of investment in urban infrastructure to total investment in fixed assets went down. The average ratio between 1949 and 1978 was 26.7 per cent. It declined to 18.5 per cent during the period of 1979 to 1983, and then increased to 23.3 per cent by 1990, which was still lower than that between 1949 to 1978. This was on account of the rapid urban development after the implementation of open door policies and a smaller increase in investment for urban infrastructure than that for total fixed assets. This indicates that the urban infrastructure needs beefing up to improve water supply and contain river pollution. The situation will worsen further if the city size continuously expands without commensurate increase in the necessary infrastructure.

Policies and Measures Ahead

The policies and measures for construction of urban water supply and sanitation in Beijing should be as follows:

The principle of To Pay Equal Attention to Broadening Water Sources, Reducing Consumption and Protecting Water Sources must be implemented. It is necessary to concentrate on saving water and protecting water sources, as well as on promoting the diversion of water from the Yangtze River to Beijing.

It is imperative to build sizable urban wastewater treatment plants. The first one to be built is the planned Gaobeidian secondary treatment plant, which will collect wastewater from the old city and the eastern suburb. The daily treatment capacity of the first phase of the project will be 500,000 m^3. A part of the treated wastewater, which will go through tertiary treatment, will be supplied to nearby industries.

The piped water supply, storm drains and sanitary sewer systems should be perfected so as to form a complete trunk and lateral pipe system. It is necessary to maintain adequate pressure in the water supply system in order to ensure the quality of water and to progressively realise the transition from a combined sewer system to a separated system.

The construction of urban infrastructure, involving urban water supply and sanitation, must be further strengthened. The investment proportion of urban infrastructure should be raised and stable investment channels must be established through further deepening the reform, and the advanced development of urban infrastructure must be vigorously achieved.

Allocation of funds for the different urban infrastructure components needs careful and skilful handling. On the one hand, it is necessary to give priority to those projects that are most urgently needed which require less investment, that have an immediate impact and greater benefit. On the other hand, we should also give consideration to the others to ensure that no serious problem will emerge later on.

In addition, designed load levels and construction standards of urban infrastructure should be appropriately adopted in order to make the best use of limited funds. Generally speaking, the designed load of urban infrastructure should be so adopted keeping in mind the long term, especially for deep sewers, submarine inlets and long tunnels. But the construction funds will lie idle too long if the load level is very high. Therefore, it is necessary to draw the line between trunk pipes and laterals, deep pipes and shallow ones, central urban areas and suburbs. In order to save the initial investment, a large-scale project may be designed but constructed in stages. Above all, the standard of urban infrastructure should be determined by the actual requirement.

REFERENCES

"The Urban Construction in Beijing since the Founding of the New China", Editorial Department of Beijing Construction History, 1986.

China Today: Beijing, China Social Science Press, 1989.

Socio-Economic Statistical Yearbook in 1990, Beijing, China Statistical Press, 1990.

7

Community Participation: The Kenyan Experience

Margaret Mwangola

THE Kenya Water for Health Organization (KWAHO) is a registered Non-Governmental Organisation (NGO) in Kenya and engaged in activities for provision of water, health and sanitation through community participation. It has been in existence since 1976 and works all over Kenya with a staff of 136 persons.

The KWAHO's main strength has been development of rural water, health and sanitation programmes. So far, nearly one million people have benefited from its activities. Through provision of water, other projects such as growing vegetable gardens, promoting income generating activities, selling and buying of agriculture produce, and dispensaries have emerged. In this paper, we shall endeavour to show two case studies undertaken by KWAHO depicting its experience in rural and semi-urban areas of Kenya. Both the studies show that desired results can be achieved through active community participation. We have undertaken both the case studies because the principles of community participation of the NGO clearly come in these case studies, even though one is based in urban area and the other one is located in the rural area.

In the promotion of 'Water for All' programme by augmenting funds from international as well as from local sources for water and in undertaking health and sanitation related projects, KWAHO serves the objectives of the Government of Kenya while remaining non-political and voluntary in nature.

KWAHO programmes cover all aspects of community mobilization and training of personnel for maintenance of water and sanitation projects and encouragement of health education and self-help schemes among women.

KWAHO's success in the implementation of community based water and sanitation projects is the result of its commitment to relevant government policies and cooperation with other NGOs. In conformity with the government policy of 'District Focus for Rural Development', KWAHO began to vest more responsibility to the districts in identification, resource mobilization, project design and implementation. Also, KWAHO's ability to live among the communities and readiness to recognize and respect their leadership, cultural background and beliefs contributed to the success. The following is the procedure for taking up projects:

First, the staff assess the preliminary needs of the area at meetings with the inhabitants and conduct baseline surveys in socio-economic and technical areas and discuss with community members. This leads to awareness among the people of the project objectives. The responsibilities of participating agencies are then clearly defined and explained. Communication channels are clearly delineated. Once the operations are known, affordability and sustainability of the project leads to its technical design and construction. The maximum use of local consultancy, manpower and technical expertise is stressed throughout. Care is taken to evolve grass-roots interest in operation and maintenance activities. Training needs and materials are identified and provided as support services.

Case Studies

1. Buguta/Makwasinyi

This project is located in Kasigau location in Taita/Taveta district lying on the extensive Nyika plateau. Most of the project area is made up of poor alluvial and deep sandy soils and lies between 510 m and 790 m above sea level. The area is semi-arid having an annual rainfall of about 480-680 mm and high temperatures averaging 22.5 degrees Celsius. The only surface water available is located at the top of the Kasigau hills in small perennial springs that only travel a short distance downstream before fading away. The population of Buguta/Makwasinyi is estimated at 10,000. It's density varies over the area, being concentrated around Buguta, Kisimenyi, Kulikila and Kasigau Hills. The Taita, Kamba and Duruma ethnic groups comprise the main inhabitants.

The project area is a newly settled area and land demarcation and adjudication processes are still being carried out. Large sections of the population, comprising low income families, rely on subsistence level cultivation and livestock farming. Some people also engage in small scale business enterprises such as running shops and posho (maize) mills, carpentry and plying hides and skin trade.

A 22 km *murram* road connects the project area to the Nairobi-Mombasa highway. There are few access roads to the project area which has three active trading centres viz. Buguta, Kisimenyi and Makwasinyi. Most of the people live in traditional houses prone to termite attack and general climatic wear. Apart from a health facility – Rukanga Health Centre, there is a mobile clinic operating at Makwasinyi and Makumbusho once a month. Inadequacy of medical services has led to increasing use of traditional medicine. Four primary schools and a secondary school located in Rukanga, and four adult literacy centres at Buguta, Kisimenyi, Kitege and Makwasinyi form the educational infrastructure. The area is administered by the Makwasinyi sub-location assistant chief assisted by village elders.

Prior to the project, there was no permanent source of surface water in the area. The residents were forced to walk an average of six to 20 km a day to fetch water from the hills of Kasigau. Livestock also had to trek similar distances in search of water. In 1984, the Buguta community formed Taita Integrated Rural Community Water Project (TIRCOWAP) funded by the African Development Fund. Under this scheme, two boreholes were sunk at the Makumbusho area but they were unsuccessful because a number of factors had not been taken into account. Discussions were held to retrace steps, involving the community, KWAHO and the collaborating government ministries. The community with the assistance of the Ministry of Water Development and KWAHO personnel planned and designed the Buguta/Makwasinyi Water Project. The community mobilized resources through membership fees, share capital, local expertise and Harambee fund raising drives. The Government of Kenya have continuously provided technical support. Water Aid (London) supplemented the community efforts and also supported the project. The construction work commenced in March 1989.

This project achievements have so far been:

35 km of main and distribution water pipelines, four ferro-cement storage tanks (200 cubic metres capacity in total),

three spring intakes, three break pressure tanks, five water kiosks and nine standpipes. Sanitation services covered four blocks, comprising in each block two toilets, two bathrooms, a washing slab as well as five VIP latrine slabs manufacturing moulds. With regard to health education, the project has developed a culture specific education manual "Maji na Afya Bora Kwa Jamii", and calendars which carry health messages. The project area has eight villages where eight womens groups and five sub-branch committees consisting of nine members each were set up. Fifteen main policy makers comprising the umbrella committee are selected from the five sub-branches. The various collaborating agencies have representation on the umbrella and sub-branch committees.

The project beneficiaries have elected a patron who acts as a chief adviser to the project and is also a link between the community and the collaborating agency. It is his/her role to encourage the community to pursue the objectives and ensure the maintenance of the project works after completion. The patron also makes sure any kind of education given to the community is seriously followed up.

As earlier mentioned, the project has registered over 1800 families who contribute an initial 20 Kenyan Shillings (KShs.) – (1 Indian Rupee = 1.25 KSh.) – and a monthly subscription of 10 KShs. per family for the sustenance of the project.

Among the lessons learnt by KWAHO from the project are:

- the need for careful study of the socio-cultural background of the people before commencement of the project;
- a successful project like the Buguta/Makwasinyi can be founded on failure;
- the undertaking of a project is possible after the patron position is established at the beginning;
- the women groups are a focal point in changing the lives of the community, and
- that a water project has no end.

2. *Maina Cillage Nyahururu*

Africa's biggest challenge is how to curb population growth. Unplanned migration to urban areas have resulted in the spread of slums with adverse effects on public health. The current population of Kenya is estimated at 23 million, with an annual growth rate of 3.4 per cent.

The village of Maina is located about two km from the centre of Nyahururu town. The area was set aside in 1961 for retired workers from surrounding settler farms. In 1965, local plot owners were granted a 20-year lease by the local council and a communal water pipe was laid, nursery and primary school was also built. Lately, then there has been an exodus of forest squatters expelled from the forest increasing the population. The village covers an area of about 45 acres with a population density of 700 people per hectare (a density of 600 or less is recommended). Local houses are built of timber pieces and corrugated iron sheets. The housing density is quite high and because of fear of vandalism and also illicit trade, windows are closed all the time. The interiors are stuffy during the day and very cold at night.

There is a high incidence of respiratory disease on account of poor living conditions. Single pit latrines used by the people are also a source of ill health. During wet weather the solid waste would overflow eventually finding its way into drainage channels. Sanitation and surface water drainage had a direct bearing on the public health situation in Maina village.

There are no major cultural barriers as regards usage of sanitary facilities. Few people remembered to wash their hands after toilet use. The pit latrine combined with the bad soil conditions made it difficult to curb the high incidence of diseases.

Most of the plots had pit latrines, however 50 per cent were filled up so that when it rained the contents were carried away by the storm water. Sometimes bathrooms were used as toilets; 25 per cent of the toilets were found to be satisfactory though most of them lacked privacy and were in a bad state of repair, in fact some collapsed during the wet season. The situation was exacerbated by the high water-table and black cotton soil in that area which floods easily.

The administrative area of Nyahururu town is 18 km^2. The local population is estimated at more than 30,000. This local authority is also in charge of water supply. The water demand coverage is about 93.7 per cent which is the highest in the country. More than 92 per cent of the local population (including Maina village) is sewered. As of 1987, the Council had 1805 refuse bins and two refuse collection vehicles with 43 per cent of the population receiving refuse collection services. We shall see later that refuse collection services at the semi-urban level are very inadequate and sometimes non-existent altogether. Billing and refuse collection covered 77.9 per cent of the area as of 1987. This performance is very good especially when compared to other local authorities which sometimes do not even know the area covered. Virtually all areas under the council have access to safe and reliable water supply. This is a prerequisite for provision of sewerage and other public health services.

Community Involvement in a Sewerage Project

There were no reliable municipal refuse collection services, hence the community used to dump garbage in heaps within the village, along paths and roadsides, creating large heaps of rotting and foul smelling of organic matter. These were perfect grounds for rats and insects to breed especially during the wet weather. During dry weather, the community used to burn the garbage causing domestic fires.

It was decided that the provision of sewerage services should benefit all municipal residents regardless of whether they live in a planned or an unplanned settlement. That was why Maina village was included in proposed municipal sewerage system mooted in the early eighties. The Danish International Development Agency (DANIDA) agreed to fund the project and in early 1989, DANIDA and the Nyahururu Municipal Council jointly embarked on the sewerage project. The physical works included the upgrading of roads, building of storm water drains and constructing sewerage network and residential sanitary units. After the placement of the contract, the local community refused to co-operate since they felt that they were left out of the project discussions and as such, it was not clear to them who would benefit in the end. It was for this reason that DANIDA decided to bring in KWAHO as an intermediary to mobilize the community.

It was agreed that two of public health profession officers from KWAHO would participate in the project. One of them a senior programme officer was to be on a part time basis while a community extension officer was to be a full-time participant. In May 1989, KWAHO undertook the responsibility of taking a cross-section of Maina village community to Homa Bay to educate and expose them to the benefits accruing from a similar project. This group was in turn effectively used to disseminate what they had learnt in Homa Bay.

The major issues raised by the community centred on poor communication about the project, its objectives and the role of the community in it. KWAHO facilitated the establishment of a site committee composed of local village leaders to serve as an instrument through which KWAHO or any other intermediary could communicate with the local community. The Committee was to take over from KWAHO at the phase out stage of the project. It was also to serve as a vital link between the steering committee and the community. Such an arrangement seemed crucial if the community was to participate in decision making and the latter was to be in line with their hopes and aspirations. It led to the revitalization of the village health committee which became a mouth-piece for the whole village. The Community Extension Officer established a lot of useful contacts with the community paving the way for the actual project implementation.

The site committee was composed of 15 members drawn from various women groups, landlords, tenants and government officials who were already working in the village. The committee was charged with monitoring the implementation of the project, mobilizing the community to appreciate, participate and later operate and maintain the facilities. The project priorities as seen by the site committee were construction of residential sanitary units, refuse disposal services and drainage of waste water.

A two-day community workshop was held to try and get the people to look at various aspects of the project such as health and sanitation and solid waste management. The schools health education programme was planned by the community extension officer in conjunction with the headmasters of the two schools for every two days of the week. Trips to Homa Bay, Nyeri and Kirinyaga were arranged.

Thirty refuse collection sites were identified in areas where the community used to dump rubbish before. These facilities are constructed of stone, have a double swing wire-mesh gate in front but are uncovered so that chicken tend to litter the refuse around and need to be fitted with ramps to make them accessible to children. Observations so far indicate that they are being used very well and have dramatically improved village cleanliness. Refuse pick-up services by the council need to be better co-ordinated in order to avoid pile up of garbage.

Thus because of the involvement of the KWAHO in both places, the communities were mobilized to a level where they voluntarily took part in the construction of facilities. Secondly, the misunderstanding between the council planners and community was sorted out, allowing the project to take off.

8

Hydro Resources and Sanitation in Sao Paulo

Renato Arnaldo Tagnin

THE township of Sao Paulo in Brazil (see Figure 1) has vast potential in economic terms but the problems besetting the metropolitan region are equally daunting. Traditionally, the responsibility of the municipal administration was limited to provision and maintenance of drainage. Sanitation, including water supply and sewerage, is the responsibility of the State government, which operates through a public sector company. It is so with most of the townships of the country. In practical terms, the conditions in which the sanitation and sewerage services are run interfere with the work of drainage. A great part of the sewerage lines are underground tunnels for the flowing of water when it is not directly released into the water streams. This procedure is basically to give priority to the implementation of networks for collecting sewage, so as to keep it away from residential areas. Adequate precautions are also taken to ensure that the disposal of the wastes is done at places sufficiently distant from water sources and that it does not affect those who dwell in areas located downstream of the contributing areas.

This point gains fundamental importance when one considers the fact that the population that dwells in these critical areas belongs to the low income category, and is most vulnerable to the consequence of insanitary environmental conditions. The location of these critical areas, especially along river-beds and their frequent subjection to inundation is, paradoxically, another extra obstacle to the setting up of the infrastructure capable of cleaning up the area. The local government is subject to pressure from the population urging solution of such problems while overcoming the sanitary and sewer systems are affected. This is in respect of sewage disposal.

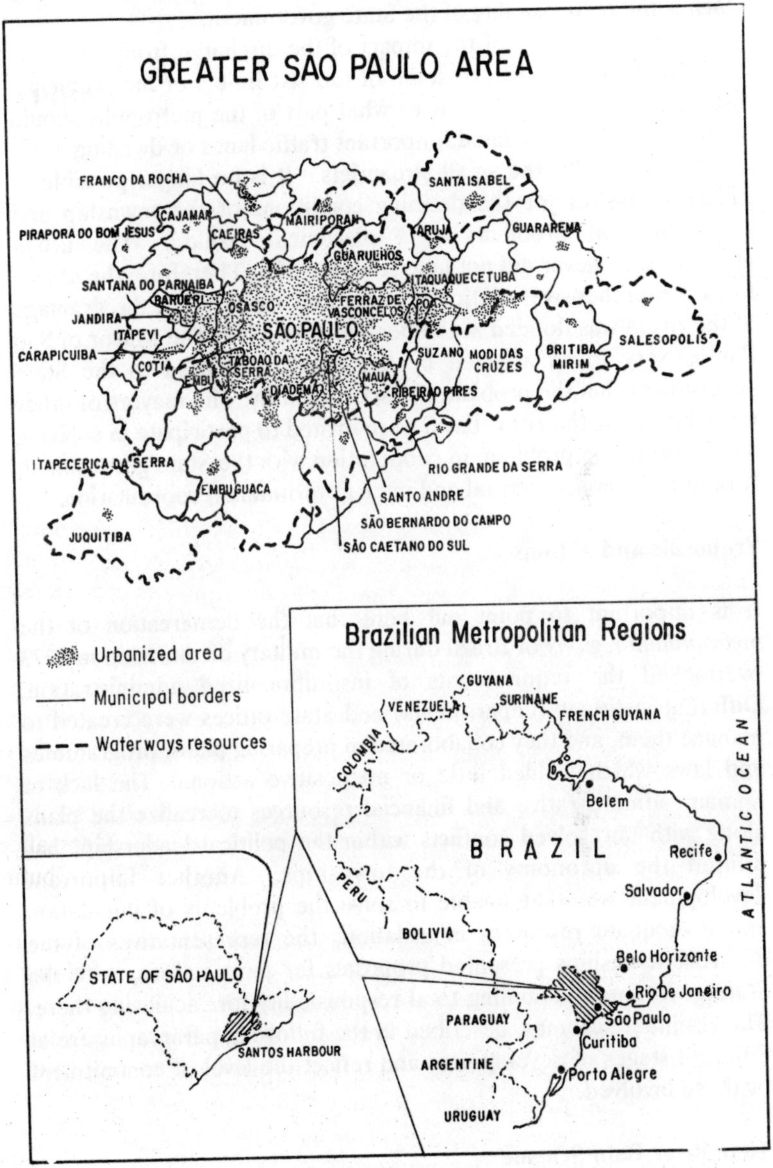
GREATER SÃO PAULO AREA
FRANCO DA ROCHA
SANTA ISABEL
CAJAMAR
MAIRIPORAN
PIRAPORA DO BOM JESUS
CAEIRAS
ARUJÁ
GUARAREMA
GUARULHOS
SANTANA DO PARNAIBA
ITAQUAQUECETUBA
BARUERI
OSASCO
FERRAZ DE VASCONCELOS
POA
JANDIRA
ITAPEVI
SÃO PAULO
SALESOPOLIS
CARAPICUIBA
COTIA
TABOAO DA SERRA
SUZANO
MODI DAS CRUZES
BRITIBA MIRIM
EMBU
DIADEMA
MAUA
RIBEIRÃO PIRES
ITAPECERICA DA SERRA
RIO GRANDE DA SERRA
EMBU GUACA
SANTO ANDRE
SÃO BERNARDO DO CAMPO
JUQUITIBA
SÃO CAETANO DO SUL
Urbanized area
Municipal borders
Waterways resources
Brazilian Metropolitan Regions
GUYANA
VENEZUELA
SURINAME
FRENCH GUYANA
COLOMBIA
ATLANTIC OCEAN
Belem
BRAZIL
Recife
PERU
Salvador
BOLIVIA
STATE OF SÃO PAULO
Belo Horizonte
Rio De Janeiro
PARAGUAY
São Paulo
SANTOS HARBOUR
Curitiba
ARGENTINE
Porto Alegre
URUGUAY

Additionally, there is the problem of drainage of the main rivers which is the responsibility of the State government.

A brief evaluation of the impact of the discharge from the rivers in addition to canalizing of some of the streamlets of the municipal district raises the question as to what part of the metropolis should be allowed to be inundated: important traffic lanes or dwelling areas located alongside the small streamlets. It is no longer possible to isolate initiatives for the draining conditions of the township and solve different problems in a piecemeal fashion. The urban authorities however did not take any note of it. Therefore, the search for a comprehensive solution became imperative when the drainage of the rivers was flooded at the beginning of 1991. The Mayor of Sao Paulo, very much affected by the event, proposed to the State government that the problem be tackled jointly. The mayors of other townships near the river basin were invited to participate in evolving a solution to the problem, in cooperation with the State government. It required a multi-sectoral and inter-governmental coordination.

Proposals and Actions

It is important to point out here that the demarcation of the *metropolitan regions* of Brazil during the military dictatorship in 1973 overlooked the requirements of institutionalized administration. Different institutes (departments) and State offices were created to manage them, and they collaborated in preparing plans, programmes and laws which yielded little or no positive action. The lack of human, administrative and financial resources to realize the plans along with unresolved conflicts within the political leadership, has diluted the autonomy of the townships. Another important development was that unable to solve the problems of inundation and inadequate resources in isolation, the representatives of the different townships presented proposals for joint actions, with the State government assuming total responsibility for achieving these. The resultant schemes, described in the following paragraphs are at different stages of development and reflect the level of commitment by those involved.

Tiete River Bain Scheme

The State government prepared a plan for water resources providing for the creation of a managing system for the hydrographic basins.

The State government is responsible for operating the water system of the upper Tiete river and is mainly engaged in generating electricity and has not paid much attention to the drainage problems as also the quality of the water basin as a whole.

Considering that urban flooding has structural causes which are difficult to solve in the short term, emergency measures taken during critical times are very important in guaranteeing the security and survival of the affected population.

One of the emergency measures was to create a civil defence service managed by the townships. The sectorial offices of the state were also simultaneously motivated towards the same goal. Since the population of the areas affected by the flooding is afflicted by water-borne diseases, preventive measures and emergency health services were also undertaken.

Most of the streamlets in the urbanized areas are unable to drain the outflow. This becomes more serious when the drainage system is interfered with to overcome other local problems. A joint effort to change the situation was agreed upon.

The necessity of centralized control over flooding was realized. Similarly, the need for efficient sanitary services to meet the requirements of the different townships was acknowledged. As a result, a forum for discussions and a representative organisation, different from the model adopted by the *metropolitan region* came into being.

The solution proposed, which has been put into practice and is one of the ways of managing the hydrographic basin in Brazil, has had interesting results.

Technical Cooperation

The techniques for flood control and sanitation suited to different townships, is usually out of reach of individual township. Therefore, access to the research and technologies developed by institutions directly or indirectly linked to the State government was become necessary.

Even within the metropolitan area there has been mutually conflicting interests. Because there are areas which have a potential for accumulating water during floods, like the Tiete river lowlands, located upstream of the central part of the city of Sao Paulo. The inhabitants of these lowlands try to put joint efforts to resist pressures for straightening of the river otherwise they will get flooded.

It was decided that the State government should once again invest in sanitation which was abandoned by the former Governor and also accelerate the projects for resuscitating water basins so as to increase the supply potential.

As already mentioned, the residents of the slums located in the lowland are vulnerable to flooding. But shifting from those areas involves building settlements for them, which adds to the cost of the drainage systems. It was, therefore, decided that the costs of resettlement of displaced persons from the lowlands should be divided between the State government and the townships. This has facilitated the modification or remaking of the drainage systems and the establishment of means for sewage collection. One of the plans elaborated years ago by an institution created to manage the *metropolitan region* focused on the same theme. The revival of the scheme, now under pressure from the townships illustrates the failure of the metropolitan management to solve the problems on its own. Apart from the responsibilities of the urban authorities, the inhabitants also needed to change their habits, such as throwing trash into streamlets and other parts of the city to educational campaigns would facilitate such change. The State Government has shown its willingness to participate in joint action programmes to lessen the instability of urban land and augment the drainage capacity of the water courses. It was decided that instead of isolated requests for funding by the Federal Government of drainage and sanitation works, the State Governments and the townships should present consolidated plans, act jointly to pressurize the Federal Government to share in the responsibility for redressing the serious situation in the metropolitan area. Finally, it should be said that the decisions taken jointly during 1991 show the strong political content of the management of water resources. Steps are also afoot to create new forms of action and relationship among the different sectors and governmental departments. The initial deadline for action could not be met, though many technicians at different levels were put to work and many evaluation meetings were held. In the context of the present political institutional set up some basic conditions for inter-governmental actions should be outlined.

State Level

The State was pressed to assume its constitutionally defined role and began to react on a case-by-case basis; in the process, the authoritarianism inherent in the hierarchical relations was aggravated. Further, there was mistrust of the critical attitudes and autonomy of the lower levels of government. The partners were not peers and the State government began to take decisions without discussing the alternative presented by some townships.

In this authoritarian atmosphere, when the tasks were passed on to the townships they did not carry them out effectively, as was to be expected. There was once again the distorted, one-way relationship that prevailed during the previous attempt at metropolitan regional management. Furthermore, the state government involved all the townships in the region, whether or not they were part of the basin or affected by flooding. This meant that the meetings and forums discussion forums were too big, creating an impression that little progress was being made. The state government attributed this to lack of effort on the part of the townships although it had been warned of the risk of including all townships. Moreover, the State representatives were increasingly at the meetings. This was sometimes because its own sectoral organs did not participate and sometimes because the decisions to be taken required prior actions about resources and policy that had not yet been taken or, if they had, it was not considered convenient to make them known to the townships. Thus, the agreement was broken and the inter-governmental meetings became fruitless. From this point on, the state took some action on its own *vis-a-vis* certain townships, reinforcing the politics of patronage so common in a municipal election year.

The townships had different degrees of interest in participating in the joint action programmes and this was one reason for its scant success. The relative lack of interest was explained in terms of involvement with other local government priorities and in some cases it meant that townships were not represented at meetings by adequately trained technicians. Some townships did not understand the need for joint action and even refused to allocate resources, including administrative resources for sharing responsibilities. They wanted the State government to take complete responsibility. There were also some cases when townships frankly opposed some collective decisions because they felt their interests had been harmed.

At the sectoral level also, there were obstacles to common action: there were conflicts about approach. The State electrical engineering industry which controlled the use of water resources of the upper Tiete Basin was found too powerful for the townships to collaborate with. In spite of scarce resources and may be even because of them, the conditions for joint action provided for the State Water Resources Policy, had to be changed. It has become law now. According to this law, the decisions on the use of water resources would be taken at various levels, starting with the hydrographic basin. The State and municipal governments will participate in the efforts on an equal footing. Furthermore, the administration costs of the schemes will be covered by charges on the use of water and fines imposed on polluters.

At the formal level, however, the State government fully maintains its administrative role for all the water resources in its territory, according to the State constitution. However, in practice the above aspect is absent, especially in the most critical areas like the Upper Tiete Basin where there is an acute and long standing lack of management.

For the townships the "decentralisation" of responsibility is still the crux of the matter because of the absence of partners and the heavy social demands placed on them every day. The decentralization of investment in the infrastructure should be seen in the context of the municipal government's efforts to democratize access to the basic services and to reverse a tradition of patronage in these services. This tradition had shaped both the State government apparatus and the configuration of high-value neighbourhoods in the city. Decentralization was necessary even within the township, as Sao Paulo has a population of 9.5 million. In practice, this means taking steps to make information about the city and its management including priorities, resources and even technological choices accessible to the population.

Municipal Level

Significant people's participation has been achieved in the content and mechanisms of the annual investment in the municipal budget. Through debates held in micro-regions, consolidated afterwards in each of the 20 administrative regions of the city, investment priorities were discussed based on initial proposals formulated by the municipal government.

The proposals identified costs and investments that may be made with the township's own resources (based on transfers of part of Federal and State taxes to the township, as well as municipal taxes), with credit operations (domestic and international loans and finance) and resources that may be obtained through increased municipal tax revenues. The municipal revenue sources as well as the regional proposals for investment, and the regular and statutory expenditures on salaries, water and electricity bills and so on are stated in simple language.

How much to invest and in which sector? These questions are raised in meetings to which the local people are invited. They may even discuss whether the township should raise its taxes to ensure greater involvement and improvement in the city's maintenance services. The proposed alterations are brought together in a new budget proposal, discussed again with the population and then sent to the town council for a vote. The involvement of the local people continues with the defence of its proposals during debates by the town councils, before being voted into law.

This process had begun in 1989. Then the present city government, saw to it that the decision-making, covering administrative financial and legal mechanisms, be made more accessible to th poorer sections of the population. There are difficulties in thi process in terms of organisation, understanding and the time avail able so that the poorer sections may attend the meetings and be abl to perceive that the demands facing the city as a whole do not nece ssarily imply meeting their specific needs immediately. The proces will be improved when the Council approves the proposed admin strative reforms, decentralizing municipal authority into thirtee regions. The regions will have infrastructure, trained staff and rel tive autonomy with regard to the budget, besides a council of electe representatives to participate in decisions, including budgetary one The council of representatives, not to be confused with the municip legislature, is provided for in the 1990 Municipal Constitution fo each new sub-prefecture, or regional branch, of city hall.

Situational Aspects

The recessive policy presently adopted by the Federal Government to control inflation (running at 520% a year), which conforms to

International Monetary Fund guidelines requiring payment of interest on the foreign debt, has caused serious harm to several sectors of the Brazilian economy and resulted in an increasing trend of unemployment. The effects of this policy on the living conditions of the already poor urban population are seen in their inability to pay rent and look for alternative housing, usually in areas without infrastructure or services. In the process the required investment capacity of the authorities already hit by the recession, is affected. A large part of its revenue is derived from taxes on consumption of goods and services.

Along with these difficulties and the increased social pressure that the local authorities are subject to, there is "modernization" of the State and decentralization of responsibilities of the federal and state governments. As a result additional responsibilities are passed on to the local government. Though this may seem legitimate from an administrative point of view, in some sectors like health and education besides basic infrastructure, funding either does not accompany responsibility or is absolutely insufficient to reclaim bankrupt and obsolete structures, maintain them or expand them to meet real demand. Conflicts have arisen, and many townships have refused to take on a school or drainage infrastructure because of its dilapidated, unusable state. Transfer to the townships of State and Federal tax revenues raised in the townships, as well as investments, have been linked to political party affiliations. For the largest township in Brazil, this means a total lack of Federal funding for investment in infrastructure over the last three years.

Among the municipal taxes, the real estate tax (IPTU) has the largest share representing 15 per cent of Sao Paulo's municipal revenues. Even so, it has not been easy to make it reach this percentage, especially in an election year, as the principle of progressiveness (in force since 1988) puts a heavier tax burden on owners of land while exempting low-income property owners. There is currently a political and judicial battle between the city government and the largest taxpayers who receive support through effective media publicity, paradoxically, from the poorest sections of society, who are exempt from the taxes and are the greatest beneficiaries of the investments to be made with IPTU funds.

New Financial Instruments

According to recent estimates eight million additional inhabitants need to be accommodated in regions with adequate infrastructure. These numbers show that instead of interminable technical discussions on how to cover an expected deficit, the distortions in allocation of present and planned infrastructure should be faced.

The development plan proposed for Sao Paulo defines its regions as being able to cope with a denser population or not, depending on environmental and infrastructural conditions; it also defines some instruments to carry out the plan.

These instruments condition urban growth to private investment, the sale of the right to expand buildings and the investment in infrastructure in poor areas, and in low-cost housing in areas where infrastructure already exists. They also ensure that low-income areas remain so, avoiding rising property values in such areas that would expel low income residents, while creating incentives for private building firms to become interested in this market segment. Another proposal that awaits approval by the city council is an "improvement contribution" (betterment tax) by citizens who have benefited from large public investments in infrastructure. The charge is prorated among all property owners (not only those along the road) whose property value has risen due to the investment, in proportion to the increase. This meets a basic requirement of the national and international lending agencies besides being a just criterion and provides for reinvestment in other areas requiring infrastructure.

Other forms of financing infrastructure include conditioning the municipal approval of large private real estate development projects to the use of part of this investment to reduce their environmental impact and helping extend the system and services to projects and residents of the areas around them.

Private investors and agencies also pay for low-income housing and even infrastructure in other parts of the city as a price for permission to build beyond what is allowed by the city development plan in force for the past 20 years. This is so in cases where the additional construction, will not have a negative impact.

Technical Adjustment

Investment in urban infrastructure in Brazil has traditionally been determined by foreign concepts, measurement methods, and technology, often unsuited to Brazilian conditions. Low investment in technology and professional training, mean that the inadequacy continues, especially in basic sanitation. Moreover, large contractors are not interested in changing building methods that are profitable to them.

Thus, during the "economic miracle" that the country went through under the military dictatorship (1964-1985), it was said that the country's grave social problems would be solved through large public works. Today, the foreign debt and extreme concentration of income show the opposite to be true. In more practical terms, the recession that resulted from the public sector's reduced capacity to invest at a time of acute social demand has stimulated a more realistic approach, less oriented to concentrated investment.

This approach by city government, less grandiose but effective, was applied to such problems as drainage and sewerage in critical areas of the city, such as shanty towns. These areas are given priority because they are critical and are densely populated. Plans are drafted, with the participation of the inhabitants, to install water and sewerage systems and eliminate the risk of flooding and landslides common in these areas. The beneficiaries of the projects participate in the redefinition of measures to reduce population density. When this is done, the residents are exclusively responsible for rebuilding their houses, though they receive constant advice about hygiene and use of the new infrastructure. Far from ideal, this is what is possible in a city with 2,500 shanty towns, of which 900 have grown up during the last four years. Large investments are also being made by city government in "formal" housing. The 420 frequently flooded areas cannot await the normal construction process of building channels for streams; this sometimes even results in transferring the flooding to other places. Gradually, critical points are being treated, obstructions removed and the effected population resettled.

To carry out these projects, the city government has taken the lead over the state government, which is responsible for the basic water and sewerage systems, forcing it to review its technical and financial parameters while again raising the need to decentralize urban management in order to meet social demands.

REFERENCES

PREFEITURA MUNICIPAL DE SAO PAULO, Organizacao Secretaria Municipal do Planejamento, "Sao Paulo: Crise e Mudanca", 218 p-il 1990

SAO PAULO. CONSELHO ESTADUAL DE RECURSOS HIDRICOS, "Plano Estadual de Recursos Hidricos: Primeiro Plano do

Estado de Sao Paulo", DAEE, 140 p.-il. 1990, ROCHA, Geroncio Albuquerque, "Agua e Vida no Cidade de Sao Paulo", Secretaria de Vias Publicas, Sao Paulo, 11p. il, 1990

PREFEITURA MUNICIPAL DE SAU PAULO, "Programa de Recuperacao Ambiental e Social de Fundos de Vale do Municipio de Sao Paulo", Secretaria Municipal de Vias Publicas, 117 p. il, 1991

PREFEITURA MUNICIPAL DE SAO PAULO, "Da Utopia a Construcao - a Participacao Popular na Politica Habitacional em Sao Paulo"
Secretaria Municipal de Habitacao e Desenvolvimento Urbano, 36p. il, 1991.

9

Drinking Water Supply and Sanitation in Latin American Towns: Some Element of Diagnosis[1]

Daniel Faudry

THIS paper puts forth a general examination of drinking water and the sanitation sectors of Latin America, by studying the economic and the institutional problems of the management services with special emphasis on the experiments of popular participation.

Taking Latin American towns overall, the number of households not connected to a source of drinking water was estimated, in 1985, to be 25 per cent (that is to say a quarter of the population or 65 million people). One hundred and five million or 45 per cent of the population were at this date without any sanitation whatsoever. These approximate data give an optimistic view of the reality: they do not take into account the quality of the services available, notably with regard to forms of restricted services. Even if the objectives of the International Water Supply and Sanitation Decade have been achieved, though these objectives were reviewed and lowered, the situation would be little better in terms of the percentage of the population serviced, because of the high urban growth rate.

The statistics, with their specious objectivity, indicate installation delays and incomplete coverage. The terms inequality and segregation in implementation would be nearer reality. Essentially such inequality is one of the elements of urban segregation.

The inhabitants of areas not connected to water and sanitation services are often at the mercy of water-sellers, there being few public standpipes in Latin America outside Mexico and to a lesser extent Colombia and Peru.[2]

The provision of water by water-sellers presents economic and sanitary problems. At the economic level, in all the cases studied, water selling was a private concern; there was little or no competition as the market was shared out by agreement among the sellers and the prices were very high. Even though, because of the high price, consumption was low, the amount spent by each household was much higher than the basic rate charged by the public service authorities. At the sanitary level, the problems arise from the contamination of the water during storage and distribution as well as from an insufficient consumption of this poor quality, over-priced water. This situation results in popular discontent and conflict.

Thus, in the most urbanised continent of the Third World the main problem of drinking water and sanitation is in servicing the marginal urban populations. The challenge is, of course, primarily human; but it is also urban. Inevitably, the lack of water and sanitary services hinders the functioning and development of the economy. The problems of sanitation and supply of drinking water therefore contribute towards the urban crisis in Latin America: they assist in a deteriorating situation.

To be more precise, the absence of financial speculation and the insufficiency of control over land utilisation have resulted in very sparsely populated cities and hence in a very high cost of equipment per habitant.

Financial Situation of the Services

The basic problem is how to finance the enormous investment necessary, when all the Water Boards have deficits and some of them cannot even cover their running costs. Under these conditions it seems illusory to expect to retrieve the total cost in order to guarantee recovering the investment. The World Bank has itself begun to consider this to be out of the question in the middle term. In fact, the deficit on the sanitation and drinking water services is chronic.[3] This deficit has many causes attributable not only to the methods of running and organising the Water Boards, but also to the general economic situation and urban management of the Latin American countries.

Unfortunately, no precise studies have been conducted on the impact of policies of structural adjustments on the water sector. The only thing one knows is the fact that these policies have led to higher prices of water, as of other public services, and to the lowering of the loan sanctioned by the World Bank and the International

Development Bank.

The level of the water rates charged, a very controversial area, is certainly one of the first parameters to be examined. It is true that in many countries during the seventies, the rise in prices was lower than the rate of inflation, the governments having refused increases for political, economic and social reasons.[4] Nevertheless, in the last few years, the price of water has risen faster than the rate of inflation in several countries.

The manner of implementing water rates does not permit their efficient administration. The rate is in fact a fixed price in most cases, either from deliberate choice, due to lack of meters, or for other practical reasons, or again through shortcomings in meter-reading or servicing. The fixed price is generally calculated on cadastral value which allows, in theory at least, redistributive pricing. In reality this way of pricing is subject to all the limitations of the cadastre and is not an exact reflection of consumption.

Unaccounted for water, which can be as much as 50 per cent of the volume produced is another source of deficit. Finally, on top of the general under-billing are the unpaid bills and here also it is not only the poorest that are to blame. The origins of the deficit must also be looked for in the extra costs the Water Boards have to put up with, which vary in importance as the case may be. Inefficiency of maintenance is, no doubt, one of the principal factors here.

The impossibility of balancing income and costs leave the drinking water facilities and sanitation dependent on external financing, both national and international. Again, the deficit is both a cause and a consequence of the dependence on the national budget since the board of the utilities generally have control over neither their budget nor their prices. They are therefore, subject to the hazards of economic policy and at present, the burden of debt disposes governments to go in for the most directly productive investments. Even in earlier times this sector has never been a government priority. International financing is therefore indispensable.

The contribution of international loans in total investment dropped from 37.8 per cent during the sixties to 30.2 per cent in the following decade.[5] For the first five years of the International Water Decade, the amount rose again to 43.5 per cent. This would have been encouraging if in the meantime interest rates had not also risen.

Administration

The crisis in the drinking water and sanitation services has an institutional element which is important from two points of view: the administration of the sector contributes frequently to the crisis and what is more, global solutions are frequently sought in institutional reforms. Thus, in most of the countries studied, reorganisation in this sector has taken place within the past fifteen years, or is presently being considered.

The institutional system can be studied from four points of view: the legal status, the level of centralisation, the level of autonomy and the functional integration of the Water Boards. From the point of view of status, public administration has for a long time been the rule, almost without exception. Discussion of privatisation has yet to come up. With regard to centralisation, the administration is carried on by a national organisation in most countries, and where the structure is federal, by a state organisation.

The most conspicuous reason for the predominance of the centralised model is the unavoidable financial intervention of the State, either through the national budget, or for obtaining external loans. This model should also be related to the tendency of centralisation of the Latin American States. However, one can observe generally a few move towards decentralisation, from the federal level to the state level, in Mexico, in Argentina and in Venezuela, whereas in Peru, these movements are noticeable at the municipal level.[6] In fact, centralisation entails quite a few inconveniences; it adds an extra difficulty to an already problematic articulation between provision of equipment and urban development which belong to the local governments. Doubtless, it also favours a management which is more social than political or economic and this damages the economic balance, especially placing demands on the state. In these conditions, decentralisation aims, without doubt, as much at the disengagement of the State as at an increase in efficiency. The state however, retains an important role, notably in fixing taxes and that too in the countries where the management of water services has been in the hands of municipal bodies for a long time.

From the point of view of sector integration, the combination of the drinking water and sanitation services is the norm. Even though the sanitation service is thus theoretically assured of resources, the equipment aspect chronically lags behind, which, it might be said, is not peculiar to Latin America. As for the functional integration, from sector planning to the collecting of bills, it rarely seems complete. This, without doubt, is due to the centralisation and the lack of autonomy of the Water Boards.

The planning and programming of the urban water sector are made very difficult by the lack of autonomy in administration and lack of control of urban development as much as by a paucity of coordination between the Water Board administrators and the municipal government. Because of this, the organisational infrastructure follows urban growth as best as it can instead of structuring it. This spatial and temporal lag creates all sorts of negative effects and extra costs.

The foregoing suggests that the problems of drinking water supply and sanitation cannot be correctly analysed by themselves; the solutions are to be found at least in part outside the sector and notably in the control of the process of urban growth. This raises a group of problems to which the solution is not obvious and it has to be admitted in consequence, that the introduction of a complete service by the networks will take a long time in the poorest countries such as Peru and Bolivia, or in those lagging behind in full coverage such as Argentina. The parameters just laid out show a background of penury on account of which determining the criteria of evaluation and the choice of priorities and techniques takes on a crucial aspect.

Where sectors are concerned the urban water network suffers from an increasing lack of official interest as the sectors descend the scale, that is to say, from the production of drinking water down to the distribution and the treatment of sewage. This neglect of sanitation naturally undermines the social and economic benefits brought about by the availability of water. It is also a source of extra costs as it is always more difficult to install a sewage network after that for water supply than it is the other way round. Furthermore, this refusal to give sanitation *a priori* consideration reduces, in the end, the range of conceivable technologies.

Within the drinking water sector itself, one can see a tendency to try to solve problems from the top, that is to say at the level of production. In a situation where consumption is uncontrolled both in quantity and localisation, this type of reaction can, more so than for distribution problems, be formulated in purely technical terms. It avoids the question of the administration of limited resources.

Community Participation[7]

For the inhabitants of the areas concerned, work participation, even self-help schemes, are the only way to obtain these elementary services, when conventional means are not accessible because of their insolvency, or because of the lack of funds of the Water Board or of a specialised bank. As much for this last reason as for the size of the role played by popular organisations, it would be simplistic to limit the objectives of this participation to merely a reduction in cost, which nevertheless it obviously is.

The participation envisaged goes beyond supplying a workforce and is more concerned with administration, the choice of technical solutions, the quality of the installation, etc.

Self-help schemes are sometimes refused participation because of the legal right to public services, or simply rejected because public works or building firms are considered more efficient.

Such schemes also face difficulties from the efforts of the political parties to control the basic organisations by clientist practices; for example, during the elections, candidates can give material gifts to a locality. In other cases, it is the party in power which tries to channellise and recuperate the popular movement by creating local committees comprising leaders chosen by the party in order to organise the participation. Moreover, the important role of women in these organisations should be noted.

In most cases, it is the inhabitants who take the initiative in prolonging the demand movement, and this popular mobilisation constitutes an implication of the technical and economical powers of the Water Board. The Water Board questions the efficiency of the programme and criticises the disrespect for technical norms which is often the case when the works are executed without any competition, or any control of the Water Board. Another argument used as much by the utility administrators as by the national and international financial organisations, is the protection of employment in the businesses that undertake such works; forgetting no doubt that, on the one hand, the self-help schemes could contribute towards enlarging the outlets for businesses in the sector by creating demand through increased solvency and, on the other hand, that the inhabitants concerned are themselves under-employed.

The local governments are generally not very active in the programmes in terms of participation and more generally in terms of finding solution to the problems of the sector. This can probably be attributed to the still very centralised nature of the administration of the Water Boards. The central governments are even less concretely involved in the participation programmes.[8]

The national and international NGOs play an active role in almost all the programmes studied, both through their legal and technical assistance and their political support, while in certain cases they, also help out financially.

Financial Aspects

The means of financing works undertaken with the participation of the local inhabitants are at least as varied as the concrete means used in the participation. It is nevertheless possible to distinguish two predominant types.

In the case of co-participation programmes the means of financing is generally negotiated case by case, since this type of programme is not officially designated as an entirely separate unit in the extension of Water Board services. The negotiations concern all aspects of financing: initial capital, purchasing of material, etc and a particular concern with the rate of interest. The work of the local inhabitants seems to be only exceptionally evaluated within the framework of the total cost. It is an element to be negotiated along with others.

In these programmes where the local organisation cooperates with the public Water Board, the source of finance, save that contributed by the inhabitants, is the Water Board itself and/or a specialist bank.

However, in the self-help construction programmes, the sources of finances are very much more varied and generally include grants or loans from the international NGOs. These contributions can constitute the best part of the external financing that is added to the self-financing by the inhabitants and to their work contribution.

Technical Choices

First of all it should be stated that the programmes undertaken with the participation of the inhabitants are, in the great majority of cases, the extension of distribution networks.

Work participation and *a fortiori* self-help schemes are obviously a factor in reducing the financial cost of these works; but the cost can also be reduced by buying materials directly in the open market at a lesser cost than that charged by the specialist business. Further reductions can also be obtained by resorting to non-conventional techniques, which is, all the same, a rare occurrence.

This last point raises the question of the quality and thus the durability of the works undertaken with the participation of the inhabitants. Both sides raise this question but for different reasons. The inhabitants often accuse, justifiably, the concerns involved, of poor workmanship or of using second rate materials and the overseer administrators of negligence in the supervision of the work sites. As for the concerns, they complain, not without reason, about non-conformity to work norms by the inhabitants.

Conclusion

Faced with the gravity of the situation, popular participation appears as an inadequate solution, even if all the potentialities are mobilised, which in turn would presuppose important political changes. In the face of the imbalance between needs and resources which is reasonable to hope for, one should underline the importance of technical choices. It is now admitted that conventional systems are too expensive to be used everywhere in the medium term, notably in the area of sanitation and that is where segregation occurs. This segregation is increased by the frequently enormous size of the projects as well as by the high technical specifications. The question of choosing less costly techniques contains a certain ambiguity, as the lesser cost is to be obtained by a lowering of the level of service and/or by another technical conception. This means the problem of choice of techniques has to be seen as a function of time-span. In the long term it is difficult to justify questioning the level of service, that is to say, to envisage a more or less permanent second class service, but the question of means is very important. On the other hand in the short term both questions are apposite. Temporary solutions are, in fact, indispensable whatever the effort made.

In fact, in the experiments of participation studied here, one observes that the community organisations choose to realise the domiciliary connections, that is, at the level of conventional service, fearing no doubt, that the provisional solutions might become permanent. So far as the choice of techniques is concerned, they are normally tributary to the knowledge possessed by the engineers to whom they apply. But there is at least one example of the application of a traditional technique which is less expensive (the work being free, to an extent) than the modern ones.

Several factors limit choices of technique to a small part of the technological range available and create a predisposition for setting up the systems dominant in Europe and the United States. In any case, these factors are not fundamentally different from those which inhibit diversification in these continents: the inhibiting factors are essentially the training methods and sources of information of the engineers and the policies of the firms in the sector.

The crisis of the Water Boards cannot be overcome solely by financial means, without there being enormous amount of resources available. The mechanisms by which costs are arrived at in the Latin American cities are in fact more disadvantageous than in developed countries while their resources are obviously very much more limited. It is the whole of the functioning and the organisation of the sector which is in question as well as its articulation with the urban system and the rest of the economy.

NOTES

1. This communication is based on a bibliographical survey as well as on several researches conducted within the CIUDAGUA, programme of decentralized co-operation among the European and Latin American cities in the field of drinking water and drainage.
2. In Mexico the public standpipes serve around 30% of the population since the important "Programme de colonias populares" of 1978-1982.
3. The record is doubtlessly held by the District Federal of Mexico where less than 20% of the cost can be recovered. Moreover, the extent of deficit is often difficult to measure considering the vagueness of the account books.
4. In Argentina, the cost for 1985 represents only 19% of that of 1960 in fixed currency. In the petroleum producing countries the cost of water can be subsidized thanks to the income from petroleum.
5. The cost for 1978 taken as an average of three years, the international finance has reduced from 193 million dollars in 1961-1973, to 120 millions in 1969-1971, and then it climbed again to 240 millions in 1977-1978 and has been maintained almost at this level during the eighties. The recourse to international finance depends on the countries and it is not equal. Relative to the number of inhabitants, the biggest borrowers are Columbia, Bolivia, Guatemala. The weakest debtors are Brazil, Mexico, Ecuador and Argentina. At the same time differences correspond to both the national differences in financial politics and priorities accorded to the water department.
6. The administration of the water department comes under the municipal bodies in Chile, Ecuador and Columbia.
7. This chapter presents the results of the case studies conducted in Uraguay, Bolivia, Peru, Ecuador, Columbia and Venezuela. Communal participation is

more frequent in those countries where the urban growth is supplemented by a recent rural immigration and where there exists a tradition of communal work.

8. Except in Venezuela where the government has established a system of popular legal organizations or in Columbia where an outstanding programme like the "Plan de Eradication de la Pobreza Absoluta" has been put to work with the collaboration of the army.

PART II

Indian Experience

10

Urbanisation in India 1951-2001

Ashish Bose

INDIA became Independent in 1947. The partition of India in 1947 and the mass migration of the refugees had its impact on urban growth and the decade 1941-51 recorded the highest ever rate of urbanization.

The 1951-61 decade was largely free from the impact of 'abnormal' circumstances such as epidemics, war and partition. It was also the first decade of planned economic development in India and a decade of rapid industrialization. Indeed, for a proper study of industrialization, urbanization and economic growth in India, this decade should be considered as the starting point. Incidentally, this is also a first decade for which fairly adequate data are available for the study of urbanization in relation to economic growth. The rural-urban dichotomy in the presentation of all basic census data was introduced in the tabulation scheme for the first time in the 1951 Census. It must also be noted that questions on "place of birth: rural or urban and the duration of residence in case of those whose place of birth was not the place of enumeration", were also introduced for the first time in the 1961 census, thereby yielding a great deal of data on migration (subject to the limitations of migration data on the basis of place of birth). The National Sample Surveys were introduced in 1950 and this decade also saw the undertaking of a large number of socio-economic and demographic surveys. Thus, there has been a tremendous improvement, both quantitatively and qualitatively as regards the availability of data for the study of industrialization, urbanization and economic growth in India since 1961.

Push-back Factor

Under conditions of rapid population growth, the 'push' factor operates *both* in rural as well as urban areas; we have called the urban push factor as 'push-back' factor.

In the context of traditional "push and pull" analysis, we wish to introduce the concept of "push-back factor", a factor which is responsible for inhibiting the potential flow of migrants from the rural areas to the urban areas. At the root of this factor is a high rate of natural increase in population leading to the growth of a sizeable labour force within the urban areas. It must also be noted that both unemployment and underemployment are increasing in the urban areas thus considerably lessening the inflow of fresh migrants.

The slowing down of the tempo of migration will mean added misery in the rural areas as there is every possibility of rural wage rates getting further depressed. At the same time, the presence of a large surplus population in the rural areas constitutes a standing threat to the comparative high wage rates in the urban areas and there is every possibility that rural-urban migration may force these wage rates down and thereby accentuate urban misery as well.

The implication of our analysis in terms of economic development is that urbanization in the face of rapid population growth has built-in obstacles in the form of a surplus labour force in the urban areas which has to be liquidated before there is any scope for a significant shift of population from the rural to urban areas. This lack of shift not only slows down the pace of urbanization, but also worsens the situation in rural areas. While the pressure of population on land goes on increasing, the channels of rural-urban migration are closed or narrowed down on account of the "push-back" factor from urban areas.

Independence and After

According to our estimate, the urban population of India in 1947 was 53 million, or 15.7 per cent of the total population.

In the wake of partition in 1947, India witnessed one of the major human migrations in history, representing roughly an influx of 10 million refugees into India and an exodus of a similar number to Pakistan. According to the 1951 Census of India, 54 per cent of the total refugees who came to India settled in urban areas. This implies that though only 17 per cent of India's total population was urban, a disproportionate number of refugees moved to the urban areas. Similarly according to our estimates, the refugee migration to Pakistan accounted for 6.2 per cent of the 41 per cent increase in urban population during the 1941-1951 decade.

1951-1961

Between 1951 and 1961 there was a marked shift in the distribution of towns by size class. There was a significant increase in the number of towns with 10,000 population and over, and a considerable decrease in the number of towns with less than 10,000 people. Similarly, the distribution of population by size class changed considerably during this decade with a shift in the direction of large towns. The proportion of total urban population living in towns with under 20,000 inhabitants declined from 32.0 per cent in 1951 to 23.4 per cent in 1961, while that of towns with a population of over 20,000 each showed an increase from 68 per cent to about 77 per cent.

1961-1971

The urban population as a proportion of the total population increased from about 18 per cent in 1961 to about 20 per cent in 1971. In terms of increase in percentage points the rate of urbanization during 1961-71 cannot be regarded as high. However, in terms of absolute numbers, the urban population increased by about 30 million from 78.9 million in 1961 to 109.1 million in 1971. In other words, during these ten years, the urban population of India increased by 38.2 per cent or in other words at the rate of 3.3 per cent per annum. Thus from the point of view of the urban growth rate, urbanization has indeed been rapid during the 1961-71 decade.

The number of class I cities (100,000 people and over) increased from 113 to 148 during 1961-71 and the population residing in these cities went up from 38 million to 61 million. In 1961, 48.4 per cent of the country's urban population lived in class I cities (population: 100,000 and over). By 1971 this proportion increased to 55.8 per cent. During the same decade, the proportion of total urban population living in towns of 50,000 to 99,999 decreased slightly from 11.9 to 11.3 per cent. All other size categories experienced small declines in their relative share of the total urban population. Clearly then, the 1961-71 decade witnessed a shift in the distribution of the urban population from smaller to larger towns and cities, a continuation of the pattern that has characterized each successive census since 1901.

1971-1981

The urban population of India as recorded in the 1981 Census (excluding Assam and Jammu and Kashmir) was 156 million. This constituted 23.73 per cent of the total population of the relevant areas of India covered by the census. If the projected total as well as urban population of the two excluded states are taken into account, then the urban population of the country in 1981 should have been around 159 million or 23.3 per cent of the total population. If this figure were to be compared with the urban population as recorded at the 1971 Census, the urban population of India could be said to have increased by 46 per cent during 1971-81.

Highlights of the 1991 Census Results: 1981-1991 Decade

According to the provisional figures for the 1991 Census, the total population of India is 844 million (as of 1st March 1991). The census was not conducted in the State of Assam in 1981 and in the State of Jammu and Kashmir in 1991. Therefore, while arriving at the total population as well as the urban population of India, the *projected* population of Assam in 1981 and the *projected* population of Jammu and Kashmir in 1991 have been considered.

The total urban population in 1991 spread over 4,689 towns and cities is 217 million. Some of the smaller towns (called census towns) are in fact constituents of larger urban aggolmerations. There are 3,768 urban agglomerations in 1991. The absolute increase in the urban population during the 1981-91 decade has been of the order of 58 million that is a decadal growth of 36 per cent.

The urban proportion in 1991 is 26 per cent of the total population. A summary picture of these figures is given in Table 1.

Trend of Urbanization

Table 2 presents a summary picture of the trend of urbanization for the nine decades of the twentieth century.

Even in 1991 the urban population of India is just over a quarter of the total population. But in absolute terms, the total urban population is very high, 217 million. Adjusted for under-count in the 1991 Census, our estimate of the 'true' urban population of India is 235 million. Thus in spite of the low level of urbanisation in India, the urban population of India is almost the same as the total

Table 1
Urban Population of India, 1991 Summary Picture

Total population of which:	- 844.32 million
Rural population	- 627.15 million
Urban population	- 217.17 million
Per cent rural	- 74.28
Per cent urban	- 25.72
Total	- 100.00
Absolute increase during 1981-91 in:	
Rural population	- 103.28 million
Urban population	- 57.72 million
Total population	- 161.00 million
Decadal increase in population during 1981-91:	
Rural population	- 19.72 per cent
Urban population	- 36.19 per cent
Total population	- 23.56 per cent
Number of towns in 1991	- 4,689
Number of urban agglomerations	- 3,768

Source: This and subsequent tables are based on data given in *Census of India 1991, Series I, India* Paper 2 of 1991: *Provisional Population Tables: Rural-Urban Distribution*, Registrar General of India, New Delhi, August 1991.

Table 2
Trend of Urbanisation 1901-1991

Census Year Urban	Total Population (in million)	Urban Population (in million)	Per cent (Urban)
1901	238.4	25.8	10.8
1911	252.1	25.9	10.3
1921	251.3	28.1	11.2
1931	279.6	33.5	12.0
1941	318.7	44.2	13.9
1951	361.1	62.4	17.3
1961	439.2	78.9	18.0
1971	548.2	109.1	19.9
1981	683.3	159.5	23.3
1991	844.3	217.2	25.7

population of the U.S.A.

Table 3 gives the trend in the growth rate of the urban population during the past nine decades.

Table 3
Growth Rate of the Urban population 1901-1991

Census Year	Number of Urban Agglomerations	Decennial Growth Rate of Urban Population Per Cent	Annual Exponential Growth Rate
1901	1827	-	-
1911	1815	0.35	0.03
1921	1949	8.27	0.79
1931	2072	19.12	1.75
1941	2250	31.97	2.77
1951	2843	41.42	3.47
1961	2365	26.41	2.34
1971	2590	38.23	3.21
1981	3378	46.14	3.83
1991	3768	36.19	3.09

It may be noted that due to a stricter definition of "urban area/town/city" adopted in the 1961 Census, the number of urban agglomerations declined in 1961 compared to the figure in 1951 and the urban growth rate was only 26.4 per cent for the decade. Our estimate of the "true" urban growth rate for the decade (having made adjustments for definitional change) was 34 per cent (Bose, 1978). For the 1961-71 decade (when the urban data were comparable), the decadal growth rate was 38 per cent. The highest ever urban growth was recorded for the 1971-81 decade, namely, 46 per cent. It is somewhat premature to comment with confidence on the growth rate for the 1981-91 decade, in the absence of detailed data. The urban population revealed by the census was lower than the projected urban figure (as per the official projection of the Planning Commission, 1983) while the total population was the same as the projected population. There are several explanations for this phenomenon.

It does seem likely that there are limits to the absorptive capacity of our cities in view of the strained urban infrastructure (and a virtual collapse of the infrastructure in several big cities like Calcutta and Kanpur) which has slowed down rural to urban migration.

Another explanation could be that in view of the rural development programmes under the five year plans, the economic condition in the rural areas has improved, there lessening the flow of rural to urban migration. Statistically speaking, the components of urban growth like natural increase in population, net migration, extension of city boundaries and the impact of reclassification of villages and towns as well as the emergence of new towns must be examined in detail before arriving at any firm conclusion. It must also be noted that increasing urbanisation and the greater mobility of persons make the census enumeration increasingly difficult. The presence of a large houseless and squatter population also adds to the miseries of the census enumerators who go from house to house during the census. We do not rule out the possibility of a much higher undercount in the 1991 Census in the big cities and towns. We have roughly estimated that in the cities with population of 100,000 and over, the undercount must have been of the order of 10 per cent, and in the other urban areas it might have been five per cent.

Adjusting for this degree of undercount, we estimate that the urban growth rate during 1981-91 must have been of the order of 47.3 per cent and not 36.1 per cent as claimed in the official figures. This is the highest ever growth rate of urban population during this century. The planners and policy-makers must take full note of this reality.

Theoretically speaking, one could argue that as a result of better urban policies, the rate of urbanisation has slowed down. Without being cynical, we may observe that there are some success stories in some parts of India but there is nothing on the urban scene which can support the theory that urban policies have made a positive impact on the demographic situation. The limited data on urban population published so far by the Registrar General confirm the earlier trend of increasing concentration of population in the big cities.

Role of Million-plus (M +) Cities

The role of million-plus cities is brought out in Table 4.

It will be seen that in spite of the slower rate of urban growth officially revealed by the 1991 Census, the proportion of population in the M+ cities has shot up from 26.4 per cent to 32.5 per cent, as the number of such cities increased from 12 in 1981 to 23 in 1991.

Table 4
Million-plus Cities in India, 1901-1991

Census Year	Number of M+ Cities	Population (millions)	Per cent of Urban Population in M+ Cities	Decadal Increase Increase in Population (Per cent)
1901	1	1.51	5.8	-
1911	2	2.76	10.6	83.0
1921	2	3.13	11.1	13.2
1931	2	3.41	10.2	8.9
1941	2	5.31	12.0	55.8
1951	5	11.75	18.8	121.3
1961	7	18.10	22.9	54.1
1971	9	27.83	25.5	53.8
1981	12	42.12	26.4	51.4
1991	23	70.67	32.5	67.8

Since the number of such cities does not remain the same in each census, the decadal growth rates of population have to be interpreted with caution. Compared to the earlier decade when the growth rate of M+ cities was 51 per cent, the growth rate in the last decade of M+ cities was 68 per cent.

In Table 5 we look at the growth rates of individual M+ cities.

Without some knowledge of history, geography, economics, demography and census methodology, it is difficult to interpret the figures revealed by Table 5 for the individual population growth rates of M+ cities during the past two decades. For example, it is difficult to explain the growth rate of Patna (the capital of Bihar) which was as high as 67 per cent during 1971-81 and as low as 20 per cent during 1981-91. We would suspect a high degree of under-enumeration during the 1991 Census in this city. There has been no spectacular development in the rural areas of Bihar to warrant a significant slowing down of migration from the rural areas to the capital city of Bihar.

The growth rate of Calcutta as an urban agglomeration during the 1981-91 decade was 19 per cent. Here too, the possibility of considerable under-enumeration cannot be ruled out. But if one sees the trend over the past several decades, the slowing down in the growth rate seems realistic. Calcutta reached saturation point quite some time back and is heading towards stagnation and decay. It has also lost its prominent place to Bombay where despite the slowing down of the growth rate during the last decade, the percentage

Table 5
Growth Rate of M + Cities 1981-91

Urban Agglomeration/ Cities	Population in 1991 (million)	Growth Rate 1971-81	(percentage) 1981-91
1. Greater Bombay	12.6	42.9	33.4
2. Calcutta	10.9	23.9	18.7
3. Delhi	8.4	58.2	46.1
4. Madras	5.4	35.3	25.0
5. Hyderabad	4.3	42.7	67.0
6. Bangalore	4.1	75.6	39.9
7. Ahmedabad	3.3	45.9	28.9
8. Pune	2.5	48.6	47.4
9. Kanpur	2.1	23.5	28.8
10. Nagpur	1.7	40.8	36.2
11. Lucknow	1.6	23.8	63.0
12. Surat	1.5	87.4	64.2
13. Jaipur	1.5	59.4	49.2
14. Kochi	1.4	48.2	38.1
15. Coimbatore	1.1	25.0	23.4
16. Vadodara	1.1	67.4	42.5
17. Indore	1.1	47.9	33.1
18. Patna	1.1	66.7	19.6
19. Madurai	1.1	27.6	20.5
20. Bhopal	1.1	74.4	58.5
21. Vishakapatnam	1.1	66.3	74.3
22. Varanasi	1.0	25.5	28.8
23. Ludhiana	1.0	51.3	66.7

increase was as high as 33.4 per cent.

In contrast with Patna, the growth rate of Lucknow (capital of Uttar Pradesh) has shown a remarkable increase from 24 per cent during 1971-81 to 63 per cent during 1981-91. Again, there has been no spectacular industrial, commercial or administrative expansion in Lucknow to warrant such a high growth rate. We believe it is the incorporation of surrounding rural areas and the urban sprawl which is responsible for this high rate of urban growth. On the other hand, it seems likely that the high growth rate of Hyderabad's population (67%) does reflect the vast expansion in the industrial, commercial and administrative base of that city. Similarly, the high rates of growth in industrial cities like Vadodara in Gujarat, Indore in Madhya Pradesh and Visakhapatnam in Andhra Pradesh reflect the economic expansion in those cities.

It is remarkable that in spite of the turmoil in Punjab, the city of Ludhiana has recorded a higher rate of growth (67%) during

1981-91 compared to the growth rate during the preceding decade (51%). Ludhiana is a symbol of economic dynamism reflected in the agricultural prosperity of the Green Revolution areas growing small scale industries and the emergence of that city as the commercial centre of Punjab, with the decline of Amritsar and other towns close to the border of Pakistan. It is worth noting that Bangalore which had shown a growth of over 75 per cent during 1971-81, as a result of its vast industrial and commercial expansion has strained its infrastructure considerably and the urban growth rate has come down to around 40 per cent. While Pune has maintained its dynamism with the growth rate of around 48 per cent during both the decades, the industrial cities of Tamil Nadu like Coimbatore and Madurai are facing stagnation, as revealed by their growth rates.

To sum up, we cannot draw solace from the fact that in several M+ cities the growth rates of population have come down. It does not really indicate that urban problems are less pressing today. More often than not, the slowing down of the urban growth rate shows lack of economic dynamism, inability to attract enough investment and generate employment, strained urban infrastructure, sky-rocketing land prices, extreme shortage of water and energy and a general worsening of urban environment. This leads us to the philosophy of the National Commission Urbanisation (NCU) which submitted its report to Prime Minister Rajiv Gandhi in 1988. This Commission comprised some of the best urban experts in India and had the distinction having a famous administrator and the initiator of the new Bhopal city project (capital of Madhya Pradesh) as the Vice-Chairman.

The NCU report argued that one should take a positive view of urbanisation in India, and the cities should be regarded as engines of economic growth and generators of income and wealth. In fact, the NCU coined acronym: "GEM" to denote Generators of Economic Momentum. The objective spelt out by NCU was to make GEMs of as many cities as possible and in their first preliminary exercise NCU identified 329 GEMs, spread over 49 SPURs (Spatial Priority Urbanisation Regions).

Urban Population in 2001

The NCU examined a number of projections of urban population and came to the conclusion that as things were, India was heading towards an urban population of 350 million which would constitute 35 per cent of the total projected population of over 1000 million in 2001. The NCU also identified 40 cities which would cross the one million mark. The report of the NCU also discussed Statewise variations in growth rates of rural, urban and total population and concluded that

> We have a variety of demographic situations which indicate that there can be no worthwhile urbanisation strategy of a blanket nature; a number of strategies are called for in the light of the sharply differing demographic situation in the country (National Commission on Urbanistion, 1988).

The projections of the total population as well as the rural and urban populations will have to be revised in the light of the final results of the 1991 Census. The official projection of the urban population in 2001 was 326 million whereas the NCU projected a figure of 350 million. It may be argued that in the light of the 1991 Census figures which show a somewhat lower rate of urbanisation, the figure of 326 million may be nearer reality in 2001. On the other hand, the recent liberalisation in the Industrial Policy (1991), and other economic measures taken by the new Government of Narasimha Rao, are likely to speed up the pace of industrialisation and economic growth in the country. This will have its impact on the pace of urbanisation also.

A rather disturbing feature of India's urban demographic scene is the high rate of natural increase in population (i.e. births minus deaths) even in the urban areas. This is because although the urban death rates are much lower than the rural death rates its *birth* rates are not significantly lower than the rural birth rates in several large States of India. As a result, the contribution to urban growth is as much from natural increase in population as it is from rural to urban migration. This highlights the role of an effective population control programme not only in the rural areas but also in the urban areas. In fact, it can be argued that unless family planning measures succeed first in the urban areas, it is unlikely that these would succeed in the rural areas. At one time, the western donor agencies held the mistaken view that the classical demographic transition in the West could be short-circuited by modern contraceptive technology. On the basis of this premise, it was thought that countries like India need not wait for the long drawn out process of demographic transition which relied on the process of industrialisation urbanisation-modernisation to trigger off the decline in the birth rate.

Table 6 gives the latest vital statistics from the Sample Registration Survey (SRS) of the Registrar-General.

Table 6
Birth Rate, Death Rate and Natural Increase in Population, India

	1971-80	1981-89
Birth Rate		
Rural	35.8	34.2
Urban	28.5	27.3
R - U	7.3	6.9
Death Rate		
Rural	15.8	12.8
Urban	9.2	7.7
R - U	6.6	5.1
Rate of Natural Increase		
Rural	20.0	21.4
Urban	19.3	19.6
R - U	0.7	1.8

Seventh Five Year Plan, 1985-90

Given that the finalisation of the Eighth Five-Year Plan (1992-97) by the new Planning Commission and the new Government which came to power in June 1991 is pending at the time of writing, we may refer to the latest Five-Year Plan (1985-90) to get an idea of the programmes for urban development in operation.

There are five major areas of State intervention:

1. *Environmental Improvement of Slums (EIS)*

It has been estimated that the slum population constitutes nearly a fifth of the urban population. Obviously, the per capita income of the slum-dwellers is very low. Given the resource constraints, it was decided to improve the environmental condition of the slums rather than thinking in terms of building proper housing units for the slum-dwellers.

2. *Integrated Development of Small and Medium Towns (IDSMT)*

This programme was launched during the Sixth Plan to provide infrastructural facilities to small and medium towns (population less than 300,000).

3. *Special Allocation for Development Projects in the Calcutta Metropolitan Development Area (CMDA)* and also for development of state capitals like Gandhinagar, Bhopal and Chandigarh.

4. *Special allocation for National Capital Region (NCR)* around Delhi to take note of development of towns located in Haryana, Rajasthan and Uttar Pradesh in order to divert migration away from Delhi.

5. *City and Urban Infrastructure Development Corporation and a National Housing Bank.* This will look after the infrastructural facilities including housing.

The Seventh Five-Year Plan also emphasised the need for suitable programmes for urban water supply and sanitation. The provision of water supply and sanitation in urban areas calls for highly capital intensive programmes with a long gestation period. This is an area which requires assistance from international donor agencies.

Recommendations of the NCU

The NCU made a series of recommendations aimed at tackling the critical urban problems of the national context. We reproduce below some of the recommendations which are relevant in the context of the demographic dimensions of urbanisation.

Dimensions of Urbanisation

1. The urban centres which can generate economic momentum and require priority in development have been identified. They include National Priority Cities (NCPs), State Priority Cities (SPCs), Spatial Priority Urbanisation Regions (SPURs) and the small towns which serve the rural hinterland. From the Eighth

Plan onwards the fullest support must be given to the development of the identified growth centres.

2. The process of urbanisation can and must be used to improve agricultural performance and create localised employment opportunities.
3. Population control measures must be made really effective in both urban and rural areas in order to stabilise the urban situation.

Land

4. Since the most disastrous feature of Indian urbanisation has been the failure to anticipate the rising demand for urbanised land, (a key resource for urban planning), the supply of such land should be given the topmost priority.
5. A settlement survey of India should be established at the national level with a Directorate of Urban Land in each state. At the city level there should be an Urban Land Manager under the control of the District Collector.
6. The urban land tenure system must be changed to ensure security of tenure.
7. Future land requirements, especially for housing the poor, should be anticipated and provided for.
8. Squatting on public land may be regularised where possible, but land required for public and social purposes must be protected.
9. The State must intervene to provide equitable access to land.
10. To bring increasing quantities of land to the market, the Urban Land (Ceiling and Regulation) Act, 1976 should be drastically amended, and supplemented by taxation measures that would discourage land owners from keeping their land vacant and encourage proper utilisation.
11. Various forms of land assembly, through land exchange scheme, layout approval and other similar measures should be encouraged.
12. The Land Acquisition Act should be amended to eliminate delay and ensure timely payment to the affected citizens.
13. All laws which inhibit or restrict the recycling of land should be suitably modified.

Water and Sanitation

14. A holistic rather than a compartmentalised view of water resource management should be taken.
15. Water, being an absolutely critical input for human survival, must be treated as such and accorded high priority in the planning process.
16. The immediate objective should be the provision, on an equitable basis, of at least 70 litres of water per capita per day in urban areas for domestic requirements.
17. To ensure better maintenance of existing water systems, an additional Rs.1000 million per annum must be provided to local bodies. Waste water recycling and its use for non-domestic purposes should be encouraged.
18. To ensure water conservation, a differential tariff on water use should be applied with a sharp increase in the rate charged for consumption in excess of 100 litres per capita per day.
19. Legislation should be introduced to control drawing of water even from private sources in order to maintain the water-table. This may include nationalisation of all water sources.
20. The collection of solid waste and its use in compositing and as an energy source should be made more efficient. Where possible the service should be transferred to private hands.
21. Laws relating to control of pollution must be strictly enforced.

Energy

22. Energy demands of urban areas must be anticipated and advance action taken to meet them and optimise energy use.
23. Energy supply planning and pricing should be used to influence activity location.
24. Land use planning should be used as a means of reducing the energy need of the transport sector.
25. Development control rules and building bye-laws should be modified to ensure the construction of energy-efficient buildings.
26. An integrated pricing and supply policy, covering all fuels, should be evolved to achieve equity and efficiency.
27. A data-base on energy use in urban areas should be built.

Urban Poverty

28. The amelioration of urban poverty should be accorded the same priority as that given to rural poverty.
29. 400,000 urban youth should bc selected from poor households every year and trained in skills for which there is a demand.
30. Self-employment of the urban poor must be encouraged by an appropriate credit-support programme.
31. Production and market support should be given to the self-employed urban poor.
32. City planning should be geared to provide shelter and sites for employment generation programmes. Local bodies should be supported in their efforts to create special employment facilities, including worksheds for small manufacturers.
33. The shelter programme should be used to provide employment to the urban poor.
34. Wage employment for the urban poor should be provided through a programme for creation of such urban assets as water supply, drainage systems, land development, etc.
35. The public distribution system should be strengthened to meet the consumption requirements.
36. Community development should be the strategy for the improvement of the living conditions of the poor and an Urban Community Agency should be set up at national level. (NCU Report)

Role of International Co-operation

Urbanisation under conditions of rapid population growth is a complex phenomenon. The large surplus urban labour force tends to deter the unending stream of migration from rural areas. In this sense, the push factor operates everywhere - *both* in rural and urban areas.

The tempo of industrialisation under such circumstances cannot keep pace with the rate of urbanisation, a phenomenon which some writers have called "over-urbanisation". In other words, the organised manufacturing sector cannot absorb the surplus rural-agricultural population, as the investment in the manufacturing sector and the employment generated by modern technology is not large enough to take care of the surplus labour from the rural agricultural sector. This gives rise to a large poverty-based *informal* sector in the urban areas, which is largely service-oriented. Thus urbanisation brings in its wake growing poverty and environmental degradation, and yet, as we have argued, urbanisation must be made a positive force in the process of economic growth, social change and modernisation of India. In short, our cities must be engines of economic growth.

International donor agencies have from time to time, supported *ad hoc* programmes like slum clearance, site and service schemes, basic urban services, etc. and also funded some capital-intensive projects in cities like Calcutta, Bombay and Madras. But the central issue in our mind is *employment generation in a big way*, both in rural and urban areas. This will reduce rural poverty and also cut down the spill-over of the rural poor to the cities. It may be noted in passing that our inability to create employment opportunities, especially for the youth, leads to social and political tension, unrest and violence.

In India, four decades (1951-91) of rapid population growth, has converted the "population problem" into an "unemployment problem". The green revolution has eased the food situation considerably but the employment scene is far from rosy. Therefore, the basic strategy recommended by the NCU was to make our cities generators of economic momentum (GEMs). Doling out money for slum improvement does not improve the state of affairs in the long run.

We would conclude by suggesting that international donor agencies should give priority to the following problems in the urban areas of India:

1. How to generate intermediate level skills which would improve the productivity of the surplus rural labour force which migrates to the cities. While doing this, priority must be given to women workers in the labour force.
2. How to tackle the growing water famine in India's cities and also the allied problem of disposal of solid and liquid waste.
3. How to handle the energy crisis in our cities.
4. What innovative technology can be evolved to meet the problems of mass transit in our cities, given the sharply escalating oil prices in India.
5. What concrete steps can be taken to meet the growing

environmental degradation of our cities.

6. How to use modern medical technology in the health and family planning programmes tailored to meet the needs of the urban poor.
7. Finally, what are the prospects of heavy capital-intensive investments, say in steel, on the lines of the first German-supported Rourkela Steel Plant, followed by Durgapur, Bhilai and Bokaro.

These are not strictly demographic issues but in the context of development, demographic and economic issues go hand in hand.

REFERENCES

Ashish Bose (1978), *India's Urbanisation 1901-2001* New Delhi: Tata McGraw-Hill Publishing Company Limited.

Planning Commission (1983), *Task Force on Housing and Urban Development.*

Report of the National Commission on Urbanisation (Issued by the Ministry of Urban Development, 1988, Government of India, New Delhi), Vol II.

Report of the NCU, *op. cit*, Vol I.

11

Urban Corridors in India

B. K. Roy

THE concept of Urban Corridors in India was evolved using the 1971 Census data (Roy, 1977). Its basis was "Typograms of Service Zones of urban areas" with reference to class I towns of 100,000 and above population on geo-cartographic grounds. It was meant to formalize a space based on "demographic" and "geometric" indices for identifying factors having both inter-urban and intra-urban linkages with surrounding regions. It is assumed that urbanization is going through the country in the form of a concentration of infrastructure, migration of rural population to urban, and resource mobilization at all such centres from various directions in a certain magnitude. This process has caused a projected zoning in a synthetic manner interlinking the hinterlands of other towns and cities according to arterial linkages and influence. Urban corridor is a concept which is used to capture these linkages. It has 24 axes throughout the country, where urbanization in the zones delineated will be continuing till AD 2001 and beyond. Further, the zones can be of assistance in streamlining future urbanization from census to census without changing the base line delineated zones to avoid losing point prevalance qualities of such areas. As per the 1991 Census data the corridors have validity since these centres have been undergoing demographic growth. Further, it is conceived that such Indian corridors will be a replica of the urban spread in the long run, say by AD 2050 available in the type of eastern sea board of the U.S. The base line research may enable scholars to test the scenario to interpret the consequences of urbanization in the urban corridors. The urban corridors may also provide a zoning for preservation of the ecological system to growing population and to assess future urban trends. In addition, it has certain policy implications also.

Since the urban corridors indicate a certain kind of urban growth, the policy-makers should try to provide adequate amount of basic services to keep sanity in those places. Secondly, infrastructural facilities should be augmented to encourage a healthy urban growth in a more decentralized manner than before.

Methodology

The above relationships were evaluated on 1:250,000 basic maps of topography, routelinkages, train/bus traffic alignment, ecological space-potentials. In turn the spaces were re-established with morphogenesis of cities/towns to form a mosaic of typogramic space (urban corridors). In some cases spontaneous contiguous areas emerged while in others isolated or terminated areas emerged at the adjunct of Class II urban neighbourhood. This methodology was suitable to focus primarily on spaces of concern of large cities and towns articulating urban and rural relationships of various categories in the local, regional and national set up. The urban corridors are hence directional and spatial.

The spatial qualities of the urban corridors are two-fold, (i) quantitative element to judge and to define the corridors with specified goal of regionalization and (ii) to strengthen space orientation of geographical elements of landscape configuration with factors of linkages. These are elaborated below:

(i) As regards the quantitative derivation of the urban corridors, the parameters are presented in the following notation with indicators:

pt	=	Population of administrative areas
xd, yd	=	Location of district headquarters and towns
xq, yq	=	Location of geometric centres in the administrative districts of first order
x, y	=	Location of geometric centre in administrative areas of second order

now:

$$DI = pt\sqrt{(xt-xd)^2 + (yt-yd)^2} = \text{Demographic Index}$$

$$GI = pt\sqrt{(xq-x)^2 + (yq-y)^2} = \text{Geometric Index}$$

Added with pp (potential population) as

$$pp = 1/2\,[(DI) + (GI)]$$

$$= 1/2\ pt[\sqrt{(xt-xd)^2 + (yt-yd)^2} + \sqrt{(xq-x)^2 + (yq-y)^2}]$$

Where xt, yt are locations of towns/cities and Urban Agglomerations (UAs) in administrative areas for population analysis to fix *inter se* relationship in a hierarchical manner.

(ii) In combination of (i) above, the geographical factors inter-related in relation to the geographical space fixation with trend of railway/transport routes, facilitate the construction of urban corridors. But factors like broad land uses in the administrative districts of orders fixed in (i) above, i.e., arability, forest and broad wasteland areas on the scale of map indicated above act as limiting factors of corridors while mapping. In addition, groundwater maps are also consulted and interpolated in the analysis of the theme on the subject which is tabulated in the paper. The result of these systems in evolving the urban corridors is transformed in the accompanying map of India for perception (Fig. 1). It is also noted that the predominant functions of the important nodes (towns/UAs) are shown as per the 1971 data. This parameter has not been updated as per the 1981 Census because the nine-fold industrial classification of towns/cities were not tabulated. However, future researchers in this field may get the opportunity to link the changes on functional status of towns/UAs as per the 1991 Census, when the statistics are available for comparison. At the same time, it should be mentioned that the urban corridors with reference to the 1991 administrative boundaries and the urban population are provisionally matched to give the contemporary reflections of such areas for perception of the internal changes over time, specially during 1981-1991 within the unchangeable limits of urban corridors fixed as base line.

Changing Phases (1971-1991)

The decade of sixties was rated as one of population explosion and that too in the large urban centres because of comparatively increased migration, establishment of new industries, requirement of skilled and unskilled labour-force, concentration and expansion of training of personnel to man such activities in almost all class I towns and UAs. It is quite relevant that the townscape which was developed by the 1961 Census on the basis of TG (Town Group) concept inflated the area expansion of morphology of urban spaces which was further remodelled as UAs (Urban Agglomerations),

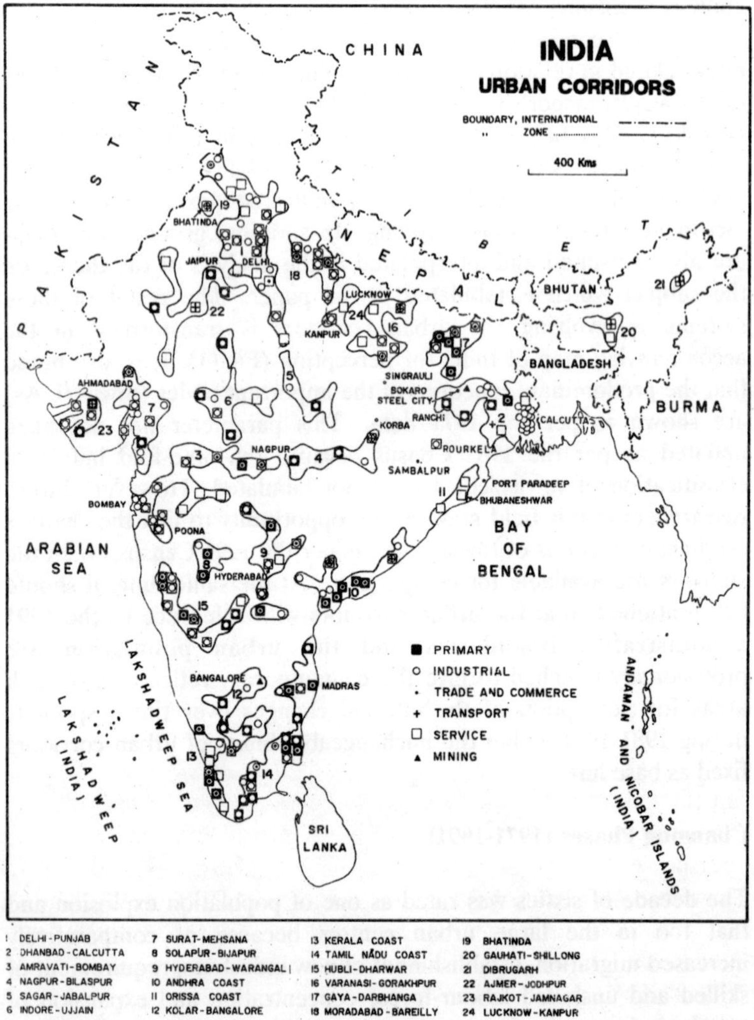
INDIA
URBAN CORRIDORS
BOUNDARY, INTERNATIONAL
ZONE
400 Kms
CHINA
PAKISTAN
NEPAL
TIBET
BHUTAN
BANGLADESH
BURMA
ARABIAN SEA
BAY OF BENGAL
LAKSHADWEEP SEA
LAKSHADWEEP (INDIA)
ANDAMAN AND NICOBAR ISLANDS (INDIA)
SRI LANKA
BHATINDA
JAIPUR
DELHI
LUCKNOW
KANPUR
SINGRAULI
BOKARO STEEL CITY
KORBA
RANCHI
CALCUTTA
ROURKELA
SAMBALPUR
PORT PARADEEP
BHUBANESHWAR
AHMADABAD
NAGPUR
BOMBAY
POONA
HYDERABAD
BANGALORE
MADRAS
PRIMARY
INDUSTRIAL
TRADE AND COMMERCE
TRANSPORT
SERVICE
MINING
1 DELHI-PUNJAB
2 DHANBAD-CALCUTTA
3 AMRAVATI-BOMBAY
4 NAGPUR-BILASPUR
5 SAGAR-JABALPUR
6 INDORE-UJJAIN
7 SURAT-MEHSANA
8 SOLAPUR-BIJAPUR
9 HYDERABAD-WARANGAL
10 ANDHRA COAST
11 ORISSA COAST
12 KOLAR-BANGALORE
13 KERALA COAST
14 TAMIL NADU COAST
15 HUBLI-DHARWAR
16 VARANASI-GORAKHPUR
17 GAYA-DARBHANGA
18 MORADABAD-BAREILLY
19 BHATINDA
20 GAUHATI-SHILLONG
21 DIBRUGARH
22 AJMER-JODHPUR
23 RAJKOT-JAMNAGAR
24 LUCKNOW-KANPUR

taking into its fold more area expansions for future development onwards 1971. Consequently, the ills of urbanization developed at a level which crystallized in the acquisition of land (both agricultural/ non-agricultural) by the Central, State Governments as well as private colonizers for habitats. With this transitional phasing of urban systems, the rural-urban landscapes changed considerably. This added additional load to the Standard Urban Area (SUA) concept of 1971 Census which in actual terms became more or less an urban region comprising an urban core of 50,000 and above population with peripheral rural components and naturally, the aspirations of man and environment changed to a notion belonging to urban.

However, in such situations the amenities and infrastructure could not change much because the basic facilities remained at a "still stage" as regards planning, with no commitment in the plans.

In this process, it is to be noted that some of the urban spaces (industrial spaces) like Rourkela were ignored in forming a typical zone because this iron and steel industrial centre acquired the bulk of man-power (unskilled) from the tribal areas and the produce was primarily to be channellised for the national utilization outside the centre. Now this space is to be integrated with the 1991 data as an exercise because this region needs full scale explanation and identification of the corridor with reference to the final 1991 census data. Similarly, Sambalpur (Orissa) also needs elaboration in this context.

Resolution of Urban Corridors

In the light of the foregoing statements, a set of 24 urban corridors as worked out on large scale (1:250,000) maps in each case having perspective qualities for the future, were recomposed on a small scale map of India for perception and published (Roy, 1984) to get feed back from scholars and urban experts regarding the strength and weakness of the design of the urban corridors. During the deliberations of the National Commission on Urbanization (1988), the concept of urban corridors was considered favourably along with other options of urban management of populations, growth restrictions and so on. However, the report on the subject remained academic rather than applied.

It is true that the areas of urban corridors at the level of intensity of urbanization in the country, still show the 1991 provisional data a dubious manifestation because, excluding a few nodes in the urban corridors, so defined, a weak urbanization level has emerged in 1991 as per Table 1. It is alarming to note that the urban corridor at the Dhanbad-Calcutta axis merely indicate urbanization level ranging from a maximum of 20-40 per cent to a minimum of 5-10 per cent in 1991. The axis of Delhi-Punjab corresponds to the 25-40 per cent level. The Varanasi-Gorakhpur axis has been dwindling along with Varanasi UA although it has achieved the million plus population mark in the 1991 enumeration as a centre of urban corridor.

The traditional urban spaces forming the ingredients of the urban corridors as defined, such as Surat-Mehsana and Bombay-Thane have shown an above 60 per cent urbanization level, in terms of percentage of urban population to total population. In general, the other urban corridors in 1991 do not range beyond the

Table 1
Urban Corridors of India and Urbanization Level, 1991

Sl. No.	Name of Urban Corridors (Axis)	Range of Urbanization Level (% of Urban to Total Population)
1.	Delhi-Punjab	60 & above: 15 - 40
2.	Dhanbad-Calcutta	20 - 40; 5-10
3.	Amaravati-Bombay	25-40; 15-25; >60
4.	Nagpur-Bilaspur	>60; 15-25
5.	Sagar-Jabalpur	25-40; >40
6.	Indore-Ujjain	25-40; 15-25
7.	Surat-Mehsana	40-60; 25-40; >60
8.	Solapur-Bijapur	25-40; 15-25
9.	Hyderabad-Warangal	>60; 10-15; 15-25
10.	Andhra Coast	25-40; 15-25
11.	Orissa Coast	15-25; 25-40
12.	Kolar-Bangalore	15-25; >60
13.	Kerala Coast	15-25; 25-40; 5-10;,>60
14.	Tamil Nadu Coast	-do-
15.	Hubli-Dharwar	15-25
16.	Varanasi-Gorakhpur	5-10; 15-25
17.	Gaya-Dharbhanga	-do-
18.	Moradabad-Bareilly	25-40
19.	Bhatinda	15-25
20.	Gauhati-Shillong	25-40
21.	Dibrugarh	15-25
22.	Ajmer-Jodhpur	15-25; 25-40
23.	Rajkot-Jamnagar	25-40; 40-60
24.	Lucknow-Kanpur	>60

25-40 per cent mark. Some of the urban corridors such as Indore-Ujjain, Andhra Coast and Orissa Coast even range between 15-25 per cent urbanization level in certain areas of the concerned corridors.

Curious Questions

A number of questions considering the initial base of urban corridors from 1971 through 1991 arise for reasonable explanations. First in addition to the 1981 million plus (M+) cities 11 were raised to the same status in 1991. At the same time in the history of Indian census, the percentage decadal variation for urban areas has come down to 36.09 per cent in 1991 as against 46.23 per cent in 1981. More curiously the corresponding figures for class II have been enumerated as 46.87 in 1991 as against 53.35 per cent in 1981. Similar trends are observed in that the smaller towns of class V and VI have shown negative growth rate of 1.27 per cent and 21.70 per cent respectively as a whole. It is further observed that the annual gain in urban population and the rate of gain per annum have come down to 3.09 per cent (1991) from 3.83 per cent (1981); 0.24 per cent (1991) from (0.34%) and 1.02 per cent (1991) from 1.72 per cent (1981) respectively in the general urban system, including the projected population (October 1989) estimate of J & K, for the nation as a whole. In the gamut, whether the urban problems are reduced due to lack of rural-urban migration or a recheck of the manual data of the 1991 Census is an important question, because the natural increase/1000 in the urban context is more or less stable 19.3 (71-80) and 19.6 (1981-89) as per the Sample Registration System (SRS). Under-enumeration may be a simple answer which can be evaluated after the migration data are available in due course.

It is a fact that besides natural increase, migration from rural to urban areas for job opportunities in the 70s was appreciable but during 80s the percentage rate of growth in the foci of urban corridors particularly M+ cities/UAs has been dwindling (see Table 2). Exceptions to this trend are a few centres like Hyderabad, Lucknow, Visakhapatnam and Ludhiana. It could be due to establishment of government, semi-government, autonomous, port development agencies and the like. This pitfall does not compress the urban problems of congestion, overcrowding, water requirements and sanitation with the present status of development.

Table 2
Present Trend of Mega Cities of India in the Core of Urban Corridors 1991

Name of Mega Cities (UA/City)	Absolute Population Increase in 1991 over 81 (in Million)	Present (1991) Actual Population (in Million)	Growth in Per cent (Rate)	
			1971-81	1981-91
Greater Bombay*	4.3	12.5	42.94	33.43
Calcutta*	1.7	10.9	23.90	18.73
Delhi*	2.6	8.3	57.09	46.18
Madras*	1.0	5.3	35.31	24.99
Hyderabad*	1.7	4.2	42.65	67.04
Bangalore*	1.1	4.0	75.56	39.87
Ahmedabad*	0.7	3.2	45.94	28.94
Pune*	0.7	2.4	48.55	47.38
Kanpur*	0.4	2.1	23.53	28.81
Nagpur*	0.3	1.6	40.80	36.24
Lucknow*	0.6	1.6	23.79	62.97
Surat	0.6	1.5	87.40	64.21
Jaipur*	0.4	1.5	59.42	49.18
Kochi	0.4	1.1	48.82	38.14
Coimbatore	0.2	1.1	25.01	23.38
Vadodara	0.3	1.1	67.36	42.54
Indore	0.2	1.1	47.85	33.13
Patna	0.1	1.0	66.71	19.55
Madurai	0.1	1.0	27.58	20.49
Bhopal	0.3	1.0	74.35	58.51
Visakhapatnam	0.4	1.0	66.08	74.27
Varanasi	0.2	1.0	25.50	28.77
Ludhiana	0.4	1.0	51.32	66.72

* Denote mega cities of 1981. Other centers (towns/UAs) declared M+ only in 1991 Census.

Source: Census of India, Provisional Totals -R-U distribution 1991, pp. 407-415.

There are apparent variations in cities and towns in the internal structure of expansion, growth and employment potentials. Taking a general note, the basic need of water at the rate of 70 lpcd for rural and 200 lpcd for urban areas for drinking and domestic purposes as suggested by the NMPE 1981-2001 A D, the population count of urban areas at 217.18 million (1991) against the projected 230 million, according to the National Master Plan Estimates (NMPE) may further affect planning and hence the 1991 Census is most critical in the sense of under-enumeration which may be affecting the positive action of urban development amenities so far conceived. The exercise of the Master Plan needs to be reoriented to some extent.

At the same time, the planning agencies, the local governments in relation to the urban corridors of India as defined in this paper may also feel the need to rectify the hazards of water (both surface and groundwater) in the interest of the health of the people on the one hand and the industrial requirements of water, in view of the forthcoming industrial policy of the government for future challenges (Roy, 1991). Also one may examine Table 3, in this perspective more inter-disciplinary results to guide the local bodies may be essential to augment development inputs for local, regional and national significance of the cores of corridors for economic articulation.

Inference

The paper presents broad framework both for academics and planners. However, it is strongly urged that irrespective of the State/Union Territories boundaries in our country, a consensus should be considered to establish inter-state and intra-state agencies dealing with a comprehensive growth of such urban corridors where most of the urban problems in relation to rural as well can be tackled at the urban corridor level. It is also urged that these urban corridors' zones as established on the small scale map in this paper, need to be mapped on large scale lay-outs in specific cases for various uses of planning, developing base profiles of urban sections to create amenities by futurstic demands of the local bodies and corridors development. This technical work can be entrusted by the State/union territory governments to the national mapping agency such as NATMO (National Atlas and Thematic Mapping Organisation). In addition, a beginning can be made by suitably amending the Indian Constitution so that the urban corridors may contribute to national growth and reduce social tensions by creating urban development and streamlining the urban spaces. This model of research may be strengthened for consideration at a micro level for detailed classical geographic evaluations of local bodies and their perspective zones in view of their expanding zoning and morphogenesis.

Such exercises, linked with probability and simple methods of prediction of space oriented regionalization can be modified with more enlarged conceptions by students and scholars. More literature need to be created with regard to the urban corridors for India considering need based and planning strategies solutions of better

Table 3
Moisture Character, General Aquifer, Water Hazards in Urban Corridors in India

No. of Urban Corridors as on Map	Moisture in cm and climatic type	Aquifer Status	Underground Water Pollutants (selected)	Alternative Deve-lopment resource for water	Remarks
A. 1,16,17,18 19,24	Dry to sub-humid (0 to -20), (0 to +20)	Good	Cyanide Chromium Agricultural pollutants	S.C./B.U.	Readers may see literature on water availability.
B. 22	Semi-arid & Arid	Good	Fluoride Tannery Waste, Dye effluents	B.U.	Water hazards and areas not having water at reasonable distance and depth. Intensive exploration needed. Consult bibliography in the paper (Roy 1991).
C. 7, 23	-do-	Good	-do-	B.U.	
D. 2,3,10,11, 13,14	Humid & Per-humid (+20 to +100)	Good Fair Poor	Dye effluents Salinity Iron & Toxic	S.C./B.U.	
E. 4,5,6 (Part of 2)	Dry to Humid	Inferior	-do-	B.U./S.C.	
F. (Part of 3) 8,9,12,15	-do-	-do-	-do-	B.U./S.C.	
G. 20,21	Humid (+100)	-do-	-do-	S.C.	

B. U. = Boring of underground resources.
S.C. = Develop small catchment to reduce water scarcity.

habitats. It is more important that some guidelines are projected by the Central Government on such issues as in the National Urbanization Commission, but the competency in implementation and execution lies in the jurisdiction of the State/UTs to create better habitats for over all development, at least in this socio-geographic issue for the future.

REFERENCES

Government of India, Census of India, 1991, Provisional Population Totals, Rural-Urban Distribution, A. R. Nanda, Registrar General, India, Paper 2, New Delhi.

———, 1988, Report of the National Commission on Urbanization, Vol. 2 (Pt. 1), New Delhi.

Roy, B. K., 1977, "Typograms of Service Zones", *Deccan Geographer*, xv (2): 281-96.

———, 1984, "Population: A major element in habitat Transformation". In *Environmental Appraisal*, 25 IGC, Paris, Alps, NGSI. Pub-32, ICRHS (Ed.), Singh R. L. and Singh R. P. B., 213-24.

———, 1991, "Water availability in India", *International Journal of Water Resources Development*, 7(2): 107-116.

12

Urban Growth in the Context of Changing Policy Perspective on Provision of Basic Amenities in India

Amitabh Kundu

INDIA experienced rapid urban growth during 1971-81, both in terms of the number of urban centres as also the urban population. The gross addition to the number of urban centres was more than 1000 (the net addition was however, only 782 owing to declassification of towns) if each constituent town of an urban agglomeration is considered a separate entity and the annual exponential growth rate of urban population worked out to be 3.8 per cent, the highest in relation to previous decades. There was an expectation, perhaps an apprehension, that the process of rapid urbanisation would continue during the eighties as well.

The Task Force on Urban Development set up by the Planning Commission (1983) had projected the population in metropolitan cities (with populations over a million) to be about 66 million, in class I cities (with population over a lakh, henceforth called simply cities) over 150 million and that in all urban centres to be roughly 235 million or about 28 per cent of the total population in the year 1991. The present census has, however, estimated the metropolitan population to be 70.6 million and the city population to be 138.8 million. The percentage of urban population works out to be 25.7 of the total, the absolute urban population being 217.2 million.

The growth rate of population in the metropolitan cities (all growth rates here are computed by taking the population of only those cities that belonged to the category in the base year) works out to be the least during 1981-91 as compared to the previous two decades. The annual exponential growth rate during the eighties is 3.09 per cent only, compared to the figures of 3.36 and 3.40 during the seventies and sixties respectively. In the case of most of the metropolitan cities, the growth rate has decelerated significantly during the eighties.

This slowing down of the growth rate of population has occurred in the lower categories of cities as well, as shown by Premi (1991). The growth rate of population in cities between 1 and 2.5 lakhs works out to be 3.01 per cent during 1981-91. The corresponding figures for the seventies and the sixties were 3.72 and 3.63 respectively. Similarly, the growth for the cities with populations between 2.5 and 5 lakhs was 3.29 per cent during the sixties. This increased to 3.96 in the following decade only to come down to 3.56 during the eighties. The only category for which the growth has increased marginally during the eighties (compared to the previous decade) is that with population between 5 lakhs and 10 lakhs. However, when we take all the cities of 1981 together, the growth rate falls from 3.56 per cent in the seventies to 3.09 per cent in the eighties.

The slowing down of the growth of cities including the metropolises may suggest a reduction in the top heavy structure of urbanisation in the country and a balanced urban development. The number of new towns in the 1991 Census being as large as 890 can be taken as yet another evidence of this structural change.

The reduction in rural-urban disparity in terms of the levels of income, consumption, infrastructural facilities and basic amenities has sometimes been put forward as an explanation. However, the relevant data from different secondary sources seriously discount this thesis. The limited industrial dispersal around the Class-I cities provides only a partial explanation for this trend. Significant explanations must, however, be sought in the reduction of public investment in basic urban amenities, particularly those directed towards the poor.

In view of the above, the present paper examines the hypothesis that the changing policy perspective, permitting or encouraging the involvement of private agencies and compelling the public agencies to ensure cost recovery and depend less and less on grants in the provision of the amenities is responsible for the slow demographic growth in urban areas through discouraging migrants. First, it analyses the organisational structure for the provision of water supply, sewerage and sanitation facilities and the system of financing the current and capital expenditures by the concerned public agencies. An overview of the government programmes and schemes and the changing priorities therein is attempted. The impact of dependence on resources from the international agencies like World Bank, UNDP, Ford Foundation etc. and the banking sector within the country, replacing the government grants, has been considered in some detail.

Organisational Structure and Maintenance System

The responsibility of providing basic services such as water supply, sewerage, sanitation and solid waste disposal lies with the State governments which they fulfil through (a) their own departments, (b) state-level boards, corporations etc., (c) statutory and non-statutory bodies at the city level, and (d) local bodies. The Central Government, through its Ministry of Urban Development overviews the developments in these sectors, lays down policy perspectives for the country, builds up data systems, promotes research and initiates actions in key areas through centrally sponsored schemes. Town and Country Planning Organisation (TCPO) and Central Public Health and Environmental Engineering Organisation (CPHEEO) are the two technical wings of the Ministry. While TCPO monitors and coordinates the implementation of Central Government schemes such as the Urban Basic Services (UBS), Environmental Improvement of Urban Slums (EIUS), Integrated Development of Small and Medium Towns (IDSMT) besides providing technical guidance to state level planning and implementing agencies, the activities of CPHEEO are restricted to the provision of technical guidance.

In the provision of water supply, sewerage, sanitation and solid waste disposal facilities, developmental and maintenance responsibilities have been separated and assigned to different agencies. Capital works in these sectors in many states are undertaken by the concerned state government departments such as the Public Health Engineering Department (PHED), the Public Works Department (PWD), the Urban Development Department, the Department of Local Self-Government and so on through their divisional and district offices. Alternatively, some states (about 11) have set up Water Supply and Sewerage Boards and much of the responsibility for building up capital assets has been transferred to them as in the states of Karnataka, Maharashtra, Kerala, Punjab and Uttar Pradesh. These boards sometimes take up development projects on their own but mostly on behalf of the state governments, the local bodies, slum boards, universities and at times private organisations. In states such as Tamil Nadu, the Directorate of Municipal Administration also takes up certain water supply projects, although the basic responsibility for this lies with the state level board. Besides these, Housing Boards, Urban Development Authorities as well as some large municipal bodies make investments in these services within their project areas or jurisdictions. Finally, several large public as well as private sector undertakings and agencies like the Railways invest in water supply and drainage projects within their townships or localities as in Rourkela, Bhilai, Jamshedpur, and Modinagar. As a rule they also maintain the facilities.

The organisational structure discussed above takes care of the capital works in the concerned sectors in most towns and cities, barring a few metropolitan cities, in which the local bodies are financially strong as in Delhi, Bombay and Ahmedabad. However, the capital projects in the latter two cities are designed and implemented by the local bodies or their subsidiaries with the approval of their state governments. Bangalore and Madras have separate Metropolitan Water Supply Boards with a structure and functions similar to those of the state level boards discussed above. The only difference here is that these boards construct as well as maintain the facilities and thus serve the consumers directly, a role which is generally played by the municipal bodies in other cities.

Besides the municipal corporations and metro level water boards, urban development authorities also invest in water supply, sewerage and sanitation facilities. In several cities both local bodies and development authorities undertake capital projects. Within Calcutta Metropolitan Area (CMA), the Calcutta Metropolitan Development Authority (CMDA), Calcutta Metropolitan Water and Sanitation Authority (CMWSA) and the Calcutta Improvement Trust (CIT) take up capital projects besides the concerned municipal bodies, the Housing Board and state government departments such as the PWD, the Irrigation and the Waterways Department. Thus, unlike the city level boards of Bangalore and Madras, CMWSA is not the only agency responsible for capital projects. Under the Calcutta Urban Development Project III (CUDP-III), a two-tier organisational structure has emerged, wherein the CMDA acts as the coordinating, evaluating and monitoring agency, while CMWSA,

CIT, Howrah Improvement Trust (HIT), Calcutta Municipal Corporation (CMC), Howrah Municipal Corporation (HMC) and other local bodies take up the responsibility of executing the projects. Most of the local bodies, because of the inadequacy of managerial and technical staff, are assisted by the CMDA and other state government departments in discharging their functions.

In the metropolitan cities of Kanpur, Lucknow, Pune and Nagpur, state level water boards are responsible for capital expenditure. In the city of Hyderabad the responsibility lies with the Hyderabad Metro Water Works whereas in Jaipur the investment is undertaken by the PHED. However, in most of the states the latter take the responsibility of capital expenditure for smaller cities and towns only.

The responsibility of maintaining the capital assets providing water supply and sewage disposal facilities, and of collecting water taxes, user charges and so on, lies with the local governments. In situations, however, where local bodies are financially or organisationally weak, state government departments or state-level boards take up the maintenance responsibility for short or long durations. In some states, the state level boards construct as well as maintain the water works including organising bulk and retail sales. They also maintain the old water delivery systems that were transferred to them by the state governments when they were first set up. In the small and medium towns of Madhya Pradesh, the water supply projects which of late have been undertaken with World Bank assistance, are being maintained by the state government, although generally the revenue is collected by the municipalities. Maintenance of water supply and sewerage systems directly by the state governments or indirectly through state level boards and other bodies is, therefore, not very uncommon.

Financing of Capital Expenditure

In the states where capital investments in water supply, sewerage and sanitation are the direct responsibility of the state government, funds are made available in state plans and budgets. In others, where there are state level boards, the state and central level projects are executed through them. Provision for funds is made in the Central and/or state budget for loans and grants for the project.

For projects undertaken by the boards on behalf of the municipal bodies, the responsibility of arranging funds is that of the latter and these are financed normally through a combination of loans and grants. The loans are obtained generally from the LIC while the grants come from the state governments. It is important to note that the local bodies do not have direct access to LIC funds. The boards draw the loans on a state government guarantee, although the responsibility of repayment lies with the local bodies. The loans from the state government to the local bodies are also routed through the board but here the repayment of the principal amount takes place via the boards while the interest is paid directly to the state government. HUDCO also provides funds for utility infrastructure schemes including water supply and sanitation projects to municipalities, corporations and other government bodies for towns with a population of not more than 10 lakhs as per the 1981 census. HUDCO finances up to 50 per cent of the project cost while the balance is to be met by the state government or the borrowing agency. The loan is to be repaid within twelve years with an interest of 10.25 per cent. For several municipalities, public contribution constitutes a portion of the total funds. The loan/grant mix varies with the status of the local body, the grant amount being higher in the case of smaller municipal bodies. In some states as in Gujarat, these grants-in-aids are made available to the local bodies on "as and when" basis depending upon the availability of funds. In many states, however, water supply projects for towns with populations of less than 20,000 are financed entirely by the state government grants-in-aid.

The boards are also called upon to take up investment or maintenance responsibility by private companies, universities and so on but then the latter arrange for funds on their own without borrowing from either the government or from other agencies. Sometimes slum boards or municipalities meet the entire project cost out of their own resources but ask the boards to undertake the projects on their behalf. In such cases, these bodies deposit the required funds with the board. The latter in turn constructs, operates and maintains the projects for the former on payment of specific charges. These are generally known as deposit contribution projects.

In addition to the above, the boards take up capital projects on their own using their internal resources, supplemented by loans from the state governments, LIC and other agencies. Besides, the boards can also raise open market loans and borrow from the nationalised banks for lending to the municipal corporations. Finally, there are international agencies such as the United States Agency for International Development (USAID) and the World Bank, which occasionally finance water supply and sanitation specific projects. Integrated urban development projects supported by the World Bank which are functioning in some states also have water supply and sanitation as major components.

Changing Policy Perspective

The organisational structure discussed above is responsible for the establishment and maintenance of water supply and sewerage/ sanitation facilities for both the poor and non-poor in urban India. It is only in the case of a few cities that the capital projects for these facilities in slum colonies are undertaken either by the concerned state government departments or by state level slum boards. The responsibility of maintenance lies generally with the local authorities. The role of vested interests and local elites in the selection of infrastructural projects and their locations within the cities cannot be ruled out as is true of any other decision making process in the country. One, therefore, finds a significantly higher investment in per capita terms and better maintenance of the facilities in relatively well-off areas. The distributional network by its very design tends to discriminate against the low income colonies, particularly those which are away from rich localities (Misra and Sharma: 1979).

In a few states, Slum Clearance Boards have been set up which relocate pavement dwellers and shanty settlements from the dense areas to the peripheries. They take up integrated housing projects for the poor that include provision of water supply and sanitation. In some of the metropolitan cities, there are Slum and Squatter Wings within the Development Authorities like the Slum Wing of the DDA or the Municipal and Anchal Development Sector of CMDA. In other large cities, development work in slums is undertaken by the regular departments of the municipality or its special Slum Wing or Bustee Cell.

It is evident that most of the urban poor draw water from public stand posts (PSP) managed by the urban local bodies. People in regularised slums as also in certain unauthorised colonies have this facility within the locality while the others have to either get it from a PSP outside the locality or from households in the neighbourhood that have domestic connections.

It is not always possible to provide water through public stand posts to all slum localities owing to their distance from the existing pipelines or because of inadequate supply of water. Water is made available in such localities through tubewells or handpumps. This, of course, is more common in the cities where the water-table is reasonably high. The Calcutta Municipal Corporation, for example, has a separate department responsible for the installation and upkeep of small diameter tubewells all over the city. In addition, it installs large diameter tubewells in a few pockets where there is water scarcity. In Delhi, too, both the DDA and the DMC have dug a large number of tubewells for the slum and pavement population.

In a few large cities, tankers are used either regularly or during periods of scarcity to provide water to colonies not covered or inadequately covered by the piped system or in areas where ground water is not potable. In Madras, Delhi and several large towns in Karnataka, water is supplied to a section of the urban poor through tankers.

Despite all these arrangements, the poor face problems in obtaining water through the public delivery system. It may be noted that water is available through the PSP for short durations at a low pressure and the supply is often erratic. As the number of persons per PSP or per tubewell is also very high in the low income colonies, long queues and many hours of waiting often result in high tempers and quarrels. Where, there is no tap in the locality, water has to be brought from long distances. As a result, the per capita water consumed in localities without tap connections is very small compared to those with connections.

Households without domestic connections do not pay any user charges but in certain cities they have to pay a water tax (which is included in the property tax) if they live in localities covered by the distribution system. The charges, however, are nominal and work out to be less than Rs. 10 a year.

A section of the urban poor has domestic connections for water supply. Most of these are unmetered and therefore the payment is minimal, generally less than Rs. 10 a month. Even for metered connections, the payment works out to be about the same since the poor belong to the lowest consumption category. The problem, therefore, is not one of non-affordability. On the contrary, since the user charge is low and does not show significant progressivity (with increases in consumption, ferrule size or value of property), non-priority use of water or its wastage becomes very high.

In many states the exemption limits fixed by the authorities are high so that the urban rich do not pay for a substantial part of their water consumption. It is unfortunate that pricing of water has not been applied as an instrument to rationalise its use, which could have increased water availability in the slums through the PSP.

The problem of affordability is, however, important for the poor in the context of the capital expenditure involved in obtaining a new domestic connection. In the old parts of large cities, several households with domestic connections need to replace their local pipelines. Otherwise, there is a risk of epidemics due to the seepage of sewer water through corroded water pipes. The cost of a new connection or of replacement even at subsidised rates works out to between Rs. 100 and Rs. 500 per household. The poor in general cannot afford this expenditure. Many among them are not able to perceive the imminent dangers while others believe that such expenditure should be borne by the government. In certain large cities, the risk of epidemics is also high due to shallow tubewells. The local authorities generally become aware of the dangers caused by these tubewells owned privately or publicly, only after the damage is done and a few hundred lives are lost.

The poor generally use the free community toilets provided by local bodies or open spaces for defecation. Slums either have open drains or do not have any drainage facility at all. Even in large cities, reported to have been fully or partially covered by the underground system, most of the slum colonies are unsewered.

The number of public toilets in low income colonies is inadequate to meet the needs of the population. This results in long hours of waiting and consequently use of public spaces for defecation. Because of the lack of proper maintenance, many of the toilets are rendered unusable. Owing to non-availability of water near the toilets, negligence, and inadequate sanitary staff and other related problems, many of these remain choked for several days on end. Defecation in open spaces, along with the overflowing toilets and drains pose a major health problem, particularly during the rainy season.

A small fraction of the urban poor have toilets in their houses. These are mostly dry latrines cleaned by municipal staff but sometimes privately as well. The maintenance is not very satisfactory owing to paucity of funds with the local bodies. The sanitation tax and the user charges together work out to be not more than Rs. 5 per month in most cities. Besides, the recovery rate is also very low.

The major problem with private latrines is not their current but capital costs which even with a subsidy component work out to a few hundred rupees. The poor are unable to get individual connections because they cannot afford them and also they are unable to appreciate the urgency of such a need. At the same time the conversion of dry latrines into flush latrines has been extremely slow despite the subsidy component in the schemes.

Given the high cost of construction and maintenance of flush or dry latrines, sanitary toilets with septic tanks have emerged as a low cost alternative. Here, the responsibility of the local bodies is much less as the tanks need to be cleaned only once in five to ten years. In many cities and towns, local bodies are now permitting the construction of dwelling units only when the individual or cooperative undertakes to build its own tubewell and septic tanks, placing no extra demand on the existing system. The inability to meet this municipal requirement often puts the settlements of the urban poor into the unauthorised or illegal category.

In recent years, some efforts have been made by the state level bodies or municipalities to extend sewer lines and provide open drains to the slum colonies. The dim prospects of cost recovery and lack of funds for urban development particularly for uneconomic projects have hindered progress in this direction. Public sector efforts in environmental improvement schemes have, therefore, been sporadic, often linked with outbreak of epidemics or the advent of an election and have not been carried out on a sustainable basis.

Conclusion

The above analysis shows that the concerned public agencies do not show the required sensitivity for the needs and paying capacity of the poor. Most of the governmental schemes by their very stipulations, norms, instalment rates etc, keep the poor out of their purview. It may also be argued that the "structural adjustments" carried out and proposed in the urban sector in the context of economic liberalisation might further reduce rural urban migration. This would stifle an important channel for alleviating the burden of rural poverty.

REFERENCES

Kundu, Amitabh (1990), "Access of Urban Poor to Basic Amenities", Unpublished Report, Centre for Study of Regional Development, Jawaharlal Nehru University, New Delhi.

Mishra, G. K. and Sharma, K. S. R. N. (1979), *Distribution and Differential Allocation or Public Utilities in Urban Delhi*, Indian Institute of Public Administration.

Planning Commission (1983), *Task Forces on Housing and Urban Development.*

Premi, M. K. (1991), *India's Population: Heading Towards a Billion*, B. R. Publishing Corporation, Delhi.

13

Status of Water Supply and Sanitation Facilities in Urban India – An Overview*

Archana Ghosh

THE most common problem facing urban population in a majority of the developing countries is the limited access to almost all the basic services like health, shelter and particularly water supply and sanitation facilities. The level of services is below the standard requirement in both quality and quantity. The inadequate services while affects all sections of the society, poorer suffer the most. The slum localities in developing countries have either no access or very limited access to piped water supply and sanitation facilities. The inevitable consequences of these environmental insanitation is diseases and high morbidity in these countries. Recent data show that 30 per cent of all reported cases of illnesses and 40 per cent of deaths in urban areas in Pakistan are attributed to water-borne diseases (Ahmed, 1984). The inadequate sanitary system in Indonesia has placed it among those countries having the highest incidence of water-borne diseases (Mitsuhiko, 1984). In Nigeria, poor urban colonies get 12 litres of water per capita per day and because of the unhygienic source of water, water-borne diseases are common. These include typhoid fever, dysentery, diarrhoea, cholera and guinea worm (Oniboken, 1990).

India is no exception. High infant and child mortality reflects the poor state of public health and environmental hygiene in urban areas. It is estimated that in India 26 per cent of child deaths are caused by water-borne diseases like diarrhoea and dysentery (NIUA, 1991). These two diseases are again predominantly

* This article forms a chapter of the Status Report on "Access to Basic Amenities in the Context of Rapid Urbanization: Drinking Water and Sanitation Issues" prepared by the Institute of Social Sciences.

responsible for child and infant morbidity. Five hundred per 1000 infants and 200 per 1000 pre-school children suffer from these diseases.

Serious concerns were expressed about the state of these two services prevailing in the developing countries at the United Nations Conferences on Human Settlement in June 1976 at Vancouver. In the Water Conference at Mar del Plata, Argentina in March 1977 it was decided that the ten-year period (1981-1990) would be declared as the International Water Supply and Sanitation Decade. The conference on Primary Health Care at Alma Ata, USSR in September 1978 approved the recommendations of the water conferences. All the participating countries in the conference emphasised the need for water supply and sanitation facilities to their people, both rural and urban.

India as one of the signatories to the Alma Ata Convention, launched the programmes with much fanfare. Detail Master Plan was chalked out and specific targets were set to meet rural and urban needs.[1] The financing pattern, institutional set-up, manpower needs, technological support etc. for the programme implementation were meticulously planned.

As the decade is over now, it is worthwhile to review the prevailing situation. The present paper is an attempt in this regard. It provides an overview of the situation in urban India as a whole and in different size-class of cities as far as these two services are concerned in terms of coverage and quality. The emphasis is on metropolitan cities, Class I and Class II towns.

The analysis shows that even with the emphasis given on these two urban services at various levels and occasions, most of the higher order cities, (even though they are better served than the other lower order towns) are deficient in service level and that there are large-scale disparities in the availability of the services at inter-city, and intra-city levels. Even within a city more affluent localities are better served than the others. In the squatter and slum settlements, nearly 40 to 50 per cent of the population of which live in metropolitan and other major towns, the services are available in name only. It also becomes clear that economic development of a state do not always ensure better availability of these services to its people. Many developed states have fared not so well in providing basic services to all sections of the people.

The sources of data for the analysis are mainly secondary viz published and unpublished reports of the different government departments and major surveys conducted during the last decade at the national level by organisations like the National Institute of Urban Affairs, Central Pollution Control Board and National Sample Survey Organisation. In addition some micro-level studies have also been referred to for corroborating the major findings. The paper is divided into three sections. The first section discusses the status of water supply facilities at different levels. The second one deals with sanitation facilities. In the third section the status of these two facilities in slum localities has been discussed.

I. Water Supply Facilities

The urban population covered by protected water supply was 72 per cent at the time of launching of the Decade Programme in 1981. The entire population was to be covered by March 1991.

The latest data received from the Central Public Health and Environmental Engineering Organisation (CPHEEO), the central monitoring authority of the Programme, reveals that the percentage of urban population covered by organised water supply, which includes piped water and tube-wells, has increased to 82 per cent in 1988. Even the reduced target of 90 per cent coverage could not be achieved by the end of the Decade. In 1990 the coverage figure reached 83.80 per cent and the Eighth Plan estimates the anticipated population coverage in March 1992 to be 84.90 (Eighth Plan 1992, p. 378). But the average figure of the coverage level does not reveal the wide disparities in the performance of different states and union territories. Table 1 shows the population covered in all the states and union terriroties in selected years during the Decade programme.

By the end of 1988, only six states/UTs could achieve the goal of 100 per cent coverage, of which two had already been at that level at the time of launching of the programme. The performance of union territories is much better than the states. In economically backward states like Assam, Orissa and most of the north-eastern states the coverage is extremely low. The achievements of states like Rajasthan and Haryana and a union territory like Chandigarh are noteworthy in that starting from a very low level they could cover nearly entire urban population by protected water supply by 1988.

The same picture of inter-state differences in the coverage of

Table 1
Per cent Population covered by Water Supply System in Urban Areas over States/Union Territories in Selected Years during the Decade

State/UTs	1981	1985	1986	1987	1988
Andhra Pradesh	55.33	52.09	62.42	62.42	71.75
Arunachal Pradesh	47.61	88.46	100.00	100.00	100.00
Assam	25.89	37.53	37.53	37.53	37.53
Bihar	63.42	59.44	63.38	63.58	69.77
Goa	93.75	81.85	79.91	81.45	83.33
Gujarat	88.94	83.14	93.36	93.35	91.87
Haryana	39.97	69.09	100.00	100.00	100.00
Himachal Pradesh	100.00	89.07	92.87	100.00	100.00
Jammu & Kashmir	97.61	86.61	94.96	94.98	95.57
Karnataka	88.81	81.17	94.88	98.72	99.60
Kerala	59.73	64.50	63.81	65.62	68.21
Madhya Pradesh	67.06	79.68	80.00	80.48	81.00
Maharashtra	94.89	87.04	89.98	99.70	99.70
Manipur	69.33	51.48	75.47	75.47	68.49
Meghalaya	24.89	22.14	19.35	49.47	47.49
Mizoram	8.19	7.57	18.56	18.57	18.36
Nagaland	58.33	46.66	46.66	43.87	43.47
Orissa	34.40	38.10	37.11	37.11	37.80
Punjab	65.61	71.16	71.28	71.17	71.18
Rajasthan	56.31	56.00	56.06	54.53	98.59
Sikkim	46.15	89.02	55.88	67.12	69.33
Tamil Nadu	80.86	83.74	86.66	88.24	88.51
Tripura	48.67	51.50	53.19	53.19	53.19
Uttar Pradesh	70.30	70.09	69.29	69.29	69.99
West Bengal	60.01	63.65	67.16	68.29	69.34
Andaman & Nicobar	100.00	100.00	100.00	100.00	100.00
Chandigarh	94.11	100.00	100.00	100.00	100.00
Delhi	81.48	98.12	97.08	96.98	97.16
Pondicherry	56.96	76.30	100.00	100.00	100.00
All India	72.25	72.88	77.25	79.24	82.28

Source: Central Public Health and Environmental Engineering Organisation, Ministry of Urban Development, New Delhi, 1990.

urban population by protected water supply is evident in the survey conducted by the National Sample Survey Organisation (42nd Round) in 1986-87, in major states. The survey ascertains the distribution of urban population across major sources of water supply (Table 2).

It is noticed that a substantial percentage of the urban population in some States like Assam, Bihar, Punjab, Uttar Pradesh, West Bengal and Kerala still do not have access to tap water and they have

Table 2
Percentage Distribution of Persons across major Sources of Drinking Water in Urban Sector for Selected States and All India

State	Percentage of Persons across different Sources of Drinking Water				
	Tap	Tubewell/ Handpump	Pucca Well	Others	All
Andhra Pradesh	70.28	13.09	14.76	1.87	100.00
Assam	44.73	38.97	12.64	3.66	100.00
Bihar	48.87	25.76	21.96	3.41	100.00
Gujarat	91.62	4.85	1.36	1.17	100.00
Haryana	79.97	19.97	0.06	–	100.00
Himachal Pradesh	96.11	0.59	1.82	1.48	100.00
Jammu & Kashmir	93.56	3.52	0.21	2.71	100.00
Karnataka	83.05	5.44	9.72	1.79	100.00
Kerala	49.74	1.16	48.08	1.02	100.00
Madhya Pradesh	80.04	7.86	10.47	1.63	100.00
Maharashtra	92.83	1.54	4.72	1.21	100.00
Orissa	52.68	13.49	27.99	5.84	100.00
Punjab	61.33	38.57	0.10	–	100.00
Rajasthan	79.69	7.66	11.72	0.93	100.00
Tamil Nadu	70.66	13.78	11.32	4.24	100.00
Tripura	83.48	11.15	1.20	4.17	100.00
Uttar Pradesh	58.73	30.14	10.02	1.11	100.00
West Bengal	54.39	33.95	6.55	0.11	100.00
All India	72.43	15.44	10.26	1.87	100.00

Source: *National Sample Survey Organisation, 42nd round, No. 361, 1986-87.*

to depend on tubewells or *pucca* wells for thier drinking water supply. Although it is not obligatory that the entire urban population must have tap water, the source of water supply is important because due to the absence of adequate sanitation and a proper check on the water quality, the incidence of water-borne diseases are also very high in these states. Kerala is the only exception where although 48 per cent of the urban population depends on *pucca* wells for its drinking water supply, it has a very good record of health performances. Although the data from the above two sources cannot be compared, it is evident from them that advanced states like Maharashtra and Gujarat have done relatively well compared to the others, with more than 90 per cent of their urban population covered by protected water supply. On the other hand, an agriculturally prosperous state like Punjab has not done very well compared to a backward state like Madhya Pradesh.

Level of Services

The state level averages as cited above do not explain the differences that exist in the level of services in terms of quantity available in different size class of towns. National level data are available in this regard at least from two sources – one is the survey conducted by the Central Pollution Control Board (CPCB) and another is the study of the National Institute of Urban Affairs (NIUA) conducted in 1988. The study of CPCB conducted in two different periods (1978-79 and 1988-89) in Class I and Class II towns, spread over 21 major towns, based on information provided by the local authorities, furnishes a comparative picture of water supply facilities available in these size-class of towns.

Table 3 shows the total and per capita supply of water in Class I towns in the major states. It is observed that although the average per capita supply in Class I towns was 147 litres per day (lpcd) in 1988-89, at least in 12 states the per capita average was much lower than this. In some states the average was not even 100 lpcd.

In states like Tamil Nadu and Rajasthan the per capita supply was as low as 68 and 89 litres respectively. The study for the earlier period (i.e. 1978-79) shows that the average per capita water supply in 1978-79 was 143 litres per day. This shows that there has been only a marginal improvement in per capita supply even with a substantial increase (43.14%) in the total water supply from 8638.48 mld (million litres per day) to 15191.88 mld during the decade. It is also noted that there has been a substantial decrease in the per capita water supply ; states like Gujarat, Maharashtra, Punjab, Rajasthan and the Union Territory of Pondicherry. This indicates that the improvement in the total water supply did not match with the rapid pace of urbanisation.

The second source of data for the level of services in different Class I towns is the study of National Institute of Urban Affairs (NIUA). This is based on survey conducted in 133 sample class I towns over twenty major states in 1986-87.

This study reaffirms that in almost all the states the per capita supply is much below the desirable norm set by different authorities.[2] The average supply is 142 litres per capita per day (lpcd) in the 133 class I cities surveyed, as against the norm of 200 lpcd.

But the similarities in the two sets of data for an equivalent

Table 3
Total and Per Capital Water Supply Situation in Class I Towns in 1978-79 and 1988-89 in major cities

Sl. No.	States/UTs	Number of Class I Towns		Total Water Supply (MLD)		Per capita Water Supply (Litres/day)	
		1978	1989	1978	1988	1978	1988
1.	Andhra Pradesh	13	17	433.77	974.80	107.00	141.00
2.	Assam	1	--	34.05	--	170.00	--
3.	Bihar	11	11	387.12	553.60	151.00	147.00
4.	Gujarat	7	11	583.74	1018.72	164.00	145.00
5.	Haryana	2	9	18.16	162.72	80.00	83.00
6.	Jammu & Kashmir	2	2	102.83	261.80	175.00	254.00
7.	Karnataka	11	14	467.61	818.48	133.00	110.00
8.	Kerala	5	6	192.49	274.52	131.00	126.00
9.	Madhya Pradesh	11	14	394.05	718.09	131.00	117.00
10.	Maharashtra	17	29	2265.73	3547.19	204.00	176.00
11.	Manipur	1	1	12.30	22.50	123.00	105.00
12.	Meghalaya	-	1	--	3.97	--	31.00
13.	Orissa	4	6	92.53	257.60	154.00	167.00
14.	Punjab	4	7	247.69	291.22	190.00	105.00
15.	Rajasthan	7	11	243.80	397.05	128.00	89.00
16.	Tamil Nadu	17	19	404.88	608.67	55.00	68.00
17.	Tripura	-	1	--	16.47	--	103.00
18.	Uttar Pradesh	22	29	1079.20	1804.27	171.00	165.00
19.	West Bengal	5	21	679.73	1384.21	87.00	151.00
20.	Delhi	1	1	885.30	1848.00	243.00	248.00
21.	Pondicherry	1	1	--	48.00	487.00	257.00
22.	Chandigarh	-	1	113.50	180.00	--	460.00
	TOTAL	142	212	8638.218	15191.88	143.37	147.00

Source: Compiled from (1) *Waste Water Collection Treatment and Disposal in Class I Cities - Status and Action Plan* - 1978-79 -- Central Board for the Prevention and Control of Water Pollution, New Delhi.
(2) *Status of water supply and wastewater collection, treatment and disposal in Class I cities, 1988* -- Central Pollution Control Board, New Delhi.

period end at the average figure for the country as a whole. Comparisons of total water supply and per capita consumption at state level gives a very diffirent picture. In some cases e.g., Kerala, Meghalaya, Manipur and Punjab etc., state level average figures in the first source are quite different from the second, even with the number of towns surveyed remaining the same. In such cases to draw conclusions based on one data source alone, may prove to be unrealistic.

Nevertheless from the NIUA survey important observations can be made: wide inter-state variations exist in the level of water supply in Class I towns (Table 4). In states like Orissa, Manipur and Tripura where the number of sample Class I towns is small, the level of service is above 200 lpcd. In some other states like Assam, Bihar, Jammu and Kashmir and Meghalaya, the per capita service level is far below even the reduced norm as recommended by National Commission on Urbanization (70 to 100 lpcd).

From Table 5 it will be seen that out of 131 class I cities only 17 per cent maintain levels of water supply as per the norms stipulated by different agencies at different points of time. It is important to mention here that the stipulated norms have not taken into consideration the social needs and demographic compositions of different urban centres. If such factors like age, sex ratio and social habits of people are taken into account, the norms would have to be revised.

Among the different sizes of Class I towns also, there are sharp disparities in the availability of services as Table 6 shows. The sample city with population more than 7 lakh is best served in terms of present population covered though not in terms of per capita supply. However, the finding cannot be generalised as the sample comprises only one city of this size. The lowest size of class I city with a population of 1 to 2 lakhs is deficient both in terms of population coverage and per capita supply. Middle order cities with population ranging from 4 to 5 lakhs are best served, both in terms of population coverage and per capita supply.

Class II Towns

The supply situation in Class II towns is much worse as established by the two surveys conducted by Central Board for the Prevention and Control of Water Pollution in 1979-80 and in 1988-89. The first one shows that the average supply for 190 towns was only 125 litres per day. The updated survey conducted by the same agency in 1988-89 covering 241 towns only shows that the per capita supply has declined to only 78 lpcd over these years (Table 7).

While there has been a nominal increase in the total water supply from 1533 mld to 1622 mld in these 10 years, the number of towns has increased from 190 to 241. It is also noted that there are large variations in the average supply of water in this size class of towns across the states. Except for Himachal Pradesh where per

Table 4
Level of Water Supply in Sample Class I Towns in Different States in 1986-87

State	No. of Sample Class I Towns	Actual Supply: Total Water Supply (MLD)	Actual Supply: Per Capita Supply LPCD
Andhra Pradesh	18	444.80	134.45
Assam	1	1.26	30.48
Bihar	3	19.91	60.60
Gujarat	9	364.77	132.91
Haryana	7	97.15	122.90
Himachal Pradesh	1	11.80	144.45
Jammu and Kashmir	1	19.50	32.67
Karnataka	11	239.62	108.18
Kerala	5	103.30	106.38
Madhya Pradesh	4	139.61	185.46
Maharashtra	21	768.94	174.62
Manipur	1	21.00	262.78
Meghalaya	1	4.00	57.14
Orissa	2	82.50	239.07
Punjab	6	264.41	170.04
Rajasthan	5	114.10	107.57
Tamil Nadu	14	221.20	93.57
Tripura	1	15.30	250.82
Uttar Pradesh	20	847.09	192.48
West Bengal	2	20.56	106.05
Total	133	3739.00	142.34

Source: *Upgrading Municial Services: Norms and Financial Implications*, National Institute of Urban Affairs (NIUA), 1988.

Table 5
Percentage of Class I Towns Having Different Levels of Water Supply

Water levels (lpcd)	No. of Urban Centres	Percentage to Total
Under 50	24	18.32
50-100	25	19.08
100-150	39	29.77
150-200	20	15.26
200-250	11	8.39
250 +	12	9.16
All	131	100.00

Source: *Upgrading Municipal Services — Norms and Financial Implications*, Vol.I, National Institute of Urban Affairs, 1988.

Table 6
Population covered by Piped Water Supply and Per Capita Demand and Supply of Water by City Size (1986-87)

City Size (Population in 1000)	No. of Sample Cities	Populattion covered	Per capita Supply
100-200	88	73.66	115.66
200-300	21	69.41	151.91
300-400	12	76.50	158.45
400-500	5	73.19	190.73
500-600	7	73.05	131.64
600-700	3	74.46	228.24
700-750	1	93.35	151.74
Total	137	73.78	142.39

Source: Compiled from *Upgrading Municipal Services: Norms and Financial Implication*, November 1988.

Table 7
Total and Per Capita Water Supply Situation in Class II Towns in 1979-80 and 1988 in Major States

Sl. No.	States	No. of IInd Class Towns 1979	1988	Total Water Supply (MLD) 1979	1988	Per capita Water Supply (Litres/daily 1979	1988
1.	Andhra Pradesh	17	26	111.14	111.03	104.16	49.00
2.	Assam	5	-	10.029	-	56.28	--
3.	Bihar	9	10	66.68	43.11	139.35	49.00
4.	Gujarat	18	23	118.80	151.56	97.07	79.00
5.	Goa	1	2	7.50	13.00	126.56	82.00
6.	Haryana	9	6	110.83	39.74	157.24	77.00
7.	Himachal Pradesh	1	1	14.00	23.61	252.85	282.00
8.	Karnataka	9	12	44.47	64.37	75.75	62.00
9.	Kerala	7	7	57.87	88.74	124.79	182.00
10.	Madhya Pradesh	14	23	145.97	162.84	167.61	82.00
11.	Maharashtra	19	22	381.75	191.82	310.49	101.00
12.	Mizoram	-	1	-	2.17	--	16.00
13.	Orissa	1	5	8.50	35.09	116.96	73.00
14.	Punjab	8	10	62.98	112.49	124.71	129.00
15.	Rajasthan	7	10	52.84	44.80	108.22	51.00
16.	Tamil Nadu	27	39	162.35	200.91	92.42	64.00
17.	Uttar Pradesh	20	27	122.70	239.73	91.47	99.00
18.	West Bengal	18	17	54.56	97.14	47.24	64.00
	TOTAL	190	241	1532.97	1622.15	125.27	78.00

Source: Surveys in the same name of CPCB for Class II Towns as mantioned in Table 3.

capita supply is as high as 282 litres per day, only four more states have a per capita supply above 100 lpcd. In states like Andhra Pradesh, Bihar and Rajasthan, the per capita supply is only around 50 litres per day. The CPCB survey has also shown that although availability of raw water is a very important factor in the city water supply system and although 168 out of 241 towns are situated in major river basins, the average per capita supply in these towns is the same as in case of towns situated in coastal or non-basin areas. It is also evident that the level of economic development of the state is not very material unless importance is given to this sector and financial allocation is made accordingly.

Metropolitan Cities

The availability of water supply services in metropolitan cities is much better than in Class I and Class II towns or the state as a whole, although there is sharp inter-city disparities. The figures in Table 8 show that cities like Madras and Bangalore have a far lower per capita supply than other metro centres and these are much below the average for all metro cities. While in Bangalore the supply reaches 100 per cent of the population, in Madras the coverage is 85 per cent. Cities like Calcutta, Bombay, Delhi and Ahmedabad score high both in terms of percentage of population covered and the per capita supply level.

However, the better service level in some metro cities is no index of the extent of differential distribution of the services among different areas within the city. There is a significant intra-city variation in the level of services provided. Banerjee, for example, has shown that the per capita availability of water is close to 'normative standard' in Calcutta but it is far below that outside the city proper, even in 1986. It is also worth noting that there exists an inter-ward disparity in terms of per capita availability (Banerjee, 1990). In 1979, Mishra and Sarma in their survey on Delhi found that per capita supply by the Municipal Corporation of Delhi (MCD) was 40 gallons per day (gpcd) or 180 lpcd, whereas in the New Delhi Municipal Committee (NDMC) area, the supply was 78 gpcd or 350 lpcd. Even within their respective jurisdictions there is differential level of access to services across localities. The same survey shows that within the MCD area, the South Delhi Zone (III) had the highest average monthly consumption of water (56.22 kl) per

Table 8
Status of Water Supply Situation in Metropolitan Cities (1988)

Name of the City	Estimated Population	Total Water supply (MLD)	Per Capita Water Supply (lpcd)	Population Covered in Percentage
Bombay	10331657	2143.0	207.8	99
Delhi	7464000	1848.0	258.0	96
Calcutta	4532213	976.1	226.7	95
Hyderabad	2700570	652.5	241.6	100
Ahmedabad	2648695	477.0	200.1	90
Bangalore	3820089	435.0	113.9	100
Kanpur	1770154	407.0	307.0	75
Lucknow	1056225	277.0	262.3	100
Madras	3880796	250.0	75.8	85
Nagpur	1549517	240.0	206.5	75
Pune	1527207	202.3	169.8	78
Jaipur	1350844	168.0	155.5	80
Total	42632367	8075.9	189.4	93

Source: *Status of Water supply and Waste Water Collection Treatment and Disposal in Class I Cities - 1988*, Central Pollution Control Board, 1989-90.

connection (Misra and Sarma, 1979).

A recent study conducted by the Delhi Water Supply and Sewage Disposal Undertaking (DWS & SDU) corroborates the above findings. It shows that the availability of water in colonies inhabited by affluent people is much higher compared to the poor localities. While 60 to 70 per cent of the households in the posh colonies record consumption levels of more than 30 kl per month, the position is just the opposite in the other category of colonies where 70 to 75 per cent of consumers do with less than 30 kl per month and nearly 50 per cent of water connections in these localities have a supply level of less than 20 kl per month.

It becomes clear from the above analysis that the availability of water is a function of the size class of the city. In the larger cities more people have access to an organised water supply system and the per capita supply is higher. In a big city even with differential distribution, the water supply level in a lowly served area is higher than the average supply in a town of a lower order. This access to better services in metro or higher order cities works as a very significant pull factor for migrants from lower order towns who move to larger ones in the same state.

II. Sanitation Facilities

a. Level of Sanitation Facilities in Urban India

The sanitation facilities comprise the following components: latrines, the sewerage/drainage system for disposal of sewage and sullage water and solid waste disposal facilities. The level of sanitation facilities in any state, or city, is to be assessed by taking into account the existing level of these three components. But the CPHEEO and NSS have provided data on the latrine facilities alone to determine the status of sanitation.

The population covered by latrine facilities as evident from the Decade Programme review by CPHEEO, has increased from 25 per cent in 1981 to 43.50 per cent in 1988 (Table 9). In other words, at the all India level the uncovered population has decreased from 75 to nearly 56 per cent. In many states like Haryana, Arunachal Pradesh and UTs like Andaman-Nicobar and Chandigarh, the sanitation programme has achieved 100 per cent population coverage, although for some states (almost all north-eastern states and J & K, etc.) the achievement is not even 10 per cent. It is also to be noticed that some of the prosperous states like Punjab, Maharashtra, Gujarat and West Bengal have not done very well in this regard. Interestingly again, only 32 per cent of total population are covered by the sanitation facilities even in a state like Kerala. In a small state like Arunachal Pradesh the figures show that achievement has been very good. It is also to be noted that performances of the states like Jammu and Kashmir, Assam, Tamil Nadu, Uttar Pradesh and Pondicherry in terms of coverage of population over this eight-year period has been either nil or very marginal. Even with the efforts by the central and state governments for total sanitation in major towns, a large section of the urban population is still has no access to environmentally safe sanitation facilities.

Information regarding types of latrine facilities is available from NSSO 38th Round (1983). It shows that nearly 63 per cent of the urban population had access to some kind of sanitation facilities whereas 37 per cent did not have any latrine facility at all (see Table 10). The higher level of coverage in the NSSO data as compared to the CPHEEO figures for an equivalent period based on Decade programme performance record, may be attributed to the former's inclusion of service latrines in the former which have been excluded in the CPHEEO data. The reason may be that service latrines do not conform to the sanitation standard set by the Decade Programme as mentioned earlier. Table 10 also shows that in almost all the states, even among those providing toilet facilities, larger percentage have shared facilities.

Table 9
Percentage of Urban Population covered by Sanitation (Latrine only) Facilities over States/Union Territories

State/UTs	Sanitation Coverage				
	1981	1985	1986	1987	1988
Andhra Pradesh	11.21	10.88	15.94	15.94	19.98
Arunachal Pradesh	47.6	38.46	100.00	100.00	100.00
Assam	14.65	15.72	15.72	15.72	15.72
Bihar	19.95	22.88	38.40	38.40	38.79
Goa	17.04	13.27	23.75	28.33	28.73
Gujarat	41.21	37.99	78.33	79.22	77.51
Haryana	12.38	28.38	31.84	35.34	100.00
Himachal Pradesh	15.33	13.66	20.00	18.57	21.72
Jammu & Kashmir	7.94	7.75	7.13	6.87	7.05
Karnataka	3.73	38.38	55.97	59.86	57.19
Kerala	6.29	28.17	29.67	29.60	31.78
Madhya Pradesh	5.10	7.81	9.66	9.73	10.32
Maharashtra	38.28	39.73	40.00	62.22	62.40
Manipur	N A	0.80	9.43	9.43	8.56
Meghalaya	N A	N A	21.50	20.90	21.28
Mizoram	N A	1.51	1.51	1.43	2.04
Nagaland	N A	N A	N A	6.21	6.21
Orissa	9.32	9.42	26.84	26.84	33.78
Punjab	35.28	48.46	51.05	51.03	52.36
Rajasthan	4.16	9.59	9.58	9.06	76.22
Sikkim	N A	32.92	26.81	26.02	33.33
Tamil Nadu	46.38	47.49	47.00	47.39	47.78
Tripura	4.42	13.15	11.33	11.33	11.33
Uttar Pradesh	12.86	14.01	13.78	13.98	14.04
West Bengal	15.50	19.43	39.49	39.60	32.12
Andaman & Nicobar	40.00	55.00	100.00	100.00	100.00
Chandigarh	94.11	100.00	100.00	100.00	100.00
Delhi	64.11	73.33	81.19	86.44	87.21
Pondicherry	37.97	39.88	38.56	38.60	38.84
All India	25.04	28.39	36.57	40.37	43.51

Source: Ministry of Urban Development, New Delhi, Central Public Health and Environmental Engineering Organisation (CPHEEO).

Table 10
Percentage Distribution of Household by Latrine Facilities in States and Union Territories

	Households with			Type of latrines:			
	No Latrine	Using Shared Latrine	Having Excessive Latrine	Service Latrine	Septic Tank	Flush System	Others
Andhra Pradesh	51.77	61.91	38.04	25.86	51.00	19.19	3.94
Assam	6.99	34.69	65.31	39.02	34.60	2.36	24.00
Bihar	45.21	45.63	45.37	24.44	62.22	7.14	6.20
Gujarat	34.12	60.84	39.16	12.37	43.00	43.29	1.33
Haryana	42.80	42.84	57.56	89.56	5.59	33.22	1.64
Arunachal Pradesh	39.13	49.16	50.64	4.79	16.29	44.16	2.71
J & K	20.66	59.69	40.31	83.04	4.23	7.38	6.15
Karnataka	44.20	54.10	45.90	9.95	20.54	61.79	7.78
Kerala	62.67	23.44	76.56	3.53	53.00	6.52	36.94
M.P.	47.48	51.43	48.57	42.49	27.08	19.46	10.99
Maharashtra	62.61	72.16	72.84	19.03	30.48	48.47	2.02
Manipur	1.90	62.76	37.24	32.77	5.54	3.67	58.83
Meghalaya	7.60	--	--	40.21	32.30	8.65	18.83
Nagaland	3.23	96.77	3.23	53.09	41.37	0.65	4.89
Orissa	56.13	38.23	61.77	25.71	61.94	7.21	5.14
Punjab	39.40	54.13	54.69	46.99	4.44	49.45	4.06
Rajasthan	49.07	56.13	43.81	37.09	25.17	30.69	7.05
Sikkim	28.40	62.09	37.91	14.24	84.11	0.75	0.89
Tamil Nadu	47.64	60.48	39.52	34.82	62.47	35.84	1.86
U.P.	33.62	53.69	46.31	59.22	8.96	29.59	2.23
West Bengal	13.29	62.29	37.71	19.04	61.02	7.85	12.09
Andaman & Nicobar	30.39	58.84	41.16	37.49	55.81	4.76	1.92
Chandigarh	14.31	25.85	74.15	4.89	1.30	93.80	--
Delhi	27.28	50.62	49.38	19.35	6.35	68.22	6.08
Goa, Daman & Diu	52.21	42.48	57.02	2.34	3.34	48.98	15.27
Mizoram	10.29	30.75	69.25	4.16	10.27	0.59	84.98
Pondicherry	66.54	52.39	47.61	13.36	61.15	25.49	--
All India	36.82	57.60	42.40	28.62	32.72	31.86	6.80

Source: "Access of Urban Poor to Basic Amenities", Amitabh Kundu, 1990, unpublished report based on NSSO-38th Round (1983).

In 17 out of 27 states and UTs surveyed more than half the population is without exclusive facilities. Even in prosperous states like Maharahstra, Gujarat and middle level states like West Bengal, more than sixty per cent of urban population does not have the privilege of toilet facilities of their own. It is also to be noted that as in case of water supply mere access to sanitation facilities do not ensure quality of services. Table 10 also shows the type of facilities available to the urban population in different states. A large percentage of the population have access to service latrines. In states like Haryana and Jammu and Kashmir, more than 80 per cent of the population use service latrines. Even in the capital city, Delhi, nearly 20 per cent of the population are using this type of facility.

It becomes clear from the above that the status of the state in terms of economic standard or industrial performance does not unduly affect the quality of sanitation facilities available to the people. This sector needs much more attention and the necessary financial allocation for removing service latrines which creates environmental hazards and definitely affects the health standard of the people of the state, and installing suitable substitutes.

b. Sewerage System

As early as in 1964, the water supply and sewerage systems were treated as independent entities which was wrong. To quote the proceeding of the seminar (GOI, 1964) "unfortunately, the practices in the country through past several decades has established a notion that water supply and sewerage systems should be treated as two separate and independent entities. It is because of this the very few waste water disposal projects are taken up concurrently with water supply projects. As a result waste water flows into open water sources which causes environmental hazards."

It was estimated that only 30 per cent of the total urban population were covered with sewerage facilities in 1964. The average figure had risen to 33 per cent of the total urban population by 1988 (National Commission on Urbanisation, NCU, Vol. II). At the same time, the distribution of sewerage facilities is very skewed according to the NCU. The upper income groups generally have a 100 per cent coverage. The urban poor, on the other hand, may have little or no coverage at all. In addition, most of the small and medium towns have no sewerage systems. The NCU (1988) concluded, "If the water supply system is unequal and unjust, being highly biased in favour of the rich, the sewerage system is even more unjust and even more highly biased in favour of the rich." The seriousness of the problem is also evident from other studies.

The Central Pollution Control Board has surveyed sewerage and sewage disposal systems in Class I and Class II towns over two different reference periods, viz. 1978-79 and 1989-90. The state level scenario as in 1988 has been shown in Table 11. Out of 212 Class I towns surveyed, only 71 centres had waste water collection systems. In terms of population coverage, the percentage figure was 63.88. It indicates that even though only 33.5 per cent of all class I towns had the facilities, a larger percentage of the population in these cities had access to the service. In case of class II towns only 32 per cent of the 19 responding cities had the facilities. The corresponding figures were 43.4 per cent and 12.46 per cent out of 142 Class I cities and 190 Class II towns, respectively, for the year 1978 when the first survey was carried out.

Moreover, a high degree of inter-state disparity in the coverage level of population by sewerage facilities as existing in the year 1988 (the year of second survey) is evident from Table 11 with respect to two size class of towns. Among other states and UTs, only Karnataka, Maharashtra, Tamil Nadu and Delhi can boast of having nearly or more than 70 per cent population covered by sewage facilities in Class I and Class II towns, while in the states like Bihar and Kerala and the UT of Pondicherry the coverage level is as low as 20 to 25 per cent only.

The data on sewerage system for sample urban centres belonging to different size class are available from the NIUA survey mentioned earlier. It shows that only on an average 31.5 per cent of all urban centres have a sewerage system and barring a few prosperous states like Haryana and Punjab where the situation is very good, in most other urban centres the population covered by sewerage facilities, in percentage terms, is either nil or very low (Table 12). On the other hand, a small state like Himachal Pradesh has 100 per cent coverage but it has only one sample town.

Even among the centres where sewerage facilities exist the percentage of residents covered by these facilities is low. According to the same survey 13 out of 50 or 26 per cent of urban centres reporting sewerage facilities have 20-40 per cent people covered by the facilities. Only 5 centres or 10 per cent among all size class of cities have more than 80 per cent population covered (NIUA, 1988).

Table 11
Statewise Details of Sewered Population in Class I and Class II Towns in 1988-89 and 1978-79

	Total No. of Towns		No of responses about sewerage systems		Estimated population of these towns (1988)		Sewered Population of these towns	
	Class I	Class II	Class I	Class II	Class I	Class II	Class I	Class II
	1	2	3	4	5	6	7	8
Andhra Pradesh	17	26	7	1	4395613	72059	2522482 (57.39)	--
Bihar	11	10	1	0	1186180	--	237236 (20.00)	--
Gujarat	11	23	7	2	6017337	172629 (60.74)	3654843 (59.41)	102552
Goa	0	2	0	1	--	96246	--	57748 (60.00)
Himachal Pradesh	0	1	0	0	--	--	--	--
Haryana	9	6	9	4	1966597	402169	1178787 (59.94)	196533 (48.87)
Jammu & Kashmir	2	0	--	--	--	--	--	--
Karnataka	14	12	5	0	5400246	--	4269330 (77.62)	--
Kerala	6	12	2	0	1221025	--	263400 (21.57)	--
Maharashtra	29	22	13	2	16639319	168323	12000727 (72.12)	--
Meghalaya	1	0	--	0	--	--	--	--
Manipur	1	0	--	0	--	--	--	--

Cont'd...165

	1	2	3	4	5	6	7	8
Madhya Pradesh	14	23	4	2	2115470 (45.32)	216512 (23.11)	958789	50044
Mizoram	0	1	0	0	–	–	–	–
Orissa	6	5	1	0	365776	–	135337 (37.00)	– –
Punjab	7	10	3	3	1154303	206116	461721 (40.00)	68681 (33.32)
Rajasthan	11	10	–	0	–	–	-	–
Tamil Nadu	19	39	4	2	5834952	155953	4050534 (69.42)	45561 (29.21)
Tripura	1	0	–	0	–	–	–	–
Uttar Pradesh	29	27	6	2	4848364	138985	2304484 (47.53)	–
West Bengal	21	17	6	0	1338966	–	591120 (44.15)	–
Chandigarh	1	0	1	0	391346	–	391346 (100.00)	–
Delhi	1	0	1	0	7464000	–	5598000 (75.00)	–
Pondicherry	1	0	1	0	186675	–	46669 (25.00)	–
Total	212	241	71	19	60526169	1628992	38664805	521119
(Per cent)							(63.88)	(32.00)
Position in 1978-79	142	190	142	190	60252039	12769930	26920970 (43.4)	1590925 (12.46)

Source: Compiled from (i) *Status of Water Supply and Waste Water Collection, Treatment and Disposal in Class I Towns*, 1979-89 and 1988-89; (ii) The Study of the same name for Class II Towns -- CPCB, 1978-79 and 1988-89.

Table 12
Statewise Distribution of Responding Urban Centres Having Sewerage System 1986-87

State	Responding Urban Centres	Urban Centres Reporting Sewerage Systems	
		No.	%
Andhra Pradesh	19	6	31.6
Assam	3	0	0.0
Bihar	4	0	0.0
Gujarat	9	2	22.2
Goa	1	0	0.0
Haryana	7	6	85.7
Himachal Pradesh	1	1	100.0
Jammu & Kashmir	2	0	0.0
Karnataka	13	5	38.5
Kerala	6	0	0.0
Madhya Pradesh	5	1	20.0
Maharashtra	22	7	31.8
Manipur	1	0	0.0
Meghalaya	1	0	0.0
Nagaland	1	0	0.0
Orissa	5	0	0.0
Punjab	6	6	100.0
Rajasthan	10	3	30.0
Tamil Nadu	14	2	14.2
Tripura	1	0	0.0
Uttar Pradesh	23	11	47.8
West Bengal	5	0	0.0
All/Average	159	50	31.5

Source: *Upgrading Municipal Services: Norms and Financial Implications*, Vol. I, NIUA, p. 30.

c. Solid Waste Management

Solid waste management is another aspect of sanitation that is neglected in most of the urban localities. The sources of solid waste in any urban area are domestic, industrial, commercial and municipal. Management of solid waste is carried out in three stages, viz., collection, transportation and disposal. There is a large gap between the level of waste generated and that disposed in all size-class of towns. The NIUA survey shows that nearly 27 per cent of the urban refuse generated cannot be collected and disposed of by the municipalities. However, it must be mentioned that although there is a large disparity between refuse generation and disposal in all classes of urban centres, this aspect of sanitation (disposal) is better available to people than the other aspects, viz., latrine facilities and sewerage/drainage systems. It is observed from Table 13 that in all categories of urban centres more than 65 per cent of the waste generated is disposed of.

Table 13
Refuse Disposal Level as Proportion to Refuse Generation by Size Class of Cities, 1986-87

Size Class	No. of Responding Urban Centres	Average Per capita Refuse (grams/day)		
		Generation	Disposal	% disposal (as proportion to generation)
I	98	302.8	217.6	71.9
II	27	479.9	319.10	66.5
III	13	375.8	288.9	76.9
IV	6	483.8	354.4	73.3
V	7	413.7	341.4	82.5
VI	2	294.4	203.4	69.1
All/Av.	153	377.8	273.8	72.5

Source: (NIUA) *Upgrading Municipal Services: Norms and Financial Implications* Vol.I, 1988

III. Slum Localities

Any discussion on the availability of two basic facilities like water supply and sanitation will remain incomplete without focusing on their availability in slum localities which comprise more than one-third and in some cases even half the urban population.

Recent data pertaining to this at national level are available from two sources: Census of India 1981 which covered the slum population in class I and Class II towns of twelve major states and the other is the NIUA survey conducted in 1983 in 79 cities and towns across 14 states.

Table 14 shows the facilities available in slum localities according to the 1981 census. At the all-India level more than 50 per cent slums have tap water facilities and more slums are served by public hydrants in Class II towns than in Class I towns. As far as latrine facilities are concerned, more slums in Class II towns have both private latrines as well as community latrine facilities than in Class I towns. However, it must be remembered that the service latrine has been included as a category but these figures do not indicate what percentage of the population in a slum is covered by this facility. The availability of better water supply and sanitation facilities in slums in Class II towns compared to those in Class I towns may be because there are fewer slums in Class II towns than in Class I towns. The latter account for 85 per cent of the total number of slums in the country.

Although, according to the census data there is a reasonable level of these services in the slum areas, the existence of such facilities does not necessarily indicate easy availability to the slum population. In terms of other indicators like distance of water source from the house sites and the quantity and quality of water available, the services have deteriorated over the years. A substantial section of the urban poor fall outside the public water supply system and has to depend upon unprotected sources, which do not always provide water fit for human consumption. Moreover, the public water supply in very often is erratic and much below the minimum level of requirement.

The NIUA survey conducted in the latter part of 1988 among 23,263 households in 589 slums, spread over 79 cities and towns, covering 14 states and Union Territories, throws light on these aspects. It reveals a hopeless situation regarding access to basic services for the slum people. Table 15 shows that out of the total number of *bastees* (slums) surveyed, 59 per cent have piped water supply, 39 per cent depend on Mark II hand pumps and 27 per cent still make do with shallow hand pumps. The table further shows that while the average number of person served by a tap is nearly twice the norm recommended by slum improvement programme (usually 150 persons per stand post), the number is more than ten times in case of Mark II hand-pumps. In such a scenario the labour and time spent by the slum people, especially the women and children, in fetching water can be imagined. Table 16 shows the availability of toilet and solid waste disposal facilities in selected *bastees* in different states. While only 29 per cent of *bastees* have toilets for women and 28 per cent for men, 41 per cent have rubbish depots. In other *bastees* the rubbish is thrown anywhere.

The inevitable outcome is environmental insanitation leading to severe health problems. As the recent UNICEF report shows "acute diarrhoeal incidence in urban areas in India is estimated to be 500

Table 14
Availability of Civic Services in Slum Areas

Sl. No.	States	Size Class of Town	No. of Slums	Private Latrines (water-borne service)	Community Latrines	Tap Points/ public hydrants
	India	Total	6741	38.02	30.20	58.02
		I	5787	32.69	29.31	54.36
		II	954	70.34	35.64	80.19
1.	A.P.	Total	850	75.76	55.06	84.82
		I	659	73.75	52.96	82.85
		II	191	82.72	62.30	91.62
2.	Bihar	Total	295	93.90	12.54	85.08
		I	258	97.67	12.40	86.05
		II	37	67.57	13.51	78.38
3.	Gujarat	Total	302	37.75	48.34	80.13
		I	197	34.01	34.01	77.16
		II	105	44.76	75.24	85.71
4.	Haryana	Total	117	31.62	10.26	45.30
		I	103	30.10	9.71	44.66
		II	14	42.86	14.29	50.00
5.	J & K	Total	12	16.67	N.A.	100.00
		I	12	16.67	N.A.	100.00
		II	--	--	--	--
6.	Karnataka	Total	311	17.36	27.65	54.66
		I	256	13.67	25.00	50.00
		II	55	34.55	40.00	76.36
7.	M.P.	Total	416	97.60	0.96	91.11
		I	233	100.00	1.72	95.28
		II	183	94.54	--	85.79
8.	Maharashtra	Total	1,478	19.22	48.44	60.62
		I	1,392	16.67	48.71	59.84
		II	86	60.47	44.19	73.26
9.	Rajasthan	Total	141	3.55	1.42	5.67
		I	136	2.21	--	2.94
		II	5	40.00	40.00	80.00
10.	Tamil Nadu	Total	1,222	29.71	27.17	61.87
		I	1,114	26.66	26.75	60.32
		II	108	61.11	31.48	77.78
11.	U. P.	Total	249	42.17	29.72	63.86
		I	202	37.62	25.74	63.86
		II	47	61.70	46.81	63.83
12.	West Bengal	Total	1,348	20.18	11.80	19.58
		I	1,225	14.53	11.59	14.69
		II	123	76.42	13.82	68.29

Source: *Census of India* 1981; Occasional Paper No.3, 1988.

Table 15
Accessibility of Water Supply in Bastees

State/Union Territory	No. of Bastees	Percentage of bastis having access to		
		Shallow hand-pump	Mark II hand-pump	Taps
Andhra Pradesh	111	19	83	81
Assam	12	58	8	8
Delhi	8	88	25	88
Gujarat	104	50	6	55
Haryana	9	56	100	89
Himachal Pradesh	5	--	--	80
Jammu & Kashmir	20	--	--	95
Karnataka	3	100	--	100
Maharashtra	53	6	21	49
Madhya Pradesh	2	--	100	100
Orissa	139	23	51	50
Punjab	56	43	50	34
Pondicherry	31	3	--	87
Rajasthan	4	--	75	75
Tripura	8	38	50	63
West Bengal	24	4	--	38
Total	589	27	39	59
Average number of persons per facility		523	1661	315

Source: *Basic Services and the Urban Poor - NIUA Study series No. 46*, 1991.

per 1000 among infants and 200 per 1000 among pre-school children and nearly 3 lakh urban children die annually due to diarrhoeal dehydration" (USAID, 1988). The figures are no doubt alarming. Recurrence of cholera and gasteroenteritis epidemics in poor localities in Delhi and in other cities shows that these diseases have become a part of the poor man's life.

In addition to the above, direct impact on health, the cumulative social and economic loss in terms of mandays lost due to health problems and the time and energy spent especially by women and children in fetching water is colossal. It is estimated that a total of 73 million workdays are lost every year due to water related diseases. The cost of treating these and the loss in production amount to Rs. 600 crores a year.

Table 16
Sanitation and Garbage Disposal Facilities in Bastees

State/Union Territory	No. of Bastees	% of Bastees with community toilets Men	Women	% Bastees with rubbish depots
Andhra Pradesh	111	23	40	65
Assam	12	17	--	25
Delhi	8	88	88	50
Gujarat	104	41	41	7
Himachal Pradesh	5	--	--	20
Haryana	5	44	33	11
Jammu & Kashmir	20	45	10	--
Karnataka	3	--	--	100
Madhya Pradesh	2	--	--	--
Maharashtra	53	87	83	92
Orissa	139	4	3	56
Punjab	56	--	4	13
Pondicherry	31	35	35	39
Rajasthan	4	--	--	--
Tripura	8	--	--	--
West Bengal	24	50	50	29
Total	589	28	29	41

Source: *Basic Services and the Urban Poor - NIUA Study Series No. 46*, 1991.

Conclusion

In conclusion some of the major observations from the foregoing analysis may be briefly recapitulated. The studies conducted by different agencies at different point of time reiterate that the situation in urban water supply and sanitation facilities is precarious and it is deteriorating with the increasing rate of urbanisation. Even with the emphasis in the Decade Programme on providing these services to the entire urban population, much headway has not been made. It is also noticed that the available services are not evenly distributed. Cities of higher order are better served than those of lower order and within a city there is large-scale differential distribution of the services among different localities and among different income groups.

The recently published Eighth Five-Year Plan document also observes, "Provision of drinking water and sanitation including solid and liquid waste management facilities in urban areas has been inadequate". The Plan has emphasised the need for extending safe drinking water facilities to the remaining urban population so as to achieve 100 per cent coverage by the turn of century. It has also specified standards of 125 lpcd for urban areas served with piped water supply and underground sewerage system and 70 lpcd for other urban areas without any underground sewerage system. It has specified 40 lpcd for towns with spot sources/standposts and also insists on at least one source for 20 families within a maximum walking distance of 100 metres (Eighth Five-Year Plan, 1991-95). It has also put emphasis on converting all dry latrines into low-cost sanitary latrines, so that the present system of scavenging is completely eliminated in urban areas.

Keeping in view the objective of bringing 94.03 per cent of total urban population under protected water supply, the Plan provides an outlay of total Rs. 16,711.03 crores which is no doubt much higher than the allocations in earlier Plans. But it must be mentioned that out of Rs. 5968 crores of central sector allocation only Rs. 488 crores or a little more than 8 per cent is earmarked for the urban sector. If the allocations from respective state governments for the urban sector are also low then it is doubtful whether the targets would be meet by the end of the Plan period.

NOTES

1. The targets of the programme for urban India was set as follows:
   Water Supply: Expected coverage of 100 per cent by piped water with service level of 70 litres to 200 litres (an average of 140 litres per capita per day).
   Sanitation: Overall average of 80 per cent in all cities and towns. Provision for sewerage and sewaage treatment facilities to all Class I cities and low cost sanitation facilities in all other size-class of towns.
   After the mid-term review of the programme in 1985, it was decided to reduce the targets in view of very slow progress of the projects due to resource constraint. The new targets for urban water supply and sanitation coverage were set at 90 per cent and 50 per cent respectively.
2. Minimum levels of per capita supply as recommended by different authorities:
   Zakaria Committee (1963): 157. 5 to 270 lpcd depending on the size-class of urban centres.
   Ministry of Works and Housing (1973): 70 to 200 lpcd
   World Health Organisation: 180 to 200 lpcd in all urban centres.
   Master Plan (India), International Drinking Water Spply and Sanitation Decade (1981): 70 to 250 lpcd with an average of 140 lpcd.
   National Commission on Urbanisation (1988): Minimum 70 lpcd and maximum 100 lpcd for all classes of towns.

BIBLIOGRAPHY

Ahmed Viqar: "Management of Urban Services for the Poor in Pakistan" in *Managing Urban Development Services for the Poor*, Ed. by G. Shabbir Cheema, United Nations Centre for Regional Development, Nagoya, 1984.

Arora P. L: "Metering of Water Supply as a Means of Checking Waste of Water" Paper presented in the seminar *Water Conservation*, March 1991, New Delhi.

Central Pollution Control Board: *Status of Water Supply and Waste Water Collection, Treatment and Disposal in Class I Cities,* CPCB, Delhi, 1989.

———: *Status of Water Supply and Waste Water Collection, Treatment and Disposal in Class II Towns - 1988*, CPCB, Delhi, 1989.

Central Board for the Prevention and Control of Water Pollution:- *Waste Water Collection Treatment and Disposal in Class I Cities - Status and Action Plan*, CBPCWP, New Delhi 1979.

———: *Status of Water Supply and Waste Water Collection Treatment and Disposal in Class II Towns of India*, CBPCWP, Delhi, 1979.

Cheema, Shabbir G: *"Managing Urban Development Services for the Poor"* in G. Shabbir Cheema (Ed), *Managing Urban Development Services for the Poor* -- United Nations Centre for Regional Development, Nagoya, Japan.

Finqueiievich Susana: "Innovative Technology for Latin American Mega Cities -- state and Community Involvement. *Cities*, Vol. 7, No. 1, Feb. 1990.

Government of India: *National Water Policy* (Draft), Ministry of Water Resources, New Delhi, 1986.

———: *Master Plan: International DrinkingWater Supply and Sanitation Decade*, Ministry of Works and Housing, New Delhi, 1983.

——— : *Census of India 1981: Occasional Paper No. 3, 1988*, Registrar General, New Delhi.

——— : *Eighth Five-Year Plan Document*, Vol.2. Planning Commission, New Delhi.

Kundu, Amitabh: *Access of Urban Poor to Basic Amenities*, Centre for the Study of Regional Development, Jawaharlal Nehru University, New Delhi, (unpublished report), 1990.

Makinwa P K, Adebuso, "Urban Services for the Poor in Nigeria" in G. Shabbir Cheema (Ed) *Managing Urban Development Services for the Poor*, United Nations Centre for Regional Development, Nagoya, 1984.

Misra, Girish K and Sharma K S R N: *Distribution and Differential Allocation of Public Utilities in Urban Delhi*, Indian Institute of Public Administration, New Delhi, 1979.

Mitsuhiko Hosaka: "Urban Services in Indonesia: A focus on Kampong Improvement Programme" in Shabbir Cheema (Ed) *Managing Urban Development Services for the Poor*.

National Sample Survey Organization: *42nd Round, No, 361*, NSSO, 1986-87.

National Commission on Urbanization *Report Vol. II*, NCU, New Delhi, 1988,

National Institute of Urban Affairs: *Basic Services and the urban Poor*, NIUA Study Series No. 46, NIUA, New Delhi 1991.

National Institute of Urban Affairs: *Upgrading Municipal Services - Norms and Financial Implications*, Volume II, NIUA, New Delhi, 1989.

Onibukun Adepoju, G: "Poverty as a Constraint to Citizens Participations in Urban Development in Developing Countries -- A Case Study", *Urban Studies* Vol. 27, No 3, 1990.

World Health Organization: *Community Water Supply and Excreta Disposal in South East Asia*, WHO, New Delhi, 1977.

14

Status of Basic Services in Indian Cities

Arup Mitra

RAPID population growth in cities often exerts pressure on the existing infrastructure, housing and other basic amenities. One way of examining the status of basic services in the context of rapid urbanisation is to consider the size of the population residing in the slums, for slums by definition are a manifestation of the inadequacy of such facilities.[1] The major focus of this paper is on the nature of relationship between the size of a city and the percentage of slum population. Besides, we have delineated some factors governing the growth of slums. Empirical evidence tends to suggest that rapid urbanisation creates considerable urban disamenities.

The organisation of the paper is as follows: Section I makes an evaluation of the existing data on slum population. Section II examines various estimates of population with practically no access to basic amenities. Some of the major factors explaining the growth of slums in the cities are highlighted in Section III and the findings are summarised in section IV.

Data-base

The available information on the number of slum dwellers or other related aspects of slums even in a particular city suffers from the drawbacks of non-uniformity and non-comparability over time. Similar problems arise in cross-sectional comparison, too, the basic reason being the non-availability of slum data from a national level organisation. Again, whatever data are available, relates to class I cities only.

It was in the 1961 Census that an attempt was made to estimate the slum population of Madras city. After that various organisations like National Sample Survey Organisation (NSSO) (1976-77), Census of India (1981), Town and Country Planning Organisation (TCPO) (1985) and Task Force on Housing and Urban Development (1983) have collected data on slums.

Since we are trying to measure the magnitude of slum population based on the above sources, it may be worthwhile to examine the definition of slum used therein, so that discrepancies, if any, in the estimates may be attributed to definitional and conceptual differences.

NSSO in its 31st Round Survey (1976-77) covered class I cities in India (i.e., population with 100,000 and above as per 1971 Census) both at the national and state levels. But the survey was limited to the "city proper" and did not include urban agglomerations. Secondly, the survey covered only the "declared slums" in the million-plus (M+) cities whereas in the rest of the class I cities it included the undeclared slums or 'slum like areas' also.[2]

Therefore, the proportion of slum population to total population in the M+ cities cannot be compared with that of other classes of cities as the exclusion of the undeclared slums in the former would obviously underestimate the ratio.

Strictly speaking, the proportion of slum population to total city population even in cities other than the metropolises may not be comparable across states since the criteria chosen by the state agencies for identifying the slums vary across states, thereby making the component of "declared slums" quite different from what would have emerged had the municipal agencies applied uniform criteria for declaring/notifying an area as slum.

However, NSSO's inclusion of 'slum like area' in the survey is likely to neutralise the error due to variations in the definition. Thus the figures for the cities other than the metropolitan ones can be considered comparable.

The National Building Organisation (NBO) provides its estimate at the national and metropolitan city levels. The former has been desegregated according to population-size classes of cities/towns. The information provided by the various state governments/local bodies to the Central Ministry of Works and Housing under the scheme of Environmental Improvement of Slums (EIS) has been used for arriving at the NBO estimates assuming certain growth rates of slum population for each size/class of towns and cities. The figures refer to the year 1981 taking 1971 population as base.

However, the definition of slum seems to be missing in the exercise (Task Force, 1983).

TCPO estimates relate only to "identified slums" in cities/towns under the EIS scheme but not all cities/towns in the urban sector of the states. Though there is some overlap between the TCPO and NBO estimates, the main difference between them is that while the NBO extrapolated the reported data as explained above, the TCPO arrived at its estimates directly based on the slum population figures supplied by the States and Union Territories under the 20-point programme. According to the Task Force apart from the limitation mentioned above regarding its partial coverage of cities/towns in the urban sector of the states, it is neither clear which year the TCPO data corresponds to, nor is the basis of the estimates provided by the state government known. Although estimates have been reported for 1981, the reference year might have been different for some of the cities. The ratio of slum population reported by the states/local bodies irrespective of the time period, is taken to be true for 1981 and on that basis the absolute numbers of slum population have been worked out for individual cities. Again, although the criterion for identifying a slum was mentioned in the EIS scheme whether it was adopted by the State authorities to assess the slum population.

The 1981 Census data suffer on account of two difficulties, namely (a) information on slum population has been collected from the municipal authorities, and (b) in several cities, information on slum population corresponding to each and every slum pocket is not available. Hence it underestimates the ratio of slum population to the total population of the city.

Based on several alternative sets of estimates, the Task Force provided the interval estimates with lower and upper limits of the population. Thus, it may be concluded that different sources of information on slum population suffer from different kinds of problems including the lack of an explicit definition of slum. As a result it is neither possible to make comparison nor is it sensible to predict the direction of bias of one estimate relative to another. However, NSSO data seem to be more organised and systematic as it refers to a particular time period and the method adopted to estimate the slum population is almost uniform for all the class I cities other than the metropolitan ones.

In the next section we make an attempt to examine the magnitude of slum population using the above sources of information.

The data have been analysed at the following three levels: (a) national level; (b) state level and (c) individual city level.

Table 1 presents the proportion of slum population to total urban population at the national level corresponding to different size classes of cities/towns as estimated by NBO, TCPO and NSSO. It also lists the estimates provided by the Task Force. As per the NBO estimate around 19 per cent of the population in urban India lived in slums. Though the NSSO and the TCPO have dealt with all-India figures they have not reported for the entire urban India.

Table 1
Proportion of Slum Population to Total Urban Population at the National Level

Size class of cities/towns	NBO-1981 (% of 1981 Population)	TCPO (% of 1981 Population)	Task Forces (% of 1981 Population)		NSSO-1976-77 (% of 1971 Population)
			Low Estimate	High Estimate	
(1) Less than one lakh	10.66		15.04	19.72	--
(2) 1 lakh - 3 lakh	18.12		17.91	24.59	13.48
(3) 3 lakhs - 1 million	19.56	21.12*			18.00
(4) 1 million and above	30.78	30.32	33.00	38.00	16.95
(5) All classes	18.75	--	20.88	26.33	--

* Combined figure for size classes II and III, i.e., cities with pop. 1 lakh to 1 million)

Note: TCPO estimates refer to those cities/towns where the EIS Scheme was applied.

Source:
1. *Hand Book of Housing Statistics*, 1981, National Building Organisation.
2. NSSO 31st Round Survey (1976-77), *Sarvekshana*, Vol. III, No. 4, April 1980.
3. Task Force on Housing and Urban Development, Part IV, Shelter for the Urban Poor, Planning Commission, 1983.
4. *A Compendium on Indian Slums*, Town and Country Planning Organisation, Ministry of Works and Housing, 1985.

The Task Force had prepared two sets of estimates, i.e., low and high with a view to indicating the possible range in the estimated magnitudes. This exercise was based on available sources of data and other information available in each state. On the basis of the "probable percentage" of slum population in each size class of cities/towns in each State, the slum population has been worked out for different size classes of cities using 1981 population figures.

At the national level, the 'low estimates' of incidence of slum population of the Task Force are almost similar to the NBO figures. However, the 'high estimates' are around five per cent higher than the low estimates (Table 1). At the state level, Maharashtra, West Bengal and Andhra Pradesh followed by Uttar Pradesh, Tamil Nadu, Bihar and Gujarat had a large proportion of slum population as per the Task Force's low and high estimates.

As noted earlier, NSSO does not give aggregate State level data. But it is seen that barring a few States, a substantial percentage of population lives in the slum areas in different size classes of cities.

Table 2
Percentage of Population in Slums by City and Town Size Across States at Different Points of Time

States	NSSO[1] Estimate: 1976-77 (% of 1976-77 Pop.)			TCPO[2] Estimate (% of 1981 Pop.)
	Million plus cities (city-class I)	Cities with pop. 3 lakh-1 million (city class II)	Cities with pop. 1 lakh-3 lakhs (City class III)	
Andhra Pradesh	12.17	40.13	16.38	34.77
Assam	--	--	4.97	17.90
Bihar	--	7.89	5.13	36.70
Gujarat	2.19	15.53	8.53	16.20
Haryana	--	--	5.28	14.69
Jammu & Kashmir	--	--	8.25	--
Karnataka	8.42	5.43	9.36	9.28
Kerala	--	7.91	6.49	7.27
Madhya Pradesh	--	8.83	12.01	--
Maharashtra	9.73	24.98	22.28	29.70
Orissa	--	--	16.52	30.45
Punjab	--	17.61	3.45	27.80
Rajasthan	--	8.42	7.75	23.50
Tamil Nadu	34.33	10.93	8.68	16.80
Uttar Pradesh	8.51	9.31	3.87	32.76
West Bengal	18.96	46.13	15.44	37.04
Chandigarh (UT)			6.90	--
Delhi (UT)	19.40	0.87	--	31.40

Notes: 1. Cities have been classified as per 1971 Census figures on population.
2. TCPO refers to cities and towns where EIS Scheme has been applied, and not the entire urban sector of the states/Union territories.
3. '--' represents non-existence of cities in that category.

Source: 1. NSSO 31st Round Survey (1976-77) on Socio-Economic Condition of the Slum Dwellers.
2. *A Compendium of Indian Slums*, 1985 (see Table 1).

Again the TCPO data confirms the above tendency though it also does not cover the entire urban area as mentioned above (Table 2).

With regard to the proportion of slum population to total city population residing in different size classes of cities (i.e. each with a population of 100,000 and above) the NSSO figures show that except in the case of million plus cities (which are not comparable with the rest) the proportion varies directly with city size. This pattern is evident both at the national level (Table 1) and in a majority of the States (Table 2).

Coming to individual M+ cities, we have a series of alternative estimates from various special surveys.[3] However, we present here the following estimates only: (a) NBO, (b) TCPO, (c) NSSO, (d) Population Census 1981 and (e) Task Force. For the rest of the class I cities, figures from TCPO and 1981 population census have been presented. NSSO estimates are not available for these cities individually, only for groups of cities across states (see Table 2).

Table 3
Incidence of Slum Population in Metropolitan Cities at Different Points of Time

Metropolitan Cities	NSS-Estimate (1976-77 (% of 1976-77 Pop.)	TCPO Estimate (% of 1981 Pop.)	NBO Estimate % of 1981 Pop.)	1981* Census Estimate (% of 1981 Pop.)	Task Forces Estimate (% of 1981 Pop.)	
					Low Estimate	High Estimate
Bombay	9.73	34.30	38.30	27.58	40.00	45.00
Calcutta	18.96	32.90	35.35	30.26	35.00	40.00
Delhi	19.40	31.40	30.19	-	45.00	50.00
Madras	34.33	32.10	31.87	20.26	30.00	35.00
Ahmedabad	2.19	20.30	26.16	0.01	20.00	25.00
Bangalore	8.42	10.40	10.02	2.90	20.00	25.00
Hyderabad	12.17	19.60	21.28	-	20.00	25.00
Kanpur	8.51	37.50	40.31	4.81	40.00	45.00
Jaipur	--	29.10	15.62	4.45	25.00	30.00
Lucknow	--	28.30	38.83	2.03	35.00	40.00
Nagpur	--	31.90	33.90	13.08	30.00	35.00
Pune	--	16.30	17.69	18.42	15.00	20.00

Note: * Incomplete coverage: Bombay, Pune, Madras
Source: See Tables 1 and 2.

Both as per the NBO and the TCPO estimates, Bombay, Calcutta, Delhi, Madras, Kanpur, Nagpur and Lucknow reported a higher incidence of slums (varying between 30 and 40 percentage points – Table 3) than the rest. In the case of Jaipur and Lucknow the estimates are substantially different because the NBO estimate refers to city urban agglomeration whereas the TCPO estimate refers to the Metropolitan Corporation. According to the Task Force's 'low' and 'high' estimates, again, almost the same set of cities (Bombay, Calcutta, Delhi, Madras, Kanpur, Nagpur and Lucknow) appear in the list of high incidence slums.

As expected, compared to other estimates, the NSSO estimates turn out to be substantially lower for metropolitan cities. Even among the metropolises (as per 1971 Census) Bombay was surprisingly far below Madras with an incidence of less than 10 per cent whereas Madras had the highest figure (35%). This is perhaps because the old dilapidated buildings in Bombay, resembling the characteristics of slums (*chawls*) and which possibly are also unique to Bombay, have been excluded from the domain of 'declared slums'.

The following is the comparison of the 1981 population census estimates of slum population for 1979 with the TCPO estimates for 1981. The 1981 census estimates are reported for around 120 class I cities from the State-specific town directories. Out of 105 cities for which we have both TCPO and census estimates, in almost 35 cities the census figures have been substantially lower than those of the TCPO and in around 10 cities the reverse is the case. In the rest of the 60 cities the margin of difference varies from 0 to 6 per cent in either direction, which is not significant. In general, the census estimates are lower than the TCPO estimates perhaps because of non-availability of information for some of the slum pockets of the cities as indicated in the town directories, e.g., Bombay, Pune, Thane, Dhulia and Madras. Besides, the census estimates as mentioned above refer to the 1979 slum population whereas the TCPO figures correspond to 1981. This could have been another reason for underestimation of slum incidence in the 1981 census, as in both TCPO and census estimates of slum incidence the denominator corresponds to 1981 population. The correlation between the TCPO and census estimates is 0.43 which cannot be considered high.

TCPO reports the percentage of slum population for around 176 class I cities in India. We have cross-classified the cities by their population size and size classes formed by the percentage of population living in the slums. Table 4 indicates that more than 55 per cent of the relatively big cities had a higher incidence of slum population. On the other hand, nearly 70 per cent of the cities falling in the population size group 100,000 to 300,000 have an incidence of slum population less than 20 per cent. We have conducted a chi-square test to test the association between the attributes, i.e., city size and incidence of slum. At 10 per cent level of significance the calculated value of chi-square is greater than its tabulated value, thus suggesting relationship between the attributes. Results from regression analysis which have been reported in the following section also confirm that a positive relationship exists between city size and the incidence of slum population. NSSO estimates may also be recalled here to strengthen the basis that the cities with population of 300,000 and above but less than one million correspond to a higher proportion of slum population compared to the cities with population of 100,000 and above but less than 300,000 (the exceptions being Karnataka and Madhya Pradesh).

Table 4
Distribution of Cities as per their Population Size and Percentage of Population Residing in Slums

Percentage of Slum Population (TCPO)	City Size			
	500,000 and above	300,000 and above but less than 500,000	100,000 and above but less than 300,000	Total
Less than 10 per cent	8	6	43	57
10 per cent and above but less than 20 per cent	8	6	33	47
20 per cent and above but less than 30 per cent	11	11	21	43
30 per cent and above	10	4	15	29
TOTAL	37	27	112	176

Chi-square = 12.33

Notes: 1. Chi-square test has been conducted to test the association between city size and incidence of slum population. The calculated value is larger than the tabulated value at 10 per cent level of significance asserting the presence of association between the attributes.

2. Million plus cities are not taken as a separate class since some of the cells have no/very few entries.

Source: 1. TCPO, see Tables 1 and 2.

2. Census of India, 1981, Population figures.

In spite of the differences in estimates of slum population by different sources, it is evident that the slum problem is serious in most Class I cities in India. Of the total slum population found in the country in 1981, 26.36 per cent as per the TCPO estimate, lived in the metropolitan cities (12 in number as per the 1981 census), and around 60.18 per cent of the total slum population lived in the class I cities. Distribution of slum population as predicted by TCPO (1985) was likely to move more in favour of the metro cities in 1990, that is, their share in total slum population is likely to go up to around 39 per cent and the share of total class I cities to around 74 per cent. The Task Force also estimated that in 1981 itself the million-plus cities constituted about 40 per cent of the 32 to 40 million slum dwellers in the country.

Another way of quantifying the population with inadequate basic amenities in cities is to examine the distribution of households by the predominant materials of roof, wall and floor of census houses occupied by them. The information on this aspect has been made available from the 1981 population census for around 42 class I cities. In 17 out of 42 class I cities, the proportion of households with walls made of mud, grass, leaves etc., is more than 20 per cent.

Information on the number of households as well as population without electricity or toilet facility in different class I cities is also available from the 1981 census (see Table 5). It indicates that the percentage of households without electricity or toilet facility is extremely high in the class I cities. The proportion of households (and population) without toilet facility seems to be larger than the proportion of households (and population) without electricity except in the case of Uttar Pradesh (urban) and class I cities belonging to the state, Bihar (urban) and some of the class I cities belonging to the state, Kerala (urban) and West Bengal (urban). The association between these two attributes as mentioned in Table 5 is quite high (chi-square = 20.25 which is greater than the tabulated value at one per cent level). Also the correlation coefficient between the percentage of households without electricity and sanitation is 0.55.

It may be further noted that in the cities the percentage of households without electricity or toilet is usually larger than the percentage of population without such facilities. This implies that the size of households without basic amenities is smaller than the size of households having access to it. In other words, there could be more single-member households like pavement dwellers and squatters in the former category. Also the percentage of households with mud-walls or walls made of grass, leaves etc. is smaller than the percentage of households without electricity or sanitation implying that even better quality housing may have slum characteristics in

Table 5

Distribution of Cities as per Size Classes formed by Percentage of Households without Electricity and Sanitation, 1981

Percentage of Households without Toilets	Percentage of Households without Electricity				
	Less than 25 per cent	25 to 35 per cent	35 to 45 per cent	45 per cent and above	Total
Less than 25 per cent	10	10	7	6	33
25 to 35 per cent	20	16	8	6	50
35 per cent and above	9	17	23	25	74
TOTAL	39	43	38	37	157

Chi-square = 20.25

Note: 1. The calculated value of Chi-square is larger than its tabulated value even at 1 per cent level suggesting the presence of association between the attributes.

Source: Census of India, 1981, Table HH-1, Part-A and Table HH-6, Part-A.

terms of inadequate basic amenities. However, information on housing conditions as mentioned above is available only for around 42 class I cities from the 1981 census; therefore, this statement needs to be carefully read. While comparing the percentage of population without electricity or sanitation with that of slum population as per the TCPO estimates, we find that in most of the 121 cities (for which both the sources of information are available) the former exceeded the latter. (Only in a few cities like Patna, Ludhiana, Jalandhar, Jaipur, Kanpur, Varanasi, Meerut, Moradabad, Saharanpur, Rampur and Delhi, the incidence of slum population as per the TCPO estimates turned out to be larger than the percentage of population without electricity or sanitation). This may be partly because non-availability of sanitation or electricity is a major characteristic of a slum. In general the term 'slum' refers to a cluster and that too a cluster of *kutcha* or semi-*pucca* houses with inadequate basic amenities. Therefore, it is quite possible that better quality dwelling units without electricity or sanitation may not come within the purview of 'slums'.

We next examine the extent of shortage of basic amenities in slums. In this regard the NSSO 31st round survey had provided some information which as per Table 6 indicates that the percentage of slum households without the provision of sanitation is quite high specially in the city classes II and III, i.e., around 50 per cent or more of the slum households did not have any access to such facilities, exceptions being Assam, Meghalaya and Maharashtra (Madhya Pradesh and West Bengal partly). Second, it may also be noticed from Table 6 that except in the case of Karnataka, Rajasthan and West Bengal the percentage of slum households without sanitation varies inversely with city size, although the incidence of slum has been found to vary directly with size classes of cities. Similar tendencies are also observed in the case of slum households without drinking water. This is mainly because investment on infrastructure including public convenience etc. is concentrated in the big cities as compared to the small cities/towns.

Inter-city Variations

In the preceding section, we have presented the magnitude of city population with inadequate access to basic amenities. It has been noted that the NSSO data on slum population for cities other than the million-plus ones are better comparable across states than the TCPO or 1981 census figures on slum population in individual cities. In this section, with a view to explaining the variations in the incidence of slum population across cities we have considered mainly the NSSO data. The TCPO data have also been used for regression analysis.

The organisation of this section is as follows: First, certain factors that govern the formation of slums are identified. Second, the available information is examined so as to construct the required variables in the model and finally the empirical results are presented.

The basic factors that govern the formation of slums are the following:

a. Population density per unit square of land and city size representing the demographic pressure.
b. Urban or city in-migration – especially the rural-to-urban.
c. Industrialisation.
d. Informal sector employment.
e. Land policy of the government and so on.

Rapid increase in population due to increasing concentration of economic activities exerts tremendous demographic pressure on the existing infrastructure and resource base of the cities and, therefore, there may arise a shortage of land, housing and basic amenities.

Table 6
Slum Households without Basic Amenities

States	Percentage of slum household without Drinking Water			Percentage of slum household without Sanitation		
	City Class I	City Class II	City Class III	City Class I	City Class II	City Class III
Andhra Pradesh	28.21	9.87	18.68	43.19	57.92	75.90
Assam	-	-	30.76	-	-	19.70
Bihar	-	13.01	13.28	-	63.09	64.79
Gujarat	11.79	30.23	33.03	10.33	30.17	61.69
Haryana	-	-	22.75	-	-	59.84
Jammu & Kashmir	-	-	1.10	-	-	79.70
Karnataka	4.82	8.09	2.54	10.91	65.45	51.92
Kerala		18.90	14.91	-	50.17	59.82
Madhya Pradesh		16.10	8.28	-	31.11	61.03
Maharashtra	4.42	11.78	19.03	9.59	35.50	38.39
Meghalaya	-	-	9.47	-	-	20.52
Orissa			7.03			71.48
Punjab		2.67	2.91		46.41	52.47
Rajasthan		2.54	17.66		73.38	45.49
Tamil Nadu	15.50	32.82	43.29	35.90	48.49	68.62
Uttar Pradesh	19.63	9.90	17.14	9.00	50.87	50.11
West Bengal	2.08	0.00	2.59	0.93	66.22	6.26
Chandigarh			11.47			74.85
Delhi (UT)	7.08	0.00	-	4.50	36.52	-

Note: City class I, II and III refer to cities with population 1 million and above, 3 lakhs to 1 million and 1 lakh to 3 lakhs, respectively.

Source: NSSO 31st Round Survey (1976-77) on Socio-Economic Condition of the Slum Dwellers.

The workers' preference to reside near the work place or the market centre of the city, the limited possibilities for the city to expand –

especially older cities where almost the entire land is already built-up – and escalating material costs and land prices in the face of rising population density compel a large percentage of city population to live in slums.

Migration to the cities from rural as well as from other urban centres adds to their population thereby significantly increasing the demand for land and housing. Even if sufficient accommodation is available at reasonable prices, it may be argued that the rural poor migrating to the cities in search of jobs either for a short while or for long periods, mostly end up in slums.

The activities that the city dwellers engage themselves in also determine the incidence of slum population. If a greater proportion of the working population is engaged in informal sector activities, the income of the workers is less. This reduces the affordability and accessibility of the informal sector workers to land and housing thereby raising the incidence of slum population. Of course, it may so happen that most of the city dwellers are employed in gainful occupations and have sufficient income to pay for healthy accommodation at reasonable prices. But in that case excess demand for land and housing, relative to its supply, raises rents as well as land prices. Rapid increase in industrialisation and commercialisation leads to keener competition for land and, thus, a faster growth of slums. Even the industrial workers living above the poverty line (exclusive of the shelter), could be the inhabitants of slums due to shortage of housing.

In the initial stages, industrialisation and commercialisation lead to an increase in the level of inequality in the urban sector. It tends to get reduced only at a later stage when the share of wage in total income increases substantially.[5] Thus, an increase in relative inequality in the initial phases of industrialisation also leads to an unequal access to land and housing in the cities. Therefore, the slum problem can be identified in the following two ways although our concern is more with the former:

a. slum problem mainly as an employment problem and
b. slum problem simply as a housing problem.

We have identified some of the variables that determine the incidence of slums in the cities. However, it may be noted that the relationship between the variables is not as simple as it has been postulated here. On the other hand, inter-connections and inter-dependence between the variables is much more complex.

Data and Variables

Information on slum population from the NSSO and the TCPO have been used to explain the variations across cities/classes of cities. We have already emphasised the relative reliability and usability of different sources of data and have mainly argued in favour of the NSSO data. However, the NSSO data are aggregative in nature as it does not give figures at the city level (except in the case of million-plus cities), whereas TCPO figures refer to individual cities.

The explanatory variables included in the equation are mainly population density, city size, rural-to-city migration rate, the share of non-household manufacturing and repair workers in the total workforce and the share of informal employment in total employment. The population census is the major source of information on these variables. Since city-specific migration rates (other than the metropolises) are not available we have approximated them, equated them to the district level rates. The share of informal sector employment is derived from the exercise suggested in Mitra (1990). As the NSSO data on slum population is available for different groups of class I cities the corresponding weighted average of the explanatory variables from city-specific observations have been calculated. Further, we have used the city-size dummy in the equation based on NSSO data.

Keeping in view the wide variability of the TCPO data, it may be argued that the few explanatory variables discussed above may not explain the bulk of the variation as several social, cultural and economic factors (other than the ones discussed here) which affect the incidence of slum population differ from State to State. The level of political intervention in improving or demolishing the slums also varies from State to State. Therefore, the State-specific intercept dummies have been included in the equation based on the TCPO data. Below we present the empirical results.

The equations estimated on the basis of NSSO data are indicative of the following tendencies. As per Table 7 the population density and rural-to-urban migration rate defined as the gross decadal inflow of all-purpose migrants from rural to urban areas as a percentage of the total urban population, appear to be statistically significant with positive coefficients. The variables representing the degree of industrialisation (i.e., share of manufacturing other than household sectors in the total workforce) and the city-size dummy also have positive coefficients though the t-ratio corresponding to these variables are not significant. Informal sector employment is also insignificant although one expects it to be significant with a positive coefficient.[6] Exclusion of this variable slightly raises the t-values corresponding to the coefficients of industrialisation variable and the city size dummy, bringing them to the neighbourhood of one. However, before ruling out the possibility of the impact of certain independent variables on the incidence of slum population, it may be noted that the unit of analysing these regression equations is a group of cities and not individual ones. In the process of such aggregation their impact on the dependent variable tends to get weakened.

Table 7
Regression Results: NSSO Data Dependent Variable - SLUM

Intercept	POPDEN	RUMIG	INFIMP	MFGNH	CTYDUM	N	R^2	F	WT
1. -2.84	0.001	1.12	-0.09	0.16	2.11	25	.72	9.72	1.6
(-0.19)	(4.59)*	(2.63)*	(-0.49)	(0.92)	(0.91)				
2. -9.94	0.001	1.21		0.16	2.39	25	.72	12.54	1.6
(-2.00)**	(4.66)	(3.17)*		(0.95)	(1.08)				
3. -9.37	0.0007	1.06		0.21		25	.70	16.16	1.7
(-1.89)**	(5.49)	(2.96)*		(1.33)					

Notes:
1. * and ** denote significance at 5 and 10 per cent levels respectively.
2. WT is White's test statistic to check heteroscedasticity. It is insignificant at 10 per cent level.
3. Unit of analysis is classes of cities in different states.

SLUM = Percentage of population residing in slums (1976-77).
POPDEN = Population density per unit square of land (1976-77).
RUMIG = Rural-to-Urban all-purpose decadal migration rate in percentages i.e., gross decade (1971-81) inflow of rural migrants into the urban areas as a percentage of total urban population in 1981.
INFEMP = Informal sector employment in percentages (1971).
MFGNH = The share of non-household manufacturing in total workforce in percentages (1976-77).
CTYDUM = City size dummy.

The equations tried out with the TCPO set of data lead to the following conclusions. Keeping in view the availability of information on all the variables included in the model only 110 class-I cities have been considered, although slum population data are available for around 200 class-I cities. In most of the equations (without the State-specific dummies) it is mainly the city size which appears to be statistically significant with a positive coefficient. Migration rate, population density and shares of industrial and informal sector employment in the total workforce, mostly turn out to be insignificant. Even the rate of growth of population which has been substituted for the migration rate remains insignificant. Keeping in view the poor comparability of the TCPO data across cities it will be erroneous to argue against the importance of these variables in the model.

In order to take care of the variations in socio-cultural factors across states, state-specific dummies have been introduced. But the coefficients of the dummies remain insignificant except in the cities of Karnataka. Among the explanatory variables in the equation with dummies, it is only city size that continues to be statistically significant. That t-ratio of the coefficient of manufacturing share in the total workforce increases to 1.91 (i.e., close to the tabulated value at five per cent level of significance) after the insertion of the state-specific dummies. The coefficients of other explanatory variables (population density, informal sector employment and rural-to-urban migration rate) all turn out to be positive, though still insignificant.

Conclusion

In this paper we have examined various sources of information on population residing in slums with inadequate access to basic amenities such as sanitation and drinking water. On the whole, most Indian cities are large slums. Even households outside slums have limited accessibility to basic amenities like sanitation and electricity. Further, we have noted that the incidence of slum population defined as the percentage of urban population residing in slums tends to increase as the city size increases. Also results from regression analysis suggest that the city size, population density and rural-urban migration rate raise the percentage of slum population across cities. It may be, therefore, inferred from this that in the context of rapid urbanisation the problem of slums and inadequacy of basic amenities would further worsen. In other words, with an

Table 8
Regression Results: TCPO DATA Dependent Variable - SLUM

	Intercept	CTYPOP	POPDEN	RUMIG	INFEMP	MFGNH	ROGPOP	N	R^2	R^{-2}	F	WT
1.	-33.14 (-1.37)	3.93 (2.69)*	0.0001 (0.38)	-0.08 (-0.18)	0.01 (0.05)	0.05 (0.41)		110	0.10	0.05	2.21	0.06
2.	-35.54 (-1.62)	4.01 (2.90)*	0.0001 (0.38)		0.01 (0.11)	0.05 (0.42)	0.08 (0.09)	110	0.10	0.05	2.21	0.06
3.	-35.87 (-1.62)	3.37 (2.63)	0.0001 (0.90)	0.15 (0.37)	0.05 (0.46)	0.24 (1.91)		110	0.45	0.34	4.10	0.5

APD	BH D	GUJD	HARD	KARD	KERD
3.07	11.01	-3.98	-9.74	-15.26	-7.77
(0.44)	(1.54)	(-0.57)	(-0.85)	(-2.34)*	(-1.06)

MPD	MHD	ORD	PUND	RAJD
-7.95	-2.03	10.61	11.57	8.93
(-1.30)	(-0.34)	(0.88)	(1.50)	(1.32)

TND	UPD
6.58	5.74
(-1.06)	(0.99)

Note: 1. 1 and 2 same as Table VII (3) Unit of analysis is city.

CTYPOP City opulation.
SLUM Percentage of population residing in slums (1981).
ROGPOP Annual rate of growth of population (percentage) over the decade (1971-81).
POPDEN Population density per unit square of land (1981).
RUMIG Rural-to-urban migration rate as defined in Table 7. VIII.
INFEMP Informal sector employment in percentages (1971).
MFGSH The share of non-household manufacturing in total workforce in percentages (1981).
APD Andhra Pradesh Dummy BHD = Bihar Dummy UPD = Uttar Pradesh Dummy.

increase in urbanisation, the existing infrastructure would tend to get overused causing considerable urban disamenities and environmental degradation.

It has been argued that residual absorption of labour in the informal sector in the face of sluggish employment growth in the high productivity sector, generates meagre earnings and does not enable the workers to have access to better quality housing. Therefore, we hypothesised that the larger the share of informal sector employment across cities, the higher is the percentage of population living in slums. Also, we argued that industrialisation and concentration of economic activities escalate land prices, forcing industrial workers to reside in slums. This phenomenon occurred in several cities of the western world, particularly in the initial phases of industrialisation. In the context of developing countries like India, informal sector employment and slum dwelling seem to have sufficient overlaps. Although the informal sector employment rate does not turn out to be statistically significant with a positive coefficient it may be argued that its impact has been captured partly by variables like population density and rural-to-urban migration rate. Rural-to-urban migration raises the percentage of slum inhabitants. The mechanism of this may be supplied in terms of the residual absorption of migrant labour in urban low productivity activities.

The policy implications of the study may be viewed in terms of the implementation of rural and urban employment programmes and the stepping up of investment in infrastructure and basic amenities as urbanisation progresses. This would tend to reduce city in-migration, dilute the situation of excess supplies of labour and their residual absorption in marginal activities and enable the city residents to have greater access to better quality housing.

NOTES

The author is indebted to Ashish Bose, K L Krishna, Amitabh Kundu, Bidyut Mohanty and S D Tendulkar for their useful suggestions. Usual disclaimers apply.

1. Bharat Sevak Samaj (1958) mentioned "The term 'slum' should be applied to those parts of the city which may (on the face of it) be considered unfit for human habitation either because the structures are old, dilapidated, grossly congested and out of repairs, or because it is impossible to preserve sanitation for want of sanitary facilities including ventilation, drainage, water supply etc., or because the sites by themselves are unhealthy.
2. A slum-like area in the survey has been defined as "an areal unit having 25 or

more inhabited *kutcha* structures mostly of a temporary nature or with 50 or more housholds residing mostly in *kutcha* structures, huddled together with practically no private latrine or inadequate public latrine and water supply facilities".

3. For details refer to Task Force on Housing and Urban Development (1983). Also see Mitra, (1985).
4. See Bharat Sevak Samaj (1958), Bhargava (ed) (1981), Desai and Pillai (1972), IIPA, Seminar (1979), Majumdar (1983), Mitra (1985), Sethuraman (1976,1978), Siddiqui (1969), Singh and D'Souza (1980).
5. See Kojima (1986) referring to Kuznet's view.
6. From our ongoing research on linkages between rural and urban poverty, we have observed that rural-to-urban migration raises the relative size of informal sector employment and urban poverty.

REFERENCES

Bapat, Meera, 1977, "Housing and the Urban Poor: The Poona Experience: 1941-1976", Mimeo. University College, London.

Bharat Sevak Samaj, 1958, *Slum of Old Delhi*.

Bhargava, G. (ed). 1981, *Urban Problems and Policy Perspective*, Abhinav Publication, New Delhi.

Clinard, M.B., 1970, *Slums and Community Development: Experiments in Self-Help*, The Free Press, New York, Collien-Macmillan Limited.

Desai, A. R., and Pillai, S. D., 1972, *A Profile of an Indian Slum*, University of Bombay.

Indian Institute of Public Administration, 1979, "Slum Clearance and Improvement", papers of the Seminar, Centre for Urban Studies.

Jha, S. S., 1987, *Structure of Urban Poverty: The Case of Bombay Slums*, Popular Prakashan, Bombay.

Kundu, Amitabh, 1991, "Micro Environment in Urban Planning: Access of Poor to Water Supply and Sanitation", *Economic and Political Weekly*, September 14.

Kojima, Makoto, 1986, "Industrialisation, Income Distribution and Labour Migration: The Case of India", VIII World Economic Congress of the Economic Association, Theme 10.

Majumdar, T. K., 1983, *Urbanising Poor: A Sociological Study of Low Income Migrant Communities in the Metropolitan City of Delhi*, Lancers Publications, New Delhi.

Mitra, Arup, 1985, "Slums, Cities and Urban Informal Sector: An Analytical Study", M. Phil. Dissertation, Deptt. of Economics, Delhi School of Economics.

——, 1988, "Urban Slums: The Rural Spill Over", *Demography India*, Vol VII, No.1.

——, 1990, "Duality, Employment Structure and Poverty Incidence: The Slum Perspective", *Indian Economic Review*, Vol. XXV, No.1.

National Centre for Human Settlement and Environment, Bhopal, 1987, *A Study for the Formulation of Poverty Alleviation Programmes for Indian Slums*, Sponsored by Planning Commission, Govt. of India.

Radhakrishna, R. et. al., 1977, *An Exploratory Study on Slums: Employment, Poverty and Liquor Consumption: A Case Study of Ahmedabad Slums*, Ahmedabad.

Sethuraman, S. V., 1976. "The Urban Informal Sector: Concept, Measurement and Policy", *International Labour Review*, Vol. 114, No. 1.

——, 1978, "The Informal Sector in Developing Countries: Some Policy Implications" in A D'souza (ed) *Urban Growth and Urban Planning*, Indian Social Institute.

Siddiqui, M. K. A., 1969, "Life in the Slums of Calcutta: Some Aspects", *Economic and Political Weekly*, Vol. IV, No. 50.

Singh, A. M and V. D'Souza, 1980, *The Urban Poor: Slum and Pavement Dwellers in the Major Cities of India*, Manohar.

Planning Commission, Task Forces on Housing and Urban Development, 1983, *Shelter for the Urban Poor and Slum Improvement* (Part IV).

Ministry of Works and Housing, Town and Country Planning Organisation, 1985, "A Compendium of Indian Slums".

15

Sanitation Situation and Garbage Management in Delhi Slums

Sabir Ali

EVEN though the overall urbanisation rate of India has apparently declined in the decade 1981-91, the Delhi urban agglomeration has grown rapidly. In 1981, the urban population was 5.7 million. In 1991 it jumped to 8.4 million. The 1981-91 decadal growth rate was 46.18 per cent in contrast to 36.19 per cent at the national level.

Although the geographical area of the National Capital has not shown any increase, the large scale immigration of people from other states to Delhi has given rise to the existence and growth of unauthorised colonies, slums and *jhuggi-jhonpri* clusters. Agencies like Delhi Water Supply and Sewage Disposal Undertaking (DWS and SDU), Conservancy and Sanitary Engineering Department (CSE) and Delhi Development Authority (DDA) providing the water supply and sanitation facilities could not meet the big challenge of providing basic services and at present almost half of the total population in Delhi lives in sub-standard areas, not fit for human habitation.

In Delhi, several residential areas called 'resettlement colonies' were developed to shelter the squatters and are known as "resettlement colonies". Several community latrines have been constructed for the use by these residents. The lack of success in providing sanitation facilities could be easily assessed from the outbreak of cholera epidemic in 1988 in these colonies. In response, new Sulabh community latrines (pay and use toilets) have been constructed.

The main objectives of this case study are to understand the sanitation situation in selected resettlement colonies and to evaluate, the performance of the Sulabh community toilets constructed for the population of resettlement colonies where the cholera epidemic had broken out. It also evaluates the solid waste management system of the two resettlement colonies.

Amongst the 45 resettlement colonies in Delhi, six colonies were the worst affected by the cholera epidemic. Trilokpuri (Phase I and II) and Himmatpuri witnessed governmental response in terms of initiating construction of Sulabh toilet complexes. Old community latrines also exist in these colonies. Again, as far as garbage collection and disposal are concerned, the colonies pose peculiar problems which would make this study useful. With this background, it was felt that Trilokpuri (Phase I and II) and Himmatpuri would be the right choice for research (see Fig. 1).

Condition of Sanitation

The condition of sanitation in 45 resettlement colonies could by and large be termed as unsatisfactory. The reasons for this are several. First, civic amenities were not fully provided. Second, they were of very poor quality and, further, were poorly maintained. The problem of inadequate sanitary facilities for the people who have been allotted plots in the resettlement colonies has become more acute on account of the emergence of squatter settlements within these planned settlements. The process of emerging squatter colonies within the resettlement colonies, can be termed as 'slums within slums', a recent phenomenon in contemporary urban housing which appears to reinforce the perception of slums as an all-prevailing cancerous proliferation and an onslaught on the urban landscape. Table 1 shows the emergence of squatters in resettlement colonies.

The Municipal authorities have started the 'Pay and Use' community toilets wherein, on payment of a token amount people can avail of neat and clean latrine and bathing facilities. No money is charged from women, children and the disabled. The local authorities provide the land and other infrastructure and the Sulabh International constructs and maintains these community toilets. The cost of construction would be met by the local authorities and the token amount collected would be used for day-to-day maintenance by the private party entrusted with the job of maintenance. The Pay and Use toilet scheme has received a wide response and several such toilet complexes have been constructed all over India. In Delhi, after the outbreak of gastroenteritis in 1988 in several resettlement

LOCATION OF RESETTLEMENT COLONIES IN DELHI

Fig. 1

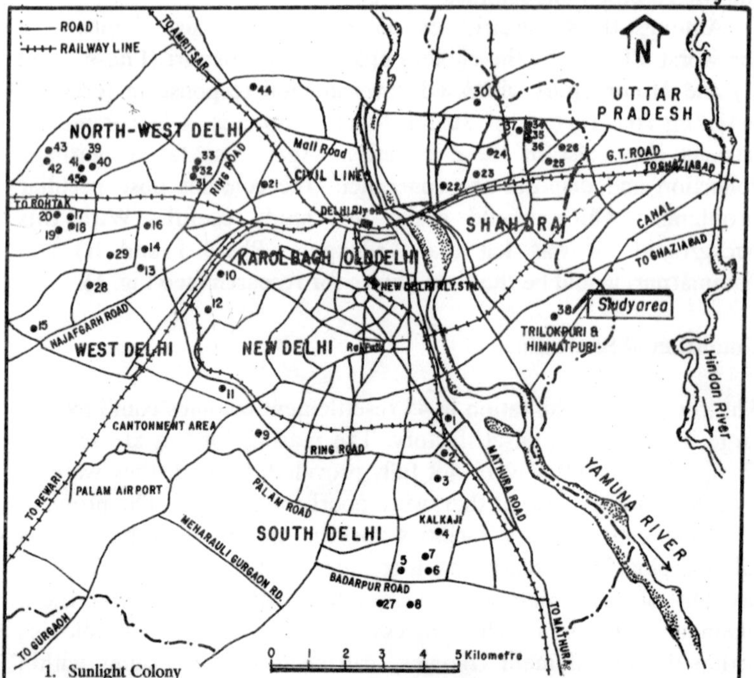

1. Sunlight Colony
2. Sriniwaspuri
3. Garhi Village
4. Kalkaji
5. Madangir
6. Dakshinpuri
7. Dakshinpuri Extn
8. Tigri
9. Moti Bagh (Ring Rd)
10. Pandu Nagar
11. Ranjit Nagar (Khanpur)
12. Naraina
13. N.G. Road (Sector A,B,C,D,F & G)
14. Addl. Plot N.G. Road (R.E. Block, etc.)
15. Hastsal
16. Madipur
17. Nangloi Phase I
18. Nangloi Phase II
19. Nangloi Phase III
20. Nangloi Phase IV
21. Wazirpur
22. Seelampur Phase I & II
23. Seelampur Phase III & IV
24. Seelampur Addl. Plots
25. Seemapuri Old
26. Seemapuri New Phase I-III
27. West of Khanpur
28. Chaukhandi
29. Khayala Phase I-III
30. Gokulpuri
31. Shakurpur Phase I & II
32. Shakurpur Phase III
33. Shakurpur Phase IV
34. Nand Nagri Phase I
35. Nand Nagri Phase II
36. Nand Nagri (Block P & G Extn)
37. Nand Nagri Extn
38. Patparganj Complex
39. Mongolpuri Phase I
40. Mongolpuri Phase II
41. Mongulpuri Phase III
42. Sultanpuri
43. Sultanpuri Addl. Plots
44. Jahangirpuri
45. Mongolpuri

Table 1
The Emerging Squatters in Resettlement Colonies[1]

Sl. No.	Name of Resettlement Colony (RC)	Year of establishment	Total No. of Blocks/sector in RC	No.of Blocks/sectors effected by growth of jhuggis in RC	No. of Squatters cluster emerging in R C	Total No.of Juggis in all clusters of R C	No. of Jhuggis occupied: Residence	No. of Jhuggis occupied: Commerce/service	Squatters emerged in spaces reserve for: Production	Housing	Praks	School	Health	Shopping	Road Berns	Religion	Any other	Housing & Park
1	2	3	4	5	6	7	8	9	10	11	12	13	14	15	16	17	18	19
1.	Jahangir Pur	1976	11	6	15	13207	10807	2400	0	0	8	1	0	0	5	1	0	0
2.	Naraina	1975	9+1&II	I&II	10	10000	9200	250	550	0	0	0	0	0	0	0	0	10
3.	Patpar Ganj Complex	1976	57	32	36	8313	7909	404	0	0	8	0	0	0	28	0	0	0
4.	Wazirpur (Phase III)	1963	13	11	11	5731	5527	154	50	0	3	0	0	0	8	0	0	0
5.	Nandnagari (Phase I)	1976	3	2	4	5386	5262	124	0	0	0	0	0	0	3	0	1	0
6.	Nandnagri (Extn) (Sundarnagri)	1976	10	3	6	5095	3756	195	1144	1	3	0	0	0	1	0	1	0
7.	Seelam Pur Ph. I & II	1976	20	11	11	5070	4435	635	0	0	1	0	0	0	10	0	0	0
8.	Kalkaji	1973	53	3	3	5000	4800	200	0	0	0	0	0	0	3	0	0	0
9.	Nangloi Phase IV	1976	3	1	1	5000	4960	30	10	0	1	0	0	0	0	0	0	0
			181	71	97	62803	56656	4392	1754	1	24	1	0	0	58	1	2	10

1	2	3	4	5	6	7	8	9	10	11	12	13	14	15	16	17	18	19
10.	Tigri	1968	8	1	1	4450	4405	45	0	0	0	0	0	0	0	0	0	0
11.	Dakshin Puri Extn.	1976	20	3	5	3564	3360	204	0	0	0	0	0	0	0	0	5	0
12.	N G Road	1964	21	9	9	2935	1965	900	70	0	5	0	0	0	0	0	4	0
	Sector A,D Raghbir B&C, F&C Nagar																	
13.	Add. N G Road																	
14.	Mongol Puri Ph. II	1976	5	4	5	2630	2090	540	0	0	1	0	0	0	4	0	0	0
15.	Pandu Nagar	1967	2	2	1	2500	2200	100	200	1	0	0	0	0	0	0	0	0
16.	New Seema Puri	1976	6	3	3	2470	2223	247	0	0	3	0	0	0	0	0	0	0
17.	Mongol Puri Ph. III	1976	16	8	38	2260	2015	245	0	0	10	0	0	0	28	0	0	0
18.	Sultan Puri Add. Plots	1982	4	1	3	2100	1500	400	200	1	0	0	0	0	2	0	0	0
19.	Sultanpuri	1976	6	5	7	3077	2017	57	3	1	1	0	0	0	3	0	2	0
20.	Nangloi Phase (V)	1980	1	1	4	1500	1400	100	0	0	0	0	0	0	4	0	0	0
			89	37	76	26486	23175	2838	473	3	20	0	0	0	41	0	11	0
21.	Nand Nagari Phase II	1976	2	1	3	886	790	17	79	0	0	0	0	0	0	0	2	0
22.	Gokulpuri	1976	4	3	3	870	695	75	100	0	0	0	0	1	0	0	2	0
23.	Seelampur Ph. III & IV	1976	36	5	5	595	595	0	0	0	2	0	0	0	0	0	3	0
24.	New Ranjit Nagar	1966	11	6	7	590	435	80	75	0	0	0	0	0	7	0	1	0
25.	Madangir	1968	25	2	2	500	0	500	0	0	0	0	0	0	2	0	0	0
26.	Seema Puri Old	1968	9	1	1	500	500	0	0	0	0	0	0	0	0	0	1	0
27.	Garhi Village	1970	12	2	1	400	400	0	0	0	0	0	0	0	0	0	2	0
28.	Nangloi Phase II	1968	5	3	3	331	276	55	0	0	2	1	0	0	0	0	0	0
29.	Sunlight Colony I & II	1966	2	2	2	170	146	24	0	0	0	0	1	1	0	0	0	0
30.	Mangolpuri Phase I	1976	2	1	1	150	75	75	0	0	0	0	0	0	1	0	0	0
31.	Moti Bagh	1958	7	1	2	100	75	10	15	0	2	0	0	0	0	0	0	0
32.	Hastasi Colony	1978	1	1	1	52	52	0	0	0	0	0	0	0	1	0	0	0
33.	Nangloi Phase III	1975	3	1	3	31	31	0	0	0	3	0	0	0	0	0	0	0

1	2	3	4	5	6	7	8	9	10	11	12	13	14	15	16	17	18	19
34.	Shakurpur Phase I & II	1976	13	1	1	12	12	0	0	0	1	0	0	0	0	0	0	0
35.	Nangloi Phase I	1967	2	1	1	6	6	0	0	0	0	1	0	0	0	0	0	0
			134	31	36	5193	4088	836	269	0	10	2	1	2	11	0	11	0
36.	Sriniwas Puri	1961	6															
37.	Chaukhandi	1975	2															
38.	Khavala (Ph. I to III)	1975	6															
39.	Madipur	1974	6															
40.	Shakurpur Phase III	1976	5															
41.	Shakurpur Phase IV	1976	1															
42.	Dakshinpuri	1976	1															
43.	West of Khanpur	1975	4															
44.	Block P&G Ext. (Janta Flats) Nandnagri	1983	1															
45.	Hyderpur[2]																	
			32															
			436	139	209	94481	83919	8066	2496	4	54	3	1	2	110	1	23	10

Notes: 1. Survey was conducted in 1989.
2. Resettlement has not taken place.

colonies in the trans-Yamuna area, 26 such toilet complexes have been constructed in 13 resettlement colonies. In the two resettlement colonies selected for the case studies (Trilokpuri Phase I & II and Himmatpuri), the Pay and Use Sulabh Community toilet complexes have also been constructed.

The Pay and Use Community toilets have three major components: (a) the community toilet building; (b) the septic tanks and (c) the soak pits. The concept of the pour-flush latrine is quite simple. The pour flush latrine consists of a pan which is a sanitary fitting made out of ceramic. The pan receives the human excreta directly from the person using it. The pan consists of a water seal which is a bent sanitary fitting which always remains full of water. The function of the water seal is to prevent the passage of obnoxious gases to pass through from the tank below and at the same time allow for the passage of excreta from the pan. The pan is connected to an RCC septic tank by means of a pipe which channellises the excreta. Within one to three days of hydraulic retention in the septic tank, the solids settle to the bottom where they are digested. The septic tank is connected to soak pits where the overflow comes into contact with the adjoining ground into which it partly seeps. The overflow also settles down to some extent in the soak pits. The septic tank needs to be emptied periodically (see Fig. 2). It is observed that the soak pits would also need attention for reasons such as faulty outlets, limited pit capacity and the ground being surcharged with higher levels of underground water or marshy conditions during rains.

The Pay and Use Community Toilet complexes constructed in Trilokpuri (Phase I & II) and Himmatpuri have a seating capacity of 84 (40 for males, 40 for females and 4 for children). The toilet complex building is a *pucca* structure with RCC roof and brick walls in cement mortar. It consists of an entrance lobby, caretaker's room, store room, bathing space, urinals, a trough for washing and latrines. The latrines are arranged in parallel rows with a common passage in between. The size of the latrine is 3'0" X 4'0" and has a door and a ventilator. The flooring is of good quality tiles and the side walls are treated with white glazed tile dado up to 6'0" height from the floor. Three water tanks, two of them 3'00" X 5'00" in area and 3'00" deep and one 3'00" X 3'00" in size and 3'00" deep are provided. Heavy duty nickel plated taps have been provided. Tube lights and electric bulbs have been provided to light the complex in the early hours of

Fig. 2

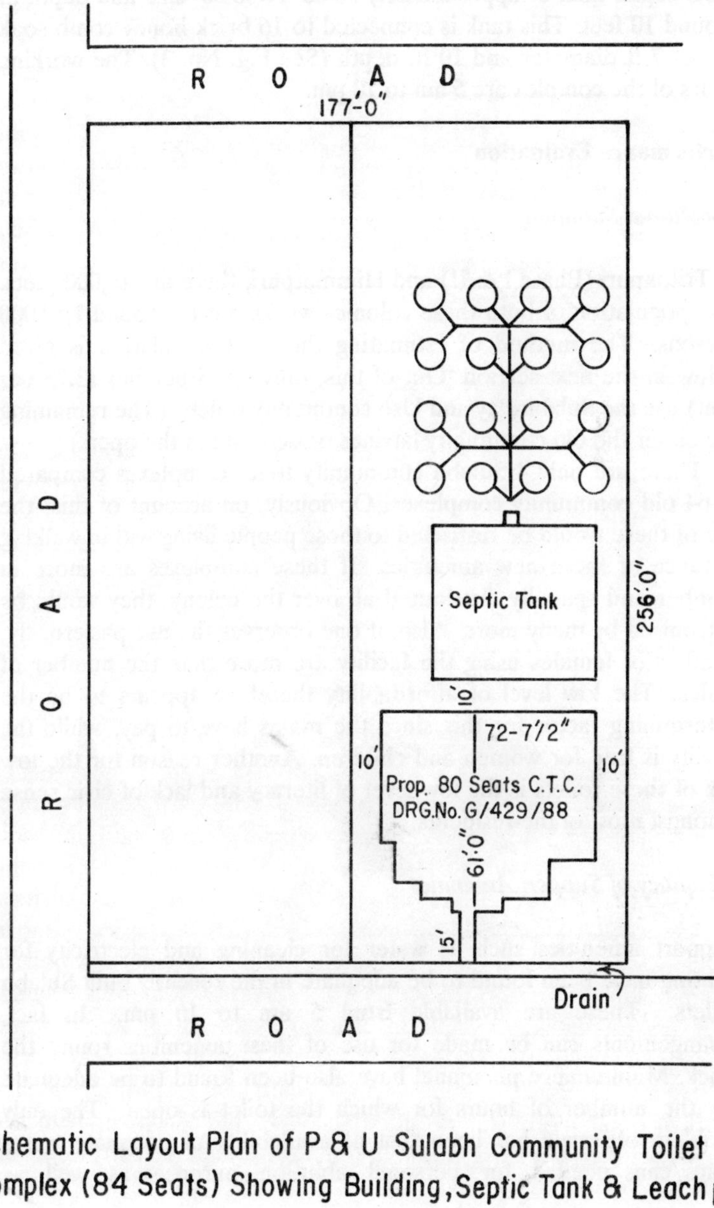

Schematic Layout Plan of P & U Sulabh Community Toilet Complex (84 Seats) Showing Building, Septic Tank & Leach pits

of the day and at night. Sintex PVC storage tanks have been installed for water storage. The toilet complex is connected to an RCC septic tank of approximately 50'00" X 30'00" size and depth of around 10 feet. This tank is connected to 16 brick honey comb soak pits of 7 ft diameter and 10 ft. depth (See Fig. No. 3). The working hours of the complex are 5 am to 10 pm.

Performance Evaluation

Locational Suitability

In Trilokpuri (Phase I & II) and Himmatpuri, there are 18,000 plots. The population of both these colonies works out to around 1,50,000 persons. The method of estimating the total population is given below in the next section. Out of this, only 4,875 persons (3.75 per cent) use the Sulabh Pay and Use community toilets. (The remaining use either the old community latrines or defecate in the open.)

There are only 4 Sulabh community toilet complexes compared to 64 old community complexes. Obviously, on account of this, the use of these would be restricted to those people living within walking distance of these new amenities. If these complexes are more in number and spatially distributed all over the colony, they would be patronised by many more. Also, if one observes the use pattern, the number of females using the facility are more than the number of males. The low level of affordability therefore appears to be the determining factor for this since the males have to pay, while the facility is free for women and children. Another reason for the low use of these toilets is the low level of literacy and lack of civic sense amongst most of the residents.

Adequacy of Support Amenities

Support amenities such as water for cleaning and electricity for lighting have been found to be adequate in the recently built Sulabh toilets. These are available from 5 am to 10 pm. In fact, arrangements can be made for use of these amenities round the clock. Maintenance personnel have also been found to be adequate for the number of hours for which the toilet is open. The only problem observed has been that of availability of adequate water mugs/cans needed for personal ablution purposes as well as

Fig. 3

PLAN OF P&U SULABH COMMUNITY TOILET COMPLEX BUILDING (84 SEATS)

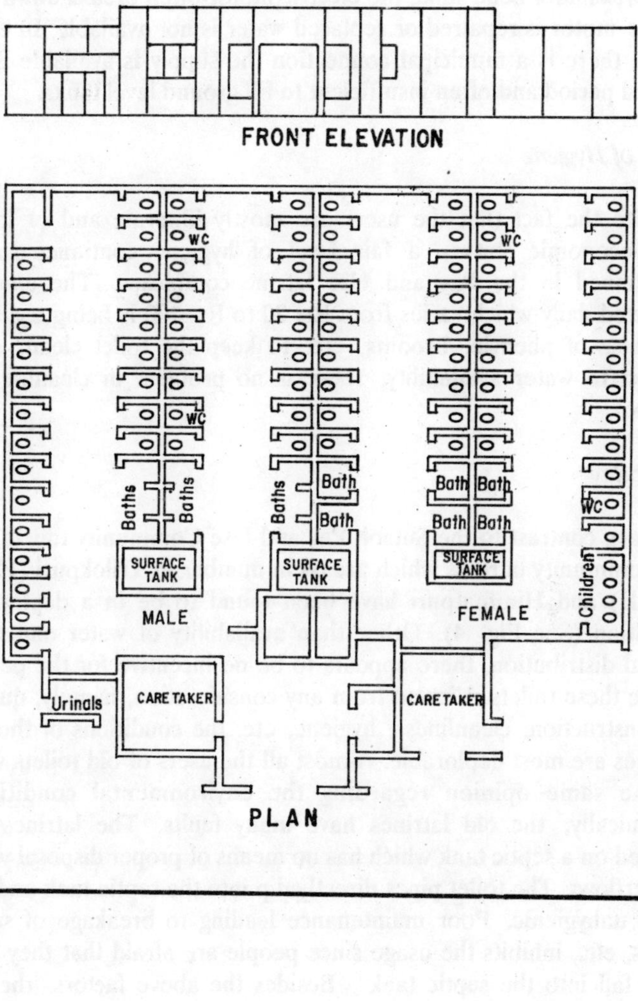

cleanliness in the latrine. The people exhibit inhibition to carry a tin of water all the way from their residence to the toilet. The caretaker therefore has to provide water mugs/tins and keep a periodic check on them. Pilferage which could be largely attributed to the low economic status of the users has also been reported. Water used in the toilets is available either from tube wells or from the MCD mains. Problems have been noticed in both the cases. Where special tube wells have been sunk, the electric motor often breaks down and till the motor is repaired or replaced water is not available. In cases where there is a municipal connection the supply is available for a limited period and often insufficient to fill ground level tanks.

Level of Hygiene

Despite the fact that the users are mostly illiterate and of lower socio-economic status, a fair level of hygiene continues to be maintained in the Pay and Use latrine complexes. The amount collected daily which varies from Rs. 20 to Rs. 100 is being used for purchase of phenyle, brooms, etc. to keep the toilet clean. Also subject to water availability, there is no problem in cleaning the toilets.

Suitability

In sharp contrast to the Sulabh Pay and Use Community toilets, the old community latrines which are 64 in number in Trilokpuri (Phase I & II) and Himmatpuri have been found to be in a deplorable condition (See Fig. 4). Other than availability of water and their spatial distribution, there appears to be no incentive for the people to use these toilets. Viewed from any consideration, namely, quality of construction, cleanliness, hygiene, etc. the conditions of the old latrines are most deplorable. Almost all the users of old toilets were of the same opinion regarding the environmental conditions. Technically, the old latrines have many faults. The latrines are located on a septic tank which has no means of proper disposal when it overflows. The toilet pipes directly dip into the septic tank and are most unhygienic. Poor maintenance leading to breakage of seats, doors, etc., inhibits the usage since people are afraid that they may even fall into the septic tank. Besides the above factors, the old latrines have outlived their life. It has been observed that the RCC

Fig. 4

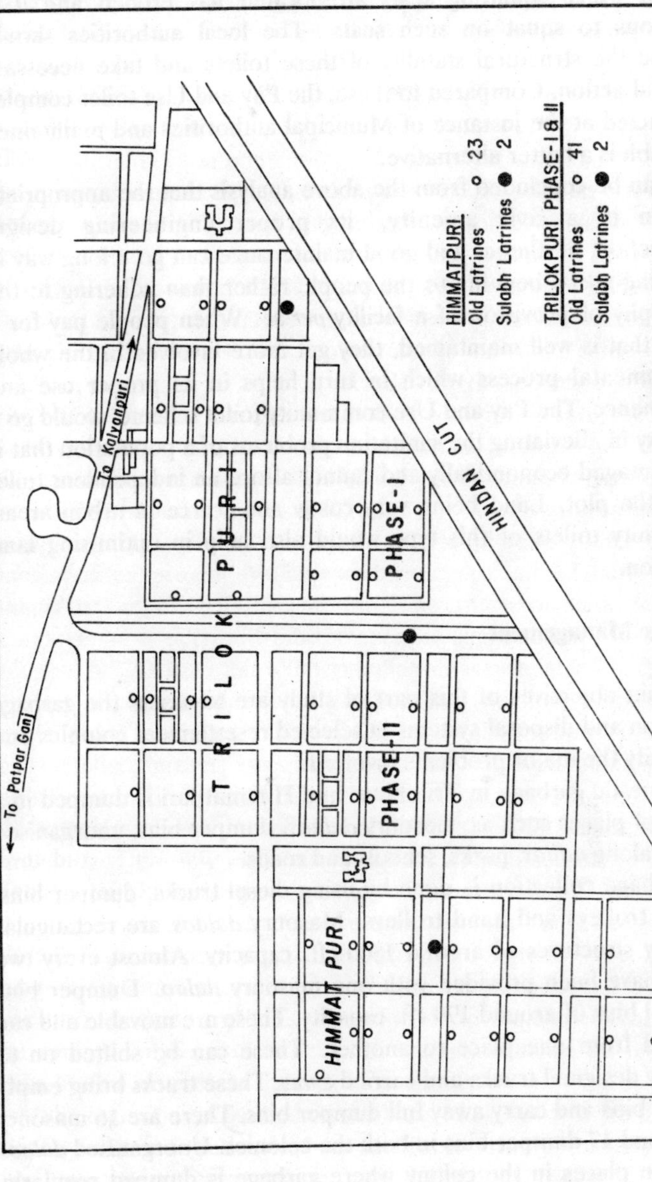

Location of P & U Sulabh Toilets and OLD Toilets in Himmatpuri and Trilokpuri (Phase-I & II)

Slab on which squatting seats are located has eroded and it is dangerous to squat on such seats. The local authorities should examine the structural stability of these toilets and take necessary remedial action. Compared to these, the Pay and Use toilet complex constructed at the instance of Municipal authorities and maintained by Sulabh is a better alternative.

It can be concluded from the above analysis that the appropriate location of a civic amenity, its proper engineering design, construction, aesthetics and good maintenance can go a long way in delivering social benefits to the people rather than adhering to the philosophy of provision of a facility *per se*. When people pay for a facility that is well maintained, they get more involved in the whole developmental process which in turn helps in its proper use and maintenance. The Pay and Use community toilet scheme, would go a long way in alleviating the sanitation problems of a population that is disadvantaged economically and cannot afford an independent toilet within the plot. Land being very costly and scarce in urban areas, community toilets of this type would also help in optimising land utilisation.

Garbage Management

The main objectives of this part of study are to assess the garbage collection and disposal systems in selected resettlement colonies and to identify the major problems involved.

Domestic garbage in Trilokpuri and Himmatpuri is dumped in a variety of places such as: masonry *dalaos*, dumper bins, unorganised *dalaos*, along *nallas*, parks, schools and roads.

Garbage collection is done by using diesel trucks, dumper bins, ox/bull trolleys and hand trolleys. Masonry *dalaos* are rectangular masonry structures of around 1800 cft. capacity. Almost every two blocks have been provided with one masonry *dalao*. Dumper bins are steel bins of around 170 cft. capacity. These are movable and can be lifted from one place to another. These can be shifted on to specially designed trucks and carried away. These trucks bring empty dumper bins and carry away full dumper bins. There are 16 masonry *dalaos* and 17 dumper bins in both the colonies. Unorganised *dalaos* are open places in the colony where garbage is dumped regularly. (see Fig. 5). Garbage in these *dalaos* is not protected and is easily accessible to stray animals. There are 34 unorganised *dalaos* of

Fig. 5

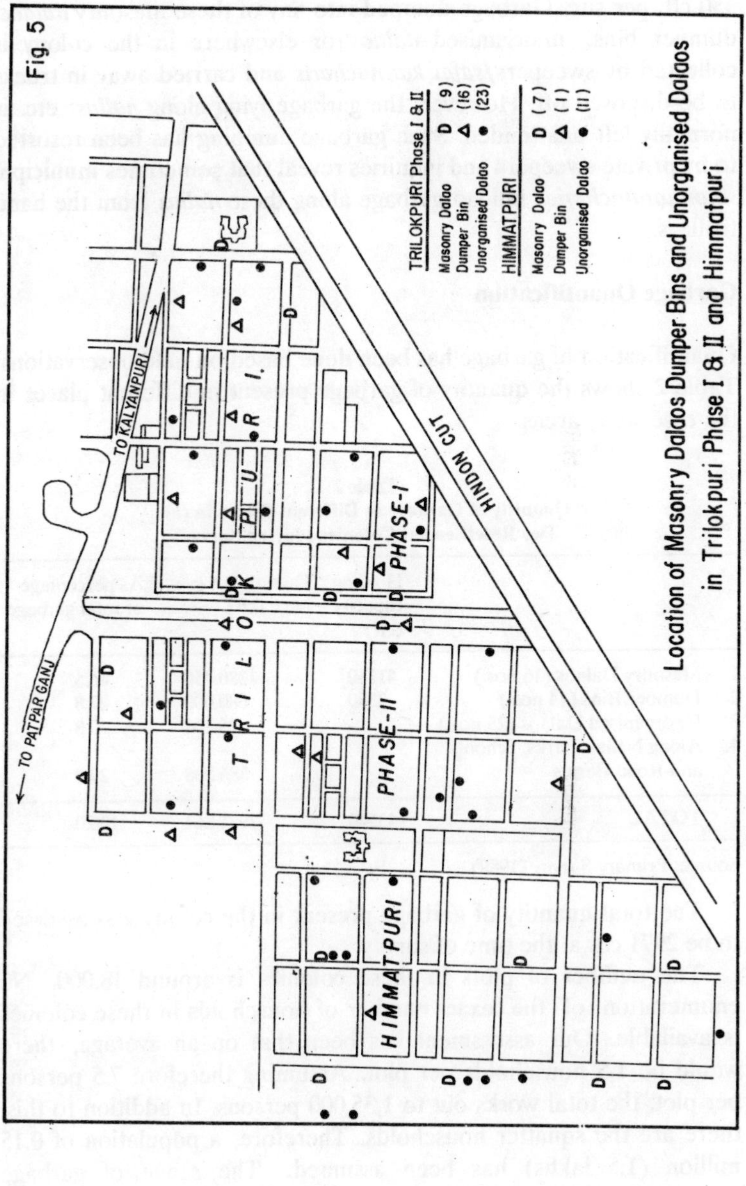

Location of Masonry Dalaos Dumper Bins and Unorganised Dalaos in Trilokpuri Phase I & II and Himmatpuri

different sizes and the garbage dumped here ranges from 12 cft. to 450 cft. per site. Garbage dumped into any of these masonry *dalaos*, dumper bins, unorganised *dalaos* or elsewhere in the colony is collected by sweepers/*safai karmacharis* and carried away in trucks to be disposed off. However, the garbage lying along *nallas*, etc. is normally left unattended. Such garbage dumping has been resorted to by private sweepers and inquiries reveal that sometimes municipal *safai karamcharies* unload garbage along these *nallas* from the hand trolleys.

Garbage Quantification

Quantification of garbage has been done based on field observations. Table 2 shows the quantity of garbage present in different places in the case study areas.

Table 2
Quantity of Garbage in Different Places in the Two Resettlement Colonies (during Survey)

	Holding capacity (cft)	Quantity of garbage (cft)	As percentage of total garbage
1. Masonry Dalaos (16 nos.)	41160	1380.450	46.5
2. Dumper Bins (14 nos.)	2380	680.000	22.8
3. Unorganised Dalaos (25 nos.)	-	25.104	0.8
4. Along Nallas, Parks, Schools and Road Berms		886.308	29.9
TOTAL	43540	2971.862	100.0

Source: Primary Survey (1989).

The total quantity of garbage present in the colony was assessed to be 2971 cft. at the time of survey.

The number of plots in these colonies is around 18,000. No enumeration of the exact number of households in these colonies is available. Our assessment has been that on an average, there would be 1.5 households per plot. Assuming therefore 7.5 persons per plot, the total works out to 1,35,000 persons. In addition to this, there are the squatter households. Therefore, a population of 0.15 million (1.5 lakhs) has been assumed. The range of garbage generated per person per day varies between 250 to 1000 grams which is the international average covering both the developing as well as developed countries. Assuming an average of 400 grams/person/ day for these resettlement colonies, the total quantity of garbage generated would be 1,50,000 X 400g = 60,000 kg. The average density of garbage in these areas can be assumed to be 570 kg/cubic metre. Therefore, the total volume generated would be weight divided by density i.e., 105 cubic metres/day or 3,715 cft/day.

Management System

Locational Suitability of Garbage Collection Bins

It is usually the women who deal with garbage at home and they exhibit inhibition in carrying garbage to the garbage bins located far away. From the point of view of accessibility of trucks to the garbage bin, they have to be placed along the wider roads. However, if several smaller dalaos/bins are placed, one at the end of each street, their use may be more intensive. The requirement of private sweepers would also thereby reduce. The people themselves would not mind walking up to the end of the street, since the street is an extension of their living space and does not pose problems of inhibition for women.

Adequacy of Capacity and Support Amenities

The holding capacity of masonry *dalaos* and dumper bins has been found to be 43,540 cft while the maximum garbage generated on an average/day is estimated to be 3715 cft (say 4000 cft). The quantity of total garbage generated/day as a percentage of the holding capacity would be 10.88. Even at full utilisation, the holding capacity is adequate for storing the garbage. However, what is lacking is the appropriate location of rationally designed *dalaos* of smaller capacity but with more accessibility to people.

As per the information furnished by the local officials of the Municipal Corporation of Delhi regarding the transportation of garbage to the final dumping site, the study areas utilise two trucks each with capacity of 330 cft. In addition there are 8 dumper bins each with capacity of 170 cft. Thus, the total carriage capacity of the trucks and dumper bins per trip works out to 2 X 330 + 2 X 170 =

660 + 340 = 1000 cft. Thus, if the two trucks and 8* dumper bins were to make just two trips every day they could remove 3000 cft. of the total quantity of garbage generated is 3715 cft. In other words even though there exists enough infrastructural facilities the garbage is not picked up properly every day.

Level of Hygiene

Conditions of hygiene in the case study areas have been found to be deplorable on account of the garbage not being properly protected before it is lifted. More than 40 per cent of garbage is strewn around parks, *nallas*, etc. The low rate of clearance, foul smell, mosquito breeding and presence of stray animals namely cows, pigs, dogs, etc. are bound to lead to several diseases.

In extreme conditions such as prolonged accumulation of garbage during monsoons, the situation definitely assumes alarming proportions. Since none of the garbage collection bins are protected from rain, the possibility of the garbage getting water logged and stagnant in the masonry *dalaos* and dumper bins is rather high.

Public Participation

Most of the people felt that the job of keeping the neighbourhood clean was that of the Municipal Corporation and they have nothing to do with it. Surveys showed that the people do not wish to participate in keeping their neighbourhood clean. There are several reasons. The sense of belonging, attachment and civic pride evolves and grows over a long period of residence in a particular area. Added to this is the literacy level of the people which is low.

It can be concluded from the above analysis that the mere provision of a facility *per se* would hardly solve the problem. In fact it may aggravate it. There appears to be a total lack of perception by the Government as far as the specificity of the needs of the low-income population is concerned. Unlike high income colonies, low-income colonies generate not only domestic garbage but also garbage resulting from a variety of informal sector activities and home based activities which they pursue to augment their incomes. There are *bazars* along many streets in these colonies where several

* Incidentally, not all dumpers are used every time every day.

items are sold. Also, these people cannot afford to employ servants who can carry the garbage regularly to the garbage bins. State intervention in terms of mere provision of a few garbage bins, sweepers, trucks, etc. would not suffice. What has added fuel to the fire has been that the garbage bins have been provided at unsuitable locations and in an unplanned manner. Despite the fact that they have adequate capacity, they are not properly utilised on account of their concentration at only a few points. The people do not bother to carry the garbage all the way to the *dalaos* and would rather dump it at a more convenient place near a park, school, etc. The bins are uncovered and during the rainy season, are liable to cause serious environmental problems. One invariably finds animals, namely, pigs, dogs, cows etc. digging into the garbage lying strewn around these *dalaos*. The situation of apathy that prevails could be attributed to a poorly conceived approach resulting in inappropriate and inadequate provision of facilities. In the field of solid waste management, it is not the lack of manual labour or transportation facilities that result in the inefficient clearance of garbage, but it is the lack of proper management of these.

The location of the *dalaos* is unscientific. These should be properly spaced so that people are encouraged to walk up to these and dump the garbage in them. This would also facilitate the periodical collection of the garbage from these bins by ear-marking a pre-designed drill for the machines and men supporting the vehicles.

Above all what is important are training programmes for different groups identified below:

a. *Training Programmes for Staff*

Training facilities are required at all levels of staff starting with *safai karmacharis*, supervisory staff and senior officers in-charge of solid waste management.

b. *Workshops for Residents of Area*

To ensure public participation and co-operation in sanitation, it is essential that special workshops are organised with the residents of the area where they are apprised, consulted and their views and cooperation sought. Residents need to be especially consulted regarding location and spacing of *dalaos*, frequency of cleaning, methodology adopted so that there is a certain amount of autonomy and participation in-built in the process. The workshops should also create awareness regarding habits of cleanliness, how to keep garbage covered even within the household both through visuals, demonstrations and films.

16

Basic Amenities and Quality of Life in an Urban Industrial Complex: A Case Study of Rourkela[1]

Rajkishor Meher

MAJOR cities have been expanding at rates of five per cent or more, and most of the world's major metropolises are now found in the less developed countries (Gilbert and Gugler, 1981:5). In this situation, in order to accommodate the increasing number of less qualified and distressed rural migrants in the urban economy, the cities of the third world have evolved a dualistic pattern of economy namely large scale, organized and highly formalised economic structures at a limited level and unorganized and informal production and service organizations at the larger level.

The studies of third world urban economy by the many authors and institutions show that quite a high percentage of the city's population earns its livelihood in the informal manufacturing and service sectors. It is estimated that the number of those employed in the informal sector constitutes around 60-70 per cent of the population in Nairobi and Kumasi, 50 per cent in Jakarta and 45 per cent in Calcutta, Bombay and Ahmedabad (ILO, 1972 & 1977, Sethuraman, 1976; Lubell, 1974; Bose, 1974; Heather and Joshi, 1976 and Papola, 1980).

In a highly populated developing country like India although only 25.72 per cent of the population lives in urban areas in 1991, this in absolute terms translates to more than 200 million persons. Since 1901 the population share of class I category of towns in India has been showing a steady increase. The percentage of urban population of this category of towns increased from 26 per cent in 1901 to 44.63 per cent in 1951, 57.24 per cent in 1971 and further to 65.20 per cent in 1991.[2]

However, it is unfortunate to note that the organized sector economic activities, which provide a quality living to the urban residents have not shown a proportionate increase. As a result, quite a large proportion of new entrants to the cities have entered the informal sector activities characterized by a very low level of earning, thereby increasing the number of slums and squatter areas in the cities. It was found that the squatter areas in cities like Bombay, Calcutta, Delhi and Madras constituted approximately five million out of a total population of 19 million in these cities in the early seventies.[3] Besides this, it was estimated that around 15 to 20 per cent of the population in the other 39 cities with a population of three lakh or more were living in squatter settlements during the same period.

This type of urbanization, characterized by high population growth, large scale inmigration of indigent and distressed people from the rural areas coupled with the growth of slums and informal sector economic activities in the class I cities in India, has put a tremendous strain on the supply of basic civic amenities by the urban local bodies, with limited investible funds, to all categories of population residing in different localities of the cities. The limited developed infrastructural facilities and basic civic amenities in these cities are further spatially distributed in such a way that they favour the relatively affluent localities, thus depriving the poor and migrant workers residing in slum and squatter areas of basic civic amenities to a great extent.

The haphazard growth of slum and squatter areas close to the work place of the informal sector workers, such as the main market and factory areas of the city expose them to serious health hazards. Further, in the absence of proper municipal laws and regulations, the industries are virtually free to discharge their effluents in open fields or normal sewerage channels, thereby polluting the environment. It is observed that the combined impact of all these factors in the urban areas of the Third World, especially India, lead to ecological degradation, environmental pollution and deterioration in quality of life of people living in cities.

Although, Rourkela is a planned industrial town which came up in the context of the setting up of the giant public sector steel plant in the early sixties, this city has also witnessed the growth of innumerable informal sector activities in the wake of large scale exodus of poor and less qualified people from various parts of the country in recent years, resulting in the growth of slum and squatter areas. According to our estimate, around 25 per cent of the city's population presently live in slum and squatter areas located near the industries and central business district of the city. This has naturally put a strain on the basic civic amenities infrastructure.

In this paper, we attempt to study the availability of basic amenities in different localities of Rourkela and its implications for the quality of life of various categories of people residing in the city. The study is mainly based on direct and intensive observations of the various localities of the city made at the time of collection of information and field data for my doctoral thesis from November 1987 to March 1989.

The Industrial City of Rourkela

Rourkela, the venue of the first public sector steel plant, is situated in Sundergarh district of Orissa and is 413 km away from Calcutta. The city is situated in a valley formed by the intersection of the Sankh and Koel rivers. It is here that the two rivers have merged together and formed the river Brahmani, the second largest river of Orissa.

The construction of the plant and the township started in the mid-fifties and with production beginning in the early sixties, Rourkela became a prominent township of the country. According to the 1951 Census, the population of Rourkela village including the *bustee* was only 2,533 and the acquired villages had a total population of 15,502. However, with the beginning of construction activities for the erection of the plant and its township, workers from various parts of the country started coming to Rourkela. With the commissioning of the steel plant in 1960 there was recruitment of workers on a massive scale. Thus, at the time of the 1961 Census the whole area was incorporated as the Rourkela steel town in the map of urban India. The new town recorded a total population figure of 90,287, registering a net growth rate of 480.18 per cent during 1951-61. The decadal growth of the town during 1961-71 was 91.06 per cent and it came down to 87.02 per cent during 1971-81 with a total population of 3,22,610 in 1981. During the 1981-91 decade, the growth rate of the town has again come down considerably to about 23.58 per cent and according to the 1991 Census, the city presently has a total population of 3,98,692. But still the absolute addition to the total population was very high.

Planning of the Township

The blue-print of Rourkela project provided for an area of 207.37 sq. kms including 10,500 acres for the township. The Master Plan of the town envisaged that when industrialization of Rourkela would be in full swing, the population of the steel township would be around one lakh including the employees of the steel project as well as the ancillary industries, the personnel engaged in various servicing institutions, commercial enterprises etc. A steel township with 19 sectors was planned and provision was made for the construction of 14,000 houses for the employees of the steel plant and their family members in these sectors.

With the Government's decision to set up the public sector steel plant at Rourkela, the original village of Rourkela and other nearby hamlets began to grow as a town close to the project site. The population of the civil town which was less than 4,000 in 1951, suddenly increased to 35,000 in the year 1961. The civil township of Rourkela, thus, started growing in a narrow wedge between the steel plant and the steel township. So, in order to stop the haphazard and sporadic growth in the immediate vicinity of the steel township and the steel plant and to reduce the congestion thus caused, the Town Planning Department of the Government of Orissa formulated another Master Plan in 1965 for the planned and systematic growth of the civil town. The projected population for the civil town after the full development of the different areas of the Civil Township Master Plan by about 1975 was estimated at 80,000.

To accommodate the growing population of the Civil town and to reduce congestion, the plan made necessary provision for the development of residential plots according to the needs of different classes of people and divided the whole area into several zones and earmarked their use for different purposes. Adequate provisions were also made for the location of educational institutions, government offices, green belts, small parks, play centres etc. in various zones.

Potable Water Supply

As Rourkela is situated in a hilly region and the Brahmani river goes dry during summer, the region faced acute water shortage and was unable to cater to the needs of the large number of people, who came there in the wake of construction of the steel plant. So, in order to facilitate the supply of water to the steel plant and the township all around the year, the Hindustan Steel Ltd. (HSL) constructed the Mandira dam, 24 km away from Rourkela on the river Sankh, a tributary of river Brahmani, and a pick up dam at Tarkera.

To meet the water requirements of the civil town the HSL in 1965 made available 80,000 gallons of water per day through its water works at Tarkera, and to serve this area a pumping station at Panposh was located. However, this was not sufficient to meet the water requirements of the people residing in the civil town. The existing capacity of the water works at Tarkera in 1965 was only three million gallons per day. As the population in the civil town was growing at a very high rate, the new Master Plan of the civil town finalized in 1965, proposed to expand the filtered water supply to six million with a per capita supply of 40 gallons per day.

Drainage and Sewerage

To facilitate the growth of a modern healthy township, the Master Plan of the steel township made adequate provisions for the laying out of a scientific drainage and sewerage system. The plan provided for the discharge of effluents into the river Koel after necessary treatment at the sewage treatment plant. Similarly for industrial wastes from the steel plant, a treatment plant was constructed so that only treated wastes would be released into the Brahmani river.

However for the civil town, intitially there was no provision of a drainage and sewerage system because it grew haphazardly in the wake of industrialisation and large scale immigration of people to Rourkela. When the new Master Plan for the civil township was, however, prepared, it made necessary provisions for the laying out of a drainage and sewerage system and proposed to discharge the sewage of the civil town near village Deongaon, so that the vast agricultural lands available there could be utilised for sewage farming.

Growth of Industries

With the functioning of the steel plant in 1960 many large, medium and small industries started growing in and around Rourkela. Besides generating forward and backward linkage effects for the growth of industries, the location of the giant steel plant in this mineral rich backward region of Chotanagpur plateau helped in the development of basic infrastructures such as rapid transport, communication system, water, electricity, drainage, sewerage and the like, thereby widening the scope for growth of a large urban-industrial complex. The steel plant has generated its multiple effects on the regional economy.

In-between the sixties and eighties a number of large and medium industries were set up. All these industries generated employment for 2,562 persons besides the 34,000 and odd directly employed by the Rourkela Steel Plant.

It is found from Table 1 that by the end of 1987-88, 2,827 Small Scale Industries (SSI) units with a capital investment of Rs. 4,594.27 lakh and a total employment capacity of 31,555 persons were functioning in Sundergarh district of Orissa.

According to the Industrial Survey Report (1983-84 and 1984-85), Sundergarh district with a share of 12.77 per cent organised sector units in the state during 1984-85 shared 48.10 per cent of productive capital, 29.12 per cent of factory employment, 61.54 per cent of inputs, 58.36 per cent of output and 49.78 per cent of value added.[6]

Consequent to the growth of many large, medium and small industries coupled with periodic expansion of production capacity of the steel plant over the years, Rourkela has grown into a large urban industrial complex of Orissa. It is seen from Table 2 that Rourkela is basically an industrial city with 49.08 per cent of workers employed in the secondary sector in 1981. Over the years the city has registered a significant increase in its percentage of workers in the secondary sector – from 46.13 in 1961 to 49.08 in 1981. The percentage of tertiary sector workers in the city on the other hand decreased from 50.88 in 1961 to 47.19 in 1981. From the trend of population growth and workers in the city it may be assumed that till 1961 Rourkela mainly comprised of single workers. The sex ratio was only 537 females per 1,000 males. After the construction of the township and the growth of basic amenities the migrant industrial workers brought their families into the city. As a result, the sex ratio in the city suddenly rose to 748 in 1971 and further to 790 in 1981. Simultaneously, the percentage growth of secondary sector workers in the city registered a negative growth and the over all increase in percentage of all categories of workers during 1961-71 was 12.71 per cent only, as compared to a 91.06 per cent increase in population.

Table 1
Category-wise Break up of Number of SSI Units, Capital Investment and Employment in Sundergarh District of Orissa by the end of 1987-88

Sl. No.	Category	No. of Units	Capital Investment (Rs. in Lakh)	Employment
1.	Food and Allied	436 (15.42)	367.83 (8.01)	2,369 (7.51)
2.	Chemical and Allied	144 (5.09)	397.62 (8.65)	1,575 (4.99)
3.	Electricals and Electronics	62 (2.19)	104.73 (2.28)	416 (1.32)
4.	Engineering and Metal based	741 (26.21)	2133.64 (46.44)	12,492 (39.59)
5.	Forest and Wood Based	184 (6.51)	146.39 (3.19)	1,357 (4.20)
6.	Glass and Ceramics	284 (10.05)	562.28 (12.24)	8,355 (26.48)
7.	Livestock and Leather	17 (0.60)	5.42 (0.12)	80 (0.25)
8.	Paper and Paper Products	98 (3.47)	134.17 (2.92)	664 (2.10)
9.	Rubber and Plastic	82 (2.90)	125.53 (2.73)	454 (1.44)
10.	Textiles	144 (5.09)	44.30 (0.96)	609 (1.93)
11.	Miscellaneous Manufacturing and Servicing	635 (22.46)	572.36 (12.46)	3,184 (10.09)
		2,827 (99.99)	4,594.27 (100.00)	31,555 (100.00)

Note: Figures in parentheses indicate percentage.
Source: Government of Orissa (1988). *Statistical Handbook, 1987-88*, Cuttack, Directorate of Industries.

At the same time, during 1961-71, there might have been a higher rate of inflow of workers to the city, but due to a change in the concept of workers at the time of 1971 Census, the growth rate of workers has been under record.

However, it is important to note that all these workers employed in the secondary and tertiary sectors of the city do not belong to the organized sector. Quite a few of them earn their livelihood in unorganized and informal sectors of the economy. The large size of organised industrial sector work force i.e., the steel plant workers and the concentration of various other large, medium and small industries have opened wider scope for the proliferation of informal

Table 2
Total Number of Workers in Primary, Secondary and Tertiary Sectors of Rourkela City during 1961, 1971 and 1981

Sl. No.	Category	1961	1971	1981	% of Growth 1961-71	% of Growth 1971-81
1	2	3	4	5	6	7
1.	Primary Sector	1,535 (2.99)	2,133 (3.69)	3,587 (3.73)	38.96	68.17
2.	Secondary Sector	23.677 (46.13)	20,443 (35.34)	47,205 (49.08)	-13.66	130.91
3.	Tertiary Sector	26,115 (50.88)	35,273 (60.97)	45,380 (47.19)	35.07	28.65
	TOTAL	51,327 (100.00)	57,848 (100.00)	96,172 (100.00)	12.71	66.25

Note: Figures in parentheses indicate percentage
Source: 1. Census of India, 1961, Vol. XII, Orissa Part II-A, *Primary Census Abstract.*
2. Census of India, 1971, Series 16, Orissa, Part II-A, *Primary Census Abstract.*
3. Census of India, 1981, Series 16, Orissa, Part II-A&BC (i) *General Economic Tables.*

Table 3
Number of Organised Public Sector Establishments and their Employment Strength at Rourkela, 1980

Sl. No.	Category of Establishment	Number of Establishments	Total Employment
1.	2	3	4
1.	Central Government Offices	18	6,494
2.	State Government Offices	150	13,913
3.	Central Government Undertakings	73	42,771
4.	State Government Undertakings	45	2,951
5.	Local Bodies	5	755
	TOTAL	291	66,884

Source: R. K. Samantrai (1981). "Social Integration in Rourkela Region", Paper presented at the Seminar on, *Problems of Integrated Development of the Steel Region*, organised by the Asian workers Development Institute (AWDI), Rourkela.

sector activities in the city. It is seen from Table 3 that in the year 1980, there were 291 public sector establishments in the city and a total of 66,884 persons were employed in those establishments including the giant steel plant. In addition to 66,884 workers employed in the organised public sector another 3,000 workers are employed in different organised private sector. Thus, the total number of workers in the organised sector comes to around 70,000 in the city out of a total of 96,172 workers in 1981. This means, 72.79 per cent of the workers in the city are organised sector workers and the rest are unorganised and informal sector workers.

On account of their better organisational strength and effective bargaining power, the organised sector workers always get higher wages and better service amenities from their employers than the unorganised and informal sector workers. So, taking into account the consumer price index of industrial workers during the year 1988-89 and the then prevailing wage rate of the organised sector workers at the minimum of the scale, we may say that workers earning less than Rs. 1,200 per month in the city of Rourkela in 1988-89 were unorganised and informal sector workers. By adopting this same norm, when we consider the percentage of unorganised and informal sector workers in the city, a figure similar to our previous estimation is obtained.

It is seen from Table 4 that out of a total of 316 sample households taken from different localities of the city, 98 or 31.01 per cent of the households earns an income of less than Rs. 12,00 per month. Of this as many as 38 households or 11.71 per cent in the sample reports a monthly income of less than Rs. 800. It is further revealed from the table that there is a significant difference in the level of earning of households residing in various localities of the city. The slums and squatter areas like Malgodam, Nala Road and Modern India Labour Colony have a very high percentage of households earning less than Rs. 1200 per month; whereas the developed localities like the Oraon Para, the Udit Nagar area and the sector area of the Steel township have a number of households in the high income group.

Growth of Slums

Although Rourkela is a planned city and it was planned to grow as an ideal industrial town with the full-fledged operation of the steel

Table 4
Monthly Income of the Sample Households in Various Localities of Rourkela during 1988-89

Sl. No.	Name of the Locality	No. of Sample House-holds	Monthly Income of the Households					
			Below Rs. 400	Rs. 400 to Rs. 800	Rs. 800 to Rs. 1200	Rs. 1200 to Rs. 1600	Rs. 1600 to Rs. 2000	Rs. 2000 and above
1.	Modern India Labour Colony	48	2 (4.17)	5 (10.42)	4 (8.33)	13 (27.08)	9 (18.75)	15 (31.25)
2.	Oraon Para, Udit Nagar	16	--	2 (12.50)	--	5 (31.25)	--	9 (56.25)
3.	Malgodam	74	1 (1.35)	19 (25.68)	36 (48.65)	9 (12.16)	4 (5.40)	5 (6.76)
4.	Nala Road	60	1 (1.67)	2 (3.33)	18 (30.00)	17 (28.33)	3 (5.00)	19 (31.67)
5.	Steel Township (Sector Area)	110	--	5 (4.24)	3 (2.54)	19 (16.10)	21 (17.80)	70 (59.32)
	TOTAL	316	4 (1.27)	3 (10.44)	61 (19.31)	63 (19.94)	37 (11.71)	118 (37.34)

Note: Figures in parentheses indicate percentage.
Source: Field Data, 1988-89.

plant and other organised sector industries, the very basis of operation of such industries led to the proliferation of informal sector activities and the growth of slums in a big way. The Western model of a planned industrial township failed to work in a labour surplus backward economy. Thus, when a vast size of organised sector workforce with their families and close relatives was brought and made to reside in the city, it paved the way for the generation of employment opportunities in the informal manufacturing and service sector of the city economy. Since, the Master Plan of the city did not make adequate provisions for basic services and accommodation for these informal sector workers, slums and squatters areas started proliferating over the years.

In Rourkela, slums and squatters are growing so fast that there is no proper official record with regard to the slum population. However, from our close observation of different areas of the city during 1987-89 we have recorded 41 localities in both civil and steel township areas which may be classified as slum and squatter localities. Of this, only 27 localities are demarcated in the voters' list of Rourkela Assembly constituency of 1984, while the voters' list of the rest of the localities is difficult to delimit because of their amalgamation with the voters' list of non-slum areas of the city. From this voters' list, it has been found that these 27 localities have an all total of 14,426 households with an approximate estimated population of 67,354. It is seen from Table 5 that out of this 14,426 households in slums, 15.53 per cent are scheduled castes, 29.88 per cent are scheduled tribes, 11.90 per cent are lower castes households and the rest of the 33.17 per cent are high and middle castes households. The percentage of minority households living in slums comes to 13.23 because the tribal Christian households have been included under both the sections in columns 5 and 8 of Table 5. Of course, one may question our delimitation of slum households on the basis of castes as the voters' list does not indicate the caste of the households. However, we wish to make it clear that from our familiarity with the surnames of different castes we have delimited the households by perusing the voters' list of these areas minutely and in case of any doubt people of these areas have been consulted to know the caste background of the household from the particular surname. It is seen from Table 5 that out of the 27 slums noted down from the voters' list, 10 localities are predominantly inhabited by the scheduled castes and scheduled tribes households. These 10 localities are namely (i) Malgodam, (ii) Old Labour Colony, (iii) Captive Power Plant area, (iv) Champagarh Labour Colony, (v) Phoolbari, (vi) Balijodi, (vii) Hathibandha Labour Colony, (viii) Kansar, (ix) Old Jalda and (x) Kaintabasa. From the table it is indicated that usually very few people of high and middle castes background live in slum areas and there is a close correspondence between caste and class in a modern industrial city like Rourkela also. Besides this, it is found that the Nala Road area is predominantly inhabited by the minority households i.e. the Muslims.

According to the 1981 Census, the Rourkela urban agglomeration had a total population of 3.23 lakh with 69,423 households. On this basis, it is found that the average size of a household in Rourkela consists of 4.65 persons and from this we may assume that the 27 localities mentioned in Table 5 have a total population of 67,354. Further, on a lower level if we estimate that the other 14 slum areas of Rourkela shall not be having less than 10,000 population, then the total population of the slum area of Rourkela comes to 77,000 approximately. This means around 23.84

Table 5
Caste and Community-wise total number of Squatter Households and their Estimated Population in various Slum and Squatter Localities of Rourkela

Sl. No.	Name of the Locality	Total No. of House-holds	No. of SC House-holds	No. of ST House-holds	No. of OBC House-holds	No. of higher caste House-holds	No. of Mino-rity-house-holds	Esti-mated Popu-lation
1	2	3	4	5	6	7	8	9
1.	ITI Industrial Estate Jhonpuri	701	93 (13.27)	161 (22.97)	87 (12.41)	340 (48.50)	91 (12.98)	3260
2.	Sector-2 Labour Colony	576	134 (23.26)	135 (23.44)	74 (12.85)	222 (38.54)	16 (2.78)	2678
3.	Gopabandhu Palli	1449	286 (19.74)	254 (17.53)	257 (17.74)	596 (41.13)	123 (8.49)	6738
4.	Madhusudan Palli	1218	302 (24.80)	259 (21.26)	269 (22.08)	351 (28.81)	55 (4.51)	5664
5.	Gualapara	280	14 (5.00)	123 (43.93)	31 (11.07)	104 (37.14)	37 (13.21)	1574
6.	Malgodam	1311	406 (30.97)	318 (24.26)	193 (14.72)	353 (25.93)	84 (6.41)	6096
7.	Nala Road	1298	39 (3.00)	13 (1.00)	37 (2.85)	120 (9.24)	1090 (83.97)	6036
8.	Old Labour Colony	247	39 (15.79)	107 (43.32)	25 (10.12)	56 (22.67)	25 (10.12)	1149
9.	Captive Power Plant	190	14 (7.37)	149 (78.48)	15 (7.89)	12 (6.32)	1 (0.53)	883
10.	Champagarh Labour Colony	292	23 (7.88)	138 (47.26)	36 (12.33)	93 (31.85)	2 (0.68)	1358
11.	Phulbari & Bricks Labour Colony	737	101 (13.70)	384 (52.10)	70 (9.50)	174 (23.61)	26 (3.53)	3427
12.	Balijodi	567	42 (7.41)	247 (43.56)	57 (10.05)	220 (38.80)	69 (12.17)	2637
13.	Tarapur	762	131 (17.19)	189 (24.80)	87 (11.42)	348 (45.67)	40 (5.25)	3543
14.	Hatibandha Labour Colony	768	10 (1.30)	697 (90.75)	38 (4.95)	23 (2.99)	37 (4.82)	3571
15.	Kansar	141	24 (17.02)	102 (72.34)	10 (7.09)	5 (3.55)	5 (3.55)	656
16.	Old Jalda	265	36 (13.58)	164 (61.89)	35 (13.21)	23 (8.68)	40 (15.09)	1232
17.	Deogaon Quarry Area	486	112 (23.04)	95 (19.55)	70 (14.40)	195 (40.12)	33 (6.79)	2260
18.	Kalinga Auto Colony	121	6 (4.96)	15 (12.39)	20 (16.53)	78 (64.46)	5 (4.13)	563
19.	Jharmunda	159	13 (8.18)	66 (41.51)	21 (13.21)	57 (35.85)	8 (5.03)	739
20.	Construction Colony	872	126 (14.45)	50 (5.73)	108 (12.38)	581 (66.63)	16 (1.83)	4055

1	2	3	4	5	6	7	8	9
21.	Kaintabasa	107	12 (11.21)	79 (73.83)	5 (4.67)	11 (10.28)	1 (0.93)	498
22.	Langrabasa	79	12 (15.19)	39 (49.37)	12 (15.19)	16 (20.25)	0	367
23.	Lal Tanki	351	73 (20.80)	81 (23.08)	52 (14.81)	137 (39.03)	34 (9.69)	1632
24.	Balipoda	87	11 (12.64)	19 (21.84)	5 (5.75)	52 (59.77)	0 (0)	405
25.	Modern India Labour Colony	721	107 (14.84)	85 (11.79)	66 (9.15)	440 (61.02)	24 (3.33)	3353
26.	Old Rourkela Labour Colony	279	35 (12.54)	34 (12.19)	28 (10.04)	172 (61.65)	17 (6.09)	1297
27.	Bijubandha Jhonpuri	362	39 (10.77)	308 (85.08)	9 (2.49)	6 (1.66)	30 (8.29)	1683
	TOTAL	14,426	2240 (15.53)	4311 (29.88)	1717 (11.90)	4785 (33.17)	1909 (13.23)	67,354

Note: Figures in parentheses indicate percentage.
* Field Data 1988-89.
Source: Voter's list of Rourkela Assembly Constituency, 1984.

per cent of the population at Rourkela lives in slum areas.

The growth of slums in many parts of the planned steel township has also made this city ugly including the beautiful sector areas. Quite a large number of slums are found located beside the plants' boundary wall on the southern and western side. In these localities such as Construction Colony, Modern India Labour Colony, Lal Tanki etc. quite a few regular workers of Rourkela Steel Plant (RSP) also reside, besides the contract labourers working inside the plant. It is found from a study on contract labour that the Rourkela Steel Plant alone employs 19.00 per cent of the workers in its various departments on contract and temperory basis (Sengupta, 1983). All of these workers are unorganised sector workers and they do not get any other facilities except the fixed wage unlike the regular workers of the plant, although they are found to be performing the same type of jobs as the regular workers. Moreover, due to acute housing shortage, workers in RSP with even 20 years of service have not been able to get staff quarters accommodation in the sector areas. As a result, some of them continue to reside in slums and old labour colonies alongwith their kith and kin.

Availability of Basic Amenities

On account of the high growth of population in contrast to the plan estimate for the city, it is observed that the availability of basic civic amenities such as potable water, drainage and sewerage, electricity, latrine, bath room etc. is very poor in Rourkela. Moreover, due to the supply scarcity there is a wide discrepancy in the availability of these amenities to the different localities of the city. In this situation, people living in slums and squatters are the worst sufferers. According to the Orissa Town Directory of 1981 Census in the year 1979, Rourkela urban agglomeration had 345 km (81.95%) of *pucca* road, 76 km (18.05%) of *kutcha* road, 31,273 (45.05%) latrines, out of which 1,237 (3.95%) were service latrines, 26,976 (38.86%) domestic electricity connection and 1,227.44 lakh litres water supply capacity. The availability of public health services per 10,000 population was 0.81 only or on an average one public health centre was rendering health services to 12,408 persons. Similarly, the availability of public road lighting per km was 16.69 or one lighting point for a distance of 59.92 metres. As referred to earlier, the civil township had no sewerage system and only some parts of the city were provided with the facilities of open surface drains, and box surface drains. However, the steel township had a developed sewerage system besides open surface drains.

The availability of potable water per individual in the city is presently 308 litres per day. Out of a total of 636.45 lakh litres of water available through the service reservoir in the steel township, 50 per cent of the water is consumed by the steel plant alone. Thus, the actual availability of water per head shall not be more than 228 litres a day for the entire urban agglomeration.

Further, it is noticed that the steel township, especially the sector area is better off than the civil township with regard to the availability of basic amenities. It was found from the census data that the households in the steel township have latrine coverage of 25,330 i.e., 56.00 per cent as compared to only 27.70 per cent coverage of latrines in the households of the civil township. It is observed that all the staff quarters of Rourkela Steel Plant (RSP) located in various sector areas of the steel township are provided with latrine and tap water facilities, underground sewerage connection and electricity connection. The whole of the steel township area has 21,400 (46.94%) domestic electricity connections out of a total number of

45,588 bouseholds recorded by 1981 census; whereas the civil township has a total of 5,526 domestic electricity connections (25.80%), households totalling 21,416 in 1981. Similarly, the percentage of *kutcha* road to total road length in the steel township is 6.07 per cent; whereas in the civil township it is 18.81 per cent. With regard to the availability of number of street light points per one km road length, it is 8.17 in case of civil township area as compared to 22.14 in the steel township. On the whole, it is observed that the sector area of the steel township is a modern planned city with well-developed basic infrastructure and civic amenities, whereas the civil township area is more congested, dirty and polluted except the posh locality like area No. 7 and 8 and Udit Nagar.

In such a situation, the slum and squatter areas of the city are found to be suffering enormously in the absence of basic civic amenities such as safe drinking water, domestic latrines, electricity, drainage system and the like. For my doctoral thesis, I have surveyed 182 slum and squatter households in three slum localities of Rourkela, namely (i) Modern India Labour Colony, (ii) Malgodam and (iii) Nala Road. Of this, the first one is a part of the steel township and the other two localities are located near the Central Business District Zone of the civil township. The Nala Road area is mostly inhabited by the Muslim population, Modern India Labour Colony by the people of Ganjam district and the tribals of Bihar state and Malgodam area has a composite population hailing from states like Bihar and Madhya Pradesh and also from various districts of Orissa. It is found from Table 6 that around 76.37 per cent of the sample slum households in these localities live in *kutcha* houses. Among these households, 43.41 per cent are single room houses, 37.36 per cent have two rooms and only 19.27 per cent of them have more than two rooms. The percentage of households with latrine facilities is only 28.02 and those with bathroom facilities 17.58 per cent. Fifty-two per cent of the sample households in these slums have domestic electricity connection. But at the same time, it is important to mention that 63.33 per cent of the sample households at Nala Road have latrine facilities and these are mostly service latrines, because Muslim women usually do not go to the open field for defecation. Similarly, it is due to this reason that 36.67 per cent of the households have bath room facilities in their living compounds also. Among all these three localities, it is observed that the worst

Table 6
Type of Houses and Availability of Basic Amenities in the Sample Households of Selected Slum and Squatter Areas of Rourkela

Sl. No.	Name of Slum Squatter Area	No. of sample House-holds	No. of *Kutcha* Houses	No. of *Pucca* Houses	No. of one room houses	No. of two room houses	No. of houses with more than two rooms	No. of houses with latrine	No. of houses with bathroom	No. of houses with electricity connection
1	2	3	4	5	6	7	8	9	10	11
1.	Modern India Labour Colony	48	30 (62.50)	18 (37.50)	19 (39.58)	22 (45.83)	7 (14.58)	12 (25.00)	9 (18.75)	20 (41.67)
2.	Malgodam	74	74 (100.00)	0	45 (60.81)	24 (32.43)	5 (6.76)	1 (1.35)	1 (1.35)	26 (35.13)
3.	Nala Road	60	35 (58.33)	25 (41.67)	15 (25.00)	22 (36.67)	23 (38.33)	38 (63.33)	22 (36.67)	49 (81.67)
		182	139 (76.37)	43 (23.63)	79 (43.41)	68 (37.36)	35 (19.23)	51 (28.02)	32 (17.58)	95 (52.20)

Note: Figures in parentheses indicate percentage.
Source: Field Data, 1988-89.

locality with regard to the availability of basic amenities was Malgodam slum area, located near the daily market area and the Rourkela Railway Station.

On the whole, it is observed that almost all the slum localities of Rourkela are affected by the inadequate supply of basic civic amenities such as roads, drainage, piped water supply, sanitary latrines and the like, although many of them are located adjacent to the Central Business District zone and the Steel Plant's boundary. Owing to the scarcity of piped water the public water stand posts are broken in many localities. The hand-pumps supplied by the urban local bodies hardly serve the drinking water needs of the people in most of the localities due to contamination of underground water, and in many localities sufficient number of these are not available to cater to the needs of slum population. As a result, quarrels and fighting among the residents over water collection is a daily event in all these localities. In the absence of drainage and sewerage facilities, domestic effluents accumulate on the roads. Solid wastes generated by households are found scattered all over the locality with stray cattle, street dogs, domestic pigs and fowls moving around in search of left over food.

In the absence of a proper drainage and sewerage system the entire civil town except Udit Nagar and Area No. 7 and 8 looks like a big slum. Even the planned housing scheme of Basanti Colony area looks like a relatively prosperous slum with open drains and sewage water spilling on to the roads at many places.

Quality of Life

The functioning of a giant public sector Steel Plant without well-developed pollution controlling measures, uncontrolled growth of informal sector activities coupled with proliferation of slums and many more large, medium and small industries in and around Rourkela have led to deterioration in the quality of life in the city. Further, the lack of a developed infrastructural base and supply scarcity of basic amenities for a large section of people residing in slums and other localities of the civil township aggravates the living conditions of the people residing in the city and its periphery. According to a study made by an engineering student of the Regional Engineering College, Rourkela, the Steel Plant produces

50-60 kg of dust per tonne of steel produced (S Mohapatra, 1988). A large amount of dust is released from the exhaust from the LD furnace. The dust (size ranging from 6 mm to 200 mm) content in the exhaust is 730 um^3 of flue gas. The dust presents a potential hazard to health and contributes to air, land and water pollution, whereas flue gas containing carbon monoxide, nitrogen oxide etc. causes air pollution too. Besides, this, the plant produces a large amount of blast furnace slag (12.15%) which creates a disposal problem and also water pollution problem, when rain water passes over it to the river. The Captive Thermal Power Plant produces 30,000 tonnes of fly ash per yçar which is a solid waste by-product and a potential health hazard. The power plant itself emits 40-50 per cent SO_2 through the chimney besides arseic and other radioactive gases into the air. From the nitric acid plant a huge amount of nitrogen oxide is emitted into the atmosphere. H_2S emission from the ammonia plant pollutes the river water. Moreover, waste steam cooling water and hot liqid steam from by-product and fertilizer plants contribute to both water and soil pollution in the region. Besides all these, the petrol pumps, repair workshops and the innumerable garages pollute the city environment with metals like chromium, copper, manganese, nickel and lead in the form of dust and solid waste. On account of release of a large amount of untreated effluent such as carbon monoxide, sulphur oxide, naptha, nitrogen oxide and hydrocarbons alongwith fly-ash, soot etc. The people residing in the city suffer from chronic lung diseases, asthma, sore throat, burning of eyes, headache etc. People using polluted water often suffer from dysentry, diarrhoea, gastroenteritis, jaundice, skin irritation and premature hair fall.

It is found from our survey of 316 households in different areas of the city that every year per thousand population in the sample, 14.8 persons suffer from various types of water borne diseases such as diarrohoea, gastric, jaundice etc., 4.8 persons from respiratory diseases like tuberculosis, *asthma*, 1.2 persons from heart diseases, 0.2 persons from cancer, 5.8 persons from malaria, 2.6 persons from eye diseases, 1.2 persons from paralysis and the like (Table 7). It is seen from Table 7 that on an average 39 persons from a size of 1,000 population in our sample households at Rourkela suffer from various types of ailments, which may be due to the high rate of air and water pollution in the city.

Table 7
Number of Persons per thousand Population in the Sample affected by Various Pollution Related Diseases at Rourkela every year

Sl No.	Name of the Diseases	No. of affected persons per 1000 population
1.	**Water Borne Diseases**	**14.8**
	a. Diarrhoea	4.0
	b. Gastric	6.2
	c. Jaundice	3.5
	d. Typhoid	0.4
	e. Skin disease	0.7
2.	**Respiratory Diseases**	**4.8**
	a. Tuberculosis	1.8
	b. *Asthma*	2.7
	c. Others	0.3
3.	**Heart Diseases**	**1.2**
4.	**Cancer**	**0.2**
5.	**Malaria**	**5.8**
6.	**Chickenpox**	**1.7**
7.	**Eye Diseases**	**2.6**
8.	**Blood Pressure**	**1.4**
9.	**Paralysis**	**1.2**
10.	**Rheumatism**	**2.2**
11.	**Other Diseases**	**3.1**
	TOTAL	39.0

Source: Field Data, 1988-89.

Also, our finding in the sample is corroborated to some extent by the study of Dr. T K Bose, Chief Medical Officer of Ispat General Hospital, Rourkela (Bose, 1987). According to him a random study of health status of 1,500 workers in RSP revealed that 6.0 per cent of them suffered from respiratory diseases and 14.9 per cent showed high Eosinophil content. A follow up study of 1,113 workers working in the dusty areas of RSP revealed that 3.2 per cent suffered from *asthma*, 4.8 per cent suffered from chronic respiratory diseases and 3.3 per cent suffered from tuberculosis (Bose, 1987: 8).

The case study of Rourkela illustrates that the planning of a modern township in the absence of proper planning of the periphery and the adjacent rural areas leads to an unintended form of urban development in the long run. Moreover, the policy of opening of large scale industries and providing a well-developed basic infrastructure and amenities to organised sector workers without making necessary provisions for the informal sector workers, who are an integral and indispensable part of the city economy in the present stage of our economic development, is a highly insensible method of urban development in the Third World countries. This creates labour aristocracy and a dualistic form of economy in the city.

NOTES

1. Report of the Inter-regional Seminar on *Slums and Uncontrolled Settlements*, New York, United Nations, 1971.
2. See, Government of India (1991) *Provisional Population Totals: Rural-Urban Distribution* paper 2 of 1991, Series 1, Census of India 1991, Statement 17, P. 32.
3. *Report of the Working Group*, Planning Commission, New Delh, 1972.
4. *Ibid*.
5. N. Senapati (ed) (1974). *Orissa, District Gazetteers Sundergarh*, Cuttack, Government Press.
6. Government of Orissa (1991). *Annual Survey of Industries in Orissa 1983-84 and 1984-85*, Bhubaneswar, Directorate of Economics and Statistics, p. 24.

REFERENCES

Bose, A. N. (1974). *The Informal Sector in Calcutta Metropolitan Economy*, Geneva, ILO.

Bose, T. K., (1987). "Occupational Health Hazards in Steel Industry", *Souvenir of Indian Association of Medical Health*, 37th All India Conference, January, 1987.

Gilbert, A and Josef Gugler (1981). *Cities, Poverty and Development: Urbanization in the Third World*, Oxford, Oxford University Press.

ILO (1972). *Employment, Income and Inequality — A Strategy for Increasing Productive Employment in Kenya*, Geneva, ILO.

—— (1977). *Employment Problems in Rural and Informal Sectors in Ghana*. Report of an ILO, JASPA Mission, Addis Ababa.

Joshi, Heather and Vijay (1976) *Surplus Labour and city — A Study in Bombay*, Bombay.

Lubell, H. (1974). *Urban Development and Employment: The Prospects for Calcutta*, Geneva, ILO.

Mohapatra, S (1988). "Pollution in and around Rourkela", *Utkal Chemical Engineer*, Rourkela, REC.

Papola, T. S. (1980). *Urban Informal Sector in a Developing Economy*, New Delhi, Vikas Publishing House.

Samantrai, R. K., (1981). "Social Integration in Rourkela Region", Paper presented at the Seminar on, *Problems of Integrated Development of the Steel Region*, Organised by the Asian Workers' Development Institute, Rourkela, (Mimeographed).

Sengupta, Nirmal (1983). *Contract Labour in the Steel Region Rourkela*, Rourkela, AWDI (Mimeographed).

Sethuraman, S. V., (1976). *Jakarta: Urban Development and Employment*, Geneva, ILO.

17

Financing Water Supply and Sanitation in Urban India

Abhijit Datta

ALTHOUGH potable water supply and sanitation are considered as 'basic needs' in the urban areas, over the years actual investments on these services have been minimal and woefully inadequate. Being 'merit goods', it is often difficult to assess the ability and willingness of the urbanites to pay for these services. This adversely affects the 'credit-worthiness' of urban water supply and sanitation projects in terms of investments – both national and international – so that a sub-optimal resource allocation takes place (WHO, 1977).

On the other hand, often due to institutional separation between investment and maintenance responsibilities, there is 'over investment' on facilities in terms of feasible revenue allocations, leading to maintenance gaps in local authority budgets.

There are indications that the concept of financial viability is being broadened to consider economic justification for project appraisal; similarly, unification of institutional responsibilities is seen to favour investment proposals based on low-cost techniques with lower maintenance outlay.

The paper would pursue these aspects of financing urban water supply and sanitation from four angles: (a) financial optimisation, (b) financing methods, (c) capital finance, and (d) private participation in service provision, to see how best to provide the two important and basic services within the existing resource environment. The main thrust and policy implications of the paper will be highlighted in the concluding section.

Financial Optimisation

This measure consists of the following components: network

maintenance, wastes recycling, distributional equity and low-cost technology to which we turn next.

Maintenance of water supply, drainage and sewerage lines is of utmost importance because it helps in substantial service augmentation without additional investment on the facilities. It is estimated that about 30 per cent of water leaks through the distribution system. Where storm water and sewage disposal have common pipes, very often they get clogged due to sedimentation. Periodic cleaning of sewage mains would also increase their transportation capacity without additional investment on new lines.

Financial optimisation could also be promoted through recycling of wastes – both liquefied waste and household garbage. Suggestions have been made to charge lower water tariffs for use of treated waste water for household and industrial use (National Commission on Urbanisation, 1988).

Trenching of excreta for producing marketable manure to farmers is being practised by many smaller municipalities; its use for producing bio-gas at sewage disposal sites or on slum locations having community latrines is another feasible option. Similarly, household garbage in India consists mainly of kitchen and vegetable wastes which could also be converted into bio-gas and manure after the solid elements are separated by licensed rag-pickers for eventual industrial use. The need for incinerators to dispose of the urban solid wastes may not be viable in most Indian cities in view of the non-combustible nature of household garbage.

The various forms of waste disposal, as indicated, offer opportunities for generation of valuable bye-products which could be marketed by the municipal authorities to recover a part of the cost of wastes disposal. Such recycling would also be environment-friendly and cost-effective at the same time.

Differential provision of urban basic services in the high and low-income localities is another problem that needs correction. For this, a minimum level of services needs to be defined and met before responding to demands for additional services. Very often planned upgradation targets are based on the requirements of high-income localities, without first meeting the service deficiencies in the slum and poorer localities. Therefore, it is necessary to plan for higher levels of service in the deficit areas so that an equitable access to the urban basic services could be achieved.

Once the minimum service levels are achieved, the municipal

authority would be free to offer additional or improved services on commercial principles. If specific high demand areas could be isolated, as in housing estates, it is possible to license private operators to offer differential services on the basis of demand.

Adoption of low-cost technology in the provision of urban basic services is another method of financial optimisation. In water supply and excreta removal, use of mobile tankers in slum locations is very often a cost-effective way of service provision.

Again, spot harvesting of ground-water would augment the central supply – this could be allowed to the householders provided the right of underground water is vested in the municipal authority to ensure regulated drawal of a common community resource. In the absence of such a right, the municipal authority could locally augment its water supply without costly investment in the centralised system of collection, treatment and distribution of water supply.

The same approach of localised provision of sewage treatment and excreta disposal may be adopted that do not call for large investments on trunk sewers. Since only a limited area in the Indian cities is sewered – not more than 25 per cent – the immediate need is to install community and household latrines, preferably of the pour-flush variety, with *in situ* disposal arrangements.

The main point arising out of our discussion on the various methods of financial optimisation for urban basic services is that with marginal investment, the equity and supply problems could be satisfactorily dealt with even under existing institutional arrangements. However, adoption of each of these methods would call for a reorientation of professional attitudes in terms of greater sensitivity to the needs of the urban poor and a continual search for adoption of cost-effective methods of organising urban basic services, such as water supply and sanitation.

Financing Methods

Financial methods consist of the following aspects namely Basic Services Tax, Water Tax, Service Charges and Budgetary Support.

An integrated approach for financing urban basic services, such as water supply and sanitation, in India has to be evolved as an integral part of the strategy to meet the minimum social consumption needs of the urban poor staying in designated slum locations. The financing sources for such services could be: (i) a consolidated basic service tax (BST) imposed on hut-owners benefiting from urban slum improvement schemes under the Minimum Needs Programme (MNP), (ii) a minimum *per capita* contribution from the municipal authority (at, say, Rs. 5 per adult per month), and (iii) twice the amount of municipal contribution by way of grants from the state government. All these sources could be credited to a Basic Services Account from which necessary expenditures on water supply and sanitation could be met. The point to note here is that (a) the BST is viewed as a benefit tax to be recovered only after the completion of an improvement programme under the MNP, and (b) the state revenue contribution would complement the capital grant for improvement of the urban basic services.

While the requirement for a special Basic Services Account follows such a provision for *bustee* services under the Calcutta Municipal Corporation Act, 1980, the twin requirements of the BST and the matching state contribution are innovations to induce tax compliance and meeting the maintenance cost of slum improvements under the MNP. The BST is in the form of a community charge of the poll tax variety; its use in the provision of urban basic services in designated urban slum locations is an innovation worth trying, especially after their upgradation. Earlier attempts to collect hut taxes in Bombay failed primarily due to the absence of any nexus between such taxation and demonstrable benefits to the slum dwellers.

In order to ensure a minimum level of water supply in the urban areas it is necessary to impose a water benefit tax (WBT) on all assessed properties as a proportion (say, 30 per cent) of the basic holding tax in return for an assured minimum supply per household (at, say, 15000 litres per month) taking into account a minimum of 100 lpcd supply needed to meet the basic water need. One water tap with the required ferrule size could thus be made freely available to those who would not demand any extra water. The same arrangement may be offered to non-assessed householders on payment at average cost of minimum water supply with a single tap. No exemptions need be granted to those having private water supply from payment of the WBT.

Apart from the WBT, there is no need to impose any other service taxes on the householders as it is difficult to specify the quantum of other basic services that would be required by a locality.

Separate service charges for extra water supply, sewerage and special garbage collection could be imposed at fairly steep graduated levels to meet the marginal cost. These charges are in the nature of fees and, as such, it is necessary to relate service provision to the fee level that approximates the cost. Given this requirement, the scope for cross-subsidy for such service provision needs to be minimal (say, not more than 20 per cent across the slab rates).

When such preconditions are imposed, it would be possible to induce private or cooperative undertakings to enter the urban services arena in competition with municipal or public utility undertakings. The failure of the latter to provide urban basic services is mainly due to the fact that the excessive reliance on cross-subsidy device fails either to meet the basic service component, or to satisfy the demand of the urbanites who are willing to pay for better quality and higher levels of urban services.

With this approach, the question of metering water supply loses much of its relevance. Similarly, the rates appropriate for institutional and industrial uses would be set by market forces, as not more than 25 per cent of total water demand is generated from such uses. The household and non-household rates would obviously be different, but the latter need not be extortionate in terms of incidence.

Charging for sewerage is to be piggy-backed on water rates (say, 75 per cent) under the assumption that most of the used water is to be transported back for treatment, after allowing for ground seepage. In order to encourage the use of recycled water, rebate may be allowed on the water charge, but such possibilities would exist only for industries using water as raw material.

It is also desirable to charge for collection of special garbage from markets, building sites, hospitals, factories and the like, at rates commensurate with its volume and hazardous nature. Similarly, increased frequency in garbage collection, when found necessary or desired by the residents in a locality, may be charged separately. There is a possibility of engaging private contractors to transport garbage to the tipping dumps at a cost lower than that of municipal expenses for the same. There are several municipal authorities moving in this direction; the practice needs to be more widespread. Local disposal of garbage in sanitary landfills or manure-trenches are alternatives to centralised dumping of garbage at the city outskirts.

The 'public good' component of urban water supply and sanitation needs to be clearly covered by adequate municipal budgetary support from the general revenues. Such services would include public standposts, watering of city streets, water storage for fire fighting, water supply to city parks and fountains, maintenance of storm water drains and outfalls, etc. About 30 per cent of the total water supply may constitute such activities, if one follows the mandatory provision in this regard under the Calcutta Municipal Corporation Act, 1980. Similarly, normal street cleaning and garbage disposal is another area needing municipal budgetary support, together with expenditure on public health.

The methods of financing urban water supply and sanitation envisages reliance on (i) a basic service tax, (ii) a water benefit tax, (iii) State grants for basic services, (iv) municipal revenue contribution for city-wide community services, and (v) fee-based charges for above-minimum level of water supply, sewerage and sanitation services. Additionally, the limited scope for cross-subsidies in these services needs to be recognised in view of the compulsions under tax and fee-financed services operating together.

Attempts at undue cross-subsidisation have not only been at the expense of limiting the municipal obligation to meet basic urban needs, but also in creating an impression that such services could be loaded on to the revenues generated on the basis of their actual consumption. The organisational implications of these arrangements are that the market component of these services could be separated under non-municipal auspices, but to expect that these 'commercial' undertakings would solve the problem of meeting the basic service needs is unrealistic, to say the least.

Capital Financing

Under this we have discussed the aspects like capital grants, market loans and plan finance. Given the possibility of a two-part system of urban water supply and sanitation services, it is obvious that the 'public and basic services' aspect would need tax-financed support for upgradation and improvement. Therefore, capital grants and municipal revenue surpluses are the preferred means of their capital finance. If increased tax collection is realistically projected for future, then it is possible to contract soft loans for the purpose.

The need for market loans, including institutional borrowings, for meeting the capital requirements would likewise depend on the prospects of raising fee-based revenues through realistic tariffs based on estimates of observed demand signals, rather than pious wishes. This would call for close monitoring of real demand on the basis of consumer preferences among various groups of householders, institutions and commercial undertakings. To the extent that there is a possibility of allowing privatised provision of these services, the need for municipal capital outlay and operating responsibilities would be less.

Loans for development are to be related to the repaying capacity of the operating organizations, so that a system of market appraisal on the basis of their credit-rating by independent non-governmental agencies may be attempted. Furthermore, all borrowings are to be properly funded through mandatory sinking funds to avoid accumulation of unproductive debt and the possibility of future debt default.

Plan financing of urban water supply and sanitation would thus consist mainly of capital grants and limited doses of institutional loans to be directly negotiated by the operating organizations under reasonable conditionalities like tariff revision, management and accounting reforms, beneficiary criteria, choice of project, utilisation schedule, etc. The existing practice of allocating soft loans to substitute capital grants should be ended so that both the lending agencies and borrowing institutions are conscious of the cost of capital and the purpose for which it is to be used.

The existing methods of Plan allocation of soft loans for financing urban water supply and sanitation projects should yield place to a more realistic assessment of the needs for capital grants and market loans to finance capital projects. Capital grants could be wholly Plan allocated, while loans could be made available through market and institutional borrowings, with required conditionalities.

Private Provision

We have already indicated the scope for private provision of water supply through local water harvesting by way of borewell and storage of rainwater etc. It would be necessary for the municipal authorities to acquire groundwater rights so that the private demands could be controlled.

The private efforts to recycle city wastes could also be

encouraged through a licensing system. This may have to be complemented by municipal disposal of semi-solid wastes in trenching grounds and bio-gas digesters for producing bio-gas and manure for lighting and agricultural purposes. The private-public interface in solid wastes management thus calls for a joint effort to convert city wastes into valuable resources for the community.

The possibility of contracting-out the non-basic parts of water supply and sanitation services to public, private and cooperative undertakings needs to be seen against the overall responsibility for providing essential civic services of the municipal authorities. Their future constitutional status would require that the commercial undertakings, whether public or private, operate within the overall municipal control and supervision (Constitution Amendment Bill, 1991). In a sense, these commercial undertakings would also be licensees of the concerned municipal authorities in any urban area and subjected to municipal taxation on their property value.

The scope for private participation in water supply and sanitation would increase under a two-part basic services system; however, such participation needs to be regulated by the concerned municipal authority in each urban area under licensing arrangements. This would not only cover the purely private ventures, it would also be equally applicable to special-purpose utilities under public auspices.

Conclusion

The main thrust of the paper rests on the removal of the existing deficiencies in the provision of urban basic services, like, water supply and sanitation, arising out of (a) failure to optimise existing resources, (b) inappropriate mix of revenue sources, (c) lack of integration between revenue and capital expenditures, and (d) inability to mobilise private efforts to complement local public responsibilities.

The paper attempts to overcome these lacuna through a series of measures from the operational and developmental perspectives. The suggestions made are indicative, to be modulated in terms of a specific urban situation; however, the major action point in effecting substantial improvements in the sector deficiencies lies at the municipal level, to be supported by corresponding enabling measures at the higher levels of government.

Policy Implications

The policy implications of the paper may be identified in terms of the following:

- the need clearly to spell out the policy parameters in the water supply and sanitation sector.
- optimisation of existing resources, including adoption of appropriate technology and measures to recycle wastes.
- adoption of a proper mix of tax and fees approach in the sector in recognition of the basic need for these services and the possibilities for pricing the demand element;
- integration of institutional responsibilities to facilitate fiscal integration for improved coverage of services; and
- implications of the impending constitutional strengthening of municipal governments for improved urban water supply and sanitation services.

REFERENCES

India, 1988, *Report of the National Commission on Urbanisation*, Vol. II, New Delhi: Government of India Press.

———, 1991, *The Constitution (Seventy-third Amendment) Bill, 1991*, New Delhi: Lok Sabha Secretariat.

W. H. O., 1977, *Community Water Supply and Excreta Disposal in South East Asia*, New Delhi: Regional Office.

18

Local Resource Mobilisation

Tapan K Banerjee

THE much debated issues in resource mobilisation by urban local bodies (ULB) show no sign of being resolved due perhaps to the diverse views held about the role of ULB in urban management. This is the fallout of the state-local relationship. The ULB being a creature of the state, with no constitutional status, suffers from ambiguity and uncertainty. Framing of policy instruments to be used by the ULB is the prerogative of the state so that the ULB, notwithstanding its democratic structure, is reduced to an agent of the State in respect of urban management. In other words, the ULB is bereft of inherent power and authority in respect of decisional choice and preferences. When an ULB is asked to collect a local tax, its fiscal efficiency is measured *inter alia* by the percentage of the assessed tax collected. When a tax is unilaterally withdrawn by the state and some compensation in lieu of that is given, the ULB is looked upon as grant or transfer dependent. Similarly, the functional domain of the ULB, particularly over the past couple of decades is being encroached upon, directly or indirectly, by the state. On the other hand, socially important functions which may be culturally alien to municipal environment and also liable to put additional financial burden on the ULB, are unilaterally passed on.

This urban scenario is not at all a revelation. Yet a brief sketch of this backdrop is necessary for visualising the perspective for mobilisation of financial resources at the local level.

The State of Municipal Finance

Before exploring the possibility of augmenting local resources by the ULBs, it is worthwhile to look at the present state of municipal finances in some states. It is a common allegation that the performance of the ULBs in revenue mobilisation is rather poor and that their dependence on transfers from the state is continually increasing.

Table 1 furnishes a comparative picture of eleven States in respect of the revenue composition of their municipalities. A similar picture is presented in Table 2 in respect of 12 municipal corporations of different States. The tables reveals that in the octroi collecting States the relative importance of tax revenue in the revenue composition of the municipalities is much higher than that in the non-octroi collecting States. In Gujarat, Maharashtra, Rajasthan and Uttar Pradesh 53 to 75 per cent of the total municipal revenue is composed of taxes alone. Among the non-octroi collecting states, however, Karnataka*, Kerala* and Orissa stand apart as regards the percentage of tax revenue (55 to 63 per cent to total revenue).

Table 1

Revenue Composition of Municipal Bodies of Some States (1986-87)

(Percentage)

Sl. No.	States	Own Source Revenue			Transferred Revenue				Total Revenue
		Tax	Non-Tax	Total	Grants	Shared Taxes	Others	Total	
1.	Andhra Pradesh	26	24	50	27	11	12	50	100
2.	Gujarat	64	11	75	14	4	7	25	100
3.	Karnataka	55	20	75	3	8	14	25	100
4.	Kerala	63	20	83	6	11	--	17	100
5.	Madhya Pradesh	42	14	56	23	2	19	44	100
6.	Maharashtra*	60	7	67	16	5	12	33	100
7.	Orissa	56	8	64	24	--	12	36	100
8.	Rajasthan*	75	11	86	7	--	7	14	100
9.	Tamil Nadu	25	35	60	9	29	2	40	100
10.	Uttar Pradesh*	53	9	62	28	1	9	38	100
11.	West Bengal	33	4	37	34	29	--	63	100

* *octroi collecting states.*

* Karnataka's high percentage of tax revenue is a bit doubtful in that the compensation is received in lieu of octroi has perhaps been included in the tax revenue. In the case of Kerala also, it is not clear whether some shared and assigned taxes have been included in the tax revenue.

Among the municipal corporations also the same pattern is discernible, of course, with some exceptions (Table 2). Among the octroi collecting corporations, the tax revenue accounted for between 62 and 84 per cent of the total revenue as compared to 20 to 57 per cent in the non-octroi corporations with the exception of Cochin (84 per cent) and Madras (67 per cent). However, possibly, the tax revenue of Cochin and Madras includes shared and assigned taxes.

Table 2
Revenue Composition of Some Municipal Corporations in India: 1986-87
(Percentage)

Sl. No.	Municipal Corporations	Own Source Revenue						Transferred revenue	Total
		Property tax	Octroi	Others taxes	Total tax	Non-Tax	Total		
1.	Ahmedabad	9	47	9	65	19	84	16	100
2.	Baroda	17	46	6	69	19	88	12	100
3.	Bombay	14	45	25	84	12	96	4	100
4.	Pune	15	52	14	81	5	86	14	100
5.	Delhi	32	16	33	71	17	88	12	100
6.	Kanpur	10	51	1	62	5	67	33	100
7.	Lucknow	22	56	4	82	6	88	12	100
8.	Calcutta	41	--	2	43	10	53	47	100
9.	Bangalore	26	--	31	57	14	71	29	100
10.	Cochin	51	--	33	84	8	92	8	100
11.	Bhopal	14	--	6	20	12	32	68	100
12.	Madras	30	--	37	67	29	96	4	100

The relative importance of non-tax own source revenue of the municipalities is higher in non-octroi States, which in absolute terms is not true in all cases. In the octroi collecting States the aggregate proceeds from all taxes being higher, for obvious reasons, the non-tax revenue, in percentage terms, is much lower than that in non-octroi States. In the municipal corporations, non-tax revenue in relation to total own source revenue does not conform to any particular pattern. While the Bombay Municipal Corporation which is better known for its relatively high level of fiscal management, collected only twelve per cent of its total revenue from non-tax sources, Madras collected as much as 29 per cent and Ahmedabad and Baroda 19 per cent each. Therefore, the distinction between octroi and non-octroi corporations seems irrelevant.

Among the sources of municipal revenue the dominance of tax revenue is pervasive. The trend that obtains now is that the lower the relative position of tax revenue in the revenue composition of municipalities, the higher is the 'dependence' on transferred revenue from the States. In other words, the municipalities by and large have been unable to bridge or significantly narrow down the budgetary (recurrent) gaps by means of non-tax revenue. Among the eleven states presented in Table 1, the dependence of municipalities on transfers was as low as 14 and 17 per cent of the total revenue in Rajasthan and Kerala respectively to as high as 50 and 63 per cent in the States of West Bengal and Andhra Pradesh respectively. The per cent tax revenue for the latter two States was 26 and 33 respectively, while for Rajasthan and Kerala it was 75 and 63 per cent. Tamil Nadu was an exception in that its low percentage of tax revenue (25 per cent) was significantly compensated by non-tax revenue (35 per cent) and thus kept the percentage of transferred revenue to a low 40 per cent. Among the municipal corporations (Table 2) a relatively low 'dependence' on transferred revenue is observed in Ahmedabad (16 per cent), Baroda (12 per cent), Bombay (4 per cent), Pune (14 per cent), Delhi (12 per cent) and Lucknow (12 per cent). These are the corporations that earn a substantial revenue from octroi. Among the non-octroi States, obviously with relatively low percentage of tax revenue, Bhopal had the highest percentage of transferred revenue (68 per cent), followed, though not closely, by Calcutta (47 per cent). Cochin and Madras were the exceptions in that even though being non-octroi corporations, their dependence on transfer was very low, eight per cent and four per cent, respectively. However, as mentioned earlier, there is doubt about these figures because it seems the shared and assigned taxes instead of being classified as transfer were added to tax revenue.

Admittedly, these percentages do not tell the entire story. In fact, some doubt may be raised about comparability of these corporations and for that matter the municipalities of different states, particularly because of inter-state disparity in critical areas of local government administration like, the delegated sources of tax, delimitation of functional domain, and transfer policy. In fine, the disparate state-local functional and fiscal relationship among the states makes comparability a difficult proposition. The above analysis, rather than inter-state comparison, provides an idea about the trend in respect of revenue mobilisation of the ULBs and their 'dependence' on revenue transfers from the states.

Resource Sharing and Functional Responsibilities

At this stage, a brief review of the policy of the States *vis-a-vis* urban local bodies may facilitate understanding the problem of resource mobilisation by the municipal bodies. The intended review will be confined to sharing of resources and functional responsibilities between the State and the ULBs.

Transfer of revenue from the state to ULBs is being increasingly used as a fiscal instrument by the states for meeting the budgetary gaps of the ULBs. The extent and composition of the transferred revenue reflect the respective states' policy orientation in sharing of resource bases with the ULBs. The financial resources at the local level, both actual and potential, have got to match the functional responsibilities of the ULBs which are somewhat in a flux since the early 1970s. The demarcation of the boundary of functional domain of the ULBs is the prerogative of the state, and the state exercises this prerogative from time to time depending on various perceived exigencies, political and bureaucratic. The fallout of the exigencies, guided by these parameters *inter alia* has, from time to time, been inter-state variations in composition of transferred revenue and also intra-state changes.

Three modalities of state-local transfer of revenue are commonly in practice: (i) shared tax; (ii) assigned tax; and (iii) grant: specific purpose grant and block grant.

The line of demarcation between shared tax and assigned tax is rather thin. The *entertainment tax* is used as an *assigned tax* in Andhra Pradesh because its entire proceeds are devolved to the ULBs, while in West Bengal and Tamil Nadu it is treated as *shared tax* because only certain portions of the proceeds are devolved. There are many similar examples. Leaving aside the typology of the shared resource bases, it is observed that a variety of tax bases are shared by the states with the ULBs in different combinations. The examples are: entry tax, entertainment tax, motor vehicles tax, surcharge on motor vehicles tax, surcharge on stamp duty, pilgrim tax, tax on profession, trade and callings, surcharge on sales tax, land revenue and non-agricultural assessment, compensation against abolition of octroi and so on.

The range of variations in the composition of the revenue grant is too wide; the only commonality is that the grants are given mostly for specific purposes. Some of the more common examples of specific purpose grants are: subvention to compensate increase in wage bills due to inflation; education grant; health grant; road maintenance grant and so on.

As mentioned earlier, whatever be the number of heads under which revenue is transferred from the states to the ULBs, its share of the total revenue of the latter varies widely among the states. It generally depends on the level of revenue mobilisation by the ULBs from their local sources, so that the higher the municipal revenue the lower is the proportion of transferred revenue. This seemingly obvious phenomenon has some wider implications. We will return to this later.

Functional Domain

The resource mobilisation effort is essentially linked *inter alia* to the municipal functional domain. The larger the functional domain the more is the resource requirement for meeting recurrent commitments emerging out of it. The ULBs have some obligatory functions or conventional functions to perform, like water supply, road maintenance, street lighting, drainage and sanitation and conservancy. Besides, there is an array of discretionary functions undertaken by the ULBs. This traditional functional domain has, over the past two decades, experienced changes as a result of policy at the state level which on some occasions enlarged it and on others encroached upon it, bringing about in its wake uncertainty in functional responsibilities and resource management.

Enlargement of functional domain is done mostly by adding to it such functions as are not only non-remunerative but are also responsible for additions to the municipal recurrent expenditure. These are, of course, not obligatory functions in terms of the statutes, but for all practical purposes are made to be so by executive orders. As such, they may be termed quasi-obligatory functions. Examples of the quasi-obligatory functions are the implementation of the two Centrtally-sponsored anti-poverty programmes, namely, Nehru Rojgar Yojana (NRY) and Urban Basic Services for the Poor (UBSP). Alien to municipal cultural environment as they are, these programmes are too demanding in terms of municipal leadership, organisation at field level and personnel for supervision, and hence on overhead expenditure. But the states expect the ULBs to go about performing these functions without additional financial support for meeting the overhead cost and, thus, they adversely affect the municipal revenue budget.

A converse trend in this context in the recent past, is the encroachment by the states on some major functional areas of the ULBs through the modalities of special purpose or development authorities. In order to justify this policy action the demonstrable achievements of these authorities needs close scrutiny because the financial implications of their performance has much to do with the concerned municipal budgets in one way or another. For, in some of the cases the concerned ULBs are the recipients of the services produced by these authorities at bulk rate for internal distribution. Even where the authorities deliver the services directly to the ultimate consumers, it needs to be examined whether the ULBs could perform this task more efficiently and could generate some surplus out of the revenue generated thereby. The situation that concerns most does arise when a development authority undertakes a capital work and hands it over to the concerned ULB after it is completed. In such a case, if the implementation of the capital works has been cost inefficient, the concerned ULB takes over it with the legacy of an unduly high financial liability for which it is not responsible.

Table 3 lists special purpose authorities in some states. Of course the information furnished in the table is not exhaustive. Enough feedback for evaluation of the financial performance of these agencies is not readily available. Performance evaluation is not the purpose of this paper either. However, an example of the contrast between the performance of the development authorities and that of the ULBs may be worthwhile to mention. While the Karnataka Water Supply and Drainage Board incurred a revenue loss of Rs. 1.50 crores in 1989-90, and all of the seven Jal Sansthans in Uttar Pradesh were persistently in the red due to their inability to collect user charges efficiently, the Bombay Municipal Corporation – an elected body – has been successful in recovering up to 70 per cent of the cost of a World Bank aided water supply scheme through user charges.

Bifurcation of functional responsibilities (unless justified purely on technical grounds does not seem to make a discernable change in the financial management of the services taken over by the states through the modalities of special purpose authorities. It rather gives rise to some serious difficulties when state level authorities fund and implement capital works and then hand them over to the ULBs for operation, which resist taking over the responsibilities due to lack of involvement, and are reluctant to collect user charges for meeting operation and maintenance costs and debt service.

Table 3
Special purpose authorities in some States

	State	Authorities/Board	Main functions
1.	Bihar	Bihar Water Corporation	Capital Works
2.	Gujarat	Gujarat Water Supply and Drainage Board	Project formulation, Consultancy and capital works
3.	Karnataka	Karnataka Water Supply and Sewerage Board[1]	Project formulation, capital works, distribution and collection of user charges
4.	Kerala	Kerala Water Authority	Production and distribution of water.
5.	Maharashtra	Maharashtra Water Supply and Sewerage Board	Project formulation, capital works and consultancy
6.	Rajasthan	Rajasthan Groundwater Authority	Production and distribution of water
		Rajasthan Water Works Department	
7.	Tamil Nadu	Tamil Nadu Water and Drainage Board	Capital Works
8.	Uttar Pradesh	Jal Nigam	Capital Works
		Jal Sansthans[2]	Operation and maintenance of water supply system.

1. There is also a water supply and sewerage board exclusively for Bangalore city.
2. Seven in number, one each for an urban area.

Policy Implication

Decentralisation of responsibilities in respect of urban services at the local level is believed to be the primary objective underlying the creation of the ULBs. It goes without saying that decentralised responsibility is not compatible with growing centralisation of financial power. The recent trend is much more disquieting. On the one hand uncertainty in functional responsibilities is taking deeper roots, while on the other hand the financial autonomy of the ULBs is gradually being whittled down. The foregoing sections briefly indicate how the states' unilateral policy actions could affect municipal revenue budgets by dampening the municipal effort for cost recovery. These are also indirect ways of interfering in the municipal fiscal management that leave ULBS with no options to express their preferences. Instances of direct interference are also gradually building up.

'Provincialization' of some local tax bases on 'strongly justified' grounds without replacement by other sources of revenue has occurred in almost all the states more than once. Taxes withdrawn by the states from the municipal domain are generally buoyant ones. The centralisation of motor vehicles tax has now the pages of history. Among the more recent ones is octroi, which has been abolished in two states, and other octroi-collecting states are being continually pressurised to abolish it. The profession, trade and callings tax has also been centralised in several states. Ironically, when, through a constitutional amendment, the ceiling rate of this tax got enhanced from Rs. 250 to Rs. 2500 per assessee, the Government of West Bengal provincialised it.

Encroaching on major functional areas of ULBs and centralisation of local tax bases together reflect the state policy orientation *vis-a-vis* the ULBs, which is tending to be skewed towards centralisation than towards local government autonomy. This trend at the state level is perhaps founded on the following policy myths:

(i) the ULBs are incapable of managing major functions like water, sewerage and drainage.

(ii) the tax administration of the ULBs is less efficient than that of the state and their efforts for tax collection are far less than adequate.

(iii) the scheme that entails collection of taxes by the state and balancing the budget largely by transferred revenue, works much better.

While no new tax base has been delegated to the ULBs over the past several decades even in the face of withdrawal of and attempt to withdraw lucrative tax bases from the municipal domain, quite a few shared and assigned taxes have appeared on the scene, e.g., stamp duty or surcharge on stamp duty, entertainment tax, entry tax, surcharge on sales tax, surcharge on motor vehicles tax and so on. Furthermore, grants-in-aid to the ULBs also show an ascending trend. Thus, the message is very clear. The states are increasingly going in for transferred revenue allocated to the ULBs from the taxes and other revenue collected centrally rather than strengthening the local fiscal base and hence local financial autonomy. Given this environment, what do the states expect from the ULBs? Do they expect the ULBs to augment their resources even as they are left with or are threatnened to be left with only one reckonable tax, i.e, the property tax, besides non-tax sources? Under the circumstances, augmentation of local financial resources boils down to dependence on four major sources of revenue:

(i) Property tax;
(ii) User charges;
(iii) Commercial enterprise; and
(iv) Transfers.

In the following sections the possibility of augmentation of revenue from these four major sources will be explored.

Outlook for the Future

As mentioned in the preceding section, the major sources of revenue of the ULBs are: (i) property tax; (ii) user charges; (iii) commercial enterprises; and (iv) transfers. The importance that may be attached to each of these sources with respect to resource mobilisation possibility is briefly explored below.

Property Tax

Undoubtedly, property tax is by far the most common form of local tax and, in fact, is the sheet anchor of municipal revenue, particularly where no octroi is collected. Theoretically, the base of the property tax is responsive to changes in the value of or income to real estate property and reflect relative locational advantages. In reality, however, property tax suffers from various drawbacks.

At the first instance, the base of the property tax is invariably narrowed by exclusion of various categories of properties like those whose annual rateable valuations do not exceed a specified amount and squatter settlements; secondly, the unorganised real estate and rental markets distort the base of the tax leading mostly to undervaluation of properties; thirdly, the base loses its buoyancy due to extra-economic reasons, e.g. in one state revaluation has been suspended for more than fifteen years and in another state even an 'independent' statutoty central valuation board has so far failed to bring the valuation of the properties in the municipalities up to anywhere near the market value; fourthly, the Rent Control Acts and their case laws have acted heavily against buoyancy of this tax. Lastly, professional expertise of the valuation staff is questionable. All these factors together have made property tax a declining source of revenue for ULBs at least in relative terms.

Efforts to improve the performance in collection of property tax have been made and in some cases have met with some success also; the most recent example is that of the Delhi Municipal Corporation. There are also instances where incidence of property tax has been increased more than once through upward revision of tariff. This method of increasing tax assessment can be practised only in those states where the Legislature empowers the ULBs to do so; the ULBs of many states do not enjoy this power.

Collection of the assessed property tax suffers on various counts, of which litigation is one. The litigants are mostly owners of large holdings who can carry on the legal battle for years together at considerable financial strain to the ULBs. Another is the hesitation of the ULBs to initiate coercive action as permitted by law against tax defaulters, due to voter proximity. And last but not the least, the compromising attitude of the collection staff. Evasion or attempt to minimise incidence of property tax by an assessee is induced by the 'most overt and direct form' of this tax, and by the difficulty to pass it on. In fine, though property tax is the single largest local revenue earner, no municipal development plan could perhaps be formulated depending primarily on the possible improvement in the performance of property tax.

Cost Recovery

Cost recovery by means of user charges is perhaps the most desirable way for a city manager to meet the expenditure on services like water supply, drainage, sanitation, etc. It is being advocated as a strong possibility of resource mobilisation. However, in this context the experience has been mixed. Water supply is the most commonly priced service in the states that have gone in for user charges. However, it is being argued that the perceived economic capacity of a municipal area sufficient to pay for urban services may have some validity but only at an aggregate level. At the level of disaggregated urban communities, while social demand for essential urban services is pervasive, the economic disparities among the communities casts doubt on the realism of full cost recovery of the services unless cross-subsidy is a realizable objective.

The overt nature of user charges increases the possibility of its evasion and thus, its efficient collection is pre-conditioned by an elaborate and intensive administration leading to a high cost collection machinary. On the other hand, the political compulsions of maintaining a low incidence of user charges on economically disadvantaged groups one cannot be sure about its responsiveness to inflation. There are instances of water tariffs remaining static for over two decades.

These difficulties with user charges notwithstanding, it cannot but be reiterated that there is both the necessity and justification to make efforts for mobilizing revenue through user charges. Its growing importance can be visualised in the light of the low elasticity of the property tax base on the one hand and the increasing demand for urban services on the other.

Admittedly, user charges alone may not recover the full cost of a service like water supply due to economic segmentation of urban households. But it should not be viewed in isolation. A cost recovery mechanism that is compatible with the social needs for urban services and budgetary implications of service delivery, ought to take into consideration:

(i) the tax bases available to the ULBs for meeting the costs of services provided or to be provided, their potentiality and incidence on different income groups;

(ii) the proportions of different income groups in a city population (or households) and the proportions of slum dwellers and inhabitants of squatter colonies who are otherwise not counted as beneficiaries of services and to whom incidence of taxes does not reach;

(iii) whether the transfer policy of the state, besides being gap filling in nature, could also address itself to subsidising essential urban services delivered to the economically disadvantaged communities in the urban areas.

The equity argument against cost recovery through user charges can be fully taken care of through a rationally designed tax-transfer-service pricing nexus as would fully recover the cost of services while ensuring realisation of the social objectives.

Commercial Enterprises

There is a belief that municipal commercial ventures have a strong possibility of generating surplus. That there exist a few success stories in this area of municipal activity can hardly be denied. But they are exceptions rather than the rule. Bombay's electric supply has not yet been replicated anywhere else or examples of some enterprises profitably run by some ULBs in Gujarat are not found in many states particularly in the northern parts of the country. Some claimed to be 'enterprises', operated by many ULBs, have certainly created useful facilities for the respective citizenry, like guest houses or dormitories, market complexes and so on, but how far these have been able to generate enough revenue for meeting the operation and maintenance costs, not to speak of surplus, needs close scrutiny. The Centrally-sponsored Integrated Development of Small and Medium Towns (IDSMT) scheme provided at least Rs. 80 lakhs to each of the selected ULBs as seed money for understanding various revenue generating schemes, to be recovered through pricing of services provided thereby and ploughed back. But there is serious doubt about the extent to which this objective has so far been realized.

Given the pressure of population on urban land, the ULBs could meet social obligations by providing facilities for housing, particularly for the middle and low income households, through land development and sub-division, and in the process generate surplus that could be utilised for providing shelter to the urban poor or for other purposes. Under the IDSMT scheme, there is separate allocation for investment in this area. However, barring a few, no ULB implemented IDSMT scheme has so far succeeded in land development or estate management.

The track record of the ULBs in initiating and running enterprises, in general, is anything but encouraging. Optimism in this regard may be unwarranted. It may be hoped that the ULBs will be more management-oriented in future so as to be able to generate surplus from enterprises. However, municipal programmes based *inter alia* on this source of revenue may be far removed from reality.

Transferred Revenue

Should the present trend of municipal finance continue, it can be confidently predicted that revenue transfers from the states will dominate municipal budget recurringly. There are various economic and institutional arguments against revenue transfers, as well as a few in its support. But the debate on this issue seems to be irrelevant as the policy of the higher echelon of the government is to meet the growing financial needs of the ULBs by transfers rather than through devolution of more resource bases. One may argue in this context that it matters little whether resources are mobilised by the state or ULBs, what matters is availability of enough funds for balancing the municipal budget. There is validity in this argument so far as it does not distort the income distribution pattern and local fiscal autonomy which is a necessary condition for strengthening decentralised local government institutions. Again, transfers do not reduce local autonomy so far as the ULBs are free to take budgetary decisions based on locally identified needs and prioritization. To counter these arguments it is said that it is too difficult to know who pays for what. May be urban tax payers bear a significant burden of financing rural development programmes.

As stated earlier, there is no point in stretching the debate. Accepting the logic underlying transfer policy, a question that seeks answer is whether the ULBs should be perceived as 'grant dependent'? This question is not as simple as it appears to be. For the concept of 'dependence' comes into conflict with the concept of the right to have a share in the state's revenue. Is it justified to call it 'dependence'? The profession, trade and callings tax has been taken over by quite a few states and the affected ULBs are compensated by increasing their 'dependence' on transfer. Examples like these are many. Suffice it to say that it is as a fallout of the state policy that the ULBs' claim to a portion of the revenue mobilised by the state is enlarging. In all probability this will be a continuing phenomenon in the future.

Having accepted the permanance of the system of transferred revenue one may try to visualise a scenario conducive to improving management of the ULBs. 'Assigned tax' should desirably be the main actor in this scenario, supported by 'shared tax' if found necessary. Grant-in-aid should play, if at all, a minor role. Assigned tax and shared tax do not interfere with the discretion of ULBs in spending while grants-in-aid generally do. The make-believe revenue equalisation capability of grants-in-aid has not worked well anywhere, on the contrary it has increased inter-municipal disparity. Again grants tend to be tied to specific purposes, which often do not conform with local priorities. The state generally opts more for grants as through it, it gets tighter control over the municipal activities.

Risking repetition it may be emphasised that the aspect of local autonomy as well as the question of accountability cannot be ignored whatever be the composition of transfer. In this context it is being held that even as a portion of expenditure is funded by transfer, the residual expenditure is funded by locally mobilised resources over which the ULBs have substantial discretion, which is most important to local accountability and autonomy. Related to the accountability issue, some states have development performance linked devolution mechanisms for block grants. West Bengal's 'revised grant structure' has an elaborate devolution mechanism that provides reward for good performance and sanction against capital assistance for poor performance, both measured in relation to standardised norms. The Gujarat Municipal Finance Board has developed a performance linked devolution formula for allocation of municipal shares in the proceeds of the entertainment tax. Both of these systems are still being experimented with. These and other methods of devolution pursued by different states, which take into account the accountability aspect may, hopefully, come out with an effective and generally acceptable devolution system in the future.

Assuming that the autonomy and accountability issues will receive due importance, notwithstanding the increasing use of transfer as a fiscal instrument for bridging budgetary gaps of ULBs, the question that seeks answer is the prospect of growth of the quantum of transfer. The state taking over a local tax (say, octroi) and compensating the ULBs for it does not add to the municipal financial resources. On the contrary, there remains the possibility of the ULBs being deprived of a portion of potential revenue of such a tax if it were not taken over by the state. In Madhya Pradesh the rate of growth of the proceeds from octroi was around 15 per cent a year, while the compensation it now receives in lieu of that has been growing at the rate of around ten per cent per annum.

In this context, the limitations of the states cannot also be ignored. Given the Centre-State fiscal relations, the states have only a few buoyant tax bases for meeting all of their commitments and thus, are left with only a few to be shared with the ULBs. On the other hand the Centre's initiative in strengthening the local fiscal base has so far been lukewarm. The capital finance available from Centrally-sponsored schemes is insignificant compared to the needs and is sporadic in nature. Undoubtedly some municipal towns and cities benefit out of it, but, at the same time, it widens inter-municipal development gaps.

It is reckonable that the Federal Finance Commission, while recommending devolution of the Central fund, does not recognise the existence of the lowest tier of 'government', i.e., the ULBs. The rationality of this practice is difficult to understand. There is hardly any reason for keeping local finance out of the purview of the federal fiscal system. In a highly centralised fiscal system, the ULBs, in an ambience of national planning and development, have all the justification for having a share in the nationally mobilised resources. Hopefully, the Finance Commissions will in future recommend allocations specific to ULBs, of course, to be routed through the states.

Conclusion

The urban local bodies including the municipal corporations have in general been unable to keep pace with the growing demand for urban services due to their budgetary difficulties. The octroi collecting ULBs although placed in a relatively good position are threatened by the strong central urge to abolish the levy.

There is a growing trend toward (i) transferring major functional responsibilities from the municipal domain to state administered special purpose authorities; (ii) increasing use of transfers as fiscal instrument for bridging budgetary gaps of the ULB, and (iii) provincialisation of local tax bases. This trend coupled with the absence of a constitutional base has brought about ambiguity and uncertainty in the municipal functional domain and fiscal management.

In the context of resource mobilisation, among the major local taxes, some ULBs are left with only the age-old property tax which has lost its buoyancy for various economic, legal and socio-political reasons. The less unfortunate ones are still able to collect octroi, but in two states the municipal bodies have already been deprived of this tax base without replacement; others are keeping their fingers crossed. Cost recovery through user charges has a strong potential but its applicability is limited by socio-political realities and administrative constraints. However, user charges rationally combined with tax revenue and state subsidy would take care of the socio-political aspects. The surplus generated from municipal enterprises could be a source of revenue for the ULBs. But their track record, with some exceptions, is not at all promising. However, even if the ULBs mobilise revenue from the above major sources in a significant way, the policy orientation at the state level is indicative of the growing importance of revenue transfers as a gap-filling device.

Transfers *per se* are not problematic because who mobilises resources, irrelevant. What is important is the growth of revenue to meet the increasing demand for local functions. Alongside this, the autonomy and accountability of the ULBs should not be ignored. So far as autonomy is concerned, the ULBs have absolute discretion in respect of spending and mobilisation of revenue from residual sources, and to that extent then accountability remains undisturbed. The accountability aspect could be additionally taken care of by a well designed scheme of performance-linked policy.

What is more important in the context of transfers is the uncertainty about the fiscal capacity of the states to keep up with the widening municipal resource gaps. Given the Centre-state fiscal relations, one can only hope that the states would be able to make increasing budgetary allocations for the ULBs. On the other hand, the Centre has so far shared, if at all, very little of its nationally mobilised resources with the ULBs. The successive Federal Finance Commissions also have ignored the need for integrating municipal finance with the federal fiscal system.

We will perhaps not be committing fiscal blasphemy in concluding that financing the services at the ULB level should not be treated as the sole responsibility of the ULB; that it requires governments at all levels work together to meet the urban needs.

REFERENCES

Banerjee, Tapan K, 1989. 'State-local fiscal transfer policy: Case of the Calcutta

Metropolitan Area' in *Urban Management in Asia: Issues and Opportunities*, UNCHS, EDI (The World Bank) and NIUA.

———, 1991. 'Centralisation of Municipal Valuation: A Case Study of West Bengal' in *Urban India*, XI (1), Jan-June.

Datta, Bhabatosh, 1981. 'Local Government Finance: Lessons from British Experience', *Nagarlok*, XIII (2), April-June.

Devey, Kenath, 1989. *Strengthening Municipal Government, The World Bank Report* No: INU 47.

Government of West Bengal, 1982. *Report of the West Bengal Municipal Finance Commission*.

Sarma, KSRN, 1985. 'Financing of Urban Services: Municipal vs. Specialist Agency,' *Nagarlok*, XVII (3), July-September.

Thimmaiah, G, 1986. 'Abolition of Octroi: Lessons from Karnataka Experience', *Nagarlok*, vol XVIII (2) April-June.

Government of India, 1989. *Report of the National Commission on Urbanisation'*, II.

19

Planning for Metropolitan Water Supply and Sewerage: A Case Study of Ahmedabad

Meera Mehta
Dinesh Mehta

MOST efforts at urban planning in the post-Independence period in India have been coloured by notions of ideal standards triggered by the visions of a newly emergent nation. Over time, however, these utopian exercises have been adopted, albeit very gradually, to the ground realities of fiscal and institutional constraints. However, incorporation of these constraints into the planning and management processes has not been very systematic. One of the most important sectors in this regard is urban infrastructure services, notably water supply and sewerage. These become very important, particularly in the metropolitan context of high densities. Frequent epidemics and persistent health problems in urban areas are largely a result of the failure of urban governments in providing adequately these services.

While lacunae in urban services are widespread, equally important are the distributional issues. For example, while a metropolitan area boasts of very high per capita water supply, almost a third of the population does not have access to adequate quantity and quality of water and, a quarter of the population in certain areas does not have access to even a public toilet. Overflowing septic tanks and cesspools of untreated sewage are common sights even in upper income localities in the urban peripheries. These suggest serious lapses in our planning and management.

In this paper we attempt to highlight four main issues in planning and financing of urban infrastructure.

Coverage Standards

- Can we continue to have very high standards for some while others lack even the basic minimum?
- Can we ensure that all have access to a societally determined minimum level of infrastructure?
- Can we continue to improve the standards of services for a selected minority while sacrificing the improvement in their coverage?

Pricing Policy

- How should we price the services so that they are not only affordable by the poorest but can also be provided, operated and maintained without any subsidies?

Service Thresholds and Phasing

- Should we relate the provision of services to smaller areas whenever the necessary threshold population or density are attained?
- Should we always wait for highly centralised mega projects to materialise or adopt interim solutions in a phased manner?

Decentralisation, Privatization and Community Control

- Should we always choose between only a highly centralised metro authority and totally individual household responses or evolve contextually relevant public-private-community partnership arrangements for provision, operation and maintenance of services?
- What forms of community control are possible to evolve in provision and operation of infrastructure services?

These issues are discussed in the third section, using the available studies of Ahmedabad Urban Area. The general situation with respect to housing and services is presented in sections I and II, following this introduction.

Ahmedabad – Population, Economy and Housing

Ahmedabad, the seventh largest urban area in India, is a major industrial and service centre in western India. The city has a long history. It was founded on the banks of River Sabarmati in AD 1411. From the time of its inception, Ahmedabad flourished as a major trading and crafts centre for almost three centuries. "Ahmedabad's story is of the survival and transformation of an impo. tant traditional centre of trade and industry into a modern industrial city, under the leadership of an indigenous financial and mercantile elite" (Gillion, 1968). The major change in the city's economy came towards the end of the nineteenth century with a rapid rise of the textile industry. The mercantile elite with their surplus capital, used this industry as an avenue for profitable investments. At its peak in the 1930s, the city had about 80 textile mills employing nearly 100,000 workers directly and a host of ancillary units and traders were dependent on the textile sector.

The past three decades have witnessed considerable changes in the economic structure of the city. Competition from unorganised textile sector using man-made fibres led to the closure of many mills with obsolete machinery used for cotton textiles. Nearly half of the mills have closed down, laying off about 5,000 workers. Despite this, the textile industry of Ahmedabad contributed to the extent of 16.3 per cent of the total income and 28.5 per cent of the industrial income of the state of Gujarat and nearly 50 per cent of the city's income (Kashyap, 1984). There is, howevei, considerable inequity in the distribution of this income, with the lowest 50 per cent of households earning only 20 per cent of the total income, and the top ten per cent cornering nearly one-third of this income (Mehta and Mehta, 1989a).

Population Changes

The downturn in the city's economy due to a slump in the textile industry is reflected in the population growth. According to the first official census, Ahmedabad had a population of 120,000 in the year AD 1872. After about six decades of moderate growth, the population had almost doubled between 1931 to 1941, as a result of growth in textile industries. Since then, Ahmedabad has had a moderate rate of growth of population, as compared to other metropolitan areas in the country. Since 1961, however, there has been a decline in Ahmedabad's growth rate. The provisional results of the recent census indicate a significant decline in the growth of population.

Table 1
Spatial Patterns of Population Growth in Ahmedabad Urban Areas

Average decadal growth rate - %

	1961-71	1971-81	1981-91	1991	
				Population	Density (persons per hectare
Walled city	5.0	-2.1	-15.0	405,904	658
East I AMC	56.0	35.3	17.4	1,349,096	262
West AMC	94.6	60.8	39.6	589,149	149
East II AMC	87.4	110.6	82.8	603,670	55
Total AMC	43.2	35.4	23.8	2,947,819	-
East Periphery	52.3	68.5	52.9	79,521	15
West Periphery	80.4	197.3	127.7	429,415	39
Total Periphery	70.2	155.1	111.2	508,936	-
Total Ahmedabad Urban Area	44.4	41.5	31.8	3,457,448	94

Source: Mehta and Mehta (1991d) based on the relevant census documents.

The walled city, the medieval part of Ahmedabad which was once enclosed by fortwalls, has been losing population over the years due to high level of congestion, conversion to commercial landuse and deterioration of residential environment, with an average density of almost 660 persons per hectare as compared to a gross density of 250 persons per hectare for the whole city of Ahmedabad. The average decadal growth rate was negative in the decade 1981-1991.

The west of Ahmedabad is predominantly a middle and high income residential area. The residents are either managerial or white collar employees in formal manufacturing or in services sector. The residential character of this part is evident from a far greater proportion of the formal housing stock here. The eastern parts of Ahmedabad, on the other hand, largely house lower income groups. A large proportion of these work in industries, in close proximity. In the past decade, the peripheral areas have grown much faster than the rest of the city. However, the general east-west divide of the poor and low income groups versus middle and upper income groups has continued in the periphery also.

The Ahmedabad Municipal Corporation almost doubled its area in 1986, by incorporating almost a 100 sq. km area. This zone (east II AMC in Table 1) has witnessed a more rapid rate of growth. The highest growth during the eighties has, however, occurred in the western periphery (127.7%). These developments have put a severe strain on the infrastructure services.

Water Supply and Sanitation

On paper, Ahmedabad has one of the highest per capita water supply in the country. A large proportion of its developed area also has the sewerage network. However, there are severe distributional problems in these facilities, both spatially and across income groups as is evident from the very limited access to facilities in the slum settlements.

The distributional problems are clearly evident when we review the availability of on-plot services for water supply and toilets.[1] Compared to over three-fourths of population with individual services in non-slum areas, only one-fourth has such services in slum areas. Equally important almost 30 per cent of the units do not have access to even a public toilet and another 45 per cent have access to only a public toilet, whose conditions, as we discuss later, are far from satisfactory. Gradual upgradation to individual services and/or better community control of shared services must receive high priority.

The other problems relate to spatial differences. It is clear that in peripheral areas trunk infrastructure[2] is inadequate, and thus access to services is also poor. More importantly, comparison of the experience in western and eastern periphery suggests that when trunk infrastructure is not available, the situation in low-income areas especially the slums is likely to be far worse. This is particularly true for access to sanitation facilities as indicated by much higher proportions without any toilet facilities. Of course, even for water supply, there is no effective control on the quality of water supply as clearly evident from the high incidence of jaundice, cholera and typhoid epidemics, frequently witnessed in recent years.

The above section does not clearly reveal the problems

associated with these services. While, the existence of on-plot services certainly denotes convenience, issues of quality of water supply and appropriate treatment and disposal of sewage remain important concerns. This is very clearly linked to the sources of, and treatment of water on the one hand, and the nature of disposal system on the other.

Table 2
On-plot Services in Ahmedabad

% to total occupied stock in each zone

Zone	Water Supply			Toilets		
	No facility	Shared facility	Individual facility	No facility	Shared facility	Individual facility
Walled City:						
Other areas	0.0	1.9	98.1	1.0	14.7	84.3
Slums	7.2	78.5	14.3	7.2	90.9	2.0
Total	0.4	6.0	93.6	1.3	18.8	79.9
East I AMC:						
Other areas	0.0	0.9	99.1	2.1	16.6	53.8
Slums	10.0	55.0	35.0	10.0	79.2	10.8
Total	3.0	17.2	79.8	4.5	35.5	60.0
West AMC:						
Other areas	0.0	0.0	100.0	0.0	0.0	100.0
Slums	8.7	60.9	30.4	8.7	76.3	15.0
Total	1.2	8.2	90.7	1.2	10.2	88.6
East II AMC:						
Other Areas	3.3	19.9	76.8	34.0	10.6	55.5
Slums	30.0	60.0	10.0	50.0	48.0	2.0
Total	10.0	30.0	60.0	38.0	20.0	42.0
Eastern Periphery:						
Other areas	5.5	28.6	65.8	37.4	13.1	49.5
Sulms	40.0	50.0	10.0	60.0	38.0	2.0
Total	11.0	32.0	57.0	41.0	17.0	42.0
Western Periphery:						
Other areas	0.0	0.0	100.0	0.0	0.0	100.0
Slums	20.0	60.0	20.0	20.0	75.0	5.0
Total	0.6	1.7	97.7	0.6	2.1	97.3

Source: For total market, Mehta and Mehta (1989) and Census of India, 1981. For slums, Mehta and Mehta (1989), VIKAS (1984) and AMC (1976). Estimates for other areas are derived as residuals.

In Ahmedabad, the Municipal Corporation had achieved almost 100 per cent spatial coverage in its old limits over one and a half decade back. Yet, almost a third of the households, has access only to shared services. These community taps do not meet the need due to inadequate maintenance and rising demand due to densification.

In areas outside of the old corporation limits, the resident population has faced considerable problems due to a total lack of any services. While some of the *gram panchayats* have provided limited quantity of water supply, there is rarely any effort at provision of sewerage system. Thus, about a third of the total population of Ahmedabad Urban Area, which resides in these areas, is not covered by the trunk infrastructure for basic sanitation and water supply services.

In the absence of a publicly provided water supply and sanitation trunk network in the fringe area, groundwater, through dug wells and borewells at residential project level, has been the main source of water available to the residents. The fact, that water is becoming increasingly scarce, is evident from geo-hydrological studies which indicate a ground water depletion rate of almost 2.7m per year in Ahmedabad (Gupta, 1985). Yet, it becomes necessary for every residential project, irrespective of its size, to provide for its own water supply. Such responses are inefficient, expensive and environmentally hazardous. The inefficiency arises because of a lack of mechanism for controlling use of a scarce resource. It is expensive because the sum total of all the investments in water supply (bore wells, pumps, overhead tanks) for the entire area are likely to be much higher than a single water supply system. Preliminary studies indicate that such scale economies probably operate at the level of about 10,000 units or about 150 hectare (School of Planning, 1989, Dalal, 1990). Lastly, individual residential projects tend to draw water at the smallest possible depths. This leads to rapid depletion of watertable and tapping of inappropriate aquifers both from the quantity and quality perspective. Further, individual systems prevent adequate treatment of water and thus cause health hazards related to water-borne diseases. This risk is even greater when there is inappropriate sewage disposal.

The extent of spatial coverage of sewerage is also very minimum. Most of the residential projects by the private sector have a septic tank linked to a soak pit for sanitation (in one project named Lakeview Apartments, the waste water flows directly into a nearby pond from the septic tank). Poor design and construction quality of the septic tanks and soak pits have resulted in considerable overflows of waste water in the fringe area. This poses a series of health hazards and is likely to effect the quality of groundwater as well. The market response to these problems has been the emergence of private firms which deploy vacuum trucks to draw waste water from soak pits and dump it in nearby ponds. Some of the local bodies (panchayats) also maintain these trucks which are rented out to housing societies. In then newly annexed eastern areas, the Municipal Corporation performs these tasks. However, with the number of cesspools running into thousands (a recent estimate puts it at 12,700 - Mehta and Mehta, 1991a) the facility provided becomes inadequate and the resultant pools of waste water frequently cause malaria and water-borne diseases.

It must be emphasised that both the Ahmedabad Municipal Corporation and the Ahmedabad Urban Development Authority have responded to the above situation by embarking on ambitious programmes. The problems may lie essentially with inappropriate matching of ambitions with the resources situations, jurisdictional problems of different agencies and misguided trade-off between better coverage and higher standards.

Municipal Corporation

The most dominant public agency in the planning and implementation of infrastructure projects in Ahmedabad urban area is the Municipal Corporation. Besides improving the lengths of pipelines in the distribution network and increasing the number of connections, it has also undertaken major projects for water source development and augmentation. Similarly for sewerage, besides achieving a cent per cent area coverage, it has also gone in for a major augmentation project in recent years.

The major problems pertain to the lack of infrastructure in the newly annexed areas. Unfortunately the very ambitious projects undertaken have already placed a heavy debt servicing burden on AMC. Therefore, the new areas are likely to continue to suffer from inadequate infrastructure.

AMC has also been engaged in the provision of certain basic amenities in the low income areas (slums and *chawls*) on a shared basis. It has continued its efforts in this sphere despite its inability to avail of the 100 per cent financing available from the central/state government due to the contextual problems. In Ahmedabad, a large proportion of the slum settlements are on private land or on reserved public land. Hence, the necessary guarantees could not be given by the local authority.[3]

AMC has, therefore, made legislative provision to give the necessary minimum infrastructure in slums out of its own resources. However, in recent years, with the rising debt-servicing obligations and changing political priorities, the expenditure in this area has slowed down considerably. This is also true for the subsidies accruing for individual water taps and toilets given by AMC. Besides the decreasing emphasis, there are serious service gaps in implementation of the Environmental Improvement Scheme. First, the services provided are generally inadequate in magnitude and often very badly located. The resultant pressure on services and poor quality in provision lead to poor maintenance and subsequent breakdown, especially for shared services. The existing scheme, unfortunately has no provision for major repairs at all. The attractive subsidies for individual facilities are often not availed of due to tenure problems since the owner's sanction is essential. In other cases, it was found that these subsidies are used by quasi-legal developers to provide shared services who then charge extra rent for these (see Boni, 1985 and Mehta and Mehta, 1989 for further details).

Ahmedaabad Urban Development Authority (AUDA)

The Ahmedabad Urban Development Authority constituted in 1978, is essentially a planning authority. While AUDA did commission a feasibility study for the provision of water supply and sewerage networks in the periphery areas, no major projects have so far been undertaken. AUDA is now planning to take up a very large sewerage project for the western periphery. The two-phase project envisages coverage of almost 80 sq.km area at a total cost of 4700 million rupees. The first phase of 1320 million rupees, covering an area of about 44 sq. km is envisaged to be completed by 1996. It is worth pointing out that while the system is designed at very high capacity (assuming daily water demand of 250 lpcd), neither AUDA nor any of the other local authorities, have any projects for ensuring that those in slums and other low income areas will have access to this system. More importantly, this massive investment would further enhance the east-west divide in Ahmedabad. The eastern areas which have now been annexed by AMC, where for 10 years, AUDA did not undertake any significant projects, are now less likely to be served effectively, as AMC is under financial stress. Such anomalies clearly hint at the need for better co-ordination amongst the different local bodies through either an effective development authority or a coalition of local bodies at the metro level.

Planning and Financing Infrastructure

The Ahmedabad case presented in the preceding sections, highlights certain major issues in planning and financing infrastructure. These are relevant for most metropolitan areas, not only in India, but also in other developing countries. We discuss a few of the major issues in this section.

Whether we review the water supply project or the slum upgradation programme, there has always been a tendency to set out very high standards. Ideally, the standards must be assessed in view of the resource constraints. This, however, is very rarely done.

This problem may be illustrated by highlighting the case of distribution of water supply. AMC has in principle decided to move away from the groundwater as the main source of water supply. Towards this end, it has contributed to the costs of Dharoi dam and is expected to receive about 435 mld of water, through its Kotarpur water works. Thus, by AD 2000, the total water supply is planned to be about 198 mld. The present plans of the corporation are to cover only about 75 per cent of its total area and completely leave out the peripheral areas from its jurisdiction.

In terms of the population coverage, about 15 per cent of the population within the corporation boundary, and over a third of the population of the entire urban area would be left out because of this approach. Alternatively, even if larger areas are covered by additional distribution networks, the total quantity of water supply would still be adequate (at 175 lpcd) to reach the entire population. It is worth emphasising that operations costs would then be also shared amongst a much larger populace. Such an approach implicity requires added emphasis on leakage detection and control.

The second illustration of this trade-off comes from the fact that at present at least 20 per cent of the households, even within the areas with services, do not have effective access either due to affordability or because of the tenure problems (in slums and *chawls*). The high level of subsidization in the water sector, therefore, completely ignores these most disadvantaged groups. The limited number of public water taps in slums means that they receive less than six per cent of the water, though their share in total housing is almost 25 per cent. While the Corporation has attempted to provide some shared services, its slum upgradation programme, initially visualised at over 350 million rupees , has been in abeyance for over half a decade. It has recently been reviewed though with a limited budget of only 20 million rupees. One wonders whether AMC has ever seriously considered the trade-off in water sector between subsidies, accuring regressively more to the affluent and that which might have gone in a limited way to the slum dwellers to enhance their affordability.

Table 3
Water Availability and Distribution Alternatives – AD 2000

Year	Source of water (mld)				Total (mld)
	Dudheshwar water works	Radial Collector	Tubewells	Kotarpur water works	
1985	100	30	359	0	489
2000	200	144	139	435	918

	AMC Proposal	Alternative for Water Distribution		
		Including remaining AMC area	Including eastern periphery	Including entire urban area
* % of total area covered	35.6	53.0	81.5	100.0
* % of total population covered	60.2	68.8	86.3	100.0
* Per capita daily water supply (lpcd)	255	223	219	173

Source: Adapted from School of Planning (1990), based on data from AMC.

Pricing of Services

The question of subsidies brings us to the second issue of appropriate pricing of services. The current pricing practices lead to a large financial gap in the water-supply and sanitation sectors, especially for the Municipal Corporation. Compared to an estimated per capita expenditure of 47 rupees in 1985-86, the revenue earned is less than 22 rupees per capita. Put in another way, the ratio of expenditure to revenue per connection is almost 2.5 (Basu and Vaidya, 1988). This means there is almost 100 per cent subsidy in these sectors.

The main reasons for these fiscal shortfalls relate to the inappropriate pricing. Pricing is linked neither to potential access nor actual consumption. The water supply and conservancy charges are linked to the annual rateable value and, therefore, the revenues are affected by under-assessment problems due to the effects of rent control legislation. The proposals for metering water consumption have never been accepted in Ahmedabad. While the reasons are attributed to administrative and technical problems, there are no studies of Ahmedabad comparing the experience of cities like Bombay which have used metering successfully.

There are several possibilities for revising the pricing policies, but we need to be clear about both the underlying objectives as well as the feasibility of such options. For water supply, it needs to be emphasised that the pricing policy has to ensure that each consumer/household, irrespective of the ability to pay, has access to a socially accepted basic minimum quantity of water. Consumption above this level should ideally be priced differentially across the user groups according to quantity consumed. The differential pricing should be based on the demand for water in each market segment. Sewerage may on the other hand be considered more of a public good. However, the choice between shared and individual services (toilet) may be based on the level of demand.

Based on the literature and available studies, three main sets of options for pricing of services may be discussed. The first relates to revisions in tax base and/or rates for service charges. The use of either site value or capital value of property for tax base has often been advocated for property taxes. Such changes can certainly enhance taxes as well as rationalise its incidence. For example, Mehta and Mehta (1991c) indicate that site value based taxation will distribute the tax burden more towards those who utilise the land far below the permissible intensity. On the other hand, the capital value base will favour those staying in smaller properties. In both the cases, even at the same tax rates, the total revenue more than doubles. Alternatively, to keep these sectors self-sufficient without changes in the tax base, it would be necessary to revise the tax rates. Basu and Vaidya (1988) indicate that for AMC, to meet the cost of

Table 4
Pricing options for Water Supply and Sewerage

	Equity effects on disadvantaged	Expenditure revenue gap	Transparancy of pricing subsidies	Feasibility of change
Option - 1 REVISIONS IN TAX BASE/RATES				
Tax Base ARV to site value ARV to capital value	-properties with better FSI utilisation and small properties gain	- Reduced but extent unknown	- Unclear	- Administrative problems
Tax rates Ad-hoc Full recovery	-All lose/pay more tax	- Fully recovered	- Clear	- Political Problems
Option - 2 DELINK SERVICE CHARGES FROM ARV				
Tax rates linked to property size	- Small properties benefit	- Reduced but extent unknown	- Unclear	- Easier
Connection sizes	- Small users benefit	- Reduced but extent unknown	- Unclear	- Easier
Water consumption	- Larger consumers lose	- Fully removed	-Very clear	- Administrative problems
Option - 3 COMBINED VALORISATION AND SERVICE CHARGES	- Poor may be cross subsidized more easily	- Full recovery possible	- Clear	- Possible with administrative changes

water supply alone, the per capita charge needs to be increased by 200 per cent. This does not even account for the additional operations and maintenance expenditure. Such extensive increases in tax rates may, however, be politically unfeasible in the short run.

This suggests that it may be worthwhile to delink the service charges totally from annual rateable value. The user charges should ideally then be linked to quality of the facility and level of consumption. For both water supply and sewerage, the annual charge may be linked to the size of connection, floor area of property being served or the site area being served by the connection. Administratively, such an arrangement may be simpler than relating the charge to consumption, for example, through water meters. Simulation analysis for Ahmedabad indicates that using property size as the tax base would tend to favour the small property owners much more (Mehta and Mehta, 1991c).

In both the options, it appears that to make these sectors self-sufficient, it would require considerable revisions in tax rates or increases in total tax incidence. A third option may be to breakup the charges linked to capital and operation – maintenance costs. Thus, the capital costs of major trunk infrastructure may be recovered through some form of valorization charges or betterment levy.[4] The crucial aspect here, however, would be to assess the incidence of benefits of a given project correctly. Secondly, the timing of provision is very crucial as the willingness to pay additional charges would decline substantially once the household has already invested in (or paid for) individual/community services.

This point may be highlighted quite effectively with the case of the sewerage project being proposed by AUDA for the western periphery. The total project cost of Part I, which serves about 4400 hectares, is envisaged to be rupees about 1200 rupees per dwelling at 1991 prices.[5] With cross subsidization from commercial and industrial uses, the cost may be reduced even further. This compares very favourably with the capital costs of sanitation systems, which have ranged from Rs. 1250 to Rs. 2000 per dwelling unit at 1985 prices (Mehta and Mehta, 1989). These costs may thus be recovered directly as connection costs. This will also ease the debt servicing problems of the local or development authority. The user charges may then be used for operation and maintenance costs. This approach would also have the advantage of the possibility of making the subsidies (through cross subsidisation) more transparent.

This approach, however, clearly demands appropriate phasing and timing of projects as well as the necessary decentralisation in order to relate the costs to beneficiaries effectively. We turn to these two issues in the following paragraphs.

Service Threshold

Both water supply and sanitation systems in a large metropolitan area have two important features which should force planners to consider the possibility of appropriate phasing.

In any given metropolis, there is always some level of existing infrastructure system in some parts. However, there are uncovered areas at various stages of development, ranging from sparse and initial development to a fully developed stage. Further, these infrastructure services are not always amenable to marginal increases in provision and extension, but are more attuned to 'threshold' additions. Thus, it may not be possible to incorporate a peripheral area into a centralised sewerage network till a certain level of density is attained. However, it may be perfectly feasible to adopt interim solutions which are suited to the low density levels.

The general tendency amongst development authorities is to envisage very large projects even encompassing large areas. Quite often, the financial and administrative responsibilities attached to such mega-projects are not feasible in the given fiscal and institutional context. This point is highlighted by AUDA's attempts in the last decade. Its large projects with centralised systems have not materialised at all. On the other hand, there has resulted a severe environmental degradation both in the eastern and western peripheral areas. If AUDA had undertaken smaller projects covering areas under more intense development, through smaller decentralised systems in a phased manner, it would have been possible to link the same systems to a more centralised system when the threshold population levels were reached. In the interim period, water could have been supplied through a series of well planned tube wells. The sewage could have been collected at smaller scales (of about 200 hectares or so) and treated in aerated lagoons. Effluent could have been sold to agriculturists.[6]

Such solutions would have been both fiscally and environmentally more conducive. As the construction costs have generally risen faster than general inflation, the present value of phased alternatives would be lower. Analysis of scale economies for water supply and sewerage also suggest that such solutions would be more cost effective (Dalal, 1990). Our studies in the Ahmedabad periphery also show that individual and community level treatment costs more than such interim solution on a per dwelling unit basis. Lastly, it would have also been possible to provide services in the slum areas more easily.

Even in environmental terms, such approaches would be more beneficial. For water supply, as it becomes easier to tap deeper aquifers, the negative effects on water-tables are minimized while getting better quality of water. For sewerage, with proper disposal, besides the health benefits, it is also possible to produce manure and use the effluent for agriculture purpose. In case a centralised system is introduced later on, prime land under the treatment plant would be available for either recreational or commercial purposes.

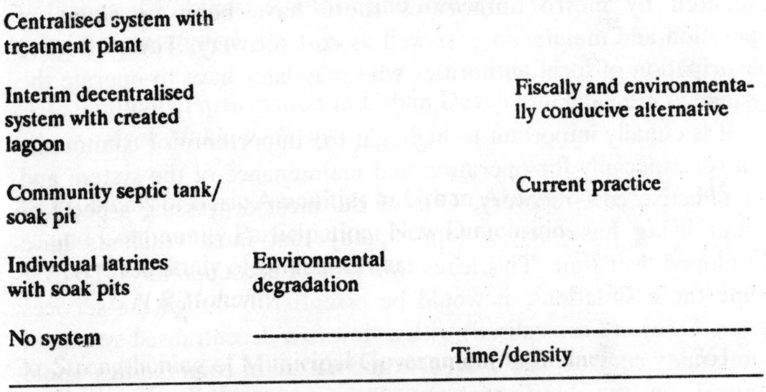

Fig. 1: Service Threshold and Phasing

Decentralisation and Privatisation

Two of the most important issues in urban infrastructure relate to the extent and nature of centralisation and the role of public, private and community sectors in the provision and maintenance of these services. While a wide variety of alternatives exist in the Indian metropolitan centres, there is inadequate discussion of these issues which would lead to more efficient, equitable and effective solutions.

The pioneering work of John Turner for housing in the early seventies, clubbed together all infrastructural services and put the responsibility squarely on the public realm at municipal levels. However, the experiences in the past twenty years and especially the more recent upsurge in infrastructure related research hints at more complex arrangements.

The present institutional arrangements cause several anomalies. In Ahmedabad, despite the presence of Ahmedabad Urban Development Authority, there has not been an adequate emphasis on the macro perspective. As discussed earlier, spatially there are clear imbalances and the current proposals will probably enhance these further.

However, it is necessary to emphasize the potential role of a macro level agency for overall planning, which functions beyond the jurisdiction of the local bodies. It may not really be necessary to create a separate authority, if the most dominant local authority can itself be given the additional powers and mandate to perform this task. In the past, when such projects have been planned and executed by metro authorities there have been problems of operation and maintenance as well as cost-recovery. Thus, effective participation of local authorities who may later have to operate the systems is crucial.

It is equally important to highlight the importance of community control especially for operation and maintenance of the system and for effective cost recovery. One of the most distressing aspects of urban living has been a total apathy that most residents have developed over time. This leads to a lack of accountability. To over come these situations, it would be essential to design the services (even if they are centralised) with a view to a decentralised system of community control. The exact size and nature of communities would depend on the local context. Thus, in a situation of good underground water potential, it may be possible to put the entire tasks of extraction, treatment and distribution of water supply under the control of a small local body. On the other hand, if water is available only from a surface source at a great distance, it may be necessary to have a centralised system with heavy investments and a metro agency to oversee the transmission. The local distribution, however, may still be with the small local body.

Lastly, in this perspective, it is necessary to review the role of the private sector as well as community groups. Ahmedabad, as we have seen earlier, has especially seen housing supply by the private sector on a substantial scale. This suggests both entrepreneurial abilities

	Centralised metro authority	Local authorities	Private sector	Local communities
Planning	. Control	. Suggestions and feedback	. Planning consultants	
Provisional execution	. Central, Resource mobilisation	For smaller decentralised systems	. Execution, total provision for decentralised systems	
Operation, maintenance and cost recovery	. Partial, if centralised	. Control, cost recovery	. Contract based operations	. Control and supervision

Fig. 2: Decentralisation and Control in Urban Infrastructure Services

	Planning	Execution	O&M	Planning	Execution	O&M	Planning	Execution	O&M
Centralised metro authority	0	0					0	0	
Local Body			0				0	0	0
Private Sector				0	0			0	0
Local Community						0			0
	Current centralised model			Current extreme decentralised			Potential decentralised model with public-private partnership		

Fig. 3: Different Models of Institutional Responsibilities for Services

and management capabilities. It may be worthwhile to extend their areas of operation by participation even in the provision of these services. A few isolated projects of land development by the private firms in the periphery show these possibilities. The areas of co-operation need to be carefully identified in a given context depending on the service demands and the strengths and weakness of different groups.

A word of caution in such attempts is, however, necessary. It would be essential to check the distributional impacts of alternative arrangements. The experience of western countries has shown that such community control has been used to create exclusive localities where the disadvantaged could have no access. It is quite likely that unless properly assessed, these measures may lead to added burden for the more disadvantaged groups. Thus, if public goods and services are offered only at market prices with no subsidies for the lower income groups, the price of services and infrastructure will increase for those urban households who can least afford to pay. At the extreme, private business can eliminate services in an effort to maximise profits and leave the poorer parts of the city unserved (Rondinelli, 1990). On the other hand, however, increased efficiency of the private sector may mean reduced costs, increased productivity and coverage and, therefore, greater scope for a larger proportion of the underprivileged to become a part of the urban mainstream. If this is backed by indirect subsidy programmes or cross subsidization through differential pricing, it is likely that the net effects can be made more equitable than the present systems. While both scenarios are equally plausible, the critical aspect lies in designing a balanced set of public-private-community partnership arrangements which maximize the net benefits. These have to be context specific and have to emerge through conscious and planned experimentation.

Conclusion

Ahmedabad Urban Area presents an interesting case for an analysis of issues in planning and financing of water supply and sewerage in metropolitan India. While these issues have been highlighted in the context of the Ahmedabad experience, they are common to most metropolitan centres in India as is evident from other studies (Mehta and Mehta, 1991a).

These issues also highlight the priorities in planning practices in the coming years. We emphasize three of these here. First, in order to interrelate these issues in a systematic manner, it becomes necessary to evolve integrated frameworks so that meaningful comparisons of alternatives become possible for decision-making. This however, also needs to be supported with a better set of planning and management related information systems. Urban planning has particularly suffered a great deal due to an inadequate information base. We would emphasise that the focus of most projects related to urban services has generally been on technical issues. The fiscal and distributional issues emphasised in this paper have received less attention.

While these methodological developments are important, the real change probably required is in the role of public institutions. On one hand, they need to become more entrepreneurial, ready to experiment and learn from these for further developments. At the same time, they need to recognise the necessity for incorporating the private and, more importantly, the community groups into the activities of provision, operation and maintenance of urban services. Innovative measures have to be tried and effective ways of supervising the private firms and communities have to be evolved. It is only through such experiments that more humane and responsive living environments will be generated. They will also provide the opportunities for the disadvantaged to demand their shares and get them. After all, it is the urban services demands which have generally been the harbingers of urban social protests the world over.

NOTES

1. On-plot services refer to the availability of taps for water supply, drainage connection for sullage disposal and a toilet with appropriate sewage disposal for each dwelling.
2. Trunk infrastructure refers to main lines linking the on-plot services to a centralised system of water supply and sewerage collection and disposal. The level of centralisation may be at the city or a smaller area level.
3. The conditions required for financial assistance are: (i) The land-owner will not evict the inhabitants for at least 10 years; (ii) No extra rent will be charged because of the improvements, and, (iii) The land owner will not ask for more compensation because of the improvement.
4. There is already a provision for imposing betterment levies under the Town Planning Act. However, this is not effectively implemented due to time delays, inappropriate costing, poor recovery and lack of any effective link between plan and implementation. Mehta and Mehta, (1989b) and Mehta and Mehta, (1991b). Also see Mehta and Mehta, (1991a) for a description of a similar approach used for determining the reserve price of land by CIDCO, Bombay.
5. It may be pointed out that the AUDA proposal is based on very high population estimates (as compared to 1991 results) and high water consumption standards. It is also assumed that about 30 per cent is under roads and open spaces, and is, therefore, not marketable. The average dwelling size is assumed to be 50 sq.m. with a FSI of 1.5
6. This is exactly what is being practised in Sardarnagar, the only locality on the eastern side which has a sewage network.

REFERENCES

Basu, D., and Vaidya, C. (1988), "Ahmedabad 2001: Investment requirements and cost recovery aspects of urban services", paper presented at the National Seminar on *Ahmedabad 2001*, by TRF, Ahmedabad, mimeo.

Boni, M. B., (1985), "Evaluation of Slum Improvement Programme: A Case Study of Ahmedabad", Dissertation, School of Planning, Ahmedabad, Mimeo.

Dalal, Ami. (1990), "Techno-economic options for water supply and sanitation: A framework for urban services", unpublished dissertation, School of Planning, Ahmedabad.

Gillion (1968), "Ahmedabad: A Study in India's Urban History", Berkeley.

Gupta, S. K., (1965), Waste water renovation for unrestricted irrigation and groundwater recharge: A perspective for Ahmedabad, PRL, Ahmedabad, mimeo.

Kashyap, S. P., *et al.*, (1984), *Facets of an urban economy*, Town and Country Planning Organisation, New Delhi.

Mehta, M. and Mehta, D., (1988), "Housing in Ahmedabad metropolitan area - 2001 AD: Policy imperatives", paper presented at the Seminar on Ahmedabad 2001, Organised by TRF, mimeo.

———, (1989a), "Metropolitan housing market: A Study of Ahmedabad", Sage Publishers, India.

———, (1989b), "Housing Finance Systems in Metropolitan areas of India", report submitted to USAID, New Delhi, mimeo.

———, (1990), "Spatial information system for housing market: Housing price studies and housing supplies for metropolitan areas", sponsored by HDFC, Bombay at School of Planning, Ahmedabad, mimeo.

———, (1991a), "Land for shelter: Delivery of serviced land in Indian metropolies", Report submitted to USAID, New Delhi, mimeo.

———, (1991b), "Appraisal of land policies and programme in selected reports", First report for Town and Country Planning Organisation (MUD, New Delhi), at School of Planning, Ahmedabad, mimeo.

———, (1991c), "Property taxation in developing countries: Situation analysis and potential reforms in Ahmedabad - India", paper presented at the international conference of *Property Taxation and Its Interaction with Land Policy*, Cambridge, USA, mimeo.

———, (1991d), "Modelling urban housing strategies: A case of Ahmedabad", sponsored by Housing and Urban Development Corporation, New Delhi, at School of Planning, Ahmedabad, mimeo.

Rondinelli, D., (1990), "Decentralising urban development programmes: A framework for analysing policy", office of HVD, USAID, Policy and research series, Washington.

School of Planning, (1990), "Housing strategies for Ahmedabad metropolitan area", student report of Laboratory programme, School of Planning, CEPT, Ahmedabad, mimeo.

Turner, John, (1976), *Housing by People*, London.

20

Pricing of Urban Water Supply

K. S. R. N. Sarma

THE central issue in the pricing of public utility services in a developing country like India is often the optimal reconciliation of financing and other objectives of those services' extension. The problems are observed to be pronounced particularly in the case of pricing of urban water supply,[1] which in turn are mainly on account of the laggard investments in that sector. The ever increasing demands for public water supply consequent upon growth in population and economic activities in urban areas, entail huge investments for augmentation of service facilities. The National Commission on Urbanization in its report of 1988[2] estimated that an investment of Rs. 1.94 lakh crore (1.94 trillion) has to be made in urban water supply projects during the next decade or so, to maintain that service provision even at the present low standards. As against the above desired level of investment of about Rs. 15,000 crore (150 billion) per annum, the investments that materialised during the Seventh Five-Year Plan were just around Rs. 587.13 crore (5.8713 billion) per annum. This laggard investment in the water supply sector is a matter of serious concern and calls for efforts on various fronts for amelioration.

Here, it is to be noted that most of the municipal and other urban water supply legislations in vogue in the country expect that service to be organised as a financially self-paying proposition, i.e., the service charges be so fixed as to cover not only the operational expenditures but also leave enough margins to attract steady inflow of capital investments into the sector. Many hold the view that the fixation of water supply tariffs as per the above requirement is not a difficult proposition to accomplish provided there is no political interference and the concerned water supply agencies are given a free hand. This contention appears to be based on a highly simplistic logic. Things in the field may not be that easy as assumed.

Besides, the argument does not seem to pay due concern for the basic objectives of public provision of water supply. Water consumption is essential for the sustenance of life and the promotion of health. It is necessary to ensure that no section of the population is priced out from availing the desired minimum level of water consumption towards meeting their basic needs. A public water supply agency has an enjoined responsibility especially towards the poorer sections[3] in the above regard. The poor constitute a sizeable percentage of urban population and this percentage is observed to be steadily increasing over the years in a number of cities.

On the other hand since water is required for performing a number of urban economic and other activities, the demands on public water supply on that count is found to exceed the capacities installed. Pricing, therefore, has to ensure that the water withdrawals are put to best use and no wastages occur.[4] There is yet another objective of pricing, namely, administrative convenience. Due note has to be taken of the parameters set out in the concerned water supply governing statute about the base, vehicle and the organisational arrangements for revenue raising.

In this connection concern for the susceptibilities of local political functionaries is an important part of the exercise as that could come handy, eventually, in enlisting the clients' cooperation, in enforcement of tariffs and of revenue collection. Though there is a general awareness with regard to the pulls and pressures that the above objectives would be exerting, no serious effort seems to have been made so far to bring in suitable policy and procedural changes, so that a less ambiguous framework could inform the exercise for determining water supply prices. The present paper attempts to highlight some of the issues involved in this regard.

Cost Calculation

In an exercise of price fixation, the first step invariably would be the estimation of the cost. According to the procedures presently laid down for the calculation of water supply costs, only the expenditures that are actually incurred (or committed) are to be taken into consideration.[5] This 'historical' or backward looking basis for the costing of service is at variance with the average 'incremental cost, approach', i.e., one with a forward looking platform for the assessment of the future cash inflows and outflows from the investments made or proposed.[6] This dichotomy in the costing approach with respect to investment decisions for establishing new capacities and then another for raising revenues from the operations of those facilities is surely not conducive for promoting financial discipline in a public service organisation.

Two typical cases may be cited here to indicate the nature of dilemma that the above dichotomy in the guidelines could cause in the fixation of water supply tariffs. The first case is from Amritsar. The financial consultants to the World Bank aided water supply project of that city, in the late seventies, observed that the water supply tariffs have to be fixed at Rs. 0.60 per kilolitre as per the average incremental cost approach, but according to the municipal bye laws in vogue, the costs would work out to only Rs. 0.30 per kilolitre.[7] The second case is from Madras. A study sponsored by the Madras Metropolitan Water Authority in the mid-eighties observed that the cost of water in that city worked out to only Rs. 1.25 per kilolitre as per the traditional accounting approach whereas according to the average incremental cost approach it had to be fixed at Rs. 4.15 per kilolitre.[8] It is thus possible that the investments on a new water supply project may appear sound, i.e. costs being fully recoverable as per the average incremental costing, but because of the different costing for the fixation of the tariffs during the operational stage, the investments in question might not realise the revenue as per the original expectation. The matter, therefore, needs urgent review and reform.

Cost Controls

Another aspect relating to cost and its calculation is the monitoring and control of avoidable expenditures. A public service agency cannot justifiably ask for tariffs revision to pass on the excess expenditure burden arising from inefficient operations. The areas where the reforms need to be particularly directed include staffing norms, unaccounted for water, capacity under-utilisation and expeditious completion of capital works. It is a common observation that the execution of capital works in the water supply sector often get delayed resulting in huge cost escalations. In a good number of cases, the principal reason for the same is observed to be the frequent changes in designs, which in turn are a result of inadequate preliminary field investigations.[9] As regards the unaccounted for water, its share is generally reported to be in the order of 30-35 per cent of the total water generated. Studies conducted by the NEERI and others indicated that with small investments on the detection operations, about 5-10 per cent of the distribution losses could be easily prevented.[10] Since water saved is revenue earned (or capacity augmentations postponed) a good deal of emphasis needs to be given for the setting up of leak detection cells under the major city water supply agencies. As regards capacity under-utilisation, a major contributing factor were the frequent power cuts. Besides that, a number of administrative inadequacies such as insufficient budget provision for repairs, inadequate arrangements for maintenance and deficient methods of demand forecasting were also found to contribute a good deal to capacity under-utilisation. The latter factors could be taken care of through suitable managerial innovations.

Revenue Raising

The discussion may now be turned to the aspect of revenue raising and its burden. The point of central interest here is the way water uses and users are classified. Most of the water supply legislations in the country classify water demands into domestic or non-domestic. A public water supply agency is required to meet the first demand as an obligatory responsibility while the second demand is left as a discretionary function.[11] Beyond this classification, the legislations do not give any further guidance as to which uses come under the domestic category and which under the non-domestic one. Nor do they specify, what has to be their *inter se* priorities for coverage under the public service network.

Such details are necessary for the fixation of tariff rates and differentials therein. The differentials in the rates would in turn be needed to achieve revenue targets while promoting at the same time the 'efficiency' and equity objectives of the service provision. For the promotion of 'efficiency' in water usage there has to be efficient price disincentive in respect of water withdrawals for (socially) less desirable uses and concessions, for encouraging more desirable water consumptions.

Community level activities such as fire-fighting and flushing of drains have to be assigned a greater share of available water than that for meeting domestic luxury demands such as shower bathing and watering of lawns. Prioritisation of water uses should strictly be as per the requirements of balanced performance of various urban activities and thus for maximisation of community advantages. If water pricing has to effectively meet the above objective, then it has to take due cognisance of the inter-relationships existing among various urban activities within different cities, their water requirements and also their *inter se* priorities as expressed in the national policy directives, and also in the development plans of the cities concerned. As against this desired approach, what is often noticed is that field agencies adopt some arbitrary classification of water uses and users for fixation of tariffs. The matter therefore, needs urgent attention and appropriate initiatives for reform.

Once the classifications of water uses and users are arrived at, the next problem to be tackled would be the fixing of prices such that they are affordable as large a section of the clients as possible. Two policy specifications would have considerable bearing on the decisions here. They are: (i) the minimum quantity (and quality) of water that has to be ensured to all sections of the population, (ii) the amounts expressed as percentage share of the family budgets that could be assumed as reasonable levels of expenditure towards meeting water supply needs.

As regards the first policy stance it may be noted that the domestic water withdrawals are normally put to a variety of uses ranging from drinking and cooking to watering of lawns and feeding of domestic animals. Surely a public water supply agency cannot extend guarantee to meet the demand for all those latter water uses in the clients' homes. Nor can such a guarantee be justified as serving the desired social purpose viz., promotion of health standards of the people. Hence the need for a policy stand demarcating the 'societal obligation' of a public water supply agency even in respect of domestic demands.

However, the views of experts as to the socially desirable minimum quantity of water that has to be assured to all the sections of the society seem to differ. An U.N. study in 1976 observed that for meeting the biological needs of the people water supply of five litres per capita per day should suffice.[13] Studies conducted in Africa in 1977, found that even with as little as 1.4 litre of water consumption per capita per day (on average) people could still lead a normal life.[14] In the study carried out by Kalbernatten *et al.*, it is noted that most health benefits of safe water consumption are attained under the public water supply systems, even in the cases where the per capita daily supply worked out to 30-40 litres.[15] In another study sponsored by the World Bank it is observed that where the public water supply agency has assumed the, additional responsibility of hygienic wastes disposal (sewerage) the per capita supplies need not exceed 100 lpd.[16] In a recent sample study carried out in five States in India, it was observed that the clients' perceptions about the minimum quantity of water that they require varied from city to city and within cities according to the type of house structure, status of the locality, type of water connections etc. The minimum requirement of water perceived by the clints drawing water from hydrants is around 65 lpcd.[17] These estimates, however, need to be verified with data from similar such studies.

Regarding reasonable levels of family expenditure on water supply, this norm is usually referred to as the 'affordability' limit and should not be confused with the term 'willingness to pay'. A client may be willing to pay a very high price for water when it has to be purchased from a private vendor or when there is apprehension of short supply. But once adequate supplies are assured under the public supply system, the clients' attitudes are generally found to undergo a radical transformation. They would now expect the service to be provided gratis or at a highly concessional price. The clients' willingness to pay price *vis-a-vis* the value of the benefits accruing to them might at times be distorted due to factors such as inadequate appreciation of health benefits flawing from consumption of treated water and expectations aroused by local political leadership. In view of these, it is imperative that a social stand in the form of a policy decision is taken about the share that the clients could easily spare from their budgets towards their water consumption without seriously affecting their other essential expenditures. In some of the World Bank-aided water supply projects, the affordability norm is assumed to be 5 per cent of the family incomes.[18] In the sample study of water supply clients referred to earlier,[19] the water supply expenditures were observed to constitute around three per cent of the household incomes. So there appears to be a need for detailed investigations and review of the norm.

Government Grants

The third major component of the framework for determination of water supply prices is the policy pursued by the higher level governments in the matter of financing the service extension. Public water supply agencies in their pursuit of the equity objective, generally provide a large share of their supplies to the poor through public hydrants. They also provide concessional supplies for community uses such as fire-fighting, flushing of drains, watering of public parks etc. The benefits from these various water provisions are wide spread and as such it is not easy to pin-point the direct beneficiaries. Besides these concessional supplies, there is revenue loss arising from factors such as unaccounted for water, capacity under-utilisation etc. A city water supply agency may thus be left with just about 50 per cent of its total water production as one with some revenue potential.

The moot point for consideration is whether the water supply agencies would ever be in a position to exploit fully even the available revenue potential, with the type of base and vehicle options that are provided to them at present. A suggestion here is that the water supply agencies should be bestowed with more elastic sources of revenue than are available at present. Alternatively, higher level governments should come forward to share a part of water supply service expenses. Subventions to the city public water supply agencies from higher level governments could be in the form of general or specific grants. They may even be in the form of shared taxes, say a share in the sales tax collected in the area concerned on sale of water related items such as pipes, sanitaryware, soaps, detergents, washing machines, and geysers. Some state governments at present provide capital grants to help water supply agencies for the execution of new water works. The pattern of assistance, however, varies from state to state and within the same state from one size city to another.[20] As most city water supply agencies are found to default in repayment of loans taken for construction of capital projects, the pattern of state financial assistance needs some changes. The changes should aim to strengthen the revenue raising efforts of city water supply agencies, rather than make them more and more dependent on doles from higher level governments. Also the grants may be tied to the efforts made by the concerned field agencies controlling distribution losses and achieving better capacity utilisation. Once policies with regard to grants are unambiguously stated, then it would be clear to the water supply agencies what revenue targets that they have to achieve through the tariffs.

Metering of Connections

The fourth area of major concern in water supply price fixation is the choice available in respect of base as well as vehicle, for revenue raising viz., whether the required revenues could be raised through a direct tax on the beneficiaries of the service or whether there should be in the form of a volumetric charge or some combinations of tax and price charge. The volumetric charging of water supplies, it may be mentioned, was strongly advocated by the GOI-WHO Seminar on 'Financing and Management of Water and Sewerage Works' way back in 1964.[21] In the follow up to that seminar, policy-makers both at the Central and State government levels emphasised metering city water supply. It was thought that metering would help increasing considerably the water supply revenues.

Unfortunately things did not happen as expected and water supply revenues continued to lagger. On the other hand, metering has resulted in additional expenditures. These have arisen on account of installation of meters, salaries of the staff recruited for periodic meter readings, issue and collection of water bills and meter repairs and maintenance. Besides, it is also noted that in all the major cities about 40 to 50 per cent of meters remained out of order most of the time. Another argument that goes strongly against the metering is that it enables rate differentiation to a limited extent only as the quantums of domestic water withdrawals are generally observed to vary over narrow ranges. As against the above negative points, the major advantage that metering offers is the controlling of wasteful uses of water. In a case study carried out on the impact of metering in Pusad town of Maharashtra[22] it was observed that universal metering had helped a good deal in preventing the pressure losses at the consumers' ends. As a result, water was available to the consumer for almost 24 hours and the need for storage was hardly felt. All these helped to postpone the capacity augmentation of the water-works by a couple of years, which got reflected in the reduced costs of the supply. Metering therefore is desirable in respect of water connections where there is an apprehension of wasteful usage and also where quantums of drawal are sufficiently large such as for industrial and commercial purposes.

Optimal Tariff Model

From the discussions in the foregoing paragraphs, and also on a close study of the sample data on the distribution pattern of water demand for different urban uses, it is observed that much reliance cannot be placed on pricing water supply as per the conventional connotation of that term. The prime vehicle for raising the water supply revenues has to be necessarily the (service) tax. The water supply tariff model best suited for Indian conditions appears to be as follows. It has to be a multi-part structure. One of the planks of the strategy should concentrate on mobilisation of funds for defraying the liabilities on capacity augmentation and another plank should be directed to earn revenues to cover routine operational expenditures.

As mentioned earlier, a number of State Governments are presently providing capital grants for execution of new water supply works. These are, however, a certain combination of loan and grants *vis-a-vis* the total cost of the project. In place of that arrangement, it may be desirable if the State Governments tie up their grants assistance to the project components, say, for the construction of facilities for abstraction of raw water, for treatment, and for transmission of treated water up to the city boundaries. The city agency, may then be asked to bear all the investments in respect of laying the distribution networks i.e. on distribution pipes, pumping stations, service reservoirs etc. To finance their part of the investment responsibilities, the city water supply agencies may be allowed to levy water supply and sewerage benefit taxes as being done by the Bombay Municipal Corporation.

For covering the expenditures on operations, they may, first, be classified under two heads: "over heads" (or fixed expenditures) and variable expenditures. The former includes staff salaries, rents on buildings, insurance etc. while the latter includes the expenditure on electricity, raw water, chemicals i.e. those that vary with the volume of water production and supply. For covering the first part, greater reliance may be placed on the water supply and sewerage taxes and for covering the second part, volumetric charging (metered charges) may be resorted to.

The advantages of revenue raising through service taxes are many. One is the savings in the cost of administration. The second advantage is that it allows for a greater scope for rates differentiation than is possible under metered charging. Regarding the criticism that revenue raising through service taxation would be less buoyant, it may be mentioned that many field studies have indicated that there is not much difference in the rates of growth in the revenues of water supply agencies that depended primarily on water and sewerage taxes and those that mainly depended on metered charges.[23] With the efforts, recently initiated, to free the municipal property taxation from the adverse impacts of the Rent Control Legislation etc., the yields from the water supply (service) taxes could also be expected to become more buoyant in the years to come.

In addition to the reforms already initiated in respect of property taxation, the municipal statutes could be amended in two other respects. One is that the restrictions, if any, for the levy and collection of water and sewerage taxes at differential rates according to the industrial classification (use) of the property involved be removed. The second reform suggested is that the simultaneous levy of water supply and sewerage taxes as well as metered charges be allowed.[24] As regards the variable part of the expenditure it may be largely covered by the metered charges. The objective of the second suggestion is to help the water supply agencies with additional revenues and also at the same time put constant pressure on their managements to monitor water consumption levels and pattern and institute appropriate measures for controlling wasteful water use, preventing distribution losses, improving capacity utilisation etc.

Table: A Percentage Distribution of Water Supplied Daily for Various Uses in Selected Cities During 1986-87

Sl. No.	City	Percentage of water supplied for the use in:											
		Total	Domestic	Hostels, Restau-rants etc.	Shops, Commer-cial Establi-shments	Ice Facto-ries	Car Garages, small work-shops/fact-ories etc.	Offi-ces	Hospi-tals	Schools	Fire protection	Municipal uses in-cluding *Dhobi ghats* etc	Public stand posts and others
1.	Bangalore	100.00	60.15	Col.	5 to 11		23.53				Col.12 to 14	16.32	
2.	Jaipur	100.00	95.50	1.40	0.11	0.05	0.09	0.24	0.06	0.02		2.52	
3.	Lucknow	100.00	55.18	3.77	2.35	3.36	3.28	0.94	1.40	0.94	1.88	14.88	
4.	Tiruchirapali	100.00	77.88	8.30	0.41	0.20	0.20	0.33	0.58	0.02	0.02	0.50	11.60
5.	Kolhapur	100.00	84.40	0.40	0.20	1.00	0.50	0.50	0.50			2.00	10.00
6.	Aurangabad	100.00	80.00	5.00	5.00	-	-	-	3.00			3.00	4.00
7.	Mangalore	100.00	46.02	Col.	5X6=	17.00	Col.7 to 13=		1.17				35.21
8.	Gulbarga	100.00	93.50	1.80	0.18	0.04	0.18	0.08	0.15	0.11			3.95
9.	Pollachi	100.00	37.70	8.35	2.36 0.45	0.45	8.60	11.80	8.18	0.27	0.27	21.30	0.28
10.	Banda	100.00	86.00	2.00	1.00 2.00		2.00	1.00	2.00		1.00	2.00	1.00
11.	Robertsonpet	100.00	86.34		Col. 5 to 13		3.66					10.00	
12.	Paramakudi	100.00	64.00	7.00	3.00 1.00		3.00	3.00	2.00	0.50	1.50	15.00	
13.	Barabanki	100.00	60.00		Col. 5 to 14 =		40.00						
14.	Ramanathapuram	100.00	50.00	12.50	12.50		Col.6 to 14 =	25					3.80
15.	Pusad	100.00	90.00	2.00	0.50	1.00	0.50	0.50	1.00			0.50	2.00
16.	Jamkhandi	100.00	88.75		Col.5 to 14		11.25						
17.	Ranipet	100.00	89.35	0.64	0.17 0.13		0.77	0.28	0.58	0.12		7.96	4.40
18.	Udupi	100.00	89.00	23.00	0.09	0.06	0.25	0.90	0.15	0.66	1.50		
19.	Murudjanjira	100.00	80.00	5.00	-	0.50		0.50	2.00	1.00			11.10

Source: K.S.R.N. Sarma, The Study on 'Urban Water Supply Tarrifs', *Op.cit.*

NOTES

1. The term 'water price' as employed in the present paper has a broad connotation which embraces both water (price) charge as well as water (service) tax.
2. Government of India. 1988. *National Commission on Urbanisation.* Vol. II. New Delhi.
3. Saunders, R.J. and Wardford J.J. 1977. *Village Water Supply Economics and Policy in the Development World* - Baltimore, John Hokins University Press 1976p. 31-34 and also WHO. 1975, *International Standards for Drinking Water*, 3rd ed. Geneva, WHO.
4. McLure, Charles E. 1977. *Public Utility Pricing — Issues in Efficiency and Equity.* Regional Report No. 77-15. The World Bank Development Economics Department, Urban Regional Economics Division.
5. e.g. Section 16, of the Bangalore Water Supply and Sewarge Act, 1965.
6. Saunders, R.J., Wordford, J.J. and Mann, P.C., 1976. "Alternative Concepts of Marginal Cost for Public Utility, Pricing problems of application in the water supply sectors", World Bank Staff Working paper No.259.
7. "Financial Consultant's Report, Punjab Urban Water Supply Project", (Amritsar) Chandigarh, Punjab Water Supply and Sewerage Board (mimeo).
8. Report of the Consultant, Madras, Madras Metropolitan Water Authority (mimeo).
9. "The Project Implementation Report of the Maharashtra Water Supply and Sewerage Board's New Bombay Project", Bombay, Chief Engineer, Maharashtra Water Supply Sewerage Board, 1986 (mimeo) p.21.
10. Paramasivam, R. 1986. "Unaccounted for water in Distribution System" - paper presented at the national seminar on "Water and Sewerage Traiffs" organised by the CPHEEO at Srinagar during Sept. 9-11, 1986.
11. Sarma, K.S.R.N. . (1991). *Urban Supply Tariffs Issues in Determination and Administration.* A study sponsered by CPHEEO, Ministry of Urban Development, Govt. of India, IIPA (Restricted) pp.77-81.
12. e.g. Sections 212 and 216 of the *Municipal Corporation of Delhi Act, 1957.*
13. U.N. 1976. *The demand for water: Procedures and Methodologies for projecting water demands in the context of Regional and National Planning.* New York, United Nations.

14a. White, A.U. 1977. "Pattern of Domestic Water use in Low Income Communities", in Richard Reachen, Michael Megarry, and Duncan Mara (eds) *Water, Wastes and Health in Hot Climates.* London, John Wiley and Sons.

b. White, G.P., Bradley D.J. and White A.U. 1972. *Drawers of Water Supply — Domestic Water Use in East Africa*, Chicago, University of Chicago Press.

15. Kalbernatten John M. *et al.* 1980. *Appropriate Technology for Water Supply and Sanitation — A Summary of Technical and Economic Options,* Vol II of the report, Washington, World Bank.
16. World Bank, 1984. *Village Water Supply*, Washington, World Bank, 1976 p.8 and also Kirke J. and Arthur J. "Water Supply Issues" in P.J. Richards and A.M.Thomson (Eds) *Basic Needs and the Urban Poor*, London, Cloom Helm.
17. Sarma, K. S. R. N. 1991. *op. cit.*
18. The poor in the urban areas are often severely constrained by several factors in availing water supplies from public supply systems and therefore the 5 per cent affordability limit is generally considered to be very high. Such norms do not give the necessary leaverage in fixing the differential tariffs. Its lowering is strongly argued for in Hubbal, Kenneth T. "Pricing of Public Utilities for the Urban Poor in Under-developed Countries" (mimeo), paper presented at the

symposium on "Organisation, Unemployment and Environmental, Quality in Latin America", Baltemore, John Hopkin University, Centre for Metropolitan Planning and Research 1977 (mimeo).

19. Sarma, K. S. R. N. *opcit.*
20. For instance in the state of Maharashtra, the Urban Water Supply schemes are financed by the State Government upto 90 per cent of the total cost. The grant/component of the assistance varies from 50 per cent to 22.5 per cent according to size of the city.
21. Government of India — WHO. 1964. "Report on Seminar on Financing and Management of Water and Sewerage Works, Proceedings and Recommendation", 1964 *op. cit.*
22. Patwardhan, S.S. 1981. 'Universal Metering of Urban Rural Town - A Case Study, *Journal of the Indian Water Works Association* Vol. xiii. Jan-March. pp. 51-60.
23. Sarma, K. S. R. N. 1983, "Financing of Urban Service Municipal Government Vs. Specialist Agency", *Nagarlok* Vol.xvii. No.3 July-Sept.
24. ———. 1983. "Municipal Property Tax Rate Structure - A critical study" *Nagarlok*, Vol.xii No.3, July-Sept.1980. pp. 36-37 and also see the judgment of the Supreme Court on "Municipal Corporation of Delhi vs. Mohd. Yasin" (SC 229).

21

Private Sector Involvement in Urban Water Supply Provision

P. S. N. Rao

PROVISION of treated piped water in our cities and towns is one of the major challenges of urban infrastructure today. While on the one hand, existing infrastructure systems have become obsolete and run down and are badly in need of replacement, there is also an urgent need for expansion to cover new urban areas. Traditionally, water supply has been in the hands of the public sector, but with increasing costs and growing needs, it has become a major burden on the public exchequer. Most countries today are facing serious constraints on public expenditure. With mounting pressures on public borrowings and inherent constraints of internal resource mobilization, the urban environment has been facing rapid deterioration in almost all areas of urban infrastructure provision. Water in the urban setting being a crucial sub-segment of infrastructure, the general deterioration of infrastructure has had untold effects on nutrition, health and well-being, on the one hand, and a multiplier effect on the economy as a whole, on the other.

The decade of the eighties has witnessed several global changes in economic philosophy and thinking which have begun to herald a sweeping and perhaps a radical shift in the course of human progress. "Privatisation" or greater involvement of the non-government sector in various areas of the economy has come to acquire great significance in many countries. The chief aim has always been to relieve the pressure on constrained public budgets and to improve efficiency in service delivery.[1] Even though it has been tried extensively in African countries as well as in some of the developed countries, the privatization effort is a relatively new area of involvement in India. More studies should be done to find out both merits and the weaknesses of the above measure. In the next section we will discuss the experiences of other countries. It will be followed by the Indian experiences and then summing up will follow.

One of the best examples of private sector involvement in water provision in the developing countries is that of Abidjan in Ivory Coast in Africa, where the SODECI (Societe de distribution d eau de la Cote d Ivoire) a private corporation based on the French model, operates and maintains the water supply systems. The SODECI provides water to more than 90,000 users directly through piped supplies. It also runs 40 public water fountains which are coin-operated hand-pumps to ensure a check against vandalism, proper supply and maintenance. In addition, there are several private water vendors who procure water from the water fountains and distribute it in the unserved parts of the city. Competition among water vendors in the water market has led to substantial service improvements. The SODECI operates at a profit and has excellent maintenance records, minimal water loss and full cost recovery.[2] A regulated monopoly, SODECI has been able to provide a good quality, reliable and acceptable water system to the people.

Another interesting example is that of Kenya where water vending in the private market through government regulated kiosks has found wide acceptance. Several low-income households avail of subsidised water through this method. The public private partnership ensures continuous operation and maintenance. Water vending has become a common feature in several African countries. Table 1 presents some details of water vending obtained by studies conducted in developing countries.[3] More details are given in Table 2 which is a comparative statement of the various forms of public-private involvement in water provision.

Private water supply provision is not limited to developing countries alone. For example, nearly 55 per cent of all water consumed in France is managed by private firms.[4] French municipalities have been long involved in hiring private firms to construct, manage and operate water supply systems under long-term contracts. Sometimes, on account of availability of concessionary finance for municipal capital investments, systems are built by the municipality and contracted out for operation to private firms. Services which are usually contracted out are leak detection, operation to water treatment plants, customer billing etc. Water authorities in the U.S. are regulated but the operation and management of water supply is usually done by a private firm.

Table 1
Water Vending in Developing Countries

Name of City/ Country	Study population	Source of Water Supply served by vendors	Per cent households served by vendors
Diourbel, Sengal	100	Open well, piped system, vending	90
Ali Matan, (refugee) camp) Somalia	16,000	River, piped system, vending	10
Mandera, Kenya	17,000	River, irrigation canal, rainwater collection, piped system, vending	90
Gankida, Nigeria	10,000	River, open well, rainwater collection, vending	15
Ibi, Nigeria	5,000	Protected well, open well, rainwater collection, vending	40
Boundiali, Ivoty Coast	15,000	Open well, rainwater collection, piped system, vending	50
Cuidan Rouondji, Niger	3,500	Open well, river, rainwater collection, vending	40

Note: Data were collected through questionnaire distribution to Peace Corps and voluntary organizations in each community.
Source: Zaroff and Okun: 1984.

Table 2
Alternative Models of Public-Private Partnerships in Water Supply Provision in Developing Countries

Form of Water Provision	Countries	Government's Role	Cost
1	2	3	4
Concession system where public authority contracts with a private company for 30 years or so for construction, operation & maintenance of drinking water. Company is a regulated monopoly, and must recover capital & operating costs.	Established in Senegal, Congo, Guinea, Madagascar, Togo, Ivory Coast in Africa. After independence, only Ivory Coast retained the system, which was converted to Affermage system in 1973.	In the Ivory Coast, government contracts with SODECI for specific source, quality & level of water supply services. Government receives around 50% of revenues and has a 4% ownership in the firm	In 1982 Ivory Coast system charged 272 CFA/(=S 1) cubic metre. Prices set at a cost plus percentage profit basis.

Cont'd

1	2	3	4
The *Affermage system* entails municipal construction of the water system and a long-term contract with a private firm to operate and maintain it. The company assumes all the risks of operation.	Morocco** Ivory Coast (as on 1973)	Government contracts for specific set of services to SODECI in Ivory Coast.	Set of rules which guide setting of price; surcharge on water fees paid to the municipality to repay construction costs.
Territorial concession for 30 years or more for water pipe network in larger cities. Company procures, purifies, distributes, meters and charges for water.	Chile Guatemala	Tariffs are approved by the Ministry of Public Works and quality control over sight is vested in three public agencies (Chile); quality control provided by Ministry of Health (Gautemala).	U.S. $30/month for 1-inch pipe. U.S. $65 for 1.5 inch pipe plus U.S. $86/cu. metre for an initial supply & U.S. $45/cu. metre for any excess. (Guatemala)
Contracting out for specific activities such as meter reading, computer services, and billing and collection.	Chile Peru Sri Lanka	Not Available	Not available.
Large-scale trucking of water, Private vendors obtained water from private sources, purify & package the water for sale.	Dominican Republic. Similar systems common in Jordan, Ecuador and El Salvador.	In the Dominican Republic, government regulates the ten firms active in water sales & inspects product weekly.	In the Dominican Republic, price varies by quality of water but all charge the maximum allowed by government.
Water Cooperatives where the cooperative usually builds & always owns the pipe network and is responsible for covering capital, operations and maintenance costs without any subsidy	Santa Cruz, Bolivia (others especially in Latin America and the Middle East)	Government approves tariffs.	U.S. $035/cu. metre (1983) in Saguapac cooperative outside Santa Cruz.

Cont'd

1	2	3	4
Water vendors at a metered standpipe (kiosks) sells water by containers. Water is sold to a licensed vendor at a subsidized rate.	Kenya	Not available	Not available
Coin operated meters at water standposts. Supplied and maintained by SODECI Sub-contract to a private company. Operator guards and maintains each unit.	Ivory Coast	Private water supply implementing company under government contract (SODECI) operates system.	U.S. $02/25 litres.
Water vendors sell water door-to-door	Documented for Senegal, Somalia, Kenya, Nigeria, Ivory Coast, Benin & Niger in Africa.	No government involvement or over-sight	U.S. $.008-U.S. 150 litre, or from 8% to over 30% of household income.

* Societe de distribution d'ean de la Cofre d'Ivore.

** Morocco's current *affermage* contract only involves supplying water to the Casablanca and Tangires water authorities.

Source: Bendix, M. and Hardy, H. P., (1982) "The Role of Private Firms in Water Supply and Waste Water Disposal — A Brief Survey of Current Practices", mimio.

The Indian Experience

India is no exception and private initiatives for water supply do exist, although in a different form and perhaps still in a very rudimentary stage.

Although the formal private sector is involved to some extent in water supply provision in India, this involvement is only limited to certain areas in the process of water supply provision which begins at tapping the source and ends at distributing water and maintaining networks. One of the notable examples is that of the city of Gurgaon in Haryana.[5] Here, private developers are involved in developing large scale composite residential areas or housing colonies under the Haryana Development and Regulation of Urban Areas Act (1975). Fig. 1 indicates the various stages in harnessing water for domestic consumption. In the private developer colonies in Gurgaon, the developer is involved only in stages 6, 7 and 8 shown in Fig. 1, i.e., development of 'internal infrastructure' works such as pumping stations, overhead tanks and water pipeline networks.

The 'external infrastructure' is to be provided by the government agency (Haryana Urban Development Authority). The housing and urban development model adopted in Haryana is a public-private partnership. The civil works are provided by the private body. After a minimum period of maintenance, the private colonies are handed over by the developer to the local municipal body for routine maintenance thereafter.[6]

Similar models are being tried out in other states with minor changes. Although these models have been successful to the extent of taping private sector efforts, they can be considered to be highly limited and restrictive as compared to the effort in the African countries where entire systems are operated and maintained continuously by private companies or a public-private partnership. In India the private sector initiatives are restricted to limited components of urban development. Government interventions for involvement of the private sector in water supply provision in India, is yet to be given serious thought.

While this is so, a great amount of potential lies among the people themselves. There are examples from some parts of India where people have organised themselves to secure water supply. In a village called Ralegaon Sidhi in the drought prone taluka of Parner in Ahmednagar district of Maharashtra the villagers have formed a cooperative to lift water from the nearby canal. Labour was provided by the people themselves as *'shramdan'*. The people have set up *'pani mandals'* which ration water to each landholder. A similar example is to be found in Purandhar taluka of Pune district where the villagers have set up *'pani panchayats'* in which all the villagers have a right to obtain water from percolation tanks built by the community itself.[7]

People's efforts in the form of water vending exist in several towns in India, although not on as large a scale as in the African countries mentioned earlier. Water vending is found in several slums of Madras city. The slum communities elect a representative who is responsible for ensuring water delivery through a truck of the

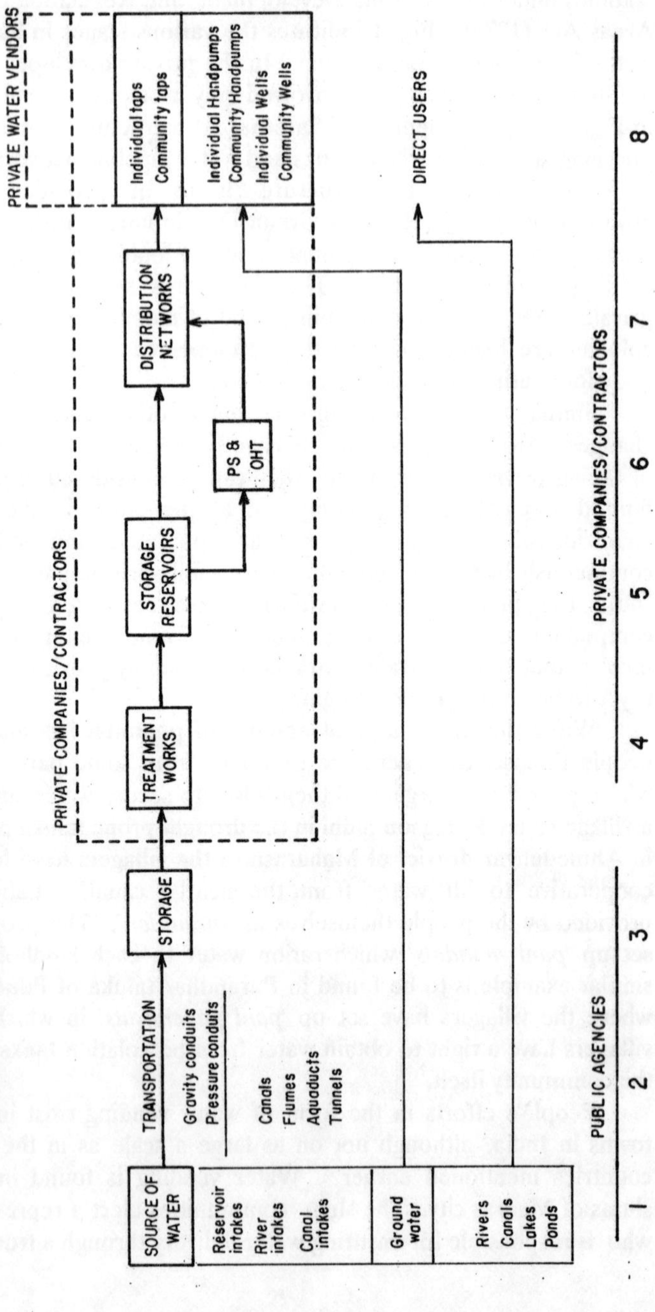

VARIOUS STAGES IN THE PROCESS OF WATER SUPPLY PROVISION

Madras Metropolitan Water Supply Board. The representative collects 10 to 15 paise per pot from the people and also ensures equitable distribution. From the amount collected, around Rs.10 is paid for every trip the truck makes. In this way, the efforts of the people have ensured them regular and adequate water supply.

Water vending by private companies is also common in New Delhi. There are several such companies which truck water for a wide variety of uses. Water is procured from private bore wells and is distributed to customers at a price ranging from Rs.100 to Rs. 150 per tanker having a capacity range of 10,000 litres to 15,000 litres. Details of these can be seen in Table 3. These companies have been operating successfully with a profit margin ranging from 10 to 15 per cent. Currently these companies receive little support from the Government and find it difficult to expand their services. What is significant here is that there is a vast potential in the private companies which are already providing a good service to the people in the absence of adequate Government support.

Table 3: Private Water Vending Companies in New Delhi, India

Sl. No.	Particulars	Jain Water Supply Co	Deep & Co
1.	No. of Tankers	6	13
2.	Capacity of Tankers	i) 4 to 12,000 litres ii) 2 to 15,000 litres	i) 7 of 12,000 litres ii) 5 of 15,000 litres
3.	No. of Trips per day	6 to 8 trips/tanker/day	6 to 7 trips/tanker/day
4.	Sources of Water	i) Own Bore Wells ii) Ali Badarpur Wells iii) Municipal Treated Water	i) Own Bore Wells ii) Ali Badarpur Wells iii) Municipal Treated Water.
5.	Price of Water	i) Bore Well Water @ Rs. 120-150 per tanker ii) Municipal Treated Water @ Rs. 1000-1500 per tanker	i) Bore Well Water @ Rs. 130 per tanker ii) Municipal Treated water @ Rs. 1000-1200 per tanker.
6.	Customers	(i) Residential Colonies (ii) Factories (iii) Hostels (iv) Construction Works (v) Hotels (vi) Marriage Halls	

Source: P.S.N. Rao, (1991), Primary Survey

Conclusion

The position of water supply coverage in India today is far from satisfactory. While is 1981, the urban coverage was 72.3 per cent and rural coverage was 20.8 per cent, the total coverage being 40.5 per cent, by 1985 the situation improved marginally to 72.9 per cent for urban areas and 56.2 per cent for rural areas, the total coverage being 60.2 per cent.[8] Further, the level of satisfaction in the areas covered has been very poor. The causes for tardy progress have been lack of funds and inefficient working of the public agencies.

Private companies can contribute to a great extent in providing efficient and satisfactory services. There are two major components in the provision of water supply. One is (a) tapping water resources from rivers, natural reservoirs, dam reservoirs, canals, etc., and transporting the same to various towns and cities and the other is (b) treatment, storage and distribution within the city. Traditionally, the former activities have been with the irrigation and state public works departments while the latter has been under water supply boards and municipal bodies. The former involves several issues related to inter-state relating, political arrangements, complex legalities and so on and are best left to the State agencies to handle. For the former, neither is it desirable to have private monopolies nor will political and bureaucratic opposition allow it.

The latter functions could easily be privatised in various forms. Fig. 1 shows the activities that could be left to public agencies and those which could be privatised. Local municipal bodies could act as facilitators to the privatisation process and be monitors. Decentralised water supply systems can also be attempted in which case the responsibility of the State would be to supply adequate quantity of raw water and the remaining functions could be taken over by the private sector which could operate and maintain its own self contained systems. Composite residential developments by private developers could be best managed in this way. Consumer interests would not be at stake on account of the recent Consumer Protection Act (CPA) of 1986 which has several features which make redressal of public complaints simple.

From the Gurgaon public-private partnership approach, a few lessons can be learnt. The private company was supposed to collect from the residential plot purchasers, external development charges which were to be transferred to the local authority for provision of external trunk services. However, in actual practice, the private company did not transfer the charges on time although it had collected the same from the residential plot purchasers. The local authorities had to ultimately resort to threatening the private companies with cancellation of licences in order to recover the charges. On this account, provision of external services were greatly delayed.

Further, the pace of development of the private companies was too fast for the public agencies to cope with. As a result, additional infrastructure had to be provided by the private companies at additional cost so as to maintain market credibility. The burden of this additional cost obviously was passed over to subsequent plot purchasers who had to pay much higher prices. One has to, therefore, realise that the success of private sector involvement rests to a great extent on the success of the regulatory mechanism that the public sector adopts. Privatisation definitely does not mean that there is no role for the public sector; in fact it calls for redefining the role of the public sector, from that of a provider to that of a facilitator.

There is, thus, an urgent necessity to undertake systematic studies of the situation, systems and structures of urban water supplies so that suitable privatisation strategies could be worked out along with clear identification of the risks involved, roles and commitments of both the private and public sectors. Various methods of private sector involvement, viz. concession system, affermage system, territorial concessions, water cooperatives, water trucking and vending, coin operated hand-pumps and community systems have a great potential for exploitation in India, more so with financial assistance for urban infrastructure coming up in a big way in the country.

NOTES

1. Rao, P.S.N. 1992. Private Sector and Housing for the Urban Poor, paper presented at the "Conference on Housing for the Urban Poor", New Delhi. April 8-10, 1992.
2. Carleene Dei. (1985). The Role of Formal and Informal Sectors in Provision of Urban Services and Housing for Lower Income Groups. Abidjan, Ivory Coast (Mimeo), October and also see Fredrick Gollady. (1983) Role of Private Organisation in Managing and Operating Water Supply and Sanitation Systems in Developing Countries. (Research Proposal), WSUDD, World Bank (Mimeo), October; and M. Bendick and H.P. Hatry. (1982). The Role of Private Firms in

Water Supply and Wastewater Disposal: A Brief Survey of Current Practices and Data Sources. Washington DC. The Urban Institute, (Mimeo), (December).

3. B. Zaroff and D.A. Okun. (1984). "Water Vending in Developing Countries". *Aqua* No.5.
4. M. Bendick and H.P. Batry, *op.cit.*
5. P S N Rao. (1987). "Public Interventions and Private Developers in Urban Housing: The Cases of Delhi, Gurgaon and Ahmedabad", School of Planning and Architecture, New Delhi (mimeo)
6. Rao, P. S. N. 1990. "Private Sector Involvement in Water Supply Provision", *Nagarlok*, Oct-Dec.
7. D'Monte, Darryl. (1989). "Jobs in Villages: Social Organisation Crucial", *Times of India*. May 15.
8. H.U. Bijlani and P.S.N. Rao. (1990). *Water Supply and Sanitation in India.* Oxford IBH Pub., New Delhi.

22

Urban Basic Services Programme in India: A SWOT Analysis

D. Ravindra Prasad

IN terms of size, the urban population in India was around 160 million in 1981 constituting 23.7 per cent of the total population. It increased to 217 million or 25.7 per cent of the total population in 1991. According to various projections, the size of urban population would almost double every two decades in the next century.

Approximately 27.7 per cent of the urban population fell below the poverty line in 1987-88 (National Commission on Urbanisation, 1988). The Task Force on Housing and Urban Development (1983) estimated that by AD 2000 the urban population of India would be 310 million of which 78 million or about 25 per cent would be living in slums. Of the 78 million, the Task Force noted that 36 million would be living in the slums of metropolitan cities alone.

The distribution of the slum population among the different classes of cities and towns is considerably skewed. For example, in metropolitan cities, they vary between 38 and 65 per cent of cities' population and these cities account for a major share of slum population of the states in which they are located. As many as 217 class I cities account for more than one-third of the slum population. An important aspect of urban poverty is that the larger the size of the city, the greater concentration of its urban poor in the slums.

Urbanisation has put a heavy pressure on the very basic needs on which there is a broad agreement. For example, one-fifth of the urban population has no access to water supply and only two-fifths have access to sanitation services. It was estimated that about 73 million lives are lost every year due to water-borne diseases. The costs in terms of expenditure on medicare and loss of production are very high.

To mitigate the problems of the poor and to make provision for basic amenities in order to improve their quality of life, several policy interventions were made and several programmes were launched. Among them, Urban Community Development Programme (1958), Environmental Improvement of Urban Slums (1972), Integrated Development of Small and Medium Towns and Integrated Child Development Services are important.

Other effective and innovative programmes include Sites and Services and Slum Improvement Projects in Madras and Hyderabad, Small Loan Programme and Community Health Scheme in Calcutta, Low Cost Sanitation Schemes in Patna and other cities, etc.

But these schemes did not have the desired impact mainly because of the sectoral approach and lack of community involvement. The impact of these programmes was examined by the National Commission on Urbanisation (1988). It was concluded that the reach of the programmes was limited; there was a high degree of inflexibility and a lack of convergence of programmes; even the main targets were often missed; and with a few exceptions the programmes are still working on a laboratory scale.

In the Seventh Five-Year Plan, the Urban Basic Services programme was launched which envisaged an integrated approach to the problems of slums and poverty by involving the slum population in the decision-making process. In the following sections we will evaluate the scheme which has had some success in Andhra Pradesh and Orissa in delivering the goods. First we will discuss the basic elements of the scheme. After that a SWOT (Strengths, Weaknesses, Opportunities and Threats) analysis will follow.

Urban Basic Services Programme

As referred to earlier the Urban Basic Services Programme (UBS) launched during the Seventh Five-Year Plan (1985-90) with the support of the UNICEF and Central and State Governments, has gained importance. When launched, the target of the programme was to cover 200 towns. By the end of 1989 it had covered 125 towns. The basic aim of the UBS programme is to upgrade the quality of life of the urban poor, especially the most vulnerable sections like women, children and the economically weak. The programme envisages development of urban slums through the provision of basic services like water, health and sanitation, education, environmental upgradation, etc.

The guiding principles of the programme are community initiative and participation, convergence, cost effectiveness and continuity. The strategy is to create awareness and promote collective action among the beneficiaries. It envisages organising the community and encouraging community management by utilising the human resource potential. Participation, therefore, is emphasised in the programme. An important feature of the programme is, that instead of the people participating in government sponsored programmes, government departments and agencies participate in the programmes organised by the people. As such the community organisers, project officers and other programme staff act as motivators and catalysts in these programmes rather than the officers implementing the programme.

In tune with its nomenclature, the programme aims at providing basic amenities and services to identified slum communities. The activities include provision of water, health care, education, nutrition, economic activities, environmental sanitation, recreation, and shelter. Each slum community, based on the local needs and resources, prepares mini-plans and implements them after approval by appropriate higher level bodies. By integrating the mini-plans of all the slums a Town Action Plan is formulated.

At the town, district, state and national levels, there are committees for coordinating and monitoring the programmes regularly. There are, however, wide variations in the nature and composition of these committees at various levels in different States.

Although the broad objectives of the programme are similar in all the states, there are variations in the nature, composition and implementation of the programme from State to State. The administrative organisation also varies. In Andhra Pradesh and Orissa, however, strong organisations to supervise, guide, monitor and evaluate the programme have been established at the State level. The programmes in these two States have attracted the attention of the academics as well as the administrators.

The UBS programme is being implemented in 16 towns in Andhra Pradesh and 24 towns in Orissa; roughly one-third of the UBS programme is being implemented in these two States covering a slum population of more than six hundred thousand and rapid strides have been made in providing a package of basic services to the slum communities. In Andhra Pradesh about 350 Neighbourhood Committees were constituted in 16 towns and there are more than 3,000 Resident Community Volunteers implementing the basic services programme. Similarly in Orissa about 250 Neighbourhood Committees were formed and more than 2,000 Resident Community Volunteers are involved.

As part of the programme, provision was made for hand-pumps or public stand-posts, community latrines, dustbins, drains and smokeless *chullas*. Loans were given to women residents to undertake income generation activities. Training and orientation in community processes, and skill development received priority in the programme. Balwadies and creches, sewing centres and adult literacy centres were established in the slums. The community leaders and resident community volunteers were trained or oriented in the participatory process, health care and sanitation, etc.

The actual impact of this programme is difficult to quantify as this is not a capital intensive programme but only a human development programme. Change in attitudes, and conscious involvement in development programmes are qualitative aspects and the programme has made considerable impact in these areas.

Central to the UBS programme is the 'Neighbourhood Committee' (NHC), serving every 200 families. The committee identifies the needs of the community, prioritises them keeping in view the resources, prepares an action plan and after its approval by the town management committee, implements it. Decision-making is thus based on the collective wisdom of the people. The NHC assumes leadership as well as responsibility on a self-help basis for the well-being of the community. One resident from every 15 to 20 families called Resident Community Volunteer (RCV) represents them in the Neighbourhood Committee. Each member of the committee looks after an important activity like health, education, etc., tries to articulate the problems of the community and ensures the proper implementation of action plans. The programme thus aims at community participation and self-management as well as building the capacity of slum communities to organise themselves to implement the development programmes.

One of the important features of the NHC is that the women members of the community constitute these committees. This was a conscious decision taken and the assumptions are:

1. UBS emphasizes improving the quality of lives of the urban poor with special focus on women and children who constitute 68 per

cent of the urban poor.

2. Women have not so far been involved in the country's developmental process though they constitute about 50% of the population.
3. The problems of women and children are better understood and better managed by women themselves.
4. If a man is educated, he alone is educated. But, if a woman is educated, the whole family is educated.
5. A housewife is a homemaker and is more affected and concerned about the lack of basic social services like health and education, and physical amenities like water, sanitation and proper shelter.
6. As a mother, a woman is more involved compared to a man in the bringing up of children who are the future citizens.
7. Women are the poorest of the poor at the family level as they are subjected to exploitation and dominated by men in the poor families due to their lack of education and freedom.
8. The status of women can be improved or raised effectively by empowering them and they can join the mainstream of society and improve their status only by shouldering responsibilities.

As we have noted, community involvement and participation are basic to the UBS programme. The key areas of community involvement are:

- forming neighbourhood groups and selecting volunteers,
- determining needs and prioritising them,
- deciding inputs (services),
- finalising mini-plans and implementing them,
- monitoring and evaluation.

What follows a SWOT analysis of this programme based upon the experience of implementation of Urban Basic Services programme and evaluation studies undertaken on the subject.

Strengths

The Urban Basic Services Programme, during the last 5-6 years has struck roots and has gained acceptance as an important programme for the provision of basic services in the urban slums. The urban poor, the local bodies and the State and Central governments have become aware of its significance as well as its potentialities for providing basic services. The municipalities have accepted the need for and significance of the programme.

Initially, there was reluctance on the part of women, though later, they began to take active interest in articulating their needs, preparing mini-plans and implementing the programme components. The slum community's involvement and participation in upgrading their own quality of life is very high. Empowerment of women has led to the realisation that they too are partners in the process of development and can mould their own lives. There is scope for further harnessing the latent potentialities of the community in improving their quality of life. Members and conveners of the neighbourhood committees are now shouldering greater development responsibilities. They maintain registers and account books on their own.

The community organisers who are directly recruited have a background of social work and understand the philosophy of UBS and so are working with zeal and commitment. They are highly motivated and are providing the necessary momentum to the programme.

The support and keen interest taken by the State Government and the UNICEF in implementing the programme has given it the much needed impetus. Finally, the training and orientation programmes for the officials and non-officials as well as community leaders has created the much needed awareness about the problems of the urban poor, the need for and significance of the participatory processes as well as implementation methodologies. This has played a very significant role in accelerating the process of implementation.

Weaknesses

Although the programme, has carved a niche in the minds of the people with regard to its need and significance, there are many problems and weaknesses which cannot be lost sight of. In the beginning, baseline surveys were undertaken hastily and neighbourhood committees constituted with disinterested and unmotivated RCVs. In the absence of adequate trained personnel in the municipalities, no efforts were made to explain the concept and philosophy of the UBS programme to the members to enlist their support and participation. The mini-plans did not reflect the felt-needs of the community rather were formulated by the project staff based on their perception of those needs of the community. No doubt, some of these basic weaknesses were overcome with the appointment of a project staff equipped with the appropriate training and orientation and who had a greater awareness of the nature and scope of the programme.

At the community level, training and orientation programmes are very few and this has come in the way of harnessing the full potentialities of the community. Similarly, the efforts in skill formation or improvement are not commensurate with the requirements of the slum communities. Coupled with the problems of marketing, the economic support programmes are not making the desired progress as this is a neglected area. In some slums, the neighbourhood committees are reluctant to extend small loans to the community from the revolving fund either because they feel that recovery is difficult or because it is an avoidable burden for them.

Frequent transfers of trained officials at various levels is halting the progress of the programme. Not all municipal functionaries, both political and administrative, seem to have fully understood the philosophy of the UBS. The UBS is being implemented as a separate pro gramme rather than as an integral part of the town development plan of poverty alleviation. Thus there does not appear to be a proper integration of UBS with other municipal services at the town level. The municipal bodies, with their very weak financial resources, quite often find it difficult to contribute even 20 per cent of their share.

Although one of the guiding principles of UBS is convergence, this appears to be its weak spot. Interdepartmental co-operation and co-ordination is very weak both at the district and town levels. This, coupled with frequent transfer of officials, is hindering progress. A closely related problem is the inability of senior officials like Joint Collectors and Municipal Commissioners to devote sufficient time and attention for monitoring, evaluating and guiding the programmes due to other pressing functions.

Involvement of NGOs in the implementation of the programme is very limited. The UBS is based upon the principle of flexibility, but the insistence on following existing procedures which is characteristic of the Indian bureaucracy has often come in the way of implementation of the programme as well as effective people's participation. Often, the municipal officials fear criticism by the audit and, therefore, insist on following the accepted administrative norms, or insist on instructions or guidelines from the Government.

Flexibility, therefore, exists only on paper in many places.

In several towns, the focus is only on certain components to the neglect of an integrated approach. Team spirit which is *sine qua non* in any programme where several agencies, individuals and groups are involved is not being forged because of the emphasis on narrow departmentalism.

The administrative structures at the state and district level leave much to be desired. The training and orientation of the municipal functionaries who have to deal with the UBS programme as well as of the district level functionaries who converge with the UBS programmes is inadequate.

Opportunities

The urban poor, for whom the programme is meant, have begun to appreciate the concept and philosophy of UBS and are participating in it actively and effectively. This is an opportunity to harness the hidden potentialities of the community, particularly, the women, in improving the quality of life and provision of basic services. The community is willing to contribute in cash, kind and labour wherever possible and necessary. The initial reluctance has given way to positive appreciation of the need and significance of their contribution to the programme. Community leaders and volunteers have begun to take pride in the ownnership of the assets created and also are keen to protect their 'assets from misuse and exploitation'. There is readiness on the part of the community to sustain the assets created through proper maintenance.

The UBS programmes, through creches, balwadies and adult education schemes have opened the doors of education to the poor, thus increasing the scope and opportunity for literacy. Similarly, there is a very good response to skill training which would augment their income. This is another opportunity to involve the community in their progress and development.

Support by the State Government and the UNICEF, has also contributed to the effective implementation of the programme. Training and orientation by the Regional Centre has brought about changes in the minds of the people towards the participatory approach. Further concentration on capacity building at various levels would ensure consolidation of gains as well as greater community participation.

Threats

There appears to be reluctance on the part of some key functionaries to understand and appreciate the concept and philosophy of UBS. To some, it is a low priority area because of the low budget involved and for a few others, it is an avoidable burden on their time and therefore unwelcome. The revenue culture which characterises the Indian administration has its own suffocating effect on programme implementation which is based on participatory processes. It is clearly antithetical to development culture.

Political pressures, interventions and unkind treatment of the project staff is a major threat. From the beginning, there have been efforts, though unintentional, to keep elected councils outside the UBS programme. The only link between the UBS and the municipal council is the municipal chairman. This created a feeling that the councillors are being deliberately overlooked, particularly when the council contributes 20 per cent of the programme costs. This has led to the feeling on the part of the councillors that the UBS programme is an infringement on their legitimate right to administer civic programmes. Some of the municipal councillors perceive the neighbourhood committees as a threat to their leadership and as well as their sphere of influence. The clash of leadership and vested interests may dampen the initiative of the neighbourhood committees.

The UBS is being implemented in some places as a government programme rather than a people's programme and the misconception that the UBS is a UNICEF programme, also poses a major threat to it. Finally, from the beginning of the programme, doubts and suspicions have been raised about the continuity of the scheme after 1990. This has had a demoralising effect and is a serious threat to motivating the project staff. A closely related issue is the absence of proper career patterns for the community organisers. They feel that they are underpaid, asked to over-work and also work under less qualified and not so committed officials. These feelings and perceptions are likely to create a gulf between the project staff and the officials and hinder the programme.

Conclusion

The foregoing clearly brings out the strengths and weaknesses as well as the opportunities and threats that underlie the programme which has been under implementation during the Seventh Plan period. During the past two years the programme has been reformulated as Urban Basic Services for the poor and is being implemented with the financial support of the Government of India. The programme is integrated with the Nehru Rozgar Yojana and Environmental Improvement of Urban Slums under the package of Poverty Alleviation Programme. The former is a programme aimed at providing employment opportunities and the latter aims at providing infrastructural facilities to the urban slums. Efforts are being made to involve the Neighbourhood Committees in the identification of beneficiaries under these schemes. The emphasis under the revised Urban Basic Services for the Poor programme is also on the participatory processes. During the last two years for various reasons the programme could not make much headway in the country. There is, need, however to redefine the roles of existing and the proposed structures and the functionaries. There is also the need to convert weaknesses into strengths and threats into opportunities and learn from the experiences in implementing the reformulated Urban Basic Services for the Poor programme.

The UBS or UBSP is not the only programme under which provision for the basic amenities is made though it gives these a high priority. Many programmes and activities contribute towards the fulfilment of basic amenities. The programme is the first serious effort to provide of basic needs to the urban poor while emphasising the participatory processes. Fulfilment of basic needs as an objective is non-controversial though there may be differences in the approaches and the strategies adopted. The UBSP should not be construed as only a programme for the provision of certain amenities. It is a development programme emphasising community participation. As the purpose of development is to develop human beings and not just things, the UBSP aims at harnessing and developing the human potential for the fulfilment and satisaction of basic amenities. This becomes all the more imperative in the context of rapid urbanisation.

REFERENCE

Government of India, (1988) *National Commission on Urbanisation*, Vol. II, Planning Commission, (1983) *Task Forces on Housing and Urban Development*.

23

People's Participation and the Cleaning of Ganga at Varanasi: Rhetoric and Reality*

Sara Ahmed

PEOPLE'S or public or community participation is often seen as *sine qua non* for the success and sustainability of development projects (Korten: 1986, Montgomery: 1988, Goulet: 1989). Yet it raises a number of questions: who are "the people'? Why is their participation sought? And how and at what level is such participation desired?

The central issue affecting participation is *power.* As a process which seeks to involve the local people in decision-making and the control of resources, including project benefits, it is not politically neutral. To be effective, participation must challenge existing power relations and preconceptions of doing things, as well as question project goals and objectives.

Thus, to argue that participation, by its very practice, reduces conflict and social tension within a community and between the community and project administrators is a fallacy (Robertson: 1984). Not only does any community have its own inherent diversities and interest groups (i.e. the community is not a homogeneous entity) which raises questions as to who participates and why, but there are also several social and institutional limitations which constrain the realization of the intended participation.

This paper seeks to examine the rhetoric of participation in the implementation of the Ganga Action Plan (GAP) at Varansi, Uttar Pradesh. Launched in 1985, as a plan to control and monitor the pollution of the Ganga, it sought in addition, to be a "people's programme" because of the powerful and deep-seated cultural and religious meaning associated with the river. Varanasi however, is indicative of its failure to deliver this promise - the GAP is only acceptable to the authorities because it does not challenge the existing institutional order and its participatory content is symbolic rather than substantive.

Varanasi: The City in Context

One of the oldest cities in the world, Varanasi occupies a central position on the crescent shaped left bank of the Ganga in the alluvial fertile land of the Middle Ganga Valley. Situated 50 to 70 feet above the river, it is a city where, to quote Mumford, "energy is converted into culture" (Eck, 1982). Nowhere is this energy more visible than along the majestic riverfront, dotted with temples, shrines, Shiva *lingams*, old houses and princely residences from which large steps called *ghats* lead down to the Ganga. It is to the *ghats* that people come everyday to bathe, to swim, to defecate, to wash clothes, utensils or buffaloes, to cremate their dead, to carry water home for drinking, cooking and ritual purposes, to offer garlands to Ganga, the goddess, or simply to walk or to sit and meditate.

In 1991 Varanasi had a population of one million but this is unevenly distributed. The inner zone of the city, which lies around the river's edge, has one of the highest population densities in the country, nearly 250-700 people per hectare. It is the oldest part of the city and is a main business area with numerous temples, narrow lanes and few open spaces.

Cultural identity in Varanasi is based on *mohallas* -- administrative groups of around 100 to 2000 people; there are approximately 50 *mohallas* to a ward (and 40 wards in the city). Each *mohalla* strives to remain culturally united and is dominated by ethnic and two to three castes or occupational groups, like Bengalis, weavers, etc. (Kumar, 1988). Most public cultural and religious activities tend to be *mohalla* based – festivals and other performances are organised around, based in, named after and identified with a particular mohalla (Freitag, 1989).

Given Varanasi's importance as a cultural, religious and educational centre, the increasing influx of visitors (pilgrims, tourists and students) has exerted demands on the limited civic infrastructure, particularly sewage, sanitation and drainage. This has affected the riparian environment, causing serious concern amongst bureaucrats, technocrats, NGOs and some individuals about Public Health. Implicit to the views underlying such concern, is the idea of *control* – who is to control whom, with respect to what aspects of life, or more specifically, what is being judged impure/polluted, who is accused of causing that impurity/pollution and who are its victims[1] (Douglas and Wildavsky, 1983).

Ganga Action Plan

The main thrust of the Rs. 430.5 million allocated to the city under the first phase of the GAP (1985-1990) has been the renovation of the five sewage pumping stations along the *ghats*, the construction of another one and the installation of sewage treatment plants to treat some of the 125 million litres of waste water discharged daily.[2]

In addition to this, an electric crematorium at Harischandra ghat provides a cheaper alternative to the traditionally expensive and energy intensive wood-pyres, while low-cost community toilets have been built along the *ghats* for public use.

But pollution control infrastructure is not in itself a sufficient solution to the problem – although there has certainly been some improvement in the quality of the water, there is much disagreement about the efficiency of the sewage pumping stations in diverting raw waste water, the main source of pollution away from the ghats.[3] Moreover, the maintenance, management and monitoring of such systems and the inability to cope with relatively minor sources of pollution (bathing, washing of clothes etc.) has been the chief reason for the continuing official buzzword: participation.

Yet, as the next few sections show, a critical examination of the issues and actors involved in the implementation of the GAP suggests that there are structural reasons for the lack of participation at Varanasi which are endemic to the nature of state-society relations in India (Guha, 1989; Shiva, 1988, 1991).

The Political Economy of the Environment in India: Institutional Constraints

According to Midgley (1986) there are four forms of state responses to participation:

- the anti-participatory mode
- the manipulative participatory mode
- the incremental mode of participation

– the participatory State

These categories are not necessarily definitive and it is possible that a state falls into one or more classifications, thus combining elements of both. Using Midgley's framework, I would argue that the response of the Indian State to participation in the context of the GAP has been both manipulative and incremental. By manipulative, I mean that the State supports participation when *it* chooses to do, largely in its own interests, to gain votes and political support. Not only was the official announcement of the GAP timed to coincide with the late Rajiv Gandhi's inaugural speech as Prime Minister in 1985, but also some of the State directed forms of participation at Varanasi involved using people as cheap (free) labour without ascribing them any power in decision-making processes.

For example, national social service camps are organised after the rainy season for students from all parts of the country to come to clean the silt from the ghats, plant trees and interact with the public on the problem of pollution through songs, slogans and discourses. While these are important awareness raising measures, the point to be stressed is that they were undertaken by volunteers who were in Varanasi for a short period of time and possibly did not see it as a chore or task they were obliged to fulfil. In addition, it was combined with other cultural activities and duly acknowledged by local bureaucrats for its social significance. This is an important factor to bear in mind for all too often the work and effort put in by NGOs and individuals is hardly recognized by the Government, which gives them little incentive to continue.

Other forms of token participation encouraged by the State include similar ghat cleaning exercises involving pilgrims and the staging of elaborate concerts – *Ganga Mahatsavs* – at the main bathing *ghat* where brochures are distributed proclaiming, "Ganga Sewa, Bharat Sewa" (i.e. to do service for the Ganga, is to do service for the country). Faded billboards along the *ghats* remind the public not to defecate along the banks of the river, nor use soap, throw garbage, dead bodies or animal carcasses into the Ganga and ironically, divert waste water in their vicinity away from the waterfront. While there are no rubbish bins along the *ghats* for people to throw garbage in, nor an incinerator where they can dispose of their dead cattle, how are they physically supposed to divert sewage?

The State's support of participation is incremental in so far as it has a *laissez faire* or ambivalent approach to implementation which fails to encourage local efforts (by NGOs and individuals) or to ensure the effective functioning of theoretically participatory institutions such as local government. Remarking on voluntary efforts, one of the ex-Divisional Commissioners of the city complained that NGOs have not come forward with concrete proposals:

> Voluntary efforts are wanting. The basic problem is that the NGOs are geared to working on a drive basis, for example, at the *Kumbh Mela* in Allahabad (1989) there were 4000 volunteers helping for a few days. But when it comes to maintaining ghats for a year they feel that they can't do it. We have tried to get NGOs to adopt one ghat each, but enthusiasm remains for a fortnight only and then starts to waver. Sustaining NGO action is difficult.
>
> (*Interview with Divisional Commissioner, Varanasi, 1990*)

There has however, been little attempt to financially support the activities of the NGOs in the city or to provide them with clear information on the GAP, its methodology and its impact on water quality. The project cell is at a considerable distance from the city centre and, therefore, inaccessible to the public at large, while project reports are usually made available after they have been approved so that there is no scope for alterations based on public debate nor any means of questioning accountability. And the bureaucracy is more concerned with achieving targets rather than building effective linkages or even communicating with the people.

The faith of the bureaucracy in their own rational, technocentric knowledge (O'Riordan, 1989) which fails to include other systems of knowledge is well illustrated in the approach adopted by the U.P. Jal Nigam, the main implementing agency of the GAP. Responsible for the renovation of the sewage pumping stations and the construction of the sewage treatment plants, the U.P. Jal Nigam did not consult local experts such as the Institute of Technology, Banaras Hindu University (BHU). Although the BHU academics offered to design the treatment facility for their campus, taking into account cheaper alternatives such as waste stabilization ponds, they received no encouragement from the higher authorities – a case of "foiled" participation or as Robertson asserts, the public are simply "not expected to offer significant *technical emendations*" (1984).

According to the General Manager (GM) of the Jal Nigam:

> People have little to contribute to the technical aspects of the GAP – they will only confuse the issue. If you open the plans for discussion, it will take longer to achieve results as they (referring to the NGO representatives who sit on the GAP Task Force in Varanasi) will discuss it for years and not do anything (Interview, 1990).

As Ingram (1976) maintains, participation increases the "cost" of receiving and assimilating information as not only does it lengthen decision-making processes, it also questions agency goals and values.

On the other hand, the GM is critical of the obsession that bureaucrats and engineers have with meeting targets (project deadlines) rather than basic objectives – keeping the Ganga clean: "Target cannot become objectives, they are simply a means of achieving a particular objective."

With regard to the "objective" side of the programme, the GM feels that there is a role for the public to play:

> "The public must be associated with the monitoring of the pumping stations (to check that there is no waste water leakage). I have brought this up at several Task Force meetings, but I am a single person and I cannot guarantee this happening" (Interview, 1990).

Such a statement reflects the "prisoner of bureaucracy" dilemma within which the GM finds himself literally trapped, that is, institutional identity (Douglas: 1987) and loyalty to the bureaucratic agency or mission orientness overrides flexibility and innovativeness (Schaffer, 1969).

Thus his conception of participation (and that of most bureaucrats in the city) is limited to "soft" options, like educating the masses so that they do not pollute the Ganga, which assumes that people are the problem rather than institutions and structures. Moreover, the mechanics of *how* people can be involved is more frequently than not overlooked in any discussion on participation. Instead, the introduction of a river police force and home guards along the ghats has further served to alienate local people from their resource base.

Patrolling the Ganga – the "Commons" Solution?

For Hardin, (1968) the "tragedy" of the Ganga is that of a system where each individual is pursuing rational self-interests (washing, bathing, defecting etc.) unable to comprehend the effects of the totality of his or her demands on other users and the ecosystem.[4] The morality of the act is determined by the state of the system when it is preformed, that is, using the Ganga to dump pollutants may have been "acceptable" when the population was small, but now, Hardin would argue, there is need for a system of *mutual coercion*. Herein, lies the problem of Hardin's analysis – that coercion must be mutually agreed upon. In actual fact, coercion is hardly ever mutual – the policing mechanism imposed on the people of Varanasi is an example of this.

Installed in 1988, the river police force is supposed to check drug trafficking, public nuisance (cheating of pilgrims and tourists at the *ghats*), and to prevent people from throwing rubbish or unburnt dead bodies and animal carcasses into the Ganga, or wash clothes or defecate along its banks. Moreover, according to the city plan document, the police are meant to "... educate, train and mobilize public opinion against various forms of pollution" (GAP, 1987).

Most people interviewed in Varanasi clearly did not like the police force as it had failed to build any rapport with them and seemed to be out to harrass them. Having a police force hasn't changed anything (least of all, the quality of the Ganga) – it simply provides more channels of corruption for the public, to those that can afford them that is.

A *pandit* explained that sometimes when the police find a dead body floating down the river in their vicinity, they just push it along to the next outpost where it becomes someone else's responsibility. Furthermore, they take money from the municipal corporation to cremate unidentified corpses, but then throw them unburnt into the river. According to one BJP legislator, "when the protectors have become the eaters, then what is the point of protection? At least 90 per cent of the unburnt bodies thrown into the Ganga are done so by the police, or with their prior consent," (Interview Varanasi, 1990).

The Superintendent of Police, however, denies knowledge of the practice, but admits that there is probably some corruption in the force as there is in any government service because of the poor conditions of pay. It is true that the river police have little incentive to work well – salaries have been irregular and they have no proper "home", living in a large make-shift tent on the steps of the main bathing *ghat* or in similar tents at other outposts.

The question is not whether there should or should not be a pollution control or monitoring mechanism, but whether it should be State imposed and more specifically, whether it should be seen as the task of the police to undertake this responsibility. In the past, mohallas used to be walled and voluntary guards were appointed by the community to keep the streets clean (Singh, 1955).

The *pandas* (ritual priests) at the *ghats* claim that they were responsible for maintaining their bit of the riverfront and used to have the power to tell people not to spit in the Ganga, or use soap and oil when bathing. Although nothing in effect stops them from continuing to do so now, they feel this so-called moral duty has been taken over by the State and that there are too many bad elements interfering with their work.

There are many who feel that the impetus to clean the Ganga should come from the people for the river police have little, if any, community education training, they do not know how to communicate with the people in a language that they can understand, nor do they respect their customs or their knowledge of their environment.

Failure to regulate means that the very reason for regulation gets discredited. True enough. But it also necessitates a search for alternative and hopefully, more effective means of resource management (regulation in a broader sense) which include resource users. Since the State and bureaucracy have been unsuccessful in mobilizing public support and involvement in the GAP, the next section considers another actor, namely the NGO, theoretically seen as intermediary actors between the micro and macro level. My discussion will be limited to the Sankat Mochan Foundation, the largest and most active of the NGOs in the city.

NGOs – People or Power Centred

Established in 1982, the Sankat Mochan Foundation (SMF) derives its name from the Sanskrit words *sankat mochan*, which mean the removal of all sufferings. It is also the name of the second most popular and largest temple in Varanasi, whose *mahant* (hereditary head), Veer Bhadra Mishra is Professor of Hydraulic Engineering at BHU. He is a particularly appropriate leader for he embodies the confrontation of religion and science surrounding the efforts to clean the Ganga.

In late 1982, *mahantji*, as he is affectionately known, launched the *Swatcha Ganga Abhiyan* (Clean Ganga Campaign), a public education programme to make people aware of the plight of the Ganga and to formulate a people's approach to the issues and problems at hand. Today the campaign organizes an annual children's painting competition on the theme of river pollution, a three-day *Kavi Sammelan* (poetry festival) and a three-day Lok *Ṡangeet Sammelan* (folk music festival) where poems, songs and hymns in praise of Mother Ganga are combined with a more important environmental message.

In addition, there is an environmental education programme in some of the larger and better endowed schools, which receives some support from teachers and schools in Sweden and more recently from the U.S.A. However, because of the sporadic nature of such efforts and the fact that awareness and knowledge are but the first steps in any environmental education programme, it is too early to judge how far such action has or can be translated into the development of attitudes, values and skills towards participation in environmental decision-making or in work at the community level outside the formal education system.

The Foundation also collects and analyzes water samples from the main bathing *ghats* at its small laboratory. According to it the data generated by Government agencies is unreliable, when it is available that is, and that there is need for an independent "watchdog body" to check their results by undertaking their own assessments. But the problem for the SMF is that they do not have the technical and financial resources (or so they claim) to disseminate their data and therefore, as an ex-bureaucrat remarked recently, "it is redundant!".

At another level, the momentum generated at public events organized by the SMF is not channelled into constructive energy. There is no structure for people to get involved in the activities of the Foundation for the office-cum-information centre maintained by them is only open in the late evenings, i.e. after 7 p.m. This means that women and children, crucial to Swatcha Ganga's objectives, are unlikely to visit unless accompanied by a male or older family member. Moreover, as all the executive and working members hold full-time jobs elsewhere, any action taken by them is difficult to sustain.

Thus, much of the public relations work rests on the charisma of one person – *Mahantji*. Effective leadership demands patience, flexibility and the ability to communicate in a language which the community can understand. There is definitely a certain aura about Mahantji, which has helped to attract not only a few local people to the campaign, but also numerous national and international visitors wanting to make films, videos and write articles. *Mahantji* speaks gently, yet his graceful demeanour can be both angry and passionate when deliberating the injustice being perpetuated to the Ganga by the human race.

> "I say to them, isn't the pollution a disrespect to your mother? Is it not (like) spitting at your mother?" That disturbs people and they are ready to do anything if you put the problem in this way," (Mahantji quoted in Berwick, 1990).

The SMF's concern for the Ganga is not far from the ecocentrism preached by the early American transcedentalists like Thoreau and Emerson (O'Riordan: 1981). It is borne out of a sense of responsibility for the earth and a plea for a basic ecological understanding of the intimate Man-Nature relationship.[6] Such an approach allows the Foundation to consider the local community as a homogeneous, culturally monolithic unity rather than to assess how different groups of people (class and caste-based) are affected by both pollution and the GAP. Thus, participation is simply equated with the numbers of people who are present at the various cultural events and meetings, who listen passively to the songs, poems and speeches, but have little opportunity to respond (Eldridge, 1984).

It is the people along the riverfront who derive an economic livelihood from the Ganga, such as the *dhobis* or washermen, and the very poor who cannot afford to pay for the various pollution control infrastructure – community toilets and the electric crematorium, who have been literally left out of the definition of participation as employed by both the State and the NGOs in the city.

Since 1988 the local administration has tried, unsuccessfully, to shift the *dhobis* to newly built washing ghats further downstream, away from the main bathing areas. Not only are these too far away for the *dhobis* to walk to on a daily basis when their only means of transport are their old and slow donkeys, but they were not designed in consultation with them, so that the structures are totally inappropriate for their needs.[7]

Explains Kanujia, the articulate leader of the well organized *dhobi* union:

> Washing clothes is my business, what else can I do – steal? All the Hindus think the Ganga is their Mother – I have no disagreement with the efforts to clean the river, though they are just eating the money. But what are you doing for my family? If we do not wash clothes, we do not get food and we are not so literate that we can find other jobs. And if we do, then who will wash the clothes? ... I am fighting for my future and that of my children – this is not just a problem for me ... but a question of survival for the community ... I have to continue this struggle," (Interview, 1990).

Although the *dhobis* have suggested numerous, *mohalla*-centred, tanks and ponds within the city which could be developed as washing places accessible to the majority of them, this local knowledge was never incorporated into the formal plans, let alone considered till after the money was sanctioned. A clear indication of the faith the GAP authorities have in their own professional expertise even if it proves to be ineffective or useless (Redclift, 1987).

Similarly the community toilets and household latrines built by the Sulabh Shauchalaya, do not serve the GAP objectives of pollution control. The practice of going outdoors to defecate, essentially a male prerogative, is part of a social ritual known as *bahari alang* which involves going outside (usually to the opposite bank of the ganga) to a quiet, less crowded venue where there is access to water, whether from a river, tank, pond or well and open air (Kumar, 1986). Defecation is an integral part of the trip thus, the need for open space, solitude and water.

Although urbanisation and changing livelihood styles have had an impact on such cultural practices, it is not uncommon to see people (men) urinating in front of the so-called low-cost toilets. Most local people find the toilets cramped and unclean and are reluctant to pay for what they feel should be free services. Argued one old woman:

> Why should we pay to go the toilet when we can go for free outdoors? Besides if I have diarrohea and have to go to the toilet ten times a day, am I going to pay 50 paise (the service cost) all the time?" (Interview, Varanasi, 1990).

Under the GAP, 17 community toilet complexes along the *ghats* were built by Sulabh Sauchalaya. In addition, there are 51 such toilet complexes in the various wards of the city. These are all maintained by Sulabh trained staff, but financially supported or subsidized by the Varanasi Municipal Corporation.

It is true that women and children are not supposed to pay to use either Sulabh or community toilets. But it seems that at Varanasi there is no such standardization – the question of payment varies with the intensity or frequency of use of the toilet. For example, at the busiest toilet complex at Dashashwamedh ghat a non-obligatoy fee of 20 paise is levied, while at Assi (where the woman I've quoted is) where there are hardly 20-25 uses in a day, there was a 50 paise charge.

Indeed the issue of payment is contentious – the municipal corporation cannot afford to meet the operational costs of the toilets because of their budgetary shortfalls, the problems they face in collecting taxes and their reluctance to increase them. However, poor users cannot be charged indiscriminately and the question of subsidizing to some extent these essential services will have to be addressed if they are supposed to play any role in limiting the raw pollutants entering the Ganga.

Moreover, there is no attempt to understand the socio-cultural practices of the local population. Rather there is an implicit assumption that such "exotic" factors (Curtis, 1978) can be removed by the introduction of technology or altered through public health education, so that the system can work. While not denying the significance of the latter, what is needed is a broader community education programme which facilitates a dialogue between the local community and project planners and is not simply limited to changing people's attitudes and hygiene behaviour. Recognizing the needs of the poor requires humility and patience, the ability to listen and to build on their initiatives, instead of imposing "development from above."

Redressing the Dilemma

In January 1992 the Sankat Mochan Foundation organized a seminar to examine critically alternative systems of transporting and treating waste water, which remains the most significant source of pollution in Varanasi. The event provided a useful forum for the exchange of ideas between waste water experts from India and abroad as well as GAP bureaucrats and technocrats (who however were the subject of much though not unfounded, criticism too).[8] Technical aspects aside, lip-service was paid to the need for greater public participation in the GAP, at least in the monitoring of the sewage pumping stations and water quality along the ghats.

However, there were no representatives from other NGOs or interest groups such as the *dhobis* to discuss the practical mechanism of participation. And while the delegates were taken to visit the landscaped sewage treatment sites, a stone's throw from the seminar was a Harijan colony where the negligence of the civic authorities had left the sewage system in a complete mess. Consequently, the once neatly paved streets had raw sewerage flowing over them, the household latrines were largely blocked and unused, and the people who had striven so hard to regain their dignity were now disillusioned.[9]

Despite the tall claims about public participation only 0.133 per cent of the total GAP expenditure between 1985-90 has been given to the voluntary sector (Kaushal 1990). Unfortunately, the NGOs in Varanasi, as well as the SMF, work within the socio-political and institutional framework of the city.

They are run by individuals "... whose views are liberal and paternalistic rather than radically egalitarian," (Midgley 1986). With respect to the SMF, the so-called charismatic leadership while important for organisation building, is rigid and hierachical and does not provide for a second echelon of leadership. In addition, it has made the NGO something of an international showpiece, "... a place of pilgrimage for international development tourists," (Midgley, 1986b). Their "participatory" efforts and that of the State, are based on the religious and cultural symbolism associated with the Ganga which does not question the nature and distribution of power in society.

Participation must recognize that the public is not a homogenous entity with a well articulated sense of the "common good". Rather it must begin from the bottom as a process of empowerment, building upon the generalized interest in a cleaner Ganga, without overlooking the specific demands of those who are being affected by such efforts. Egalitarian leadership which understands both the quantitative and qualitative aspects of pollution control is necessary. Some measure of State intervention will continue, but in order that it is sustainable, the State and the NGOs will have to readdress their discourse on participation. Otherwise the the Ganga will flow on, murky as ever.

NOTES

* This paper is based on field work undertaken for the author's doctoral dissertation at Cambridge, 1991.

1. Cultural perceptions of dirt and pollution — for most Hindus the Ganga is a pure and holy river — are significant in determining people's responses to the GAP, but they are not limiting factors in terms of participation which is constrained by socio-economic and institutional structures.
2. The sewage treatment plants which are currently working include the one at BHU (8 MLD) and the other at the Diesel Locomotive Works (12 MLD). The main treatment plant under construction at Dinapur, downstream of Konia was to be commissioned in August 1990, but it has been further delayed till March 1992.
3. The pumping stations often do not work because of power shortages, poor maintenance and the lack of technically trained personnel. Moreover, they do not pump all the waste water flowing to the ghats — there are several minor drains and illegal household connections.
4. For Hardin (1968) the tragedy briefly, was the inevitability of destruction of communally owned resources — his classic example was that of a common pasture open to all herdsmen where population checks were kept in balance by natural causes. If one herdsman was to maximise his personal utility by adding another animal to his herd, it would bring ruin to all — a Malthusian assumption based on the nature of ownership, the scale of management responsibility and the degree of collective trust in the polity.
5. There are many who dispute the *pandas* claim, maintaining that there was (and is) a lot of infighting between powerful families for control of the *ghats* and hence income.
6. This is also elaborated upon in the Upanishads and Vedas; see Dwivedi 1988.
7. The *dhobis* took me to see these *ghats* (near the sewage pumping station at Konia). Not only is there no space for them to dry clothes, the design consists of little cubicles having an inlet and outlet for water, in which they are meant to stand at least knee-deep in water. They felt that they would end up splashing each other (little elbow space) and that this would lead to needless fighting.
8. One of the main alternatives being put forward by the SMF is a deepwater, bypass sewage network which would complement the existing pumping stations, transporting the wastewater which currently flows into the river through gravity flow to the main pumping station at Konia. The technical and financial feasibility of such a system still needs to be worked out.
9. I visited the Harijan colony in the village of Nagwa at the behest of Father Francis who has been living in the area since 1979 and has done much to provide

the population with basic education, health care and alternative sources of income (a co-operative farm for example). According to him, the municipal corporation ignores their demands and instead passes derogatory remarks about their caste status. The diverted Assi rivulet (diverted from *Assi ghat*) now cuts through Nagwa and is an open carrier of pollution — people defecate along its embankments — as well as a hazard to children playing in the area. Another case of development for whom and at what price?

REFERENCES

Berwick, D. (1990) "Sacred and Profane," *The Sunday Times*, London, (Sunday Magazine).

Curtis, D. (1978) "Values of Latrines Users and Administrators," in A. Pacey (ed.) *Sanitation in Developing Countries*.

Douglas, M. (1987), *How Institutions Think*, London: Routledge.

———, and A. Wildavasky (1983) *Risk and Culture — An Essay on the Selection of Technical and Environmental Dangers*. Berkeley: University of California Press.

Dwivedi, O.P. (1988) "Man and Nature: An Holistic Approach to a Theory of Ecology," *The Environmental Professional*, Vol. 10, No. 1.

Eck, D. L. (1982) *Banaras — City of Light*, New York: Alfred A. Knopf.

Eldridge, P. (1984) "The Political Role of Community Action Groups in India and Indonesia: In Search of a General Theory," *Alternatives*, Vol. 10, No. 3.

Freitag, S. B. (ed.) (1989) *Culture and Power in Banaras — Community, Performance and Environment 1800-1980*. Berkeley: University of California Press.

GAP (1987), *Ganga Action Plan — Varanasi Chapter: An Introduction*, New Delhi, Ministry of Environment and Forests.

Goulet, D. (1989) "Participation in Development: New Avenues," *World Development*, Vol. 17, No. 2.

Guha, R. (1989) *The Unquiet Woods — Ecological Change and Peasant Resistance in the Himalaya*. New Delhi: Oxford University Press.

Hardin, G. (1968) "The Tragedy of the Commons," *Science*, No. 162.

Ingram, H. (1976) "The Politics of Information: Constraints on New Sources," in J. C. Pierce and H. R. Doerksen (eds.) *Water Politics and Public Involvement*.

Kaushal, A (1990) *A Review on People's Participation in the Ganga Action Plan*. Mussoorie: National Academy of Administration.

Korten, D. ed. (1986) *Community Management: Asian Experiences and Perspectives*. Connecticut: Kumarian.

Kumar, N. (1986) "Open Space and Free Time: Pleasure for the People of Banaras," *Contributions to Indian Sociology*, Vol. 20, No. 1.

———, (1988) *The Artisans of Banaras: Popular Culture and Identity*. Princeton University Press.

Leys, C. ed. (1969) *Politics and Change in Developing Countries*. Cambridge: Cambridge University Press.

Midgley, J. (1986a) "Community Participation: History, Concepts and Controversies," in J. Midgley *et. al.*, (eds.) *Community Participation, Social Development and the State*.

———, (1986b) 'Community Participation, the State and Social Policy," Ibid.

———, Hall, A., Hardiman, M. and D. Narine (1986) *Community Participation, Social Development and the State*, London: Methuen.

Montgomery, J. D. (1988) *Bureaucrats and People — Grassroots Participation in Third World Development*. London: John Hopkins.

O'Riordan, T. (1981) *Environmentalism*, London: Pion Ltd.

———, (1989) "The Challenge for Environmentalism," in K. Peet and N. Thrift, (eds.) *New Models in Geography*, Vol. 1.

Pacey, A. ed. (1978) *Sanitation in Developing Countries*, Chichester: John Wiley and Sons.

Peet, R. and N. Thrift eds. (1989) *New Models in Geography*, Vol. 1, London: Unwin Hyman.

Pierce, J. C. and H. R. Doerksen (eds.) (1976) *Water Politics and Public Involvement*. Ann Arbor: Ann Arbor Science.

Redclift, M. (1987) *Sustainable Development: Exploring the Contradictions*. London: Methuen.

Robertson, A. F. (1984) *People and the State — An Anthropology of Planned Development*. Cambridge: Cambridge University Press.

Schaffer, B. (1969) "The Deadlock in Development Administration," in C. Leys ed. *Politics and Change in Developing Countries*.

Shiva, V. (1988) *Staying Alive: Women, Ecology and Survival in India*. New Delhi: Kali.

———, (1991) *Ecology and the Politics of Survival — Conflicts over Natural Resources in India*, New Delhi, Sage.

Singh, R. L. (1955) *Banaras — A Study in Urban Geography*, Banaras: Nand Kishore and Brothers.

24

Community Participation in Urban Development

Asok Mukhopadhyay

GOVERNING urban areas is a specialised job which differs from the art of national/regional administration and from governing rural areas. The nature of national/regional government is essentially different in that it is concerned with a different kind of problem and the administration's relation with the people is not necessarily direct and intimate. Urban governments differ from rural governments as their socio-economic environment and the nature of the problems to be addressed are different.

Urban government has to work in the midst of a set of peculiarities of its own, namely first, the concentration of a large population in geographically small areas creates congestion in the living pattern: slum life is intrinsically an urban phenomenon; second, urban people are engaged in heterogeneous occupations and professions; third, urban people are conscious of their rights and dues; fourth, urban life is atomised and marked by a sense of anonymity and aloofness, hence it is difficult to generate strong community feelings; fifth, urban life is heavily dependent on organised infrastructure of civic services.

Hence improvement in the standard of infrastructural services requires planning and would be aided by the involvement and participation of people in urban government. It is not enough to elect the government but it is necessary to devise institutional mechanisms for community participation in urban planning and development. The success of urban development and civic service management depends on the cooperation and active participation of the people, especially the poorer section.

Urban Community Development

Urban Community Development (UCD) seems to be a useful approach for providing community services with grassroots participation in identification, execution and maintenance of development projects. It is suitable for the decentralised delivery of selected community services at a relatively low cost and is replicable in other areas of urban planning and development. For some time now urban community development projects have been undertaken in Delhi, Bombay, Calcutta, Madras, Baroda, Ahmedabad, Hyderabad, Kanpur and other cities by such agencies as the Central Social Welfare Board, Bharat Sevak Samaj, American Friends Service, Ford Foundation, Swedish Swallows, Lutheran Services and others.

Generally projects for community welfare have been started in deprived or backward areas and slums. A sense of patronage usually enters in service management and delivery, and the local people normally seek external assistance for ameliorating local environmental conditions. This state of affairs is not conducive to the efficient management of urban services. The local community needs to be awakened to its potentialities for self-organization, mutual cooperation and sharing of responsibility in managing urban development through the active participation of the area or *mohalla* committee. Project organisation will not only have to be undertaken by the community itself but the municipal and state authorities would have to encourage and promote it by rendering active assistance and extending appropriate facilities so that people could come together and work for the improvement of their physical and social environment. The institutional support of the municipal authorities and the government is part of the urban community development because the nature of urban living and its demands are too complex and gigantic to be tackled by voluntary community efforts only.

Development of urban services requires planning and implementation in the context of a well-thought-out national urban development policy. Urban community development assumes importance with respect to motivating people for an optimum use and careful maintenance of services, furthering urban development, and enrichment of local life. However UCD should by no means be held as a panacea for all the weaknesses and failures of urban government in providing services.

There are many underutilised resources in any urban area, for example, well-established local branches of international organizations like the Lions and Rotary Clubs, local groups like university service organizations or neighbourhood sports and cultural groups. The challenging job of identifying and systematically involving of such groups can be performed through appropriate organisations of urban community development.

In the urban development process, it is very much necessary to establish a link between the underprivileged and the formal sector of the urban economy like banks. Much of the economic activity of the urban poor in the Third World countries takes place in the informal sectors of the economy through the personalised services, such as those rendered domestic servants, washer-men, milk-men, vegetable vendors, rickshaw-pullers etc. Some enterprises in the informal sector, like *bidi*-making, *agarbatti*-making, basketry, leather work, carpentry, tailoring and even light industries feed larger enterprises in the formal sector of the economy. UCD projects should try to integrate this informal sector with the formal sector.

The possible areas where development projects can be organised with community participation include shelter-building, health and family planning, special nutrition programmes, informal and pre-school education, training for imparting skill, economic support programmes involving the giving of *pattas* of house-sites, organising development committees, *mahila mandals*, welfare councils etc. and community-oriented social and cultural activities.

The essence of the action strategies followed in any UCD programme is that they must be voluntary and creative in nature. The first task is undoubtedly to motivate the underprivileged community to undertake some action programme. For achieving this, it is necessary to enlist the cooperation of the privileged community, involve the potential beneficiaries at the decision-making level, identify and select the leadership in the community that would receive training, establish understanding and cooperation with outside organisations, share the people's way of life and make them understand the nature of problems and, finally, to build optimism for carrying out the programme.

Ingredients Organisation

The important ingredients of UCD programmes are (i) selection of the right kind of staff and their training; (ii) effective coordination between the community's internal and external resources, and (iii) linkages between voluntary organisations and the target community, between the target beneficiaries and financial institutions in the formal sector of the urban economy, and between physical improvements of living conditions and community development process as such.

These functional ingredients cannot be satisfactorily taken care of by the municipal authorities alone. The Indian urban scenario is crowded by a large number of authorities engaged in their respective sectoral functions. The municipal authorities have to mostly depend on the Central Government and the state government for planning and development, finance, and even personnel for discharging basic municipal functions. There is a four-level linkage in urban planning and development: (a) at the level of ideology where the link with the national government's thinking on urban development is found in repect of defining goals, assessing resources and framing the broad contours of policies; (b) in respect of direction where the state government is empowered to play the key role; (c) at the level of planning where, again, the state government or its agencies of regional or metropolitan development are concerned in respect of both strategic and structural planning; and (d) at the level of implementation where the local municipal authority either by itself or in collaboration with higher-level authorities is concerned with implementing development projects.

Moreover, because of the colonial legacy of administration and professional partisanship, a number of other kinds of functional authorities are found to be engaged in planning and development of urban areas, for example, improvement trusts, development authorities, housing boards, slum clearance boards, water supply and sewage disposal authorities, transport corporations etc. They share the functions of urban governance with the municipal authorities and thereby limit the role of the municipal government in urban development.[1]

It has to be borne in mind that some pattern of organisation and behaviour seem to be more appropriate to certain environment and task characteristics. None of the conventional organisations engaged in urban planning and development can establish a proper liaison and understanding with the poor and the underprivileged section of the urban population. Nor do these organisations play an appropriate role in the urban environment which has its own peculiar characteristics. Due to variations in environmental factors, different organisations need different management technologies, which are concerned with the ways in which organisations may be re-designed to take into account more fully the energies and competence of the people concerned. The urban environment in India – physical as well as socio-political – is characterised by certain special features: (i) rapidly growing population, (ii) general poverty and high unemployment, (iii) high density of population (iv) unauthorised settlements, especially on roadside and vacant public land, (v) growing concern for public welfare, (vi) institutionalised democracy including agitational activities of political parties and frequent intervention by courts of law in matters of policy-formulation and policy-implementation, (vii) widespread popular misgivings about officials, and (viii) chronic shortage of basic urban services like water supply, drainage and sewerage, housing, electricity supply, and health.

In this context the process of urban planning and development has to enlist community participation in order to advocate successfully some development ideas, identify the most urgent programmes and implement projects with minimum distraction and interference. That is to say, organization for urban development needs a management technology based on community participation; otherwise wastage of human and financial resources would be inevitable and even a modicum of success would elude the most energetic planner and administrator.

Andhra Pradesh

The UCD project in the Municipal Corporation of Hyderabad was sanctioned as a Centrally-sponsored scheme in 1967 and was initiated in one ward of the corporation covering about 50,000 people. The expenditure was shared by the Central Government, state government and municipal corporation on a 2:1:1 percentage basis. The programme was transferred to the state sector in 1969 and was conducted under the direct functional control of its Director, with the Municipal Commissioner exercising general administrative supervision. The programme was extended later to more wards of municipal corporation. Subsequently, the main project was supplemented by two satellite projects to cater to the demands of people in the adjacent areas. The UNICEF has provided financial assistance to this UCD programme. It is no longer an experimental project, but has become a department of Hyderabad Municipal Corporation.[2]

The highlight of the programme has been the acceptance of the principle that no development project planned and designed at the higher level without any regard to the felt needs at the grassroots is to be thrust upon the people. Appropriate strategies have been evolved to achieve close involvement of the beneficiaries. The experiences have shown that people responded with enthusiasm.

The UCD organisational structure at Hyderabad is top-down. The organisation is headed by a Project Officer, assisted by a Deputy Project Officer appointed by the municipal authorities, who provides the essential leadership in selected areas of urban development. Below this official level are the grass-roots levels functionaries viz. Community Organisers (CO) assisted by Social Workers (SW) who are a sort of urban counterparts of the Village Level Workers (VLW) in the erstwhile community development projects in the rural areas. These lower level functionaries ensure community participation in urban development by widely mixing with the poor and the underprivileged and establishing the link between the urban people and the officialdom and the formal sector of the economy.

The Community Organisers (CO) and Social Workers (SW) under the UCD programme are not given any formal training. They learn and get trained on the job. The CO is to act as a catalystic agent and not as a school master or religious preacher. His intervention in the lives of the people is in the nature of persuasion about designing development projects. Flexibility in approach is the greatest strength of this methodology of introducing changes in economic activity, health and nutrition programme, housing, education and environmental projects. The CO and his SWs record and document the felt needs of the community and discuss the probable solutions in their group meetings with the people. In Hyderabad the UCD methodology has been successfully implemented in slum improvement and slum housing programmes. Since 1989-90 the Slum Improvement Project, Phase III is being implemented under the UCD funded by the Overseas Development

Administration of the U.K. The neighbourhood committees of the people concerned are always consulted at every stage of implementing action plans. The UCD coverage has subsequently been wide and varied indicating the different levels of social, economic and educational conditions of various communities. The Neighbourhood Development Councils now run pre-primary schools and supplementary nutrition centres on a self-help basis.

Earlier different communities within the same city lived in isolation from one another and thier interrelation was marked by prejudices, contempt, jealousies and hatred born of poverty and mutual suspicion strengthened by the barriers of caste, creed and religion. The civic authorities provided the basic civic services free of any charge but still faced non-cooperation from the poor and the under-privileged communities. There was previously no rapport between municipal employees and the local community. The CO and the SWs helped to stimulate, guide and sustain the whole process by working intimately with the individuals and groups in the community, motivating them to improve environmental sanitation and living conditions, and organising outside help when needed. Undoubtedly, the essential skills needed are, patience, sensitivity and commitment to the project aims. The UCD projects of Hyderabad have since been replicasted in two other municipal corporations in Andhra Pradesh, namely, Visakhapatanam and Vijayawada, for providing improved social services cheaply and also for tackling the basic problems of poverty.

West Bengal

Since 1989-90 West Bengal has started implementing the Centrally-sponsored programme in urban development called Urban Basic Services for the Poor (UBSP), which is an improved version of the earlier programme called Urban Basic Services (UBS) launched under the Seventh Plan in 1985. The Eighth Plan envisages bringing the whole of urban India under the UBSP programme. West Bengal's success story in UBS (since renamed UBSP) is found in Siliguri municipality in Darjeeling district.[3] Twenty-five more municipalities in five districts have been identified for UBSP programmes in 1990-91.

The objective of the UBSP programme is to enable the urban poor to have access to basic social services such as non-formal and pre-school education, mother and child health care, a referral system in health administration, nutrition supplementation and immunization. The programme also aims at providing assistance to the needy sections of society and organising cultural and sports activities geared at promoting communal harmony, national integration and civic consciousness. The UBSP is designed to work in harmonious convergence with two other programmes of urban development namely Environment Improvement of Urban Slums (EIUS) for improving physical amenities and Nehru Rojgar Yojana (NRY) for generating income and employment for the urban poor. The target group of UBSP is the urban poor living in poverty pockets or low income neighbourhoods or slums, especially the women, children, scheduled castes/tribes, backward castes and minorities. The most novel feature of the UBSP is community participation, implied in organisation of local communities into neighbourhood committees nurtured by the field-level staff of municipalities.

The organisational leadership for UBSP is to be provided by from the municipal authority but the pre-condition for this programme is enlisting the participation of the beneficiaries in fixing priorities, formulating projects and in their implementation. The entire emphasis has been on building organisations at the grassroots level in such a way as to ensure community participation for community development.

The first stage in the UBSP organization is to constitute a Neighbourhood Group (NHG) comprising the adult females of 20 to 25 families. These women members are to elect the Resident Community Volunteer (RCV) from among themselves. The minimum requirement for the RCV is that she must be literate but her essential qualification would be her capacity to motivate local people to participate actively in development projects at all stages. It is her main responsibility to arouse in the local people a sense of self-confidence, development-consciousness and self-dependence. The RCV has to establish the vital grassroots linkage between the beneficiary group and the project functionaries. She is not a paid employee of the municipality and she must enjoy the full trust and confidence of the community she serves.

Next in the organisational hierarchy is the Neighbourhood Committee (NHC) for 200 to 250 families, comprising 10 RCVs who would elect a chairperson from among themselves. Ten NHCs form a *bustee* (community)-level committee comprising 100 RCVs. Thus each *Bustee* Committee works for 2000 to 2500 families, and is assisted by a paid full-time Community Organizer (CO). As the key functionary in UBSP, the CO is responsible for maintaining regular contact with the families under her charge and with the mass organisations, women's organisations and voluntary associations active in the area, for identifying the priorities in the socio-economic development of the slum-dwellers concerned. As the leader of the RCVs, the CO has to organise the different services under UBSP and draw-up a Mini-Action Plan at the *bustee* (community) level. Recruited by the municipality, the CO must be a woman, preferably a graduate and a bustee-dweller and she receives a consolidated monthly pay of about Rs. 1,000. For every five COs there is a Project Officer (PO) looking after 500 RCVs and 10,000 to 12,500 families in *bustee* areas in the town. He draws up the larger *bustee* action plan called Town Action Plan. Recruited by the municipality as an *ad hoc* project employee, the PO has the dual responsibility of ensuring that the COs and the RCVs discharge their responsibilities at their respective levels, and of keeping the municipal authorities regularly informed about the progress made and the difficulties encountered in implementing different UBSP projects. A bigger municipality with large number of bustee-dwellers may appoint an Area General Manager (AGM) if the number of POs is three or more.

At the municipal level, the responsibility for UBSP squarely lies with the municipality's chairman who entrusts one of the elected municipal commissioners solely with the UBSP programme. He is advised by a municipality-level UBSP Committee with the municipal chairman as the president and prominent social workers, representatives of mass organizations, officers of concerned departments of the municipality and the representative of the lead bank in the area and others, as members. This committee is primarily responsible for the coordination and smooth implementation of the UBSP projects. It submits the Town Action Plan to the appropriate district-level committee for approval so that necessary harmony can be achieved between other development plans and UBSP programme.

The thrust of the UBSP programme is on the fight against urban poverty through community participation of the urban poor themselves so that the traditionally exploited and deprived urban poor, especially *bustee*-dwellers, can gain self-confidence and become self-reliant. Initially the UBS used to be financed through matching contributions of the UNICEF (40%), state government (40%) and the central government (20%). Recently it has been proposed that the central government provide hundred per cent assistance for UBSP under the Eighth Plan, while UNICEF finance the training components (personnel and equipments) of the programme.[4]

In West Bengal the Siliguri municipality has been implementing the UBS/UBSP programme since 1985. From the experience gained so far two conclusions emerge: one, the degree of popular response is quite encouraging with a high level involvement of the urban poor at the grassroots level; and two, the political parties in a democratic polity can easily reach the urban poor and achieve considerable success in political mobilisation and political recruitment. Mobilization of 500 RCVs working at the grass-roots level and building rapport with more than 10,000 families for ensuring community participation for urban development has by itself proved to be a great political success.

Community participation has today become an essential component of urban development strategies in developing countries. Recently, another *bustee* improvement project in Calcutta, sponsored by the Overseas Development Administration (ODA) of the British Government, on the occasion of the city's tercentenary, has placed emphasis on it. The ODA has gifted Rs. 100 crore exclusively for improving the living conditions in Calcutta's slums, which is to be spent towards (i) improving physical infrastructural amenities, (ii) developing community health services, and (iii) ensuring community development through community participation.

Politics of Community Participation

In recent times, the concept of community participation in the development process has been advocated by a number of social philosophers and political leaders like Rabindranath Tagore, Mahatma Gandhi, Jayprakash Narayan, Willy Brandt, Robert McNamara and others. Apart from these development ideologues, the idea has also been advocated by the UNICEF, UNDP, ODA, World Bank and other international development agencies. In India both the liberals and the Marxists have also accepted the idea. But the meaning, purpose and implications of community participation differ among various people and institutions. Today the issue is no longer one of 'why' community participation but rather 'when' and 'how' to achieve it. The political motives and the structural institutional set-up differ from country to country and also across time within the same country. Across the political spectrum, it is felt necessary to place the common man at the centre-stage of the development process, from the point of view of political recruitment and mobilisation. But perceptions differ as to what constitutes "development" and who are to be the target group of beneficiaries from this development.

The liberals advocate community participation as an instrument of democratic governance but take care to define "development" in the overall context of their chosen model of development. Sometimes it is advocated on the utilitarian grounds of cheap labour, less agitation and maximization of private profits. The enlightened non-government organisations (NGOs) advocate community participation out of the ethnical considerations of self-reliance and empowerment of the dispossesed and disadvantaged sectors of the society. On the other hand, the Marxists promote community participation as a technique of development as they find in it one of the best ways of reaching the poor and the underdogs and propagating the socialist slogans and rhetoric. For them, it is an efficient political technique of mass mobilisation. Organising community participation among the poor would help to promote the political goal of staging social protests and advocating correctives against the exploitation of the poor and the underprivileged. Community participation can thus be used for to fight against the powerful establishment called the modern corporate state and its development policies.

The point is this that the nature and degree of local community participation depends largely on the nature local politics or the local power situation. In recent times, it has been amply proved that a homogeneous political power situation in the locality induces more development because the probable challenges and conflicts are either eliminated or effectively managed for particular development projects to be pushed through as in West Bengal. By any definition "development" always has a political slant and power-seeking politicians are bound to take interest in the development process. In India's case, a pro-poor slant would bring more political support because this section constitutes about 40 per cent in any big urban conglomeration. The private sector in India has not been a consistent model of efficiency and therefore there is always a strong case for public intervention in development-related investment and service-delivery to the poor.

With adequate political imagination and appropriate strategies the poor can be organized into pressure groups possessing effective electoral clout in a democratic set-up. The common man and the poor man has his own perception of development, which sometimes differs from that of the expert. The political strategists can use this pressure group for furthering social welfare as well as for broadening their support-base. A classic example of this technique can be found in the prolonged battles for adequate, wholesome water supply for the middle class and the urban poor in Victorian London.[5] Through sheer local electoral pressures and political campaign it was possible to force the leading national-level political figures to take interest in the issue of water supply for London.

Once the poor and disadvantaged sectors are effectively organised through community participation, they can function as a check on the bureaucracy-technocracy-contractor nexus in the development process. By exercising sufficient vigilance the organised community would also be in a vantage position to fight against administrative corruptions. However, whether and how far these goals would be achieved depend on the extent of functioning of the basic democratic institutions like the competitive political system, free press and independent judiciary. Empowerment of the community through its participation in development process would also necessitate empowerment of local government, which is an essential condition for building a democratically organised plural society. Of all political values for which local government is regarded as desirable, participation is the most important.[6] Community participation would secure public accountability by ensuring a better understanding of the felt needs of the community and introducing flexibility in the delivery of services to the satisfaction of the local community. This would undoubtedly be a great gain for both development and democracy.

Conclusion

Urban development through community participation is a useful approach for providing community services at the grassroots level as regards their identification, implementation and maintenance. Community participation as a development technique is extremely suitable for decentralised planning and delivery of selected community services at relatively low costs and is replicable in other fields of socio-economic development. The Hyderabad scheme took a long time to promote community organisations on a self-sustaining basis, to look after a limited range of community-level services and amenities. The West Bengal scheme aims at achieving this objective on a wider scale from the beginning. Perhaps the different political orientations of the two state governments explain this difference. The Marxists in West Bengal want to use community participation as an instrument of urban development as well as party-building through popular mobilisation, whereas the ruling parties in Andhra Pradesh seem to have taken up this programme on a practical administrative basis. Experience of urban community development through community participation suggests that such efforts constitute a useful process of training the poorer sections of society in self-help and mutual cooperation. The importance of basic linkages between voluntary efforts and environmental improvement, and between community initiative for development and financial institutions in the formal sector of the urban economy has been well demonstrated through the UCD and UBS programmes.

It has also been found that community participation can bring about considerable improvement of the physical and social environment of the locality, and develop inner strength, organisational discipline, and self-reliance of the community which learns to solve day-to-day problems through concerted voluntary community efforts, seeking outside assistance wherever necessary. In a country like India where the urban population is highly heterogeneous, a large part of which is economically as well as socially under-privileged, and community cohesion is not very high, this approach has definite sociological relevance. The concept of community in urban India will be strengthened through this technique of environmental and social development. And the theory of democratic representation will gain an additional dimension if community-level interests are institutionally represented at the municipal level. Community participation must not be viewed as a sectoral representation of the poor only. It helps civic society as a whole and enables the ordinary citizen to face squarely the demands of the modern corporatist state.

Given the basic support of the governmental and municipal authorities, local community efforts can go a long way in improving the physical environment and enriching the social and cultural life of its members. In a sense, basic amenities are culture relative but if services like water supply, garbage removal, drainage and sewerage, lighting and are not provided urban community development would suffer proportionately and popular frustration would be inevitable.

REFERENCES

1. The municipal government in India does not possess sufficient power and sophistication as regards organisation, nor is its management structure strong enough for undertaking the full responsibility of urban development. See Asok Mukhopadhyay (1983), "Status of Municipal Government", *Nagarlok*, IIPA, New Delhi, July-Sept.
2. Mohammed Mahmood Ali (1991), "Community Participation in Slum Improvement: The Hyderabad Experience", paper presented at the International Seminar on Basic Amenities in Third World, New Delhi.
3. *A Handbook on Municipal Administration*, ILGUS, Govt. of West Bengal, March 1991.
4. Institute of Local Government and Urban Studies (ILGUS), Govt. of West Bengal.
5. Asok Mukhopadhyay (1981), *Politics of Water Supply: The Case of Victorian London*, The World Press, Calcutta.
6. L. J. Sharpe (1970), "Theories and Values of Local Government", *Political Studies*, Oxford, June.

25

Problems of Basic Amenities in Urban Areas and Community Participation: New Dimensions – A Case Study of Bhubaneswar

L. N. P. Mohanty

IN the tide of change that will engulf the developing countries by the end of the twentieth century, the most dramatic and fundamental trend is that of urbanization. No less striking is the tempo of change: a four-fold increase in urban population in developing countries in a period of thirty years from 504 million in 1970 to 2020 million by 2000 A. D. Thus, the developing nations must come to grips with the problems and challenges of urbanization. The effects of this urban explosion are dramatically manifested in the teeming slums in the centre of cities and mushrooming shanty habitats at their periphery. In most of the cities one-fourth to one-half of the population live in poverty and are deprived of their basic needs. Shocking malnutrition is simultaneously a contributor to and a consequence of the urban poverty syndrome. The basic poverty continuum demonstrates itself in low incomes, inadequate nutrition levels and basic services, limited or no education and low skills. Secondly, there is the environmental poverty continuum manifesting itself in inadequate services and housing or the inability to pay for them, over-crowding, pollution, exposure to disease and low productivity. There are also the psychological dimensions such as insecurity, stress, depression, deviant social behaviour, lack of ambition or aspirations, lack of opportunity to demonstrate one's productivity, and the consequent inability to ensure family security.

The urban poor, according to many studies in India, are those with a household income of Rs. 650-700 a month, who live in low income settlements which mostly lack adequate water supply and sewerage facilities and health care. Congestion and over-crowding further exacerbate the conditions of an unhealth environment and increase the probability of infectious diseases.

The magnitude of the problems of housing, unemployment, water supply, transport, sanitation as well as the supply of other urban consumer goods and services and the deteriorating urban environment indicate a crisis. The nature of the urban crisis as stated above is itself a strong rationale for citizen participation in measures for resolving it. The new approach that is needed rests primarily on the realisation that ensuring an acceptable quality of life to all citizens, including low income and other socio-economically disadvantaged groups, requires major changes in the macro as well as the micro sphere. The former calls for reorientation in the nature, direction, strategy and goals of economic growth which must aim at reducing disparities between groups and classes, and eradicate poverty. In addition, necessary efforts are required to grapple with micro realities, such as strengthening the financial and organisational capacity of the local bodies, providing, maintaining and adequately extending environmental and social services to all sections and areas within the urban jurisdiction, and improving the environment. However, all these will not yield the desired results without popular awareness and acceptance of, and participation in the implementation of remedial and development measures.

A major thrust for integrating the poor in the urban fabric is the community management approach – a principle to execute schemes and projects through the community. This paper aims at examining in perspective the problems of basic amenities in the city of Bhubaneswar in the context of rapid urbanization, where the community management concept has been experimented within a relocated locality inhabited by persons displaced from two inner city slums. The paper also seeks to highlight the status of basic services and the differential access to these services within the city. Besides, the system has been analysed comparatively in relation to the system implemented in Hyderabad and Siliguri and has been critically evaluated in the light of its workability in Orissa.

Urban Growth in Orissa

Orissa is one of the least urbanised states in India with only 13.43 per cent of urban population as compared to 25.72 per cent for the whole country. The urban population of the state at 4.2 million in 1991, registered a growth rate of 36.08 per cent during 1981-91.

Even at such a low level of urbanization, an analysis of the distribution of urban population in towns of varying size in the State indicates a significant concentration of urban population in seven Class I towns (above 100,000 population each). These towns with a combined population of 1.9 million contain 44.4 per cent of the total urban population, registering a growth of 70.15 per cent during the decade 1981-91.

Bhubaneswar, the capital city of Orissa, has a rapid rate of population increase. The city had a population of only 38.2 thousand in 1961, which increased to 0.11 million in 1971, 0.22 million in 1981, and 0.41 million in 1991. The growth rate during the decades 1971-81 and 1981-91 have been 107.8 per cent and 87.74 per cent respectively (higher than the state urban average and Class I town average).

Immigration is one of the main factors for the expansion of the city and its population. The percentage of urban migrants Bhubaneswar is higher than that in many other cities in general. According to Census data most of the immigrants (60.48) are from the rural areas, whereas only 39.52 per cent have migrated from other urban communities.

At present there are 70 identified slum pockets in the city, inhabited by 67,972 persons living in 13,594 households. Compared to cities in other States and other Class I towns of Orissa, namely Cuttack, Rourkela, Sambalpur and Puri, the slum population of Bhubaneswar is relatively low comprising 16.5 per cent of the total population of the city.

Out of the total slum households 39.78 per cent have been built on slum holders' own land, 52.33 per cent are encroachments on government land and the rest 7.89 per cent live in rented houses or on pavements.

Basic Amenities

The water supply to the city is through pipes supplemented by a good number of bore wells. The Kuakhai river on the east of the city is the main source. The total installed capacity is about 21.00 MGD of which 18.00 MGD is available for domestic consumption. The per capita supply of water in urban Orissa (mostly bigger towns) is less than 110 litres a day whereas the per capita supply of water for Bhubaneswar for all purposes is slightly higher. This average, however, does not apply to about 30 per cent of the city's people who have access only to about 25 litres or less per head per day. The per capita availability of water varies as much as 5 to 10 times between marginal settlements and residential localities.

There is no equitable distribution among the areas on account of the topography of the city. It is found that water is available in lower zone areas for a longer period than in higher zone areas. At the same time since there is no meter system, the people tend to keep taps open continuously which results in wastage.

Although the slums do have some infrastructure like tube-wells, wells and stand posts, many of them are often out of order. The availability of piped water is restricted due to the inadequate pressure and insufficient duration of water supply. Besides, the existing pipelines are old and have eroded in many places.

An integrated water supply scheme for supply of water from the Mahanadi river at Naraj about 20 km from Bhubaneswar, is being undertaken, financed through a loan provided by HUDCO.

Sewerage

Underground sewerage is available only in a few limited areas. Sewage disposal is one of the major problems of the city. At present it is disposed of in three different ways, namely through septic tanks, oxidation ponds and by the open discharge of raw sewage into the low-lying 'valleys' on the outskirts. Such a sewage disposal system is neither proper nor adequate for the capital city. It is in dire need of comprehensive underground sewerage system.

The land topography of Bhubaneswar fortunately is conducive to good rain water drainage. The city is slopes and has a few valleys running from west to east. This is a boon because after a heavy shower the rain water finds its way to the low-lying areas in a very short time and ultimately joins the Gangua Nalla (the ancient Gandhabadi river) which flows on the eastern fringe of the city and finally meets the river Daya in the south.

Pucca covered drains were constructed by the sides of foot-paths of some main roads such as Rajpath, Janpath and Sachivalaya Marg. These drains for the outflow of rain water are clogged with *mulba* and garbage causing inundation of the roads.

Most of the slum areas are not covered by the drainage system and whatever little drainage exists is not being maintained properly.

As a result the slums suffer from water logging. In the water logged areas even after the water is drained out through a slow process, pools of water remain in the depressed pockets in and around the slums in which mosquitoes, flies and other insects breed. Only 113 small drains have been constructed in the slum areas many of which, again, do not function properly.

To overcome this problem an Integrated Drainage Development Scheme (IDDS) prepared by the Bhubaneswar Development Authority is under implementation.

The morbidity pattern of the slum population is closely connected to the poor environment in which they live. The lack of adequate latrines and the absence of drainage and safe garbage disposal methods endanger the health of the inhabitants. In the slum areas less than a third of the households are reported to have their own latrines. The rest either use public toilets or open spaces. Lack of finance and physical space are cited as the principal constraints. The condition of a few community latrines is bad, making them unserviceable. Besides, irregular cleaning and lack of water in the lavatories are responsible not only for their poor use but also their bad maintenance.

Solid Waste

The community-bin system is adopted for the collection of refuse in all the localities including the slums. Community-bins are generally provided for 10 to 20 houses in areas having a population density of less than 1000 persons/sq. km. In areas having a population of more than 1000 persons per sq. km, the system covers 15 to 25 houses. Some households put their domestic garbage inside the community dust-bins whereas some others deposit the same on the ground outside the dust-bin. The municipal vehicle collects the same and dumps it in the low land area near Khandagiri in a most unscientific and unhygenic manner. The garbage dumps are a breeding ground for the vectors of communicable diseases, create bad odour and seriously mars the aesthetic environment of a tourist centre like Bhubaneswar. Information from the Bhubaneswar Municipality reveals that the quantity of solid waste generated is 30,000 cft/day (850 cum/day). Taking the density to be 450 kg/cum, the daily generation of solid waste is 382.5 M. T. out of which the municipality dispose-off work only 102.15 M. T. by adopting the land-fill method.

Housing

The decaying tenements of the slum dwellers and the hutments of squatters are the most pervasive symbols of urban poverty. The poor quality of housing in the slum areas is due to the *kuccha* nature of the dwellings in which a large proportion of slum dwellers live. The average house has one living room without any windows and hardly any kitchen space. The houses are mostly built of materials such as mud, straw, poles, plastic sheets etc. and hence not fireproof. Basic amenities like electricity, running water, and latrines are non-existent for a majority of the households.

Health

The primary health care facilities are provided by dispensaries located on the periphery of the slums. The most commonly reported diseases in the slums are diarrhoea, skin infections and malaria which are directly attributable to the poor environmental conditions. Child deliveries are still conducted largely at home by untrained attendants. The services of a doctor/nurse are reported in very few cases.

There are a number of *balwadis*, *anganwadis* and community centres. While 4,625 children are covered by the immunization programme, 1951 children are medically checked in the balwadi centres.

Education

The level of literacy in the slum pockets is low, particularly among women. There are 16 community centres catering to the entire slum localities. The existing pre-school centres are not adequate. Similarly, there are primary schools only in a few slums. There are a few adult literacy, sewing and non-formal education centres as well as creches but they are not enough.

Training programmes are organized for different sections of slum dwellers. About 542 community volunteers, 15 *dais*, 133 housewives, 14 *balwadi* teachers, 542 RCVs, eight hand-pump caretakers and 13 masons (trained in low cost sanitation) have benefited from the different training programmes.

Under the adult education programme 8,735 adults have been

educated in growth monitoring, 14,336 in family spacing, 7,390 in nutrition and food preparation, 4,947 in administering first-aid and 10,625 in oral rehydration therapy (ORT). Besides, 956 health education sessions and 765 sanitation education camps have been held, benefiting 22,721 and 17,947 participants respectively. Furthermore, 24 audio-visual show-*cum*-discussions were held which benefited 888 participants. Apart from this, six television sets have been installed in different slum localities.

Income Generating Activities (IGA) for Women

Considering the fact that a majority of slum households live in abject poverty, there is a strong case for supplementing their family income. As the male members (15-59 age group) are already pursuing some economic activity, the women are a potential group for generating additional income for the families. Manual jobs or self-employment are the two alternatives available to them. The former includes domestic services while the latter involves making *bidis*, paper bags and doing embroidery. So far 348 women have received loans for such income generating activities.

Poverty Alleviation Programmes

The scheme for slum development which are being implemented include (i) UBSP (Urban Basic Services for the Poor), (ii) EIUS (Environmental Improvement of Urban Slum), (iii) NRY (Nehru Rozgar Yojana), and (iv) Low Cost Sanitation.

The multi-dimensional and community-oriented UBS scheme started operating in 1986 in 25 towns of Orissa. The scheme was then funded by the UNICEF, the Central and State Governments and the urban local body in the ratio of 40 : 20 : 40. The programme received a new thrust when the Central Government in its action plan announced on January 1, 1990, accorded high priority to substantial expansion of the existing programmes for the urban poor. The UBS programme was named the Urban Basic Services Programme (UBSP) without UNICEF assistance. The UNICEF now finances only its training components (personnel and equipments) and the expenditure on it for on going scheme is equally shared by the Central and State governments. The expenditure for new towns is met by the Central Government fully.

The principal aim of the programme is to improve and upgrade the quality of life of the urban poor, especially the women and children. Community participation, convergence, child and mother focus, cost effectiveness, continuity and coverage are the guiding principles of the above schemes.

The programme components include (i) immunization of all infants against diphteria, whooping cough, tetanus, poliomyeletis, tuberculosis and measles; (ii) nutrition education on low cost recipes based on locally available foods, (iii) health care including growth monitoring of children, disease prevention, care for expectant and nursing mothers, (iv) Pre-school learning, that is development of cognitive, aesthetic, physical and psychic potentialities in children under six, (v) functional literacy for mothers, learning the three 'Rs' as well as vocational trades, (vi) non-formal education for school drop-outs, working and street children, (vii) community based rehabilitation for the physically and mentally impaired by providing them opportunities to attend schools and work with others, (viii) hygiene and sanitation – inculcating personal hygiene and environmental sanitation by providing low cost latrines and hand pumps, effective disposal of garbage and sewage; (xi) behavioural adjustments – juvenile delinquents, alcoholics and drug addicts to be dealt with empathy and firmness, (x) special assistance to children and the aged, and (xi) cultural sensitisation that is the urban poor to be made aware of our national heritage.

While the above programme components are included under UBSP, the EIUS covers seven basic services, namely drinking water, street lights, roads, drains, community bath, community latrines, and sewers, to the urban poor keeping in view the per capita cost of Rs. 300 as fixed by the central government.

The Nehru Rozgar Yojana aims at providing employment through micro-enterprises, and creation of public assets. The low-cost sanitation scheme involving the provision of pit or pour-flush latrines is financed by loans, grants and beneficiary contributions involving the local bodies.

Community Management at Bharatpur

A major thrust for integration of the poor in the urban fabric is attempted through community management. The government has accepted the principle of execution of schemes and projects by the community through awareness, involvement, independence and effectiveness. The system involves people at the grass-roots level where the beneficiaries are empowered with authority, responsibility and control to manage their own affairs. The community is associated in the process of planning, implementation and evaluation of the projects. A model bye-law to lend legality to the community has been framed.

The concept of community management as devised by the Government of Orissa was initially implemented in Bharatpur, a relocated locality of Bhubaneswar. Here 1761 families from some centrally located sectors of the city, such as Madhusudan Nagar and Satyanagar, parts of which were developed as slums, were rehabilitated in 1988 on a plot of 65.36 acres of land lying towards the western periphery of the city, at a distance of about 10 km from the railway station. 685 families came from Madhusudan Nagar and 1076 from Satyanagar.

The relocated locality of Bharatpur accounts for a population of 7678, the average family size being 4.4.

A random survey conducted in 300 households indicates that a majority of the people are Hindu Oriyas. The sex ratio is 887. As many as 59 per cent of them constitute nuclear families whereas 41 per cent belong to the category of joint families.

As regards occupational status, 32.9 per cent are engaged in business sectors, 26 per cent as daily labourers, 20 per cent as masons, 7.3 per cent as trolley/rickshaw-pullers, 4.7 per cent as tailors, 3.3 per cent as service holders, 1.4 per cent as carpenters and 7.3 per cent in sundry occupations. On an average, 1.5 person per household earn their livelihood through different occupations.

Each of the households has been given legal ownership of a plot measuring 600 sq. ft. The average plinth area works out to be 300 sq. ft. A majority of the houses are semi-*pucca* (39 per cent), followed by 34 per cent *kuccha* and 24 per cent *pucca* houses. Three per cent of the houses are under construction or are damaged.

Organisational Structure

The entire *basti* is divided into neighbourhood groups (NHG). Each NHG comprises of about 15 to 20 households, and 10 to 12 neighbourhood groups constitute the neighbourhood committees consisting of the *bastee* development committee (BDC) and the *bastee* management committee (BMC). At present nine BDCs and nine BMCs have been constituted by election, each NHG electing from among the women folk a resident community volunteer (RCV) to the BDC, and from either sex a resident community manager (RCM) to the BMC.

BDCs are constituted under the UBS framework with a view to promoting the welfare of the inhabitants, with special attention being given to women and children. They are comprised of all the RCVs taken together (all women) while the BMC – formed in each BDC area to look after social, economic and physical infrastructural problems in the *basti* – is comprised of all the RCMs taken together (from either sex). The BDCs and BMCs have elected presidents and secretaries.

All the BDCs and BMCs constitute the community management group (CMG), wherein the presidents of the BDCs and BMCs are members. The CMG has a legal structure under the Societies Registration Act. Its general body comprises the RCVs and RCMs of all BDGs and BMCs taken together, co-opted members from Government and NGOs and ex-officio members, like the community organisers of *bastis* and the project officer of the municipality. It is authorised to approve the annual budget, audit report and annual action plan.

The management of CMG is vested in a governing body consisting of eleven members including a chairman, a vice chairman, a secretary and an assistant secretary elected by the non-official members of CMG from among themselves. The remaining members are from the BDCs and BMCs.

The CMG prepares and extends action plans on the basis of mini plans prepared by the BDCs/BMCs to cater to the felt needs of the *basti* people. It is empowered to plan, implement and manage all the poverty alleviation schemes for the healthy growth of the community.

The action plans are approved by the project office of the municipality. Both the physical and financial components of the town plans are ultimately integrated into the district plan.

The district urban development agency (DUDA) at the district level has the district magistrate as chairman and formulates the capital investment plan by consolidating the action plans prepared by the CMG and allocates funds. The concerned agencies implement their respective schemes with the assistance of the DUDA. The

CMG implements the plans in collaboration with the municipal body. The slum development cell of the local body prepares plans and programmes and provides various urban services schemes for slum dwellers. It formulates action plans/programmes (physical/financial) for various relevant schemes (e.g. UBSP, NRY, EIUS, Low Cost Sanitation) and submits action plans to the state urban development Agency (SUDA) through DUDA for approval. The SUDA constituted at the state level, is the principal coordinating body to monitor, evaluate, finance and supervise the activities of DUDA.

In order to motivate the people and create an awareness among the RCVs and RCMs a training programme was organised in April 1991 in which 148 RCVs and RCMs participated. The first meeting of the CMG was held on August 25, 1991 when a decision was taken to implement various poverty alleviation schemes in the area. As per the bye-law every household contributed a sum of Rs. 3 per month towards community participation. A budget for Rs. 1.5 lakhs for 1991-92 was approved. The funds of CMG are kept in a bank account operated jointly by the secretary of the CMG and the project officer of the municipality.

The UBS scheme started operating in the area soon after the slum dwellers were rehabilitated in November 1988. Out of a total population of 7678, 1235 are children among whom 179 are of less than one year, 434 within the age group of 1 to 3 years, and 622 are 3 to 6 years. Besides, there are 71 pregnant women and 82 nursing mothers. Out of the total number of children 957 are fully immunised, 204 partially protected and only 74 remain unprotected.

Learning opportunities for child and mother are provided in eight *anganwadi* centres, eight *balwadi* centres, four adult literacy centres, 11 non-formal education centres and two sewing centres, all located within the area.

Water is made available through six wells, 38 tube wells and 34 standposts. The sanitation programme includes provision of 255 individual latrines, 20 smokeless *chullahs*, and 18 dustbins for 910 families. There is a community centre with a TV set.

Under the Nehru Rozgar Yojana, 1171 units for shelter upgradation have been sanctioned by HUDCO at a cost of Rs. 13.1 million. A total number of 395 applications were sponsored for bank loans under the micro enterprises scheme of which loans have been sanctioned in 124 cases and disbursement made in 65 cases.

Under the EIUS, construction of 15 km of road and drain at an estimated cost of Rs. 7.743 million has been provided for in the action plan for 1991-92. Street lighting has been extended to a part of the basti and the entire area is expected to be covered during the current year. A *pucca* school building is under construction at an estimated cost of Rs. 70,000. Its design keeps out rodents with a built-in rat trap bound. A low-cost sanitation proposal has been submitted to HUDCO for construction of 1500 latrines.

Community Participation in Other Cities

Community participation is being tried in some other cities like Bombay, Delhi, Madras, Baroda, Hyderabad, Vijayawada, Visakhapatnam and Siliguri. It is worthwhile to compare the workability of the concept in the two neighbouring States – Andhra Pradesh and West Bengal.

In Hyderabad, the UCD project is implemented by the constitution of neighbourhood committees for every 200 families. Although the Municipal Corporation seems to have succeeded in eliciting a considerable amount of popular enthusiasm by harnessing the hidden potentialities of the community, particularly the women, political pressures and interventions are a major hindrance. Further, the project suffers from a top down approach with UCD officials leading the way rather than the community exercising the leadership. The scheme did not bring about community organisation on a self-sustaining basis to participate in a wide range of community level services and amenities. The base line surveys were undertaken hastily and NHCs were constituted with disinterested and unmotivated RCVs. The mini-plans prepared did not reflect the felt needs of the community, but rather the individual perceptions of the staff was given importance. Furthermore, besides the lack of adequate resources, managerial skills and public co-operation to provide civic amenities equitably and efficiently, no serious thought was given by the community to develop and make use of its resources and energies. In the process, the urban poor were left out.

In Siliguri (West Bengal) community participation has been ensured since 1985 through NHCs, nurtured by field level staff (community organizers and project officers) of the municipality. The RCVs have motivated the local people to participate actively in the development projects and inculcated among the local people a sense of self-confidence, development consciousness and self-dependence. The community organisers have acted as catalytic agents and their intervention has been in the nature of assistance in designing development projects.

The experience gained so far is two-fold: (a) the degree of popular response is encouraging with a high level of involvement of the urban poor at the grass-roots level and (b) the political parties in a democratic polity have easy access to the urban poor and achieve considerable success in political mobilisation and recruitment. Ensuring community participation for urban development has also by itself proved to be a great political success.

The community management model as implemented at Bharatpur in Bhubaneswar, has split the neighbourhood committees into the BDC and BMCs, thus separating the development and management functions. The BDCs organise themselves to implement development programmes for women and children while BMCs ensure the concept of self-management in the socio-economic and physical infrastructural problems. The community management group (CMG), is democratically constituted and is governed by the concept of democratic decentralization.

CMG, a new concept in the model, as a tool for development and a management technique, is extremely suitable for decentralised planning and delivery of selected community services at a relatively low cost. It is applicable in other fields of socio-economic development as well.

While in the case of Hyderabad and Siliguri, the neighbourhood committees were constituted for the management of the UBSP programme, the community management group concept as implemented at Bharatpur aims to plan, implement and manage all the poverty alleviation schemes, like UBSP, NRY, EIUS, low cost sanitation and income generating schemes, infrastructural development and other types of development schemes for the healthy growth of the community.

The project at Bharatpur has been well received by the slum dwellers and has inspired in them a new enthusiasm and spirit for collective efforts towards the development of healthy community life.

In attempting an evaluation of the growth and development of the community management experiment in the planning and implementation of poverty alleviation schemes it can be said that the people who initially had a perception of the role of the Government as a provider of various services and finances, are gradually realising that they themselves need to manage their own affairs with the assistance of the government – a significant change in attitude.

In the beginning when the scheme was implemented the BDCs, BMCs and the CMG were constituted with nominated members in which there were many disinterested and unmotivated RCVs and RCMs. Though there was reluctance on the part of women in the initial stage, they now take active interest in electing their representatives and have gradually learnt to articulate their needs. They have started preparing and implementing mini-plans and programmes. Training programmes for the officials, RCVs and RCMs have brought about the much needed awareness about the problems of the urban poor and the plans for their mitigation.

Since an important feature of this programme is community involvement and participation right at every stage, the BDCs and BMCs are consulted and their acceptance obtained before finalising the action plans. An agreement is entered into with these HNCs on post project sustenance, clearly specifying the responsibilities to be shared between the NHCs and the municipal Government Departments regarding maintenance of assets provided under the programme. The NHCs have been playing an effective role in identifying the needs of the people and in resolving problems. The decision making is based on the collective wisdom of the people. Community leaders and volunteers have begun to take pride in the ownership of the assets created and are also keen to protect them from misuse and exploitation.

Several agencies involved in the delivery of urban services are working through inter-departmental cooperation and displaying team spirit with the municipality providing effective coordination as the nodal agency. The State Urban Development Agency (SUDA) and the District Urban Development Agency (DUDA) created and made functional since 1990 have provided a proper institutional framework for the integration and coordination of various schemes and projects and to make the delivery system effective and cohesive.

Comparing the quantifiable achievements of the various poverty alleviation schemes of Bharatpur with those of the entire city, it can be said that the magnitude of beneficiaries under the different schemes in Bharatpur is quite high as compared to the number for all the slums in the city.

At the same time it may be noted that some problems have come in the way of implementation of the CMG concept at Bharatpur. The grassroots level functionaries, the COs, whose task is to ensure effective community participation are not given adequate training. Therefore, the training and orientation of municipal and district level functionaries has to be increased. Coupled with the problem of marketing of products, the economic support programmes are not making the desired progress. There should be some scope to increase for skill formation of the people which would augment their income in the community.

Finally, it can be said that any improvement in the management of poverty alleviation programmes depends, in large measure, on improvement in the knowledge and skill of the political leaders, who have been elected as chairmen and municipal councillors, as well as the administrative managers and the dwellers, elected as representatives in community management bodies. All of them have the combined responsibility of tackling problems, promoting and experimenting with innovative methods of management and improving existing ones.

REFERENCES

Ali M. M., "Community Participation in Slum Improvement: The Hyderabad Experience", paper presented at the international seminar on Basic Amenities in the Context of Rapid Urbanisation", November 14-16, 1991, Institute of Social Sciences, New Delhi.

Austin J. E., (1980), *Confronting Urban Malnutrition*, World Bank Staff Occasional Papers, Number 28, John Hopkins University Press, London, 1980.

Knutsson K. E., 'The Poor Make the City Work: Can the City Work for the Poor', *Perspective on the Child*, UNICEF Statement.

Mohanty L. N. P., and Mohanty S., (1988-89), "Slum and Squatter Settlements in Class I Towns: Orissa Experience", *Journal of the Institute of Public Administration*, Vol. 4, No. 1 to 4, Regional Centre for Urban and Environmental Studies, Lucknow University.

Mukhopadhyay A. K., "Community Participation in Urban Development", paper presented at the international seminar on "Basic Amenities in the Context of Rapid Urbanisation", *Op. cit.*

Patra, G. (1991), "The Present Water Supply, Sewerage and Drainage System in Bhubaneswar, with some suggestions for improvement", paper presented at the seminar on Infrastructure for Urban Development" held at Bhubaneswar (unpublished).

Prasad D. R., "Urban Basic Services in India, A Swot Analysis", paper presented at the international seminar, "Basic Amenities in the Context of Rapid Urbanisation", *Op. cit.*

Sharma R. C., (1991), "Metropolitanization and Urban Crisis and Conflicts", *E. N. Weekly*, 30 March - 5 April, New Delhi.

Wishwekarma R. K., (1989), "Managing Urban Basic Services for the Poor",

Development Programmes for Urban Poor", in G. K. Misra and M. K. Narain (Ed.), Indian Institute of Public Administration, New Delhi.

A New Thrust in Housing and Urban Development in Orissa, State Urban Development Agency, 1992.

Census of India, Provision Population Totals, series 19, Orissa, 1991.

Course Material for Training on Solid Waste Management held from 6.1.1992 to 10.1.1992 (unpublished), All India Institute of Local Self Government, Bhubaneswar Regional Centre.

Guidebook for Implementation of Schemes Towards Integrated Development and Management of Urban Centres, Government of Orissa, Housing and U. D. Department, 1990.

Model Bye-Law of the Community Management Group (An Unique People's Organisation).

Report of the National Commission on Urbanisation, Government of India, Ministry of Urban Development, Vol. II, 1989.

Urban Basic Services for the Poor, Spot Light, Mother and Child, Poverty Alleviation Division, New Delhi.

26

Strengthening of Municipal Government in India: Options for Reform

Gangadhar Jha

THOUGH only a little over one-fourth (25.72 per cent) of India's population is living in urban areas, the total urban population living in 4689 cities and towns is sizeable (India, 1991). It has increased from about 160 million in 1981 to about 217 million in 1991. The total urban population in India even at this seemingly low level of urbanisation is larger than the total population of many countries of Europe and America taken together. According to Task Force Report of the Planning Commission, the increase of about 50 million of urban population between 1971 and 1981 itself was larger than the total urban population of all the countries of the world except those of China, USSR, USA, Japan and Brazil (India, 1983 A: III). The increase in the last decade was to the extent of about 58 million. At the end of this century, India is expected to have an urban population of about 330-340 million (India, 1983 B).

The size of urban population as also its rate of growth has serious implications for the municipal authorities who are required to provide basic civic services and urban infrastructure. Every person coming to urban areas puts a direct demand for civic services and infrastructure, thereby putting additional pressure on an already over stretched supply situation.

Municipal authorities are not in a position even to maintain the existing levels of services; an augmentation of these in the existing circumstances, seems beyond their capabilities. This has been reflected in the level of deficiency in services (NIUA, 1989; Jha, 1991), agitation and violence in the streets of cities and towns due to inadequate urban services (CSDS, 1974), no-tax campaigns by the citizens as a matter of protest, strictures by the courts of law for non-performance of basic functions (AIR, 1980), and supersession of a very large number of municipal bodies (Datta, 1991). To quote from National Commission Report (India, 1987)

> There is no doubt that most of our large cities are showing signs of serious overstress. Under pressure of population growth, the essential infrastructure of cities has reached the verge of collapse. Housing, water supply and drainage, city transport, local employment and the availability of land on which to locate city activity have all suffered grievously because the city management systems have not been able to react adequately to the problem of growth.

The paper first looks into the status of some of the basic civic services with a view to ascertaining deficiencies in urban services. It then analyses the existing capabilities of municipal authorities and, more importantly, the factors which have weakened them over the years. Finally, it suggests policy options by critically evaluating various amendment bills for strengthening the organisational and functional capabilities of municipal bodies.

Status of Urban Services

The analysis of status of urban services is confined to a few core municipal services like water supply, sewerage, drainage, refuse collection, street lighting and urban transport.

Water Supply

Water is a basic requirement for the very survival of human beings. Yet, it has not been possible to provide potable water to all the urban dwellers. By the year 1985, about 73 per cent of urban population had accessibility to water supply (Bijlani and Rao, 1990). There is wide deviation at the State level from this national average. Almost in half the States, the coverage of population is less than this. Again, out of 31 States and Union Territories, in as many as 18 States, the coverage has declined. Water supply situation in some of the States like Tamil Nadu and Andhra Pradesh is critical. In the towns with less than 1,00,000 population, piped water supply scenario is grim. In most of the small and medium towns, water supply is taken care of through private initiatives and by taking recourse to alternative sources, on an individual or community basis (India, 1988).

Sewerage and Drainage

A mid-term review of the water and sanitation programme in India revealed that only about 28 per cent of urban population is served by a sewerage system (India, 1985). In the States of Jammu and Kashmir, Madhya Pradesh, Orissa, Rajasthan and Manipur, the sewerage system is available only to 10 per cent of the urban population. A study conducted by NIUA for the Ninth Finance Commission shows that of 159 class I towns (with a population of more than 1,00,000), as many as 100 did not have any sewerage system (NIUA, 1989:18). Out of a total number of 3849 urban centres of different size, only 217 urban centres were fully sewered. An estimate of the Planning Commission indicates that hardly 20 per cent of the urban population have access to water-borne toilets connected to septic tanks, 33 per cent use bucket or dry latrines and the remaining 33 per cent do not have access to any facility whatsoever (Bijlani and Rao, 1990: 80). Access to a sewerage system by different income groups presents an even more glaring situation. The facility presently exists only for high income groups. The urban poor and the low income groups have hardly any access to the sewerage system. To quote from the Report of the National Commission on Urbanisation. "If the water supply system is unequal and unjust being highly biased in favour of the rich, the sewerage system is even more unjust and even more highly biased in favour of the rich" (India, 1988).

The NIUA study reveals that out of 127 towns and cities surveyed, drainage covered about 66 per cent of urban population was covered by drainage. Thus, about one-third of total urban population is not served by any drainage system.

Garbage Disposal

The amount of solid waste generated in India on an average varies from 300 to 500 grams per person per day. At this rate, the total amount of solid waste generated in the towns and cities is very large. The NIUA study revealed that about 27.5 per cent of the total waste generated is not collected. As much as 41 per cent of the towns and cities had a refuse disposal level which was below the sample average of 72.5 per cent. In 12 urban centres, 50 per cent or even more of the waste was not collected. The situation is bad especially in small and medium towns where even a rudimentary hygienic disposal system does not exist.

Street Lighting

The NIUA study reveals that out of 153 sample urban centres, in about 50 per cent of them 100 per cent of roads were provided with street lighting. In as many as 88 per cent of them, the number of lamp posts compared favourably with the accepted norm. However, in as many as 29 towns and cities (out of a sample of 153), the proportion of lighted roads was below 50 per cent. The situation is also grim in the secondary cities especially in the north-eastern States.

It should be obvious from the above analysis of the existing status of some of the basic urban services that the situation is deplorable. This, to a very large extent, is due to organisational incapability of municipal authorities brought about primarily by structural deficiencies of the system. The structural capability does not enable them to perform their statutory functions efficiently and effectively. The municipal authorities have been weakened considerably by structural deficiencies of the system.

Weakening of Municipal Authorities

The institution of municipal government has suffered a great decline over the years. This is due to the indifferent attitude of State governments. Prolonged neglect by the State governments even after Independence has made the municipal bodies static organisations which are not in a position to deal with a dynamic situation created by rapid urbanisation. The decline from Lord Ripon's concept of local self-government to a situation of fragile and morbid local administrative units is so pervasive that the municipal authorities have come to acquire a negative connotation. They are identified with everything that is inferior and second grade.

A host of factors have brought about a decline in their organisational capabilities. These, among other things, include an undefined role resulting in the erosion of their functional domain, an inadequate resource base, a weak executive system, state control, lack of motivated staff and work culture, all of which flow from the structural deficiencies of the Indian local government system itself. We will discuss these factors in some detail.

Erosion of Functional Domain

Curiously enough, in post-Independence India, the role of municipal authorities has not been clearly defined officially. The constantly on-going debate during the colonial rule on the role of urban local bodies became, at best, latent in free India. Lord Ripon had initiated the institution of local self-government with the avowed objective of promoting "political education" among the grassroots level political functionaries. Afterwards, the objective shifted to promoting efficiency in local public administration in the wake of Royal Commission on Decentralisation appointed in 1906 (Tinker, 1967). Their role as nurseries of political education again came to the fore under the Montague-Chelmsford Reform of 1919.

However, after Independence, the debate came to a dead end. The role of municipal authorities finds only lip service in the Five Year Plans and their problems have been examined by a couple of Commissions and a few Committees, Task Forces and Expert Groups. The primary emphasis has been on promoting a viable system of local government in rural areas with the specific ideal of "development from below" and "people's programme with government participation". The enactments for constitution of municipal authorities, at the most, enumerate a list of obligatory and discretionary functions. They do not define their role (Mukherjee, 1972).

The undefined role of urban local bodies has led to considerable erosion of their functional domain. There has been encroachments by the State Governments and para-statal organisations on the legitimate municipal functions. Over the years, gradually some of the functions have been taken away from the municipal arena and entrusted to specific purpose and development authorities created at the State and local level. Planning and development of new areas, water supply, sewerage and drainage, slum improvement etc. are some of the functions which have been taken away from municipal authorities and entrusted to the new organisations on the plea that the traditional municipal authorities lack substantial resources and qualified personnel to perform such functions. One wonders if the newly created organisations which take over some of the municipal functions are born with these. These inputs are provided to them on the basis of re-allocation only. The same if diverted to municipal authorities would have substantially strengthened them, to effectively perform such functions.

Weak Local Resource Base

Encroachment of municipal functions is, to a very large extent, due to the weak local resource base of the municipal bodies which adversely affects their fiscal capabilities. Though the increasing pace of urbanisation has generated substantial demand for urban services, the local resource base, on the other hand, has shrink. The share of the municipal sector in the total public sector expenditure has declined from eight per cent in 1960-61 to 4.5 per cent in 1977-78 (India, 1983 B). The mismatch between the availability of financial resources and the demand for municipal services has led to an inadequate and deficient level of services. The municipal authorities are undergoing serious fiscal stress which does not permit them to perform their functions effectively. A large number of them are not in a position even to pay salary to their staff for months together. It is, therefore, not unusual that garbage is not collected, drains are not laid out, sewers are not provided or kept in an operational condition, and street lighting is not provided and maintained. Between 42 to 97 per cent of municipal authorities are incurring expenditures on various services which are below the norms suggested by the Zakaria Committee (NIUA, 1989). Municipal authorities, by and large, are not in a position to eliminate the deficiencies in municipal services for the existing population, let alone augment them to meet the anticipated increase in urban population.

Weak Executive System

Barring a few States in eastern India, the executive system at the municipal level is highly fragmented as it is based on the separation of executive powers and functions. Whereas the executive powers are vested in the Council and its executive committees, all the executive functions are performed by the Commissioner in a municipal corporation and an Executive Officer in municipal councils, who are appointed by the State Government. Under colonial rule, as per the Montague-Chelmsford Reform of 1919, the dominant position and role of the District Collector was withdrawn to enable the local bodies to function as the real and effective institutions of democratic self-government. However, the substantive executive powers enjoyed by an appointed executive, rather than an elected body, led to bureaucratic control and hence erosion in local democracy and self-rule. This is an anathema and in contradiction to the institution of self-government.

Other Forms of State Control

Barring the Municipal Corporations which enjoy relatively high autonomy, other local bodies are subject to an elaborate system of control by the State Governments. In practice the District Collector and Commissioner have extensive supervisory powers over municipal authorities. These powers are frequently exercised through inspection, calling of records and giving directions for performing civic functions. Besides these, the State Governments also possess overwhelming powers of control and supervision in matters of appointment, approval of contracts and estimates above a pre-determined amount, sanctioning of new posts, and framing of bye-laws and rules.

In the fiscal sphere as well, the control mechanism is stifling. Financial controls relate to imposition of new taxes, approval of tax rates and expenditure incurred. It sounds incredible that the municipal authorities do not have the powers to approve their own budget and decide the tax rates. Even the Municipal Corporations are required to obtain State approval of expenditures beyond certain limits. In Kerala, for example, the limit is Rs. 1,00,000. In Andhra Pradesh, it is Rs. 50,000 and in Himachal Pradesh, it is Rs. 20,000 only. In the case of municipalities, the limit is still less. In Tamil Nadu, for example, expenditure exceeding Rs. 8,000 is to be approved by the State Government. Obviously, such control is crippling and with these constraints civic bodies are hardly embodiments of self-government.

The most drastic form of control applied generally is the act of supersession without reconstituting the Council on the basis of fresh elections. As a result Councils have been under prolonged suspension. Even the Madras Municipal Corporation, one of the most efficient corporations of India, has been under supersession since 1974. The abounding regulatory and punitive provisions in the municipal enactments smack of the French system of administrative tutelage which the French themselves have abandoned under the new wave of decentralisation in President Mittarand's regime.

Units of municipal government are a British legacy. But whereas the local authorities, their structure, powers and resources in Britain have been constantly and regularly reformed, rationalised and reorganised, the municipal authorities in India are no better than what they were when the British left the country. Extensive reforms in their role, functions, organisational structures, executive, fiscal, and personnel systems have become imperative. At present municipal authorities have by and large lost their legitimacy.

Strengthening of Municipal Authorities

There are three options *vis-a-vis* strengthening of municipal authorities: (1) introducing reforms within the existing system; (2) giving municipal authorities a coordinate status; and (3) giving them a constitutional status.

Reforms within the Existing System

As explained earlier, much of the malady afflicting municipal authorities is due to the deficiencies in the local government structure itself. Introducing reforms within the existing system of governance would be, therefore, only in the nature of cosmetic changes; which would not improve their institutional capabilities. What is required are basic and fundamental changes in the whole gamut of powers and functions, resource base, fiscal transfers, structure of municipal authorities in terms of executive and personnel systems, periodicity of elections and, above all, in their very existence as units of local self-government. Such changes require a pro-active stance on the part of the State Governments. This has been conspicuously lacking in the past. Attempts have been made to introduce reforms in bits and pieces without adopting a holistic approach. Barring the Government of West Bengal, which introduced a political executive system in the Municipal Corporations of Calcutta and Howrah by providing for a

Mayor-in-Council and also sustained the practice of constituting the Municipal Finance Commission on a regular basis, not much has been done by other State governments. Even in West Bengal, these reforms have been introduced without providing for other critical parameters of desirable reform for strengthening the municipal authorities.

Coordinate Status

A coordinate status would need to recognise the local bodies (both urban and rural) as a separate level of government in the Constitution of India so that the Indian Union would consist of Central, State and Local Governments. Although it appears as an ideal option, the existing political milieu is too conscious of conserving the powers and "autonomy" of the State Governments to be receptive to such a radical system. Persistent demands made by the State Governments for more autonomy, powers and resources will not permit the installation of an altogether new federal system consisting of Central, State and Local Governments.

Constitutional Status

Granting municipal authorities a constitutional status is advisable on several counts. Conceptually, a well defined functional domain, and earmarked sources of revenue in proper relation to functional responsibilities would enable the municipal authorities to function effectively and independently within the specified functional and financial limits. A system of prudent supervision and control by the states could ensure responsibility and accounting on part of the local bodies. A constitutional status would provide a blend of independence and accountability. If left to State Governments, it is unlikely to materialise due to their lukewarm and indifferent attitude as has been observed in the past. The urban local bodies, therefore, need to be given a constitutional status. In order to do this, local functions, local sources of revenue, a rationalised system of fiscal transfers and devolution of funds, and a refurbished executive system need to be spelt out in the Constitution of India itself. It will enable the local governments to derive their powers, functions and their very existence from the Constitution itself. It will also prevent the existing trend of state control on local functional domain and on the legitimate sources of revenues. A step was taken in this direction in 1989 in the form of the 65th Constitution Amendment Bill which could not be pushed through due to its politicisation and on the ground that the step was taken in a great deal of hurry. Its usefulness and relevance in the strengthening of municipal government got lost in the political heat generated by attributing a political motive to the Bill.

As for the "great haste", ever since the enactment of the Government of India Act of 1935 when the local list containing the sources of local revenue which was earlier introduced in 1919 was removed from the Act, there has been a clamour to give a constitutional status to municipal authorities by restoring the Local List in the Indian Constitution. The Central Council of Local Governments and Urban Development constituted by the President of India under Article 268 of the Constitution and which consists of Ministers of local self-government of various States, has been adopting resolutions ever since 1970 for according constitutional recognition to the urban local bodies by delineating their powers, functions and resources (India, 1989). Likewise, the All India Council of Mayors has been adopting resolutions for inserting a Local List in the Seventh Schedule of the Constitution for restoring the provisions of the 1919 Act. Recently, the National Commission on Urbanisation suggested strengthening the urban local bodies by taking shelter under Entry 20 of List 41 of the Constitution of India (India, 1988). It also suggested the amendment of Articles 280 and 281 for setting up of a Finance Commission by the State Governments on a regular basis for suggesting principles of fiscal transfers to them. Viewed in this context, the 65th Amendment Bill seemed to be an actualisation of a prolonged debate for strengthening the civic authorities. It was not done in a 'great haste' as has been alleged. A close look at the various provisions of the Bill, however, would reveal that there are still many gray areas and it falls short of expectation on several counts. Still, whatever was striven to be achieved through this constitutional amendment was completely diluted and even washed away by the subsequent two Constitution Amendment Bills (74th Bill of 1990 and 73rd Bill of 1991) introduced in the Lok Sabha by the two successive regimes. A critical evaluation of these bills have been taken up next.

Structure

The institutions of local self-government are said to be the grass-roots level of government where the interface between the citizens and the government is very close and intimate. The existing proximity between the two has somehow been obliterated especially in the large and metropolitan cities. Consequently, the town hall stands alienated from the citizens. Even though attempts have been made in some of the metropolitan cities like Bombay and Delhi to decentralise local administration by constituting zonal committees, the distance has continued to persist. The 65th Amendment Bill by providing for three types of urban local bodies, viz. a Nagar Panchayat in a "transitional" area from rural to urban with a population of 10,000 to 20,000, a Nagarpalika (Municipal Council) in towns with a population of 20,000 to 3 lakhs, and a Nagar Nigam (Municipal Corporation) in the cities with a population of more than 3 lakhs, tried to reduce this distance. This was further intended to be reduced by decentralising the Nagarpalikas up to the ward level by constituting Ward Committees for two or more wards and by providing for a three tier local self-government in the cities of more than 3 lakhs, viz., the Municipal Corporation, Zonal Committees and Ward Committees. It would have brought the units of local self-government to the door steps of the citizens. The 74th Amendment Bill (introduced in 1990) and the 73rd Bill (1991) have made a complete departure from such a decentralised structure. The extent of decentralisation has been left to the discretion of the State Governments. The experience of the past suggests that anything left to the State Government is unlikely to materialise as civic governance has been the most neglected subject in the scheme of things of the State Governments. Had it materialised in the past, there would not have been any need for pushing through a Constitution Amendment Bill.

Powers and Functions

The 65th Bill had enumerated a very long list of functions to be devolved to the municipal bodies. A new Twelfth Schedule was appended to which had an unusually wide array of functional areas to be entrusted to the municipal bodies. But having done that it was again left to the State governments to provide for the actual devolution of functions to them. The 74th Bill completely abolished the new Schedule and left everything to the sweet will of the State Governments which was like coming back to square one. The 73rd Bill (1991) is an improvement in this regard as it has not only revived the 12th Schedule of the 65th Bill but has also condensed the scope of the 12th Schedule by providing only for such functions which are of direct relevance to the urban local bodies. It has reduced the number of items from 37 (in the 65th Bill) to merely 16 and all of them are germane to the functional domain of the urban local bodies. However, instead of making the 12th Schedule mandatory, it has made it illustrative and left it to the discretion of the State Governments, thus perpetuating the existing practice. The nature and extent of relevant functions could have been provided for in the Constitution in unambiguous and explicit terms.

Resources

Devolving of functions without devolution of adequate sources of revenue will not in itself own, be able to empower the municipal authorities. Even though the 65th and the 73rd Bills has provided for a long list of functions to be performed by the urban local bodies, there is no mention of the revenues to be devolved to them. The 73rd Bill and for that matter, even the earlier Bills, talk of levy of taxes and duties by and assigning of such taxes and duties to, the municipalities "as may be provided in the State laws". Obviously, it again leaves this vital aspect of local government autonomy to the discretion of the State Government. It also talks of setting up of a Finance Commission by the State Governments to determine taxes which may be assigned to them and also the principles for sharing of taxes between the State and the Municipalities and for giving grants-in-aid. The way this provision is presently worded in the 73rd Bill again leaves these to the discretion of the State Governments who may and may not do so. Here was an opportunity to actualise the suggestions given way back in 1966 by the Rural-Urban Relation Committee. The Bill should have defined the sources of local revenue so that encroachment on these could have been prevented and the municipal authorities would have been entitled to an exclusive area of local taxation.

Planning

It is a sad commentary on the Indian planning system that despite having more than four decades of planned development, the municipal bodies are still operating outside the planning framework. In order to integrate them into the national planning framework, they need to prepare their own five-year development plans which could be aggregated into the District Plan to be formulated by the districts in which they are located. The District Plans could then be integrated into the State Plan and thus the flow of funds could be ensured to even the municipal authorities within the existing framework of devolution of plan funds from the Centre to the State. This is presently constrained by the lack of resources at the disposal of municipal bodies who do not have the necessary expertise and qualified planners to do the job. An innovative step was introduced in this regard in the 65th Bill (1989) by providing for setting up of a District Planning Committee at the District level to consolidate the plans prepared by the Panchayats and the Municipalities in a District and to prepare a draft development plan for the District as a whole. If the municipal bodies do not have the expertise to formulate a plan, the District Planning Committee could train them in this regard. The subsequent Bills (74th of 1990 and 73rd of 1991) have not even peripherally touched upon this vital aspect of capital development programme.

Executive System

Barring the Calcutta and Howrah Municipal Corporations in West Bengal, where under the new Corporation of Calcutta Act 1980, a political executive has been installed and except for the Municipal Councils in some of the eastern States where the Municipal Acts provide for the political executive in the form of President/ Chairman, in other States, the executive powers are still vested in the appointed functionary and not in the elected representatives of the people, as referred to earlier. Even in the Municipal Corporation, which enjoys a relatively large degree of autonomy, the executive powers are vested in the Commissioner who is appointed by the State Government; the Mayor who is an elected representative, has to be satisfied with presiding over the deliberations of the Council and acting as a ceremonial head, devoid of any executive power and functions whatsoever. The existing system has an in-built scope for conflicts arising between the people's representative and the executive officers.

Curiously enough, none of the above-mentioned Amendment Bills talk of this glaring inherent contradiction in a "self-government" institution. In fact, this is supposed to be taken care by the State Governments on their own. It does not require a constitutional guarantee. But as no initiatives have been taken by the State Governments except the Government of West Bengal, this contradiction should have been dealt with in the Constitution Amendment Bills.

Conclusion

It should be obvious from the above analysis that the three Constitution Amendment Bills introduced by successive governments at the centre to seemingly strengthen the urban grassroots level government have been found to be inadequate. Therefore, if there is going to be a constitutional amendment, it should be done in such way as to take care of the aforesaid deficiencies.

Again it is worth mentioning that granting of constitutional status to the municipal bodies will not be sufficient to strengthen their organisational capabilities. In addition to the aforesaid external measures municipal bodies need to improve their work culture by developing and sustaining modern management techniques so that the revenue sources assigned to them are efficiently collected and administered the functions entrusted to them are effectively performed.

REFERENCES

Bijlani, H. U. and Rao, P.S.N. (1990), *Water Supply and Sanitation in India*, Oxford and IBH Publishing Co. Pvt. Ltd., New Delhi.

Datta, Abhijit (1991), "Local Government Finances: Trends, Issues and Reforms", paper presented at the seminar on "State Finances", National Institute of Public Finance and Policy and World Bank, New Delhi, April 19-20, 1991.

The Hindustan Times (1990), News item in January 15 Issue.

India (1983 A), Task Forces on Housing and Urban Development, *Planning of Urban Development*, Planning Commission, New Delhi.

India (1983 B), Task Forces on Housing and Urban Development, *Financing of Urban Development*, Planning Commission, New Delhi.

India (1985), *Mid-term Review of Water Decade Programme*, Ministry of Urban

Development, New Delhi.

India (1988), National Commission on Urbanisation, *Interim Report*, Ministry of Urban Development, New Delhi.

India (1988), National Commission on Urbanisation, *Report*, Vol. II, Ministry of Urban Development, New Delhi.

India (1989), *Urban Local Bodies: A Summary of Recommendations of Selection Commissions, Committees and Conferences*, Ministry of Urban Development, New Delhi.

India (1991), Census of India, *Provisional Population Totals*, Paper 2 of 1991.

Jha, Gangadhar (1991), "Integrated Management of Urban Services in India: Fiscal Dimensions and Policy Options" paper presented of the Seminar on "Integrated Management of Urban Public Services", Lyon (France), May 27-June 7, 1991.

Mukerjee, G. (1972), "Problems of Urban Government", in A. Awasthi (ed.), *Municipal Administration in India*, Laxmi Narain Agarwal, Agra.

NIUA (1989), *Upgrading Municipal Services: Norms and Financial Implications* (Mimeo), Vol. I, New Delhi.

Tinker, Hugh (1967), *The Foundation of Local Self-Government in India, Pakistan and Burma*, Lalwani Publishing House, Bombay.

27

Empowerment of Urban Local Government in India (With Special Reference to Seventy-third Constitutional Amendment Bill, 1991)

H. M. Golandaz

IN recent years, governments in most of the developing countries have come to appreciate that one of the primary obstacles in meeting the challenge of urbanisation and implementation of national development policies and programmes has been the absence of capacity and skills, whether financial, managerial or technical, at the urban local government level that is at the municipal government level. These deficiencies have been, more often than not, a consequence of the constitutional status of urban local government bodies and the extent of political, administrative and financial autonomy enjoyed by them.

Urban local government is an integral part of the system of government of a country. As such, it is subordinate to the Central and State governments with respect to legislation, policies and other matters of national interest. However, what is needed is an optimum balance in the distribution of functions and powers between various levels of governments.

In this article an attempt has been made to discuss the status of urban local government in India and the changes, if any, which need to be introduced to strengthen them. The provisions incorporated in the Seventy-third Constitutional Amendment Bill, 1991 are also discussed in this article.

Status of Local Self-Government in the Indian Constitution

After Independence, the Constitution of India was framed on federal principles, where it was assumed that the provision need be made only regarding the structure, functions and powers of the state and the union government. As far as the municipal government was concerned, it was assumed to be a State "function".

Entry 5 of the State list in the Seventh Schedule of the Constitution of India gives power to the State to legislate on the municipal laws, establishments, constitution and powers of local governments. Except for recognizing local self-government as an essential part of the system of Government of the country, the Constitution does not confer any independent status or powers on the local government bodies. The urban local bodies are created by a statute passed by a State Legislature and by the Union Parliament in the case of such bodies in Union territories. The organisations, power and functions of these municipal bodies are dependent on this statute.

Statutory Status of the Urban Local Government

There are two kinds of statutory provisions for creating a municipal authority. Either the statute itself may establish a municipal authority (like the Bombay Municipal Corporation Act, 1888, City of Nagpur Corporation Act, 1948, Delhi Municipal Corporation Act, 1957), or it may empower the State Government concerned to create a Municipal Corporation (municipality/municipal authority, municipal council/municipal board) for an area, for example, Bombay Provincial Municipal Corporations Act, 1949, the Gujarat Municipalities Act, 1964, etc. The extent of the municipality's power as well as the extent of governmental control over a municipality/municipal council depends on the statute enacted for its creation. Presently, the statutes confer wider controlling and supervisory powers on the state government. This is due to two reasons; firstly, the Constitution does not demarcate the powers and duties of the municipal authorities. Secondly, in the absence of any clear cut demarcation, it is obvious that the municipal authorities are controlled by the higher level of government – the State government. Most of the Municipal Acts in India have been enacted during the past two and a half decade and thus are of recent origin. Nonetheless, some of the provisions in these Acts are out-dated and negative, such as, the power to supersede and obtain sanction of the State Government for minor matters which continue to exist in the Acts.

State Government Control

The State government exercises varying degrees of control over the municipalities through state level agencies – the respective department of Urban Development/Local Government and the Directorate of Municipalities/Municipal Administration/Local government. In general the following are the state controls on the municipal bodies:

(a) appointments to superior posts and prevention of extravagance in the expenditure on establishments.
(b) control over municipal budgets, accounts and audit, taxation and municipal borrowing.

Besides these, the other kinds of control exercised through the administrative channel are:

(c) the right to be informed
(d) the power to sanction
(e) inspection and action in case of default.
(f) the right to suspend the execution of orders of the municipal body.
(g) the power to supersede a municipal body in the case of incompetency, default or abuse of power.

Thus, the sweeping powers of state control have continued even after Independence. Local governments, local administration and urban development being State subjects, neither the state governments nor the central government have taken proper and adequate steps to introduce certain important changes to strengthen the local bodies. On the other hand, the activities and functions of the local government bodies have vastly changed under the impact of rapid urbanisation. It has been pointed out that local governments can no longer remain merely instruments of political education and civic conscience, but have to become institutions for promotion of social and economic development of the local community as an integral part of the national government. (Rural Urban Relationship Committee Report, 1966).

Initiatives to Strengthen Local Government Bodies

Although various committees and commissions were set up which have given recommendations to strengthen municipal bodies (Taxation Enquiry Commission Report, 1955) the major efforts were those of the Central Government which in 1989 introduced the Nagarpalika Bill in the Parliament. Later the Bill was modified twice and at present the Parliament is planning to enact the Nagarpalika Bill by introducing the Seventy-third Constitutional Amendment Bill, 1991.

The following are the important provisions incorporated in the Constitutional Amendment Bill:

a. Constitution of municipalities.
b. Composition of municipalities.
c. Constitution and composition of committees at ward level.
d. Powers, authority and responsibilities of municipalities.
e. Setting up of finance commissions.
f. Audit of accounts of municipal corporations.
g. Adequate representation for the weaker sections: Scheduled Castes, Scheduled Tribes and Women.

The existence of the local self-government as a viable democratic unit can only be justified if it has sufficient political, executive and financial autonomy. In the following paragraphs an attempt has been made to discuss the existing condition of the municipal government in India with regard to those aspects. In the course of the discussion, an attempt has also been made to discuss the provisions of the Seventy-third Constitutional Amendment Bill, 1991. Chart I shows the conditions which are necessary for the existence of the urban local government as a vibrant democratic unit.

Political Autonomy

Local government is distinguished by being carried out directly by elected authorities with responsibility for a local area and by being a general organisation carrying out many functions, rather than a functional organisation limited to a single primary responsibility. This means that local authorities exercise not merely their statutory responsibilities but have the capacity for a concern that goes beyond the routine administration of their services. Local government has a wider role than that of administering a series of services. It is a political institution for local choice as well as a provider of services.

There is a closer relationship – geographically and probably, socially, – between the elector, the council and the councillors. It is much easier to contact the local authority or the appropriate councillor; the latter requiring to be a local ratepayer to be eligible for election than the political leaders of other categories.

POLITICAL AUTONOMY	EXECUTIVE ADMNI-STRATIVE AUTONOMY	FINANCIAL AUTONOMY
a. Hold regular Municipal Elections	a. Devolve as many functions as possible	a. Municipal Taxes a.1 Taxes to be assigned a.2 Power to tax devolved
b. Prevent prolonged supersession	b. Grant powers matching the functions devolved	b. Sharing of taxes
c. Composition of deliberative wing should enable more members to get-elected directly	c. Planning and implementing authority	c. Grant-in-aid c.1 Mandatory c.2 Optional/discretionary.
d. Chief Officer under the control of the Municipal Body.		

Fig. 1: Urban Local Government: As a Vibrant Democratic Unit

Local authorities share a common legislative base. They are controlled by political parties which contest election locally but these parties are normally local branches of national parties. Above all they belong to a national economy, a national society and a national climate of ideas. National, social and economic trends are felt locally and ideas generated nationally are also tested locally. Similarly, local ideas are disseminated nationally. There is a national world of the local government as well as a local world. Thus, one of the most critical concerns is the legitimacy of the local government and the nature of its representative character.

Although most of the Municipal Acts in India have made provisions for holding municipal elections, it has been noticed that these are not held regularly. Similarly, urban local "self-government" bodies have experienced a phase of prolonged supersession in most of the states in India. Most of the Municipal Acts in India have vested the power of dissolution and supersession in the State Government. This power is exercised in the event of (a) incompetence of duties, (b) persistent default in performance of duties, and (c) excessive or abuse of power. Dissolution and supersession appear to be quite drastic correctives for on erring municipal bodies.

Most of the Municipal Acts empower the state government to appoint the Administrator in certain circumstances (Gujarat Municipalities, 1990). The use of this power by the State Government shows that it has been mostly used by the Government on the expiry of the terms of the municipal bodies on the ground of dissolution and supersession. There is a tendency on the part of the State Governments to exercise this power repeatedly and municipal bodies are kept under the control of the administrator for a long period.

Even in the states where the President/Mayor of the Local Bodies is directly elected, such political executives though elected with the clear verdict of the voters are not given adequate power. (Andhra Pradesh Municipal Act, 1965).

Provision regarding co-option of members also exists in many Municipal Acts. However, it is yet to be ascertained to what extent the said provision has served the purpose. Since most of the co-opted members are affiliated to political parties the contribution of these members in the municipal bodies may not be unbiased.

As per the recommendations of various committees and commissions (Maharashtra Municipal Act, 1965) the cadrization of certain categories of Municipal employees/officers has been introduced in some of the states like Rajasthan, Karnataka, Uttar Pradesh, Tamil Nadu and Maharashtra. Although the expenditure on the salary of the cadred officers is borne by the Municipalities, the elected wing of the municipal body has no control on the cadred staff. In some of the states, the elected president and councillors are at the mercy of the municipal officers.

The Seventy-third Constitutional Amendment Bill has provided for the composition of the municipal bodies, and the constitution and composition of committees at wards level etc. However, unless certain mandatory provisions like holding of regular municipal elections, prevention of prolonged supersession and accountability of chief officers to the elected wing are incorporated in the bill, the purpose of decentralisation will not be served.

The accountability for the performance of municipal bodies lies with the elected wing. In the event of non-performance, the state governments do not hesitate to exercise the power of supersession or dissolution of the municipal body. The paradox of the Indian situation is such that while the elected wing does not have any substantial power to control administration, it is held responsible for the non-performance of municipal bodies.

In short, political autonomy of the municipal bodies in India presupposes the inclusion of measures such as, holding of regular municipal elections, prevention of prolonged supersession, provision for election of more representatives, and accountability of the chief executive officer to the elected body.

Executive Autonomy

An urban area requires not only continuity but also change – technological, economic and social – to be able to prosper. Government is not merely the means of maintaining and ordering an area in its present form, but a means by which that area changes without undue conflict or without a breakdown of continuity. Change can be responsive or directed.

The services of local authorities have a role in maintaining and in ordering their locality and its communities. The processes of maintenance involve the provision of necessary physical conditions, maintaining roads and allied services, collection and disposal of refuse, provision of health facilities etc. Thus, a local authority is a political institution constituted for the local choice with the potential for ensuring change and also a provider of services.

The local authority uses the powers conferred on it by the system of government but also has the right to vary - within limits - its use of those powers. The degree of variation differs from service to service, but in both, the amount of resources devoted to services and in their form, there are variation from one authority to another. This variation is not accidental but inherent in the nature of urban local government. it derives from the exercises of local choice.

All the Municipal Acts in India provide for functions as well as for duties and responsibilities to be carried out by the Municipal government. Some of the Acts demarcate these duties and responsibilities as obligatory and discretionary. Potable water supply, sanitation and sewerage, drainage, street lighting, street cleaning and refuse collection, street paving, health services etc, are obligatory functions whereas urban transport, construction and maintenance, of parks, playgrounds, etc. are some of the discretionary functions or duties.

The Constitution Amendment Bill has incorporated the entire Twelfth Schedule (enclosed) as the list of functions to be performed by the municipal bodies. Some of these are of a highly technical nature and would definitely render municipal bodies ineffective. The Bill has a provision regarding devolution of powers and responsibilities. However, the devolution of powers commensurate with such responsibilities are left to the discretion of the state government concerned. Thus, municipal governments are required to provide for services irrespective of their administrative capacity to do so.

In pursuing the objectives of decentralisation, it is important to ensure that the existing municipal structures are up-dated to accommodate added responsibilities. Where, the administrative functions of state government for development of urban infrastructure are transferred to the local level, it will become necessary to examine whether the local government is capable of handling such responsibilities. If such capacity is not existing, it will have to be created or where it is non-sufficient it will need to be strengthened. Such a task might involve the establishment of a special agency, capable of planning programmes and projects as well as implementing them with minimal dependence on the from state government.

While modalities for resolving the issue of local autonomy vary from country to country depending on the political, historical, and cultural antecedents and traditions, there are some measures which can minimize intragovernmental conflict at the institutional if not at the political level.

Till now local governments have remained an implementing authority; they should also be involved in planning. The purpose of restructuring an institutional organization should be to minimise programme work at the state government level and to maximise it at the local government level. This means that each local authority should decide upon its own development programme independently, depending upon the local requirements, thus allowing for a greater degree of responsiveness to the needs of the local constituency.

Financial Autonomy

Local government is also a taxing authority like the Central and State government with the right to tax. In addition, the local authority can also charge for some of its activities or services because it increases its capacity for choice. It can make its own judgement of expenditure needs.

Municipal Acts in India provide for sources of revenue. Municipal revenues come from property tax, octroi, other service taxes, fees and grants-in-aid. In some of the states the amount of grant determines and affects the municipal expenditure. In addition, certain schemes and programmes, such as Integrated Development of Small and Medium Towns (IDSMT) are often financed by loans.

Grants and other resource transfers have been tied more and more to centrally sponsored schemes, such as Integrated Development of Small and Medium Towns (IDSMT), Nehru Rozgar Yojana (NRY), Urban Basic Services for Poor (UBSP) etc., on the disbursement of which the states and local government have no control.

Future steps must be taken to endow the states with the necessary administrative authority and financial resources to enable them to discharge their constitutional role. A policy of systematic decentralisation must be based on a clear distribution of the developmental responsibilities of the centre, the states and the local self-governments. With progressive decentralisation planning, the resource funds of the local bodies will increase substantially. In order to ensure that these are met by adequate devolution from the national and state level, there must be constitutionally guaranteed minimum transfers from the Centre to the state and on to local government. This requires strong and independent finance commissions both at the centre and in the states.

It is a well-established fact that the structure of local government finances and deficiencies in the local governments' revenue collection affects capacity to meet routine obligations and to generate resources. Effective financial management by local governments requires adequate resources to operate and maintain public services and given that local government revenues are generally constrained, new measures will need to be devised to supplement existing resources.

Article 243V and Article 243T of the Amendment Bill envisages that the Legislature of a State may confer such powers and authorities on the local bodies including the power to levy, collect an appropriate tax assigned to the local bodies and the power to tax. However, sharing of such taxes as entertainment tax, vehicles tax, sales tax, etc., do not find any place in the Bill.

A provision has been made in the Bill for the establishment of a Finance Commission to review finances of the municipalities and to recommend principles for (i) determining taxes which may be assigned to the municipalities; and (ii) sharing of taxes and (iii) grants-in-aid. The Finance Commission (Centre-State) has the status and powers of an advisory body and hence the recommendations are not obligatory. Similarly, the Municipal Finance Commissions will also have the same status as the former. Considering the number of municipal bodies in India, and their relationship with the concerned state government, an advisory body like the Finance Commission will have a tough task in finding an acceptable solution.

The Bill has made provisions regarding audit of the Accounts of the Municipal Corporations by the Comptroller and Auditor-General (C&AG) of India. The audit of municipal accounts by the C&AG may minimise the probabilities of negligence by the municipal bodies. However, it may also maximise the evils of bureaucratisation in the municipal administration.

Critical Evaluation of Urban Local Government in Different Forms

Figure 2 shows the existing situation, changed situation and desired condition of Urban Local Government in India. It is observed from Fig. 2 that if the changed situation is shown on a continum, it will be closer to the existing situation and would not ensure empowerment of local government.

An expanded role for local authorities implies local autonomy and this increases the risk of conflict between local and state level authorities. If the Central Government adheres strictly to the role and functions assigned to it by the Indian Constitution the state

EXISTING SITUATION	CHANGED SITUATION AFTER THE ANACTMENT AND IMPLEMENTATION OF SEVENTY-THIRD CONSTITUTIONAL AMENDMENT BILL, 1991	DESIRED CONDITION
1. Less Constitutional administrative, financial autonomy. Strong constitutional administrative financial control by the State government including exercise of power of supersession of municipalities for unlimited period	1. No specific provisions a. Power vested with the State government to decide about constitutional administrative autonomy of local body	1. Strong Constitutional political/administrative status a. Lesser control of the state government. b. Regular Municipal election. c. No prolonged supersession. d. More number of elected representatives. e. Municipal Chief Officer under the control of an elected body.
2. Increased responsibilities and expectations. Responsibilities not commensurate with the powers	2. Increased responsibilities and expectations Twelfth schedule of the Amendment Bill, 1991	2. Devolution of functions commensurable with the responsibilities
3. Limited Financial resources.	3. Fincl. Resources a. No specific taxes/grants are made available to the urban local bodies b. State governments have been vested with the power to determine local financial resources	3. Specific Revenue Sources: a. Increased Tax Income a.1 Specific taxes to be assigned. a.2 Power to tax devolved a.3 Sharing of taxes b. Specific grant-in-aid b.1 Provision for Mandatory grants b.2 Provision for Optional/dis cretionary grants

Fig. 2 Urban Local Government in India
(Existing situation, Changed situation and Desired Condition)

cannot endow any local authority with adequate political and economic autonomy.

The Constitutional Amendment Bill would have definitely introduced some positive changes in Urban India, if it had assigned to the local government the status of a third tier of government with certain exclusive political, administrative and financial powers in the Constitution itself. In the absence of such revolutionary changes which could incur the displeasure of the State Governments and a demand for more decentralised Centre-State relations, the changes introduced will be cosmetic changes "sans" desired results.

Finally, it must be emphasised that the implementation of effective decentralisation policies is often frustrating and long drawn out. Therefore, success depends largely on a sincere and determined commitment by all parties involved. This requires incremental processes of institution – building at the local level, so that, solutions can be found to resolve pressing problems faced by most towns and cities. Failure to do so can lead to further deterioration of living conditions in urban areas.

REFERENCES

Government of Andhra Pradesh, the Andhra Pradesh Municipalities Act, 1965, section 23 (1-a).

Government of Gujarat, (1990), Gujarat Municipalities Act, 1963, section 263, Gandhinagar, Government Central Press.

Government of India, 1988, Report of the Sarkaria Commission, Nasik, Government of India Press.

Government of India, (1983), Report of Task Forces on Housing of Labour Development, New Delhi, Planning Commission, 4 volumes.

Government of India, (1955), Report of the Taxation Enquiry Commission, 1953-54, New Delhi, Manager of Publications.

Government of India, (1966), Rural Urban Relationship Committees (RCUES) Report, Vol 1, New Delhi, Ministry of Health and Planning.

Government of Karnataka, (1974), Karnataka Municipalities Act, 1964, Bangalore, Government Press.

Government of Maharashtra, (1990), Maharashtra Municipalities Act, 1965, Section 313, Bombay, Government Central Press.

APPENDIX

TWELFTH SCHEDULE
(Article 243 V)

1. Urban Planning including town planning.
2. Regulation of landuse and construction of building.
3. Planning for economic and social development.
4. Roads and bridges.
5. Water supply for domestic, industrial and commercial purposes.
6. Public Health, sanitation, conservancy and solid waste management.
7. Fire services.
8. Urban forestry and promotion of ecological aspects.
9. Safeguarding the interests of weaker sections of society.
10. Slum improvement and upgradation.
11. Urban poverty alleviation.
12. Provision of urban amenities and facilities such as park, gardens, playgrounds.
13. Promotion of cultural, educational and aesthetic aspects.
14. Burials and burial grounds; cremations and cremation grounds.
15. Cattle pounds; prevention of cruelty to animals.
16. Vital statistics including registration of birth and deaths.

28

The Politics of Providing Basic Amenities to the Urban Poor[1]

Saraswati Haider

THE paper[2] aims at exploring and documenting the dynamics of the political process at the level of the urban poor as observed during the tenth Lok Sabha[3] elections in May 1991 and demonstrating that the political process at the local slum level has as its content the provision of basic amenities. This is the dominant theme as opposed to other themes like the provision of a stable government, secularism, nationalism etc. The paper attempts to show the linkage between the electoral process, the provision of basic amenities and the urban poor with a crucial part being played by *Pradhans* (headman of a group) who emerge as performing a double role – that of a patron of the slum dweller and also that of a middleman of the politicians. Their basic characteristics and *modus operandi* which involve continuous hoodwinking and defrauding of their gullible clients for personal ends is also explored and the conclusion reached is that the urban poor are exploited for partisan ends by both the politicians and the *Pradhans*. A higher level tentative generalisation is put forward i.e. the principles of a market-oriented economy of the country have penetrated the democratic processes resulting in a political market where the commodity for sale is the vote and where competition for personal profit is also cut throat. Some of the players, however, are ignorant of the market rules.

Politics, for the purpose of this paper, is taken to mean the values, principles and actions involved in determining the form, organization and administration of a state or part of one and the regulation of its relations with other States. In a democratic set up, elections to its institutions form a crucial process, for it is through this process that a democracy becomes a government of the people, by the people and for the people.

Basic amenities involves a descriptive definition. There is now considerable consensus on what are the universal basic needs of a human being to help him or her survive. In contemporary India, the basic needs include food and potable water, first of all, because without these the human organism would perish. The basic amenities needed for fulfilling these needs would be provision of enough cheap food and taps and hand pumps. Two other universal basic needs are shelter and clothing. Lower down the scale we have the need for proper sanitation, meaning efficient, cost-effective, clean lavatories, proper sewerage and garbage disposal systems, medical aid, with doctors, hospitals and medicines being made available at low costs.

Who are the urban poor? These are people living in a city in relative deprivation on several counts. The majority of the urban poor in a city are found living in slums and squatter settlements, economically, socially and culturally deprived.

In order to test the above hypothesis the following procedure has been adopted. First we have discussed the setting of Rajpur colony, a *Jhuggi Jhompri* area. After that we have taken up the socio-economic characteristics and the status of basic amenities of the urban poor of the locality. Then we have discussed the political activities of the *Pradhans* in some detail during the tenth Lok Sabha election. Finally, we have summed up.

The Setting

Rajpur *Jhuggi Jhompri* Colony is situated in an industrial area of Delhi--the industries consisting of garment factories, factories manufacturing leather goods, furniture shops, laboratories and electronics. The Colony has a large proportion of the Scheduled Castes – about 75 per cent I am told.[4] The majority of the dwellers are from Uttar Pradesh followed by Bihar, Rajasthan and Haryana. According to information gathered there are about 150 to 200 Muslim families in the cluster.

As per the Delhi Development Authority's Slum Wing[5] data, the following are the figures showing the growth of the cluster:

Growth of Jhuggies in Rajpur Jhuggi Jhompri Cluster

	1960-65	1965-73	1974-76	1977-80	1981-85	1986-89	Total
Number	1	6	20	1344	1208	129	2708
Per cent	0.0	0.2	0.7	49.6	44.6	4.8	100

The *Pradhan*, Krishna, a *Jatav* (scheduled caste) from Haryana and by profession *Jamadar* (labour contractor) claims that in 1976 an electronics factory was to be constructed in the area. He took up the contract and he and his labour erected their tents in the vacant hillock which is now the Rajpur Colony. Construction work in the area increased and soon other contractors came in with their gangs and camped in the open space. In 1977 there were about 200 tents in the area. Krishna was advised by a politician that he should arrange functions and invite influential people so that the area could become a cluster. Functions were organized and politicians invited, as a result of which, ration cards were issued to the dwellers and their names appeared on the voter's list. Tents were converted into *jhuggis* and since 1977 the cluster went on increasing, with original inhabitants calling their relatives over. Other people from nearby areas who were living in rented accommodation and saw this opportunity to get rent free accommodation started making their *jhuggis* on the hillock. Thus Rajpur Colony grew.

Shiv Shankar, a *Chamar* (scheduled caste) from Ballia district of Uttar Pradesh now engaged in *kabadi ka kaam* (explained later) and a well-to-do entrepreneur had a different story to tell. According to him, the cluster came into existence through the efforts of another *Pradhan* Tirath Ram a *Chamar* (scheduled caste) from Haryana who was engaged in the *Kabadi ka kaam* also. In a nearby slum lived the *Gujjars* (milkman) with their cows and buffaloes who had given on rent many *jhuggis* which they had built before the influx to the area. Tirath Ram, eager to establish a cluster where his influence would be paramount asked the tenants of the *Gujjars* to move on to the hillock where he lived. He sold the land initially for Rs.25 and later for Rs.50 per *jhuggi* thus killing two birds with one stone – amassing wealth and gaining influence. Fights ensued with the *Gujjars* but in the end Rajpur Colony grew as the industrial area expanded and more and more jobs were created. The most rapid growth was experienced from 1980 onwards uptil 1985.

The Rajpur *jhuggi-jhompri* cluster occupies a fairly large area and is situated on a rocky *pahadi* (hillock). On one side of it is a metalled road, and on another side a wide dirt road. On the third side is an area covered with jungle bushes while an area comprising residential buildings converted into small-scale factories overlook the fourth side. There are many grocery shops, *pan* (betel) shops, tea stalls and *dhabas* (roadside eating places) on the metalled road and the dirt road. Grocery and *pan* shops are found within the residential cluster also. Vegetables and fruits are sold mostly on *thelas* (push carts).

Quite a significant proportion of the population seems to be self employed. One trade that is very common is called *kabadi ka kaam* (work which involves buying of junk). Cloth cuttings obtained from garment factories are sorted out and sold to buyers in Panipat and Sonepat in Haryana for making *durries* (thick woven mats for spreading on floors or ground for people to sit on).

According to a personal communication of the Delhi Development Authority's Slum Wing in Rajpur Colony there are 13 per cent unskilled, 5 per cent skilled, 13.2 per cent self employed, 30.7 per cent service workers and as many as 37 per cent are unemployed. It seems a little odd that in an industrial area dominated chiefly by the informal sector there should not be more people employed in factories and that such a high percentage should be unemployed. This point needs to be investigated.[5]

Males in the Rajpur Colony outnumber females, with the male population being 58 per cent and that of the female, 42 per cent. Illiteracy is high at 50 per cent.

The Urban Poor

In 1981, India had a population of approximately 658 million. Of this the urban population constituted 23.73 per cent. The percentage of the population living in slums[6] was 20 per cent of the urban population i.e. over 31 million.

In the same year, Delhi had a total population of approximately six million of which the total urban population came to 93 per cent. The slum population constituted 30 per cent i.e. 1.8 million[7] of the total urban population.

In 1991 Delhi's urban population is eight million. The slum

population has increased to 2.10 million people, a sizeable 'vote bank'.[8]

According to a list of the Delhi Development Authority's Slum Wing[9], Delhi has 929 *jhuggi-jhompri* clusters spread all over the city. These include about 2.6 lakh *jhuggis*. According to another personal communication of the same authority, the average family size of the 457 *jhuggi-jhompri* clusters surveyed was found to be 3.59 persons which does not seem credible hence we have to go to another source which estimates the figure at 4.7[10] and according to which the total population of squatter settlements in Delhi works out to be 1.2 million.

It is difficult to estimate the total number of *jhuggis* and population of Rajpur *Jhuggi-Jhompri* Colony because of the inconsistent in information obtained from different sources. The *Pradhan* Chotey Lal who is backed by the Congress (I)[11] gave a figure of 4000 *jhuggis*. The number given by the officers of the Urban Basic Services Programme[12] was 3770 while the figure quoted by Delhi Development Authority's Slum Wing[13] is 2950.

Taking an approximate figure of 3000 *jhuggis* and the average number of persons in a household as 4.7, the total population of the cluster works out to be about 14,000.

Elections

The author had the opportunity to observe the process of the tenth Lok Sabha election held in May 1991 in Rajpur Colony. Election for the Delhi Municipal Corporation and the Metropolitan Council[14] were held several years ago and both these bodies stand dissolved as of 1990.

Rajpur *jhuggi-jhompri* colony falls within the Outer Delhi constituency for the Lok Sabha. During the 1991 Lok Sabha elections the tussle for power in Delhi was between candidates of five parties - the Congress (I), the Janata Dal,[15] the Samajwadi Janta Party,[16] the Bharatiya Janta Party[17] and the Bahujan Samaj Party.[18] In all there were 70 candidates in the fray and the main fight was expected to be between Sajjan Kumar of the Congress (I) and Tarif Singh of the Janta Dal. Sajjan Kumar finally won the seat and according to the *Times of India*[19] this was because of the enormous support he received from slum clusters, unauthorized colonies and villages.

Basic Amenities

Rajpur Colony is an unauthorized settlement on Delhi Development Authority land and the *jhuggis* can be demolished any day. There are only 12 water taps - these are not actually taps but cuts in water pipes (which amounts to one pipe for 1167 people). Water comes for just one-and-a-half hours in the morning and one-and-a-half hours in the evening. The queues at the water pipes are long and often are the venue for quarrels. There are also about 35 hand pumps in the slum i.e. one hand pump for 400 people. The Delhi Development Authority commissioned Sulabh International (an organization known for manufacturing pour flush latrines economically) to build 200 *pucca* (brick-made) latrines in two blocks - 120 for men and 80 for women. These have been constructed. There are also 20 *pucca* bathrooms for men and 20 for women though no water is available. Of the latrines only 100 were operating i.e. one latrine for 1400 people. The maintenance of the latrines being carried out by a private organisation. The men using the latrine have to pay 25 paise every time. Most of the *jhuggi* dwellers prefer to use the open space.

The people of the Rajpur Colony, like all other such illegal colonies are first and foremost concerned about the illegality of their occupation of land and the basic amenity of water. The Rajpur Colony voter is disturbingly unconcerned about the ideologies of various parties. He or she lives almost totally insulated from national issues. The political discourse in the slum is a discourse relating almost entirely to authorization of jhuggis and provision of water with the former figuring at the very top.

Politicians have rightly perceived the dominant mood of the slum electorate and are well aware of the large vote bank that they form. Therefore, when they came canvassing for votes as did Sajjan Kumar and Tarif Singh to Rajpur Colony, they assured the slum dwellers that they would get the basic amenities, that their ownership of *jhuggis* would be authorized or plots would be given to them along with suitable loans to build a house, and that most certainly it would be seen to that the *jhuggis* would not be demolished without the consent of the owners. Sajjan Kumar in his meeting promised plots of 32 sq. yd and also confirmed that a tubewell would be installed in the cluster. The *jhuggi* dwellers, however, are fast losing faith in the promises of the politicians for these seem to evaporate once the elections are over.

One day, before the elections, I came across Dulare, a man of about 30. He is from Ballia district of the state of Uttar Pradesh and was unemployed He knew a little about carpentry and did odd jobs here and there. His wife and children were with him. He was very bitter and proclaimed "The elections are a big *dhong* (farce). This time no party will come out fully victorious since this time nobody can make up his mind about whom to vote for. Leaders come to us when they need votes otherwise nobody is bothered about the welfare of the *jhuggi-jhompri* dwellers".

I asked Murli from Ballia district who should be given the vote. He was visibly upset. "The elections are a *tamasha* (show). When votes are needed the *netas* (leaders) come to us and make all sorts of promises – we will see that the *jhuggis* are not demolished, that water taps are provided – but these promises are never kept. Money is everything in the world. If you are rich you can get everything done but if you are poor nobody helps you. I will not vote at all". The woman standing next to him said "We will give our vote only to that person who has helped us". I asked who had helped them. She said "No one". Then who will you give the vote to? She repeated "To the person who helps us".

The waning interest in elections is also confirmed by the low voting turn out. Chotey Lal *Pradhan* backed by Congress (I) said that only about 50 per cent of the eligible voters voted. Shiv Shankar was also of the opinion that the voting was not more than 50 per cent.

Patron-client Relationship

James Scott writes that "the patron-client relationship - an exchange relationship between roles-may be defined as a special case of dyadic (two person) ties involving a largely instrumental friendship in which an individual of higher socio-economic status (patron) uses his own influence and resources to provide protection or benefits, or both, for a person of lower status (client) who for his part reciprocates by offering general support and assistance, including personal services to the patron".[20]

The distinguishing features of a patron-client relationship are its basis in inequality, a face to face personal quality and its diffused nature rather than an explicit interpersonal contractual bond.[21]

The traditional patron-client relationships and structures still have vitality in several spheres of life including politics in India and other developing countries. This is so because of the persistence of marked inequalities in the distribution of wealth, status and power which have been accepted as more or less legitimate and the relative absence of firm impersonal guarantees of physical security, status, position and wealth. For the urban poor in India the situation is doubly compounded by their illiteracy which is a major hinderance to their becoming self reliant.

Politicians have been perceptive enough to realise that the patron-client relationship can be a useful tool in their pursuit for power. They, therefore, project themselves as persons who have access to resources which can ensure to the slum dweller the basic amenities which he needs in exchange for his vote which would put the politicians in a position to tap the resources. The relationship remains a patron-client relationship primarily because the urban poor acquiesce to it. They do not realize the power of the vote that democracy bestows on them and which can make the exchange an equal one and break the vicious mould of patron-client relationship embedded in a submissive sense of obligation on the part of the client. There should be a equal sense of obligation on the part of the patron to deliver the goods on his part, but politicians often default or fulfil obligations only when expedient. However, as pointed out earlier, this defaulting is fast becoming detrimental.

Nowhere is the patron-client relationship more generally invoked than in the electoral process. However, it must be noted that one of the distinctive features of the patron-client relationship is its face-to-face interaction. This is not physically possible for the politician at election time or at any other time for that matter. Thus comes into existence the "patron-client pyramid" which is a hierarchy of patrons and clients which apexes at the main patron. For the *jhuggi* dwellers the immediate patron is the *Pradhan*. He is, therefore, the key person at the grassroots level.

At this stage a distinction should be made between the patron and the "broker" or "middleman" with which it is sometimes confused. Acting as a "broker" or "middleman" – terms which can be used interchangeably – means serving as an intermediary to arrange an exchange or transfer between two parties who are not in direct contact, in this case the politician and the individual slum dweller. The role of a middleman then involves a three-party exchange in which the middleman functions as an agent and does not himself control the thing transferred i.e., the vote and basic amenities *vis-a-vis* the *pradhan*. A patron by contrast is part of a two party exchange and operates with resources he himself owns or directly controls.[22]

Important as the distinction is, it is easily lost sight of for two reasons. First, it is not always a simple task to determine if someone personally controls the resources he uses to advance himself. What of the case in which a civil servant distributes the subordinate posts in his jurisdiction to create an entourage? Here it would seem that he is acting as patron, in as much as the jobs he gives out are meant as personal gifts from the store of scarce values he controls and are intended to create a feeling of personal debt and obligation among recipients. The social assessment of the nature of the gift is thus crucial. If we were to find, on the other hand, someone who had acted as an agent of job seekers and put them in touch with a politician who controlled the jobs then he would be acting as a broker. It is only natural that many an ambitious public official will seek to misrepresent acts of brokerage or simple adherence to the rules as personal acts of patronage, thereby building his following. To the extent that he succeeds in representing his act as a personal act of generosity he will call forth that sense of personal obligation that will bind his subordinates to him as clients, as often happens in the case of the *pradhans* and the slum dwellers.[23]

Another potential source of confusion *vis-a-vis* this distinction is that the terms designate roles and not persons, and thus it is quite possible for a single individual to act both as a broker or and a patron. Such a role combination is not only possible but is empirically quite common. When a local landowning patron, for example, becomes the head of his political party at the village level he is likely to become the middleman between many villagers and the resources controlled by higher party officials. In this case he may have clients for whom he also serves as broker. The diffuse claims of the patron-client tie actually make it normal for the patron to act as a broker for his clients when they must deal with powerful third parties – much as the patron saint in folk Catholicism who directly helps his devotees while also acting as their broker with the

Lord[24] and nearer home the *guru* and the Prophet.

Since the politician cannot maintain direct contact with his clients he chooses middleman or brokers to fetch him the votes in exchange for his promise to provide basic amenities in the case of the slum. The *Pradhan* of a cluster is thus one such broker for the politician who is also a patron to his slum dweller clients. He gains money through this transaction, albeit indirectly, as also influence through the politician, and status from obligation of the slum dweller which he can call upon when the need arises.

Vote Brokers

Talking to the *up-pradhan* (deputy headman) of the *Samiti* (committee) of which Chotey Lal is the *pradhan*, backed by the Congress(I), I was told that there were about 35 *pradhans* in the area.

From what I gathered it is apparently very easy to become a *pradhan*. One gets the support of five to ten people that *pradhans* can easily muster using primordial ties and patron-client relationships. Chotey Lal, I was told, was the only properly elected *pradhan* and his *samiti* was duly registered.

There is bitter rivalry among the *pradhans* for it is only after they have demonstrated their sizeable support and following that they can catch the eye of the politician and bargain for brokerage thus entering the lucrative business of politics.

I was told by one of the *pradhans* that they form a nexus with the police and *Dadas* (gang leaders) and together intimidate the *jhuggi* dwellers. The same *pradhan* told me that in the beginning when the cluster was developing, the *pradhans* settled early and then started demanding a payment of Rs.200 for construction of a *jhuggi* plus Rs. 20 to be paid to the police constable and Rs.20 to the local *Dada*. Today when the *jhuggi* cluster is chock-full the amount being demanded is Rs. 2,000 with Rs. 200 for the police and Rs. 200 for the *Dada*. The nexus is so powerful, as I was told by the supervisor of a survey conducted by a non-governmental organization in the cluster, that no man can build a *jhuggi* without making the payments. If he does so he will be hounded out of the cluster.

Chotey Lal Pradhan is a *mali* (gardner) by caste, from Varanasi district of Uttar Pradesh. His bitterest rival is Ram Kumar Agarwal who was, when I had first met him, the chosen man of the Janata

Dal party then in power and a staunch supporter of V. P. Singh. He is a *dhimar* (water carrier) by caste, I am told. However, Ram Kumar has adopted the surname of the *Bania* (trader) caste which is of higher rank in the caste hierarchy.

Shiv Shankar, a *chamar* (untouchable and who deals in leather work) who has become rich in the business of selling cloth cuttings and has been inhabiting the cluster for nearly fifteen years, told me that earlier when the inhabitants were few they had made Chotey Lal the president of a broad based society for pressing their demands. Chotey Lal (was working as a *chowkidar* (watchman) in a factory which had a tubewell and the *jhuggi* dwellers through his aegis could get the much needed water. But soon Chotey Lal started becoming too big for his boots so he was replaced by Ram Kumar Agarwal. There arose a quarrel between Chotey Land and Ram Kumar over this issue and the society, according to Shiv Shankar, is now in a limbo, entangled in an on-going a court case.

Ram Kumar is a graduate from Banaras Hindu University. Chotey Lal is only "Inter pass" (studied up to 12th grade) as it is called.

Chotey Lal always dresses in a white *kurta* (loose shirt) and *dhoti* (a piece of cloth tied at the waist with one end drawn in-between the legs and tucked at the waist), the attire of rural *pradhans*. The *kurta* and *dhoti* are made of *khaddar* (thick woven cloth).[25] Ram Kumar Agarwal wears a *khaddar kurta* and *pyjama* – a more urbane dress.

Chotey Lal still works as a helper in a factory which gives him enough time to indulge in politics. Ram Kumar is unemployed. Chotey Lal lives in a very small room built of white-washed bricks. His wife and children are in his village. He says that his family is quite well off but he has come here and lives in the cluster to serve its people! He fancies himself to be a *samaj sudharak* (social reformer)! He says he does not do this for any personal gain. However, both Ram Kumar Agarwal and Shiv Shankar consider him a crook. They say that he collects Rs.2 per month per family as donation for the committee of which he is the *pradhan*; but what happens to the money nobody knows. He also regularly ask for donations for constructing a temple or for a function which never materialises for providing better water facilities which never get better. He is supposed to have made for himself a neat Rs. 10,000 out of the elections which is the reward for being a broker of the politicians.

Ram Kumar Agarwal showed me a cyclostyled form which Chotey Lal is supposed to have got filled in by each household, taking Rs.15 per family for ensuring legalization of their *jhuggis* and for provision of basic amenities. Where the money went, again nobody knows. Chotey Lal recently got involved in organizing a cooperative society in league with an ex-Delhi Administration worker and collected Rs.115 per household but this cooperative has not become operative till date though about Rs.30,000 are supposed to have been collected. The cooperative again was meant to help *jhuggi* dwellers claim ownership of their dwellings and to provide basic facilities.

At the moment there is a rumour going round the cluster that the *jhuggis* are going to be demolished. This rumour does the rounds quite regularly. Who starts the rumour nobody knows. It could be started by the powerful *pradhan* (backed by the ruling party) himself who is sure that the *jhuggis* will not be demolished but wants to create a scare among the people and end also show them that it is due to his actions and running around that the demolitions were prevented.[26] Or the rumour could be started by a rival *pradhan* to rattle, embarrass and undermine the position of the ruling party backed *pradhan*. At present with such a rumour rife, Chotey Lal's prestige is at stake. He is the *pradhan* being backed by the ruling party. As soon as the rumour reached his ears he ran up and down and came back with the news that the local Member of Parliament (from henceforth referred to as MP) would visit the area and assure the dwellers that no such thing was in the offing. For MP Sajjan Kumar's welcome a donation was collected. However, for some reason Sajjan Kumar could not make it but what happened to the money nobody knows. The same thing happened a second time. This kind of hoodwinking, I am told, is not the forte of Chotey Lal alone. Apparently all *pradhans* indulge in it. I believe that during the Janata Dal regime when Ram Kumar Agarwal was *pradhan* and was backed by the ruling party, he floated a similar rumour for personal gain.

All political parties back some *pradhans* or other and this should make for checks and balances which minimise fraudulent activities. However, *pradhans* are wary of exposing rival *pradhans* openly because their own hands are not quite clean and the exposure of a rival *pradhan* as a crook could lead to their exposure in some other sphere. The *pradhans* are also not solely committed to any one party. They like to keep their options open and take advantage of any situation which would be personally most beneficial for them. If they embarrass the *pradhan* of one party today they might in the future jeopardise the chance of being backed by that same party in case such a chance becomes a possibility. Hence, there are a few direct challenges and a lot of rumour mongering. *Pradhans* are all birds of the same feather and thus avoid too aggressive a posture towards each other. There are of course also possibilities of forging an alliance with some rival *pradhan* if this is more gainful or of even defection from one party to another. In such a situation discretion is indeed the better part of valour.

Ram Kumar Agarwal disclosed an incident to show how the *pradhans* fool the *jhuggi* dwellers in making them believe that they are in a position to get favours for the dwellers from the higher echelons of the political set-up. This was in connection with my having made an observation that the *pradhan* does not seem to have a direct relationship with the higher level politician who casts him (the *pradhan*) in the role of middleman during the elections but seems to distance himself from him once the elections are over.

There was a man called Binda Din, a *Yadav* (backward caste), from district Gorakhpur in Uttar Pradesh who applied for the post of peon in the Delhi Municipal Corporation. He believed he could not get the job without the help of a source. Binda Din, therefore, sought the help of the *pradhan* who was supported by the ruling party. The *pradhan* in order to make the right impression agreed and said that the next day he would take Binda Din to the area MP but since one has to meet the MP early in the morning they would have to go by a three-wheeler scooter rickshaw. They went in the morning with Binda Din paying the fare. At the MPs house the *pradhan* was not immediately received but had to go through the MP's Personal Assistant and was told that the MP was busy in a meeting and to come the next day. On the way back again a three-wheeler was hired. The *pradhan* told Binda Din that he had to meet two important persons that very day and the three-wheeler was used to visit these persons with Binda Din footing the bill. The next day the same thing happened because this time the MP had gone out of station. It was only on the third day that the MP finally gave them an audience after making them wait for four hours and then too only after the *pradhan* had requested a member of the party's cell looking after the affairs of *jhuggi jhompris*, with whom he was in direct contact, to intervene on his behalf. The MP did not give a letter but merely phoned the Chairman of the department where there was a vacancy and said that he was sending a man called Binda Din and asked the Chairman if he could see if anything could be done for him. The *Pradhan* and Binda Din then went to the Chairman the next day. The *Pradhan* told Binda Din to wait outside. He came back after some time and said that the Chairman was willing to help but the wise thing to do would be to give some money as a gift which is done customarily because the Chairman was doing a great favour. Binda Din gullibly swallowed all this and gave the money to the *Pradhan*. The *Pradhan* told him that his call letter would come soon. It never came and Binda Din had spent a cool Rs.800.

It is apparent that the political leader does not make himself readily available to all the middlemen whose help he may have taken during his election campaign. As far as he is concerned, the deal more or less ends once the elections are over. After that he becomes selective *vis-a-vis* his accessibility.

The *Pradhan* in fact is a very insecure person for he is not quite sure that his requests for provision of basic amenities promised to the slum dwellers would be granted since he is quite far removed from the apex of the political hierarchy. It is only by ensuring that election promises are kept that he can establish himself as a powerful *Pradhan* and retain his patron identity as far as where slum dwellers are concerned. The *jhuggi jhompri* dwellers are compounding the situation for the *Pradhans* as they get steadily wiser to their tactics.

On the metalled road on one side of the cluster a water pipe was spouting water. Everybody filling water was grumbling. Near the pipe people were standing with their push carts selling iced candy, bananas, *chana* (grams), puffed rice and other eatables. A thin woman sitting atop a push cart was shouting "We poor people are not entitled to anything. Nobody is bothered about us. Nobody comes to see how we live. We drink filthy water, live in dirt and therefore are falling ill all the time. Every other day the police comes threatening to demolish our *jhuggies*". The woman refused to tell me her name and continued in the same vein. "The poor are not expected to have any honour. Our *bahus* (daughters-in-law) and *betis* (daughters) are constantly harassed by the police. If the police dislikes our *jhuggis* where should we go? We are also human beings, we also need food, clothes and shelter. The police even objects to our selling eatables on push carts on the road". On her push cart were some over-ripe bananas for sale. When I asked her whom she would vote for she became even more angry. "Here, see this knot in my *sari*. I have taken voter slips from all parties but will vote for none. What is the point of voting". I asked her why she did not approach the *Pradhan* for help. "They are all swindlers and *chors* (thieves). They only want to serve their own purposes". I asked her who her *Pradhan* was. She said "Krishna" and pointed to a room of bricks down the road decorated with the Congress (I) flags. I asked her which party he was supported by. She spread out her palm and said contemptuously *"Panja/Hath"* (palm/hand - the symbol of the Congress (I)).

Mansa Ram, a *chamar* by caste, from Haryana engaged in *kabadi ka kaam* and whose brother was instrumental in populating the cluster said with candour and anger "The *pradhans* are *dalals* (brokers) of the politicians and the police. They do not have the interests of the *jhuggi* dwellers at heart but are on the look out to make a quick buck anyhow. They have no honour".

The *pradhans* I talked to were all full of bluff and bluster and liked very much to be praised and flattered. This is presumably a sign of their inherent insecurity resulting from the tight rope walking they are engaged in between the unapproachable political leader and the disillusioned *jhuggi* dwellers. Chotey Lal at the moment is the butt of many jokes because he has invited Sajjan Kumar to quell the rumours regarding the demolition of the *jhuggis* twice but Sajjan Kumar has not come and also because he has been unsuccessful in getting the inoperative hand-pumps repaired.

The eunuch *pan wala* (betel seller) said right in front of Chotey Lal "Arre Chotey Lal Ji (Here, Mr Chotey Lal) Sajjan Kumar won't come but the police will come to demolish the *jhuggis* and then you will be seen running in the opposite direction. Sajjan Kumar has got the votes he needed. Now what does he care".

As mentioned above, all *pradhans* want to take credit for the amenities provided in the cluster and boast about it even though this may have occurred via the decision making process and bargaining at a much higher level. Taking credit for the provision of basic amenities puts a stamp on the *pradhan's* status as a patron.

Obligation of the slum dwellers on this count is even greater than that earned by the *pradhans* on bestowing such favours as filling up forms for pensions and ration cards, settling quarrels and intervening in police cases in which the slum dwellers may be involved.

Ram Gopal who irons clothes is from Ballabhgarh, Haryana. He has five children. At the birth of the fifth child his wife underwent tubectomy. They are *jats* (landowning caste) but landless. Ram Gopal was evasive when he was asked who he would vote for. He said "I am not sure which is the *hawa*[27] this time. Many candidates are in the fray. I know the names of Sajjan Kumar (Congress (I)) and Tarif Singh (Janata Dal). Competition is between the *panja* (hand – the symbol of Congress (I)) and the *chakra* (a circle with spokes – the symbol of the Janata Dal). One should vote for the person who has done something for the colony". On further probing he went on to say "In fact it is V. P. Singh who has done most for the colony. He had ration cards made for all the *jhuggi* dwellers and was also behind all the other improvements in the colony."

A tailor Raghuvir Sharma, a *Brahmin* by caste, with his own shop and foot pedalled sewing machine, next to Ram Gopal's *thela* (push cart), repeated what others had said before – "Every now and then people come to us for votes but nobody does anything to improve the cluster once the elections are over. There is dust and filth all around, no proper drainage system and worst of all no water". He was also of the opinion that it was V.P. Singh who had done something for them.

According to Chotey Lal, *Pradhan*, the improvements regarding basic amenities now available in the colony had been effected during V. P. Singh's time and ration cards had also been issued during his tenure which is seen by perceptive people as only a populist gimmick but the *jhuggi jhompri* people consider it as a big favour. In actual fact, the ball was set rolling by the Rajiv Gandhi government after the outbreak of the cholera epidemic in the Delhi slums in 1988. In the elections of 1989 the Congress (I) lost and the Janata Dal Government was ushered in. The work of provision of basic amenities was therefore, completed, during the time of V. P. Singh who naturally took all the credit for it. The ration cards, according to the Congress (I) supporters, are *kutcha* (temporary) and not *pucca* (permanent) and they are useless if *zamanat* (surety) is required or loans have to be applied for to make them permanent. The Janata Dal supported *Pradhan* at that time – Ram Kumar

Agarwal – of course gave all credit to the V. P. Singh Government and buttressed his position by giving the impression that it was at his intervention that the amenities had been provided.

At election time it is very important for the *Pradhan* to get the candidate of his party to hold a meeting in his area and lend credibility to the promises made by the *Pradhan* to the *jhuggi* dwellers regarding provision of basic amenities. Mr Sajjan Kumar, Mr Tarif Singh and Mr P. N. Singh (the candidate for the Samajwadi Janata party) – visited the cluster for about 5 to 10 minutes each. I was there when Sajjan Kumar came. Chotey Lal that day was seen in a state of heightened excitement, here, there, and everywhere, bare-footed and clad in a *banyan* (vest) and *dhoti*, getting posters of Indira Gandhi, Rajiv Gandhi and Sajjan Kumar pasted on every available space on the wall of the opposite building. Arrangements were being made as if a wedding was going to take place. A tent was erected, chairs brought, a *dais* prepared, cold drinks ordered. Sajjan Kumar was garlanded. The crowd comprised a meagre 100 people, brought no doubt by Chotey Lal's contacts in the squatter settlement. Chotey Lal has his own network of workers in the cluster which include, a mid-wife who is instrumental in bringing clients who still fell a sense of obligation to her despite having paid for her services; a woman who deals in the supply of illicit liquor, mustering up the support of her clients many of whom are her debtors and thue vulnerable; a grocery shop owner who also has many clients buying from him on credit and, thus, beholden to him and reciprocating by voting according to his instructions; the clientele of many smaller *pradhans* having aligned themselves with Chotey Lal. These contacts of the latter also provide the crowds for meetings and various demonstrations and rallies organised by the party to which the *Pradhan* belongs.

Chotey Lal was not recognized by Sajjan Kumar until he was introduced by another higher level party worker. *Pradhan* always try to keep themselves to the latter in the public gaze. Chotey Lal did his best to be seen near Sajjan Kumar obviously to impress the crowd that he was on good terms with the politician. He also tried to look very busy, probably to convey to Sajjan Kumar that he had taken great pains to organise the meeting. Sajjan Kumar listened to the grievances of the people repeated like a ritual at every election and made the suitable promises as made ritualistically each time.

It is very obvious that the *pradhan's* patron-client relationship with the *jhuggi* dwellers has become very fragile. He is not able to lord it over them most probably because he is afraid that they might withdraw their support and jeopardise his position resulting in a personal loss of both money and status. The higher level party workers who see the *Pradhan* in the role of a middleman have no such fears and qualms. They know that the *Pradhan* needs them and are, therefore, able to admonish him. During the time of the Lok Sabha election when Sajjan Kumar was to come to the cluster, many of his party's workers came to see if the arrangements had been properly made. These organisers treated Chotey Lal like a minion and were positively domineering in their attitude.

The lengths to which the *Pradhans* go to see that their candidate wins at the hustings – and their position thereby strengthened and sources for making money opened – can be seen during the polling.

On polling day at about 2 p.m., suddenly there was commotion when information was received that at one of the booths only 40 per cent votes had been polled. On hearing it the *Pradhan* of one of the parties hastily organised bogus polling. Lists were scrutinised to identify those who had been expected to vote for the party but had not turned up. Their ages were noted and a hunt launched to contact people of those age groups. When a person was found a bogus slip was written out for him giving the name of the person who had not turned up. The bogus voter was then asked to go in and vote. He was told not to sign but put his thumb impression. Messages were sent to people of those age groups who had not voted so that they could come and vote. One man boasted that he had voted 18 times. I asked him how he removed the indelible ink mark. He said it was easy. A young boy also said that he had voted seven times. He just wiped out the ink mark as soon as it was put. He decided to go and vote again. The whole thing seemed to be a naughty prank. A rumour was also started that the Bhartiya Janta Party was trying to buy votes by promising liquor, money and meat in return. How far this was true is anyone's guess.

I was told by Shiv Shankar, however, that the slum voter is naive and can be bribed cheaply. The *jhuggi* voter even today is quite oblivious of the power of his vote. The *Pradhans* of every party, Shiv Shankar told me, frequently, resort to bribing to serve their ends.

It is obvious that neither the *Pradhans* nor the politicians who condone their methods serve the interests of the slum dwellers by indulging in corrupt practices and preventing the elections from being fair and free.

The *Pradhans* do not openly exploit their clients, but do so subtly by building up credit for themselves in the form of obligations which the *jhuggi* dweller still feels even though the exchange between him and his patron may be on equal terms and fully reciprocated. To prevent the *jhuggi* dweller from neglecting his obligation when the need arises the *Pradhans* practice a subtle form of coercion. However, as has been pointed out earlier, this ploy is recoiling and though the *jhuggi* dweller may out of obligation for favours done, do the *Pradhan's* bidding, resentment is building up against him. The clients have started chafing. They are becoming increasingly restive which does not a bode well for the *Pradhans*.

The *Pradhans* seemed to want to keep the *status quo* intact in the cluster for in that lies their gain. They are wary of any attempt on the part of anybody to unite the people to press for their rights by direct action. When the question of the threat of demolition of *jhuggis* was being discussed, I asked Chotey Lal why the *jhuggi* dwellers did not organise a demonstration. Pat came the reply "We must use the *seedha rasta* (the correct way) and not this *ulta rasta* (wrong way)". The *Pradhans* most probably also convince the *jhuggi* dwellers of this. Apparently they do not want the *jhuggi* dwellers to become self-reliant lest they should lose their hold and be swept aside. Their aim, therefore, seems to be to maintain the poverty of the *jhuggi* dwellers so that their power base is not disturbed. Even the *Pradhans* supported by the opposition parties did not appear to be in favour of direct action. They are shrewd enough to realism that once the *jhuggi* dwellers become conscious of their collective power the *Pradhans* of all parties would be affected.

Conclusion

A fact which emerges very strikingly from the above account is that politics at the level of the urban poor is the politics of basic needs which forms the pivot around which all political actions revolve. The main political issues are the provision of such basic amenities as taps, electricity, lavatories, sanitation, schools, and, most important, legalisation of their dwellings rather than abstract issues such as socialism, secularism, nationalism, stability, etc.

One also gets the impression that the political behaviour as witnessed in the Rajpur Colony is a micro-model of political behaviour at the national level. There is the same quest for power for personal gain, the same rivalries and factions, a similar political culture with its blatant emphasis on private good rather than public welfare, with the higher level politicians only adding finesse and sophistication to it. There is the same one-up-manship, bribing, rumour mongering and character assassinations which characterize the national situation.

Another conclusion is that the role of the middleman is becoming an important element in our social structure as the society changes from one based on informal relationships to formal ones. The contractor is a middleman, so is the lawyer, the bureaucrat, the tax consultant. These are, however, professionals with their relationships well defined, business-like, and contractual, devoid of affective ties. However, in India, in the political sphere specially, the feudal vestiges of patron-client relationships still come in handy though it is becoming more and more tenuous as is seen in the case of the *Pradhans* in the Rajpur Colony who are playing a double role at present-that of the broker or middleman as also that of a patron. These relationship would perhaps start weakening considerably as the urban poor become conscious of the powerful resource that they have with them – their votes. The balancing act of the *Pradhans* is becoming precarious and he is being compelled to be a supplicant of the *jhuggi* dweller.

One can also surmise that the divisive activities of rival *Pradhans* and their aim of maintaining the *status quo* are a definite obstacles to the unity of the *jhuggi* dwellers. These also interfere with the development of a strong social movement of the urban poor which would not be merely need-based but also based on a higher level ideology that can sustain the movement and that would not be content with getting the basic amenities but would strive for changing the social structure, the inequalities within which make the urban poor marginals.

Another point that emerges clearly is that the *Pradhans* are unscrupulous con-men and aim at exploiting the gullible, politically naive, illiterate poor who form a large chunk of the electorate and who can still be coerced into voting in a particular way. The issues involved in the political tussle, as mentioned earlier, relate to the provision of basic amenities. These, in fact, should have been a right of the poor in a State that professes to be promoting a just, socialist and equitable society. That the poor will be provided the basic amenities if their candidate wins is doubtful considering that the resources are limited and usually siphoned off to the upper and the upper middle classes who help maintain and sustain the basically capitalist market oriented system of the country.

The question that arises is, how has such degeneration come about in Indian politics seeping down to the grassroots level? A tentative hypothesis is that the principles of a market-oriented or market friendly economy as they would have it, have penetrated the democratic processes of the country. It is a market where the participants have unequal resource base and limited knowledge regarding the functioning of the same. The main principle of a market friendly economy is the pursuit of personal profit which can be accumulated at any cost. There are no compunctions. If these come into play they would undermine the very basis of private profiteering. A market friendly economy, of course, has a market where every commodity including labour can be bought at a price. Everything is saleable and everything can be purchased. These principles which have been imbibed by the country at large cannot but find their way into the nation's polity. There cannot be one set of principles for the economy and other antithetical principles for the polity. The market culture of India's economy has given rise to a "political market" also with its buyers, sellers, private profiteering as the strongest motive, cut throat competition and brokers of the commodity-the vote. If the above hypothesis holds then we need to think very seriously whether a market friendly economy can co-exist with the principles, values and behaviour of an ideal, moral democracy.

NOTES

1. I would like to acknowledge my gratitude to Professor M N Panini of the Centre for the Study of Social Systems, School of Social Sciences, Jawaharlal Nehru University, New Delhi, my supervisor, without whose guidance and constant encouragement this paper would not have been written. I would also like to thank Dr(Mrs) Bidyut Mohanty, Research Coordinator of the Project under which the seminar on "Basic Amenities in the context of Rapid Urbanisation: Drinking Water and Sanitation Issues" was organised, for her most insightful observations and constructive suggestions.
2. This paper is the outcome of field work done in a *jhuggi jhompri* cluster

(squatter settlement or hutments) of the Indian capital and metropolis, Delhi, as a part of the process of writing a Ph.D dissertation which is expected to be the outcome of a holistic, ethnographic study of an Indian slum. The techniques used will be both anthropological and statistical. The field work in the *jhuggi jhompri* cluster is still in its infancy. This paper is based on data collected through participant observation and informal interviews which will be augmented by data received from a structured schedule. This schedule has not been administered yet so the data is soft and the presentation impressionistic. Hence, the use of terms like majority, minority, some, few etc. The names of the squatter settlement and the people who appear in the narrative have been changed in deference to the need for confidentiality.

3. Lok Sabha: The House of the People or the lower chamber of the bicameral Indian Parliament.
4. The untouchable castes who fall outside the *varna* system are classified by the Government of India as Scheduled Castes. The untouchable castes are considered to be India's original population whom the Aryans coming from outside subdued are categorized as untouchables, through whose touch one gets polluted. In some areas even their shadow was considered polluting. They lived segregated from other castes.
5. Personal Communication of the Delhi Development Authority's Slum Wing.
6. Here the descriptive term slum is used coterminously with the more precise term squatter settlements. Whether squatter settlements can also be subsumed under the term slum is still a debated question. See Gans, Herbert 1965, *The Urban Villagers*, New York, Free Press; Mangin, W. (1967), "Latin American Squatter Settlements: A Problem and Solution", *Latin American Research Review* 2 (3), Lloyd, P., (1979), *Slums of Hope*, Oxford, Billing and Sons Limited.
7. Nangia, Sudesh (1988) "Slums of Urban India" in Frank J. Costa, Ashok K. Dutt, Laurence J.C. Ma and Allen G. Noble, (eds.), *Asian Urbanization* Stuttgart, Berlin, Gebruder Borstraeger.
8. Census of India, 1991, Provisional population totals, series 1, paper 2. Also see *Times of India* August 1 1992 (Delhi edition).
9. Personal Communication Delhi Development Authority's Slum Wing.
10. Nangia, Sudesh *op.cit.*
11. Congress was the party which won for India its freedom from the British Raj. It was the party to which Pandit Jawaharlal Nehru belonged. Later splinter groups were formed from the party of which Congress (I) was the group led by Mrs Indira Gandhi.
12. A Government of India programme started recently to coordinate the efforts of various departments in Delhi slums
13. Personal Communication Delhi Development Authority's Slum Wing.
14. Delhi City Government Bodies. For more information see, Sundaram K.V. "Delhi: The National Capital" in *Million Cities of India*, (1978), New Delhi, Vikas Publishing House Pvt Ltd; Datta, Abhijit and J N Khosla 1972 "Delhi" in William Robson and D E Rogan, (eds.), *Great Cities of the World: Their Governments, Politics and Planning*, Vol I, London; Oldenburg, *Big City Government in India: Councillor, Administration and Citizen in Delhi*, New Delhi, Mahohar Publications; Pandit V.L. (1954). *Elites and Urban Politics: A Case Study of Delhi*, New Delhi, Inter-India Publications; Mehra A.K. 1991. *The Politics of Urban Development: A Study of Old Delhi*, New Delhi, Sage Publications.
15. Coalition of the erstwhile Janta Party and Lok Dal under the leadership of V. P. Singh.
16. A breakaway group of the Janta Party with Shri Chandrashekhar as its leader

17. The former Jan Sangh Party with *Hindutva* as its concept of national identity and establishment of a Hindu State as its chief plank.
18. A party of the untouchable castes floated a few years ago.
19. *Times of India*, New Delhi, Tuesday, June 18, 1991.
20. Scott, James C. (1972). "Patron-Client Politics and Political Change in South East Asia". *The American Political Science Review*, Vol LXVI No.1.
21. *Ibid.*
22. *Ibid.*
23. *Ibid.*
24. *Ibid.*
25. Spun and handwoven clothes which became very popular during the Independence movement of India with Mahatma Gandhi's call to all Indians to give up wearing foreign clothes, *khaddar* has now become the hallmark of politicians in India.
26. The Pradhan as middleman is not a peculiar feature of the Indian squatter settlements. Manuel Castells talks about the *caciquesmo* in Latin America "In this traditional, long standing squatter settlements on the periphery of big cities, the key element is a very strong community organization under the tight control of leaders who are the intermediaries between the squatters (*colones*) and the administrative officials. In the early stages of process this form of community organization can be considered to be dominated by the *caciquesmo*, namely by the personal and authoritarian control of a leader, himself backed and recognized by the local authority". Lomnitz, L. A., (1977), *Networks and Marginality: Life in a Mexican Shantytown*, New York, Academic Press. Larissa Adler Lomnitz also talks about *cacicazgo*. She writes that *cacicazgo* is the emergence of a patron or broker--*caciques* are intermediaries between the settlers and the urban industrial society". Castells, M "Squattors and Politics in Chile, Peru and Mexico in A. R. Desai and D. Pillai (eds.), *Slums and Urbanization*, 1990, Bombay, Popular Prakashan.
27. Indian elections are usually contested on the pre-dominant issue. The support to this issue is called *hawa* in Hindi meaning wind, signifying a wave.

INDEX

Urban Studies Series-1